UNDERSTANDING ISRAEL

The State of Israel is an unlikely powerhouse in a troubled region. Since 1948, Israel has retained its status as a democratic state without interruption. An investor-friendly environment and skilled workforce have led to a thriving economy, whilst the Israel Defense Forces are one of the most powerful armed forces in the world. Yet Israel is also blighted by a plethora of foreign, domestic and security challenges, some of which threaten the very fabric of the state. The cost of living continues to soar; political corruption appears endemic and the conflict with the Palestinians divides domestic opinion and sours Israeli foreign relations. Thus, contemporary Israel remains perplexing, resisting any straightforward categorizations or generalizations.

This book provides a comprehensive, multi-disciplinary analysis of the external and internal threats, opportunities and issues facing contemporary Israel. The book comprises sixteen chapters written by recognized authorities in the field of Israeli Studies. Together, the chapters offer a detailed overview of Israel while separately they provide stand-alone coverage of specific topics under discussion. Part I examines the Israeli Political System, such as the Knesset, political parties and extra-parliamentary politics; Part II addresses issues in Israeli society, including the Israeli economy, the divides between Jews and Arabs, religious and secular Israelis and the struggle for gender equality; and Part III focuses on security, geopolitical and foreign policy challenges, looking at relations between Israel and the Jewish Diaspora, Israeli foreign policy, borders and settlements and regional security threats.

By filling an important gap in the study of contemporary Israel, this book is of interest to multiple audiences, most notably students and scholars of Israeli politics, the Middle East and comparative politics.

Joel Peters is Director of the School of Public and International Affairs and Professor in Government and International Affairs at Virginia Tech, USA.

Rob Geist Pinfold is a Neubauer Research Associate at the Institute for National Security Studies (INSS) at the University of Tel Aviv. He holds a PhD in War Studies from King's College London, UK.

'This amazingly engaging edited book is unique, both in its scope and the critical yet constructive ways in which the various chapters, written by top scholars, provide in-depth analysis of Israel. This book will be useful for scholars, graduate and undergraduate students alike, and will also be essential reading for anyone interested in unpacking the puzzle of Israel.'

—**Gad Barzilai**, *Vice Provost, University of Haifa, Israel, and Former President, Association for Israel Studies*

'In this fine collection of essays, Peters and Pinfold successfully interrogate the multiple meanings of Israel's security dilemmas, highlighting the paradox that at the very apogee of its power and success as a nation-state, the internal struggle between piety, power and identity reveal tensions that cannot be easily reconciled by Israel's claim to be both Jewish and democratic. With its interdisciplinary approach very much to the fore, this volume will be essential reading for not just students of Israel, but for anyone concerned about its future trajectory.'

—**Clive Jones**, *Professor of the Regional Security of the Middle East, Durham University, UK*

'This sweeping and nuanced collection provides an excellent introduction to the complexities and contradictions of contemporary Israeli politics, society and external relations. It is the most updated primer on Israel today.'

—**Naomi Chazan**, *Professor Emerita of Political Science, Hebrew University of Jerusalem, Israel*

UNDERSTANDING ISRAEL

Political, Societal and Security Challenges

Edited by Joel Peters and Rob Geist Pinfold

Routledge
Taylor & Francis Group

LONDON AND NEW YORK

First published 2019
by Routledge
2 Park Square, Milton Park, Abingdon, Oxon OX14 4RN

and by Routledge
711 Third Avenue, New York, NY 10017

Routledge is an imprint of the Taylor & Francis Group, an informa business

British Library Cataloguing-in-Publication Data
A catalogue record for this book is available from the British Library

Library of Congress Cataloging-in-Publication Data
Names: Peters, Joel, editor. | Pinfold, Rob Geist, editor.
Title: Understanding Israel : political, societal and security challenges /
edited by Joel Peters and Rob Geist Pinfold.
Description: Milton Park, Abingdon, Oxon ; New York, NY : Routledge, 2018. |
Includes bibliographical references and index.
Identifiers: LCCN 2018015573 | ISBN 9781138125643 (hbk) |
ISBN 9781138125650 (pbk) | ISBN 9781315647357 (ebk)
Subjects: LCSH: Israel–Politics and government–21st century. |
Israel–Economic conditions–21st century. | Israel–Social
conditions–21st century. | National security–Israel–History–21st century. |
Israel–Foreign relations.
Classification: LCC DS128.2 .U53 2018 | DDC 956.9405/5–dc23
LC record available at https://lccn.loc.gov/2018015573

ISBN: 978-1-138-12564-3 (hbk)
ISBN: 978-1-138-12565-0 (pbk)
ISBN: 978-1-315-64735-7 (ebk)

Typeset in Bembo
by Out of House Publishing

CONTENTS

ACKNOWLEDGMENTS

The editors would like to acknowledge the support of the Israel Institute, Washington D.C. and the Institute for Society, Culture and Environment at Virginia Tech towards the research and publication of this book. They would also like to thank Rebekah Molloy for providing invaluable research assistance, and in getting all the chapters ready for publication.

This book is modeled on *Whither Israel: The Domestic Challenges* published twenty-five years ago and edited by Keith Kyle and Joel Peters. Joel Peters would like to acknowledge his personal and intellectual debt to Keith Kyle. Keith was an extraordinarily gifted journalist and scholar. His intellectual curiosity was only surpassed by his generosity of spirit. He is still sorely missed by those who knew him, and had the privilege of working with him.

CONTRIBUTORS

Eitan Y. Alimi is an Associate Professor of Political Sociology in the Department of Sociology at the Hebrew University of Jerusalem. His research interests cover social movements, contentious politics and conflict resolution.

Chen Friedberg is a member of the Political Reform research group at the Israel Democracy Institute, which is looking at the workings of the Knesset and the Israeli electoral system. She is also a Senior Lecturer in the Department of Israel and Middle Eastern Studies at Ariel University.

Charles D. (Chuck) Freilich is a Senior Fellow at Harvard's Belfer Center and the author of *Israeli National Security: A New Strategy for an Era of Change* (Oxford University Press, 2018) and *Zion's Dilemmas: How Israel Makes National Security Policy* (Cornell University Press, 2012). Previously, he was a Deputy Israeli National Security Adviser, as well as a Senior Analyst at the Israel Ministry of Defense.

Itzhak Galnoor is a Herbert Samuel Professor of Political Science (Emeritus) at Hebrew University of Jerusalem and a Senior Fellow at the Van Leer Jerusalem Institute. From 1994–1996, he was Head of the Civil Service Commission in Itzhak Rabin's Government and served on the Israel Science Foundation's Executive Committee. In 2015, Professor Galnoor was awarded the Lifetime Achievement Award of the Association of Israel Studies. His latest book (with Dana Blander) is: *The Handbook of Israel's Political System* (Cambridge University Press, 2018).

Galia Golan is Professor of government and chair of the Program on Diplomacy and Conflict Studies at the School of Government, Diplomacy and Strategy at the Interdisciplinary Center in Herzliya and Professor Emeritus of the Hebrew University of Jerusalem. Her latest book is *Israeli Peacemaking Since 1967: Factors Behind the Breakthroughs and Failures*.

Reuven Y. Hazan is the Chair in Israeli Democracy and Politics at the Department of Political Science of The Hebrew University of Jerusalem. His expertise centers on the historical and current analysis of democratic institutions, specifically placing Israeli democracy in comparative perspective. His research focuses on Israel's electoral system, political parties and its legislative branch.

Reut Itzkovitch-Malka is an Assistant Professor in the Department of Sociology, Political Science and Communications at the Open University of Israel. Prior to joining the academic faculty of the Open University, she was a Postdoctoral Fellow at Stanford University's Center on Democracy, Development and the Rule of Law. Her research interests include gender and politics, legislative studies, political representation, electoral systems and candidate selection methods. Her articles have appeared in journals such as *Political Studies* and the *European Journal of Women's Studies* and *Representation*. She is the co-author of *The Representation of Women in Israeli Politics: A Comparative Perspective* (The Israel Democracy Institute, 2016).

Amal Jamal is the Associate Professor and former Chair of the Department of Political Science at Tel Aviv University and head of the Walter Lebach Institute. He has published extensively on state structure and civil society, democratization, social movements, minority nationalism and other topics. His books include *Arab Minority Nationalism in Israel: The Politics of Indigeneity* (Routledge, 2011) *and The Arab Public Sphere in Israel: Media, Space and Cultural Resistance* (Indiana University Press, 2009).

Rebecca B. Kook is a senior lecturer in the Department of Politics and Government at Ben-Gurion University, Israel. She has written widely on the question of identity and Israeli society. Her most recent publication focuses on the political representation of the Palestinian citizens in Israel, and she is also currently involved in a research project that focuses on local government and minority women in Israel.

Pinchas Landau is an economic and financial analyst, serving as a consultant to major financial institutions in Israel and abroad on domestic and global developments.

David Newman holds the Chair of Geopolitics at Ben-Gurion University in Israel, where he founded the Department of Politics and Government and co-founded the Centre for the Study of European Politics and Society. From 1999–2014 he was chief editor of the international journal, *Geopolitics*, and from 2010–2016 he was Dean of the combined Faculty of Humanities and Social Sciences at the University. In 2013 he was awarded the OBE for promoting scientific cooperation between Israel and the UK. His research focuses on territorial dimensions of ethnic and national politics, with a particular emphasis on the Israel/Palestine arena. He has published widely on the changing role and significance of borders in a globalized world.

Rob Geist Pinfold holds a PhD in War Studies from King's College London and serves as a Neubauer Research Associate at the Institute for National Security

Studies (INSS) at the University of Tel Aviv. Previously, he held a Predoctoral Fellowship at the University of Haifa and taught at the Joint Services Command and Staff College in the United Kingdom. His work has been published in the academic journal Mediterranean Politics and the British newspaper The Daily Telegraph, amongst others. His research interests primarily lie within the fields of territorial conflict and grand strategy.

Joel Peters is Director of School of Public and International Affairs and Professor in the Government and International Affairs program at Virginia Tech. He is also a Policy Fellow at Mitvim: The Israeli Institute for Regional Foreign Policies and for the past three summers a Visiting Research Fellow at the Leonard Davis Institute for International Relations, Hebrew University, Jerusalem. His research interests and publications cover Israeli politics and foreign policy, the Israel–Palestinian peace process, regional cooperation in the Middle East and Europe's relations in the Middle East and the Mediterranean. He is the co-editor (with David Newman) of the *Routledge Handbook on the Israeli–Palestinian Conflict* and is currently completing on a book on Israeli foreign policy since the end of the Cold War.

Arieh Saposnik is an Associate Professor at the Ben-Gurion Institute for the Study of Israel and Zionism at Ben-Gurion University in the Negev. He is a historian of Zionism and Jewish nationalism, interested in the construction of national cultures and identities in the modern world. He is the author of *Becoming Hebrew: The Creation of a Jewish National Culture in Ottoman Palestine.*

Colin Shindler is Emeritus Professor at SOAS, University of London and founder-chair of the European Association of Israel Studies. His book *The Rise of the Israeli Right* was awarded the gold medal as the best book for 2016 in The Washington Institute's for Near East Policy's Book Prize competition. His most recent book *The Hebrew Republic: Israel's Return to History* was published by Rowman and Littlefield in 2017.

Dov Waxman is Professor of Political Science, International Affairs, and Israel Studies, and the Stotsky Professor of Jewish Historical and Cultural Studies at Northeastern University. He is also the co-director of the University's Middle East Center. His research focuses on the Israeli–Palestinian conflict, Israeli foreign policy, US–Israel relations, and American Jewry's relationship with Israel. He is the author of three books: *The Pursuit of Peace and the Crisis of Israeli Identity: Defending/ Defining the Nation, Israel's Palestinians: The Conflict Within,* and *Trouble in the Tribe: The American Jewish Conflict over Israel.*

Ofer Zalzberg is a Senior Analyst with the Middle East Program of the International Crisis Group. His research interests and publications cover the religious and national facets of conflict, the Arab–Israeli conflict and Israeli domestic politics and regional foreign policy.

INTRODUCTION

Israel—a nation of contrasts and cleavages

Rob Geist Pinfold

"If you will it, it is no dream": so wrote Theodore Herzl in his seminal work, *Altneuland*. Whilst the book was a work of fiction, its goals were anchored in a vision for reality, as Herzl was referring to the need to translate lofty ideological norms into action, in order to engender Jewish statehood. Herzl passed away in 1904, long before the founding of the State of Israel in 1948. Thus, the Zionist visionary died unaware of the impact and significance that his writing—and the above quote in particular—would have in forming the core foundations of the mythology underpinning the modern state of Israel. Millions of individuals were spurred into action by the commentary of Zionist thinkers such as Herzl and prompted by the perils facing Jewish life in the diaspora, particularly in the mid-twentieth century. From places of birth as far apart as Latin America, Europe and Asia, individuals with nothing in common bar the shared religion of Judaism poured into Israel in droves, realizing Herzl's vision of Jewish sovereignty. Thus, over a hundred years after the 1902 publication of *Altneuland*, Jewish statehood is far from a dream: the State of Israel is an established, indisputable reality.

Contemporary Israel is an unlikely powerhouse in a troubled region. Beginning life in 1948 with less than a million citizens, surrounded by hostile actors dwarfing the young state in geographical size and population, modern Israel now boasts over eight million citizens and was famously described by current Prime Minister Binyamin Netanyahu as "an island of stability in the Middle East." Indeed, whilst local autocrats buckled under the so-called "Arab Spring" of 2010, Israel retained its status as a democratic state without interruption. Though domestic debates are often bitter, the level of animus cannot be compared to the internecine bloodletting of the Syrian Civil War. Israel sometimes fares better than the Western countries it often seeks to emulate, surviving the 2008 Global Financial Crisis—which devastated Western economies—relatively unscathed. Similarly, Israel's "hi-tech" industry has earned it the nickname "the start-up nation," as global companies exploit the investor-friendly environment and skilled workforce, turning the country into a world-leading, technological powerhouse. Concurrently, the strength of Israel's economic and social institutions rests on the indisputable local military supremacy of the Israel Defense Forces, which transformed from a rag-tag force of volunteers and new immigrants into one of the most powerful armed forces in the world.

Yet *Altneuland* portrayed a future Jewish state governed by European liberalism and co-existence with indigenous Arabs. This normative vision sits uncomfortably with the 2015 Israeli general election, where the incumbent Prime Minister of the right-wing Likud Party—Binyamin Netanyahu—appealed to the racial prejudices of the electorate, by warning that "Arab voters are heading to the polling station in droves." At the time of writing, the Knesset continues to debate a proposal known as "the Jewish State bill"; supporters argue it would strengthen societal cohesion, detractors claim the bill will further de-legitimize Israel's beleaguered Arab minority. Additionally, late 2015 saw the Israeli Education Minister—Naftali Bennett—ban schools from studying a book portraying a love affair between a Jew and an Arab. Finally, in their normative visions of national liberation and self-determination, no mainstream Zionist visionary ever advocated uninterrupted military rule over several million non-Jewish Palestinian Arabs. Yet over seventy years after Israel's victory in the June 1967 "Six-Day War," no Israeli government has managed to extricate itself from the problem and geographical space commonly and ambiguously referred to within Israel as "the territories."

Concurrently, societal divides within contemporary Israel extend far beyond the simplistic dichotomy between Jew and Arab. The traditional Israeli historical and social narrative frames the state as "the ingathering of the exiles," where Jews are molded into a fraternally-bound nation. Indeed, contemporary Israel is composed of Jews and their decedents from around the world; Ashkenazi Jews of Eastern European origin rub shoulders with Russian newcomers and Mizrahi Jews of Middle Eastern origin. However, beyond this one-dimensional picture of co-existence lie tangible, exigent tensions, which frequently bubble over into open racism and assertions of ethnic supremacy. In the early decades of statehood, the Ashkenazi elite often subjected Mizrahi immigrants to institutionalized, racial prejudice, with discrimination continuing in the contemporary era. However, 2017 also saw incitement against Ashkenazi Jews from the highest echelons of government, as the Chair of the Coalition, David Amsalem, claimed: "the Ashkenazim and the leftists are always allowed to break the law." Internally, Israel is a nation divided, between secular and religious, male and female, Ashkenazi and Mizrahi, Jewish and Arab, left wing and right wing; ideological, cultural and social chasms underline the Israeli domestic arena.

Though in its early years, the State of Israel was characterized by the dominance of social-democratic parties in the Knesset and the cultural hegemony of the Kibbutz movement, contemporary Israel boasts one of the most salient gaps between rich and poor of any modern, developed country. Whilst Herzl envisioned a secular state, shifting demographics and the burgeoning ultra-orthodox population suggest that religion will play an increasing role in policymaking, much to the chagrin of many avowedly secular Israelis. The complicated relationship between religion and state rests on "the status quo"—an uneasy arrangement where the state is a mostly secular entity, though most businesses close on the Sabbath and Kosher food is served at official functions. However, increasing numbers of Israelis reject the involvement of the state-funded rabbinate in their weddings and life cycle events; conversely, late 2017 saw a law passed allowing the Interior Minister (from the ultra-orthodox Shas Party) to close supermarkets opening on the Sabbath. Regardless of the outcome of these latest "Shabbat wars," religious–secular tension and growing disparities of income will continue to be a constant in Israeli social and political life.

The institutions of the state are under exceptional stress, with multiple campaigns to weaken the power of Israel's Supreme Court, which often vetoes parliamentary legislation. Equally, entrenched animosity characterizes the debates between the Israeli political left and right; unlike other nations, this divide is primarily determined by attitudes towards the "peace process" with Israel's neighbors. The contemporary Israeli reality is therefore defined by a host of problems common to many nations—spanning gender and racial inequality, to the high cost of living—with unique, local traits. Israel is no dream - though its existence is an established fact, the contemporary state is far from the utopian construct envisioned by early Zionist thinkers.

Externally, Israel faces significant challenges, unusually prominent for a state with such a small population and geographical expanse. Despite testy US–Russia relations, the crisis facing the European Union and North Korean belligerency, the Israeli–Palestinian conflict retains its traction in op-eds, news reports and academic studies. Israelis often perceive the global community as disproportionately hostile, noting the growth of the Boycott, Divestments and Sanctions (BDS) movement in Western campuses and political forums. Regionally, policymakers grapple with the perceived existential threat of the Iranian nuclear program and the growing encirclement of Israel by Hizbollah and Hamas. Israel began the 1990s with an unusually optimistic and positive perceived strategic outlook, due to the collapse of the Soviet Union, the beginning of a nascent peace process with the Palestinians and the extension of US influence in the region. By contrast, Israel's contemporary geopolitical reality—though greatly improved from the perceived existential threats of its early decades—remains far more uncertain in recent years, with caution and conservatism resultantly dominating foreign policymaking.

Additionally, the occupation of the West Bank remains the elephant in the room, whenever Israel is mentioned. Over fifty years after the 1967 "Six-Day War," many questions concerning Israel's long-term vision for the territory remain unanswered. No matter what their position on the necessity of the occupation of the West Bank, Israelis of most ideological stripes are unlikely to perceive the territorial status quo as ideal. Israel ended its military and civilian presence within the Gaza Strip in 2005, whilst subsequently expanding settlements and entrenching control in the West Bank. Divergent governments have expressed radically different views on the acceptance of a two-state solution, whether to annex the West Bank or with-draw from most of it; Israelis are equally divided on the question of the fate of the millions of Palestinian inhabitants within the territory. Regardless of the political bombast, the myriad of peace plans and multiple failed negotiations, the status quo of occupation remains unexpectedly tenacious in its longevity, generating further tension between Israel and the international community, including previously sup-portive allies.

Modern Israel: the need for a comprehensive analysis

The above analysis of contemporary Israel raises a plethora of divergent questions. Will Israel ever withdraw from the West Bank? How significantly does Israel's occu-pation imperil its relations with the international community? Can Arab citizens ever be fully integrated into the patchwork of Israeli cultural life? How did Israel transition from a socialist-inspired economic model, to a "hi-tech" investment hub? What does it mean to be both a Jewish and a democratic state? Is Israel the center of global Jewish life, or is "Jewishness" very different from "Israeliness?" Rarely do these searching questions elicit definitive answers. Equally, this volume does not purport to provide solutions to the myriad of dilemmas facing the State of Israel. Instead, it seeks to trace the evolution of the key debates in modern Israel, within both the domestic and foreign arenas, whilst critically analyzing existing cultural trends and policy paradigms. Each essay within this volume links history to critical analyses of the present, whilst providing projections for the future.

Israel is a country of which much ink has been spilt, but which—paradoxically—is so often misunderstood. Within academia, the study of Israel continues to spawn a vast and ever-growing literature. Numerous books and journal articles have been published on various micro-aspects of Israeli policy and society. Nevertheless, authors frequently analyze one issue or level of analysis alone. Rarely do diver-gent fields and scholars of history and social science interact, to provide a multi-disciplinary picture of the challenges facing modern Israel. Concurrently, outside of the so-called "ivory tower," coverage of the Israeli–Arab conflict continues to dom-inate the news cycle and occupy prominent space in newspapers worldwide. Whilst policymakers and pundits frequently focus on Israeli foreign and security policy, the external relations of the state are often inseparably linked to internal perceptions, beliefs and alignments of political power and vice versa.

Thus, this book provides a comprehensive, multi-disciplinary analysis of the salient external and internal threats, opportunities and issues facing contemporary Israel; an accessible guide for students, scholars and policymakers alike. This book is comprised of sixteen chapters, each providing the reader with a critical analysis on a specific critical issue facing the State of Israel, and could be considered as a stand-alone volume of the topic under discussion. Additionally, each chapter blends an introduction to the issue or arena analyzed, with an in-depth analysis corresponding to the author's expertise. Taken together, this volume is multi-disciplinary, blending approaches spanning international relations, economics, history and sociology, amongst others. Nevertheless, this volume adopts a "theory-lite" approach in order to increase accessibility to a wider audience, including policymakers, political commentators and the general public.

Reflecting the multi-disciplinary foundations of this volume, the chapters are divided into three, broadly-defined sections, spanning both internal and external challenges. Part I examines the "Israeli political system" (such as the Knesset, political parties and extra-parliamentary politics); Part II addresses "Issues in Israeli society" (including the Israeli economy, divides between Jews and Arabs, religious and secular Israelis and the struggle for gender equality); and Part III focuses on "Security, geopolitical and foreign policy challenges" (relations between Israel and the Jewish Diaspora, Israeli foreign policy, borders and settlements and regional security threats). Despite this division into three separate sections, significant overlap exists between chapters. This is inevitable in the study of Israel, where the formation of foreign and security policy is closely linked to the domestic distribution of power and vice versa. Thus, this volume provides a comprehensive analysis, unpacking the plethora of diverse challenges and opportunities facing Israel in the early twenty-first century. Each of the sixteen chapters provides an original, unique contribution to understanding the patchwork that is modern Israel.

Chapter descriptions

Whilst political divides in Western liberal democratic states are often characterized by disagreements over levels of government spending, state intervention in the economy and cultural issues such as LGBT equality, the key cleavage defining contemporary Israel is the almost inconsolable salience of several competing conceptions of Zionism. Most Jewish Israelis across the political spectrum define themselves as Zionists. However, the consensus ends there: definitions of Zionism are fiercely contested. Do Zionists prioritize Jewish sovereignty over the "Land of Israel," or alternatively, does Zionism entail the preservation of a Jewish majority at the expense of territorial minimalism? The first chapter of this book—"Zionism in the twenty-first century"—addresses these key conflicts, with Arieh Saposnik examining the contested nature of terms such as "Zionism" and "Jewish statehood," tracing the tension within Israeli society that is salient throughout this volume. With the election of US President Donald Trump, the retrenchment of the European Union following the British "Brexit" vote, and unprecedented "culture wars" within the developed world, it is an open question as to whether Israeli society and political culture—rife with bitter, possibly irreconcilable divides—is a trailblazer in a new, global trend of unstable domestic politics.

The increasingly contested nature of political norms and institutions are a persistent undercurrent in Part I of this volume, which analyzes the workings of Israel's political system and the contemporary distribution of power within it. In the opening chapter—"Israeli democracy under stress"—Itzhak Galnoor demonstrates that the existing political contract in Israel, whereby competing parties and interest groups adhere to commonly respected rules of the game, is under unprecedented threat. This chapter charts the mainstream legitimization of right-wing populism, defined by currents termed "anti-politics" and "anti-democratic," alongside more long-term trends such as the stability of coalition governments in Israel and the challenges to the status quo posed by demographic changes. Concurrently, in the second chapter in Part I—"The rise of the Israeli right"—Colin Shindler examines the growth of revisionist Zionism, chronicling the emergence of the political right, out of obscurity and into a hegemonic position as the dominant political force in Israel. This chapter comparatively analyses early ideological torchbearers, such as Vladimir Jabotinsky, with the contemporary Israeli right wing, encapsulated by parties such as the Likud and HaBayit HaYehudi, demonstrating the divergences between classic right-wing Israeli doctrine and its contemporary adherents.

With these changes in mind, how relevant are traditional conceptions of the political "left" and "right" and accompanying party loyalties? This question is addressed by the third chapter of Part I—"Political parties and parliamentary politics"—which scrutinizes shifting electoral cleavages within Israel. Reuven Hazan and Chen Friedberg link the rise of the right to social and demographic trends, such as the decline of the labor-voting secular, Ashkenazi middle class and the rise of previously marginal groups, concentrated in Israel's "periphery." Concurrently, this chapter also notes the pivotal role of uniquely Israeli societal cleavages, such as Jewish and Arab, secular and religious, in determining electoral preferences. Similarly, the final chapter of Part I—"Extra-parliamentary politics—the settlement movement's success story"—continues to explore the implications of the declining monopoly exercised by Israeli political parties in determining policy. Though the term "civil society" often possesses left-wing, activist connotations, Eitan Alimi provides a case study of the most successful extra-parliamentary group in contemporary Israel: the settlement movement. The chapter employs the settlers to demonstrate the transmission belt between political elites, the military and civil society, charting the success of the movement and its resilience against external challenges, such as the 2005 disengagement from the Gaza Strip.

Though Part I highlighted developments within the domestic Israeli political arena, these examinations of changes in the domestic balance of political power frequently led to the identification of causality within broader, societal and cultural trends. Therefore, Part II of this volume digs deeper to identify the socio-economic, demographic and societal challenges facing Israel. Though foreign coverage continues to be monopolized by the conflict with the Palestinians, the largest demonstrations in Israeli history were not about the contested "peace process," but instead focused on public demands in 2011 to lower the cost of living. Conversely, the first chapter of Part II—"The Israeli economy: success as the new normal"—notes that many commentators overlooked the successes of the Israeli transition, from a social-democratic system to a champion of private enterprise and the "high-tech" bubble. Nevertheless, Pinchas Landau is equally explicit in identifying potential challenges for "the poster boy of the Washington consensus." Indeed, the cost of living continues to dominate Israeli current affairs, precipitating the rise of the Kulanu Party led by Likud rebel Moshe Kahlon in the 2015 election, on a flagship policy of lowering the cost of housing for middle-class Israelis.

Whilst radically altering the economic makeup of contemporary Israel, the decline of statism had profound societal effects, leading to the rise of individualism and the diversification of voices within the societal sphere. In a landmark speech in 2016, Israeli President Reuven Rivlin argued that society has transitioned from a monocultural model to that of four "tribes": Arabs, ultra-orthodox Jews, national-religious Jews and secular Zionist Jews, of whom only the latter two usually self-define as "Zionist." These trends are explored by the second chapter of Part II—"Multiculturalism and identity politics"—wherein Rebecca Kook warns that, though the decline of a monocultural monopoly is to be celebrated, the lack of a common denominator between divergent societal groups risks deepening existing divides. The twin phenomena of the pluralization of civil society and the political and societal rise of the conservative, Israeli right are enjoined by the third chapter of Part II—"Religion and state." Ofer Zalzberg examines where these two trends converge, such as the increased inclusion of growing orthodox Jewish groups within the mainstream, and where they diverge, as represented by the growing assertiveness of secular Israelis in life cycle questions of marriage and diet.

In multiple studies of Israeli civil society, existing literature often focuses on the Jewish Israeli population; Israel's Arab citizens are framed as either outside the societal mainstream or are portrayed as a monolithic group. However, the 2015 elections demonstrated both the collective assertiveness and diversity of Israel's Arab citizens, with a plethora of parties claiming to represent Arab interests winning an unprecedented thirteen Knesset seats. Thus, the fourth chapter of Part II—"Emerging elites and new political ideas amongst Palestinians in Israel"—scrutinizes internal Arab divisions. Amal Jamal examines the incongruity of increased Jewish Israeli pluralism and the continued socioeconomic challenges and discrimination faced by Israel's Arab citizens. The final chapter within Part II—"Political representation of women and gender (in)equality"—addresses a problem that is not limited to Israel, yet possesses many unique local characteristics: the struggle for women's equality. Reut Itzkovitch-Malka employs female representation in Israeli politics as a fulcrum for which to gauge the status of women in contemporary Israeli society, demonstrating that an increase of female representatives does not inherently correlate with enhanced gender equality. The local contradictions vis-à-vis women's rights are delineated critically: Israel has consistently styled itself as an egalitarian state, recruiting women for military service, yet Israeli society is often unusually masculine, partly due to the predominance of military culture.

In an oft-quoted aphorism, ex-US Secretary of State Henry Kissinger allegedly claimed that: "Israel has no foreign policy, it only has a domestic policy." Israel is frequently accused of lacking a grand strategy, with diplomacy playing second fiddle to the Defense Ministry. The tension between foreign and security policy continues to generate controversy, with Israel's Ministry of Foreign Affairs subject to significant budget cuts in recent years. Thus, the final five chapters of this book, which comprise Part III, are concerned with the nexus of security, geopolitics and foreign policy challenges. Analyses of Israeli national security often thinly-mask the ideological biases of authors, framing Israeli policy through a wholly negative prism or solely emphasizing Israel's regional primacy in military strength. By contrast, the first chapter of Part III—"Security challenges and opportunities in the twenty-first century"—provides both a positive and negative "balance sheet" of Israeli security doctrine, spanning the peace treaties with Egypt and Jordan to the Iranian nuclear program and the continued indecisiveness vis-à-vis the Palestinian question. Charles Freilich also examines the shift from state-level to non-state, "asymmetric" threats, whilst assessing how the changes in the Middle Eastern geostrategic environment impact Israeli security paradigms.

Though national security remains a salient topic in analyses of Israel, no subject has generated more commentary than the flipside of this subject area: the Israeli–Arab peace process. Thus, the next chapter—"The challenge of peace"—provides a historical overview charting the successes and failures of Israeli–Arab peacemaking. Galia Golan gives the most weight to initiatives following the Six-Day War of June 1967, contrasting the peace treaty with Egypt with stillborn Israeli–Syrian negotiations. Appropriately, substantial coverage is afforded to peace efforts between Israel and the Palestinians, beginning with United Nations Security Council Resolution 242 and ending with US-mediated talks under the Obama administration. Inevitably, the transformation wrought by the Six-Day War also plays a salient role in the subsequent two chapters: "Borders and the demarcation of national territory" and "Settlements and the creation of political landscapes," both of which are written by David Newman. In the first chapter, Newman provides a macro-analysis of how Israel's borders were delineated, taking into account topographical factors, history and conflict. Subsequently, Newman focuses on the creation of settlements in the West Bank and how the settlement movement affects Israeli policy in the territory. This chapter also maps the "facts on the ground" established by the settlement movement since 1967 and their impact on normative future territorial configurations and border arrangements with the Palestinians.

Israeli foreign policy is not limited to its regional milieu. Commentators are increasingly attributing importance to ties with countries in Latin America and Asia. This broader thread of Israeli foreign policy is unpacked by the next chapter—"Israel in the world: the quest for legitimacy"—which also assesses Israel's relations with supra-national bodies, such as the European Union and the United Nations. Joel Peters dissects Israel's "pivot" to emergent powers such as China and India and the "special relationship" between the US and Israel. Alongside relations with foreign countries, Israeli relations with the Jewish Diaspora have been dominated by complex influences. Notwithstanding their vast contributions of financial and political support to Israel, that many millions of Jews refrained from emigrating to Israel fueled suspicion of their foreign co-religionists. The final chapter of this volume—"Israel and the Jewish people"—addresses this relationship, focusing on American Jewry: the largest, non-Israeli-Jewish community. Dov Waxman argues that Israel–Diaspora relations are only becoming more complex. Whilst demographic changes are engendering a more right-wing, orthodox American Jewish community, Diaspora Jews in the US and worldwide are increasingly critical of Israeli policies, focusing their ire on the peace process and questions of religion and state.

In sum, the division of this book into three parts and sixteen chapters ensures that no stone is left unturned in a critical examination of the issues and opportunities inherent to modern Israel. The processes of change and fluctuation within Israeli society and domestic politics are equally as contested and contentious as Israeli foreign policy. Changes in the distribution of domestic political power reflect societal shifts and economic strength; simultaneously, foreign and defense policy is linked to communal perceptions. Broadly, the macro challenges facing Israel remain relatively static: societal rifts, demographic competition, lack of gender, racial and religious equality, questions concerning the public role of religion and the ever-present Israeli–Arab conflict. Nevertheless, the perceptions and perspectives within and about Israel are constantly in flux, both responding to events and setting the agenda.

Contemporary Israel constitutes an interacting, enigmatic mass of conflicts and contradictions. Israeli society remains bitterly divided regarding whether the occupation of the West Bank mortally imperils the state, or whether the conquest of the entire Land of Israel is to be celebrated. Foreign policy norms are dichotomized between conceptions of Israel as a "nation that dwells alone," doomed to be distinct or "a light unto the nations," reaching out to the west, regional powers and the developing world. Domestically, does the term "Jewish state" refer to demographics, or does it require an enhanced public primacy for religion? Will the gap between Mizrahim and Ashkenazim be overcome, or— like the growing disparity between rich and poor—will it continue to divide domestic politics and undermine societal cohesion? Similarly, will the Israeli body politic remain committed to the organizing principles of liberal democracy, or will the country continue its descent into authoritarian populism? This book addresses these questions, amongst others, providing a holistic analysis of the contemporary reality, whilst offering predictions concerning the internal and external struggles of tomorrow.

1

ZIONISM IN THE TWENTY-FIRST CENTURY?

Arieh Saposnik

The walkway to the exit gates of Ben-Gurion International Airport in January of 2017—as Israel prepares to mark its seventieth anniversary year—is adorned with an exhibition of photographs and images from the history of Israel and Zionism. At its culmination, the largest of the posters seems to be not only a summary of the history depicted in the images, but a proclamation of the state's most fundamental message to itself and to those passing through the halls of this main port of entry and exit (ironically, perhaps, it is those who are on their way out who get to see the exhibit). "I once called Zionism an infinite ideal," the poster quotes the early Zionist leader, Theodor Herzl, who is depicted, larger than life, stating that:

> it will not cease to be an ideal even after we attain our land, the Land of Israel. For Zionism[…] encompasses not only the hope of a legally secured homeland for our people […] but also the aspiration to reach moral and spiritual perfection.

This is a striking quote from the Zionist thinker perhaps most closely identified with the idea of a Jewish state as the most central *endziel*, Zionism's most important goal. It seems a worthwhile starting point to explore what Zionism might be and what it might mean in the twenty-first century.

This essay sets out to propose some thoughts concerning the theme of "Zionism in the twenty-first century." It is an essay, in other words, that is more about the present and future than it is about the past. It is written, however, by a historian, fully aware of how difficult it can be to interpret, make sense of, and paint a picture of the past, let alone attempt to envision the future, or to understand the passing present. These are, then, musings about where Zionism might go, where it might *wish* to go, and how it might attempt to understand itself in the coming decades.

Stepping away from writing that is strictly historical in focus, and concentrating instead on present and future, it is necessarily also the musings of an Israeli Jew, hoping to suggest some directions for meaning in the increasingly trying and challenging times that the early twenty-first century is turning out to be. In order to begin to consider where Zionism might turn, then, and what it might seek to be in the coming century, this essay will attempt to provide some clearer understanding of what it has been in the foregoing century.

The quote from Herzl that begins this essay is remarkable, not only given its presentation of statehood as a station along the way, rather than the ultimate end of Zionism. It is also striking given the contrast with an opposite current that appeared in embryonic form even before Zionism had attained its goal of statehood, and then in fuller form after it had been attained. In the immediate wake of the Israeli declaration of independence, there were those who proclaimed that now that the state had been established, Zionism as an ideology, as a movement, and as a set of institutions that had been erected, ostensibly in order to attain statehood, had fulfilled its historic mission, and it no longer had a *raison d'être*.

To be sure, it would only be some decades later—in the 1990s—that the term "Post-Zionism" would come to refer to a more ideologically ripened position that held that Zionism had become obsolete after 1948 (this would be one among a range of ideological positions associated with the term). As early as the 1950s, however, internal Zionist debates surrounded the notion that the establishment of the state had been a dramatic watershed moment in Jewish history. So profoundly revolutionary was the existence of a Jewish state after two millennia of Jewish statelessness, this argument went, that it raised a host of questions regarding the continued existence of Zionism.

In the early years of the state, even David Ben-Gurion, the towering leader of the Zionist Movement and Israel's first prime minister, stopped just short of suggesting that Zionism had outlived its usefulness. The institutional structures of the Zionist movement, he claimed, had reached the end of the road, now that a sovereign Jewish state had come into being. The World Zionist Organization, Ben-Gurion famously quipped in 1960, had been but "a scaffold to aid the construction of Israel," adding that "scaffolds are taken away when the building has been completed."[1]

Going deeper, Ben-Gurion questioned the meaning of "*galut*," or "exile" and the status of those Jews who chose to remain outside of Israel after the foundation of the state. The so-called Zionism of Jews choosing to live outside of the state of Israel after 1948, Ben-Gurion famously determined, was at best a "pseudo-Zionism" (Shimoni 1995, pp. 11–36). Faced with the paucity of American Jewish immigration, Ben-Gurion stated that he could no longer distinguish between Zionist and non-Zionist organizations or Jews. For Ben-Gurion, a central meaning and implication of commitment to the Zionist idea entailed the personal choice to live in Israel. Faced with a Zionist organization whose core and leadership continued to be based in the Diaspora (out of choice, now that the state had been established),

Ben-Gurion would consequently go so far as to proclaim on occasion that he would no longer consider *himself* a Zionist.[2] Even the historiography of Zionism has at times evinced the notion that Zionism came to an abrupt end on May 14, 1948. As Gideon Shimoni has pointed out, some historians have presented the history of Zionism as ending with the establishment of the state, after which only a history of the state of Israel, or histories of those international bodies known collectively as "Zionist," remain possible.[3]

If such understandings of Zionism began to develop as early as the 1950s, and were given renewed emphasis during the 1990s when the discourse of "post-Zionism" was at its height, it seems hardly possible to shy away from similar questions in the early twenty-first century. Perhaps historical Zionism—whether it is assessed negatively or positively—has run its course and we are today in a "post-Zionist" age? Can there be any possible meaning to the word today, other than as an indication of some form of Israeli patriotism or, as some would have it, unquestioning loyalty to (usually right-wing) government policies? Of course, disagreements over the reality or desirability of the continued existence of Zionism after 1948 is really a debate over what Zionism in actual fact was (or is), and what it can or cannot be, should or should not be, in historical circumstances in which one of its key desiderata has been fulfilled.

Modern Zionism emerged in the nineteenth century, in an age of ideologies and "isms." It was conceived in response to what was known during that century (and into the first half of the twentieth) as "the Jewish question," or the "Jewish problem." In addition to casting itself as a response—in its more ambitious forms, a solution—to the Jewish problem itself, it was also as a response to previous responses, which Zionists deemed to have been partial or complete failures.[4] Zionism, in short, was in its very essence a child of the nineteenth century, and an attempt to provide solutions to the predicaments and distress confronting Jews and Jewish life in the nineteenth century. Its aims—though various and at times conflicting—can collectively be deemed revolutionary: It sought a total and complete transformation of Jewish life, culture, social structures; everything from Jewish geography—where Jews lived—to the language they spoke, to so intimate and fundamental a matter such as the Jew's body itself—were all to be transformed.

Despite constituting a child of the nineteenth century, the bulk of Zionism's achievements would come about over the course of the twentieth century, most notably during its first fifty years, before the ruptures of World War II, and then in its immediate aftermath. By the second half of the twentieth century, it was already a very different world—the changes in Jewish life were particularly dramatic with the transfer of the centers of Jewish life from Eastern Europe to North America and Israel, the establishment of the Jewish state, and the extermination of six million Jews at the hands of the Nazis. The dramatic events that shaped the end of the twentieth century and the beginning of the twenty-first have come at an ever-accelerating pace. All of this raises a critical question regarding Zionism: As a set of proposed solutions to a list of nineteenth- (and perhaps twentieth-) century problems, in what sense can we talk about Zionism in the twenty-first century? Some seven decades after the establishment of the State of Israel, any attempt to assess Zionism in the twenty-first century is equally bound to begin with an attempt to understand just what Zionism has meant and what it might mean today and in the future.

Which Zionism?—the "problem of the Jews" and the "problem of Judaism"

The critiques that engendered the rise of Zionism were, from the outset, extremely diverse and focused on differing aspects of Jewish life and culture. Zionism emerged from divergent and often conflicting understandings of just what the "Jewish question" was, and different currents within Zionism consequently offered differing visions of the solutions they sought to offer. One of the defining divergences, as early Zionist leader and philosopher Ahad Ha'am phrased it most famously, was based on the question of whether Zionism aimed to create a solution to the "problem of the Jews" or to the "problem of Judaism" (Ha'am 1997, p. 266). This distinction remains an important one in understanding Zionism (and what the word might mean) in the early twenty-first century.

The problem of the Jews: Zionism and the elimination of anti-Semitism

It is probably most common to think of Zionism primarily in political terms, as a political movement that set out to establish a state for the Jews in Palestine (or, as some suggested in Zionism's earliest years, anywhere on the globe). As understood by Theodor Herzl, the anticipated result of establishing a state for the Jews would be the elimination of anti-Semitism and the end of the kinds of social discrimination faced by many individual Jews in late nineteenth-century Europe. To Herzl and others, it was this that was the fundamental problem that Zionism would and should set out to rectify. Herzl's Zionism, in other words—although more complicated—was aimed principally at addressing the problem of the Jews.

Echoing his own biography, Herzl had become convinced by the final decade of the nineteenth century that although Jews had "sincerely tried everywhere to merge with the national communities in which we live […] It is not permitted us" (Herzl 1896, p. 209). Most integrated and Western-educated Jews in the nineteenth century understood anti-Semitism as an unfortunate remnant of the so-called "dark ages," a morsel of religious prejudice that had accidentally found its way into their age of enlightenment and progress. Even Herzl himself, in his foundational *Der Judenstadt* (*The Jewish State*, 1896—the work widely seen as the starting point for political Zionism) still holds onto at least pieces of this notion, characterizing "the Jewish question" as "a misplaced piece of medievalism which civilized nations do not even yet seem able to shake off, try as they will" (1896, p. 208).

Nevertheless, Herzl had come to see that, medieval though it may be in its origins, anti-Semitism was far from a spent force. Indeed, anti-Semitism in his own day, he wrote, was only increasing in strength and was making "the position of Jewish lawyers, doctors, technicians, teachers, and employees of every description

[...] daily more intolerable" (1896, pp. 215–216). Indeed, for many Western Jews such as Herzl, the conversion to a Zionist stance stemmed in large measure from a radically new understanding of anti-Semitism as something that was fundamental to modernity, and that bore the clear marks of the modern age—whether through the addition of racialized thought (a point explicated as early as Moses Hess' 1862 proto-Zionist pamphlet *Rome and Jerusalem*) or as the outcome of opposition to emancipation, as Herzl also stressed.

The idea of Jewish statehood was, perhaps, the most immediate and obvious Zionist response to the problem of anti-Semitism. Out of this renewed understanding of anti-Semitism as a permanent feature of the modern age, Zionism—and the State of Israel in its wake—was conceived by some of its proponents as a project aimed at providing a safe haven for Jews who might need a place of refuge. Indeed, evaluated from this perspective, Zionism's response to anti-Semitism appears to have been a very successful one. Since Israel's establishment, numerous groups of Jews— Holocaust survivors in the early years of the state, alongside Jews from various parts of the Islamic world, and in later years Jews from such disparate places as the former Soviet Union and Ethiopia—have immigrated to Israel en masse and have made it their home (an increasingly multilingual, multicultural and diverse home as a result).

Yet Zionism's response to anti-Semitism went beyond the creation of a refuge. At least in some of its interpretations, Zionism was expected not only to offer Jews shelter, but to have a deeper impact as well: In the long run, many (Herzl among them) assumed, the realization of the Zionist aim of establishing a Jewish state would eliminate the need for such shelter, by eliminating anti-Semitism itself. As it turned out, anti-Semitism has proven more persistent than such predictions anticipated. A range of indicators suggest that not only has it failed to disappear in the wake of the establishment of the State of Israel, but anti-Semitism has also in recent years undergone a resurgence.

The fact of its persistence, however, now in differing form, is not to say that Zionism and the establishment of a Jewish state have not had an impact on the history and manifestations of anti-Semitism. The use of at least some expressions of anti-Zionist and anti-Israel stances as a camouflage for what some scholars have argued is a new anti-Semitism[5] suggests that if anti-Semitism has not disappeared as Herzl hoped, it has certainly been dramatically transformed. (This is not to suggest, of course, that any and all criticism of Israel or Zionism is tantamount to anti-Semitism.) Although some of the old tropes remain (the internet has countless versions and interpretations of the famous anti-Semitic forgery, *The Protocols of the Elders of Zion*, for example), one of the new characteristics of anti-Semitism today is to be found in its target and imagery: At its center now one often finds an image of "the Jew" that, at least in certain key respects, has been transformed by the Zionist project of creating a "new Jew." The target of anti-Semitism today, in other words, is often no longer the emasculated, effeminate, weak exilic Jew of the nineteenth century (admittedly also conceived as covertly and furtively powerful), but rather a Jew who is now conceived as *overtly* powerful—politically, through what has often been labeled as "the Israel lobby" or "the Jewish lobby" interchangeably (referring primarily to the United States), or militarily, with the image of the Israeli as militaristic oppressor often taking center stage.

To be sure, this reflects a change in Jewish reality as well. The American Jewish commentator Peter Beinart rightly notes that "we live in a new era in Jewish history in which our challenges stem less from weakness than from power" (Beinart 2012, p. 161). It is not only the imagery that has undergone a shift, in other words, but the very tangible reality in which anti-Semitism operates. The impact of Zionism in transforming the reality and imagery of Jewish life, manifested so clearly in Israel's emergence as a significant regional and military power (contrast this with the eighteenth-century notion that Jews could not be emancipated because they were unfit to serve in the military) has not eliminated anti-Semitism, but it has undoubtedly transformed its discourse, imagery, and thinking.

The problem of Judaism: Zionism as Jewish cultural revolution and renaissance

But to see Zionism as fundamentally reducible to a response to the question of anti-Semitism is to fail to understand the multi-vocality that was always part of Zionism. This approach fails to understand the deeper, underlying motivations that led some Jews to become Zionists, as well as the goals that stirred much of Zionism, most of the time. To be sure, the push of anti-Semitism, inevitably tended to ensure that statehood was perceived as a key objective. The Zionist enterprise of cultural renaissance and revolution, on the other hand—rooted not in the external push of anti-Semitism, but rather in an internal critique and self-criticism that led to a diagnosis that held that Jewish life and culture in the Diaspora had reached a dead-end—did not reject statehood, but laid its major stress elsewhere. Central though the goal of statehood was for many currents of Zionism at important historical junctures, what motivated and served as the principal focus and desiderata for many Zionists was in fact the cultural renaissance for which the projected state was a vehicle, a means (albeit a necessary means) rather than the ultimate end. This Zionism strove for the creation of a vibrant Hebrew culture. Not only its central goal, the creation of a vibrant Hebrew culture, moreover, is surely Zionism's most astonishing and—given the fact that little more than a century ago, there was not a single individual who spoke Hebrew as a mother-tongue—its most counter-intuitive achievement.

Indeed, as preposterous as the idea of the establishment of a Jewish state seemed when Theodor Herzl proposed it in *Der Judenstadt* in 1896, the idea of a Hebrew culture was arguably less likely still. Herzl himself famously noted in *Der Judenstadt* that Hebrew could not conceivably be the language of the state he envisioned. "Who amongst us has a sufficient acquaintance with Hebrew to ask for a railway ticket in that language," he asked rhetorically. Indeed, Hebrew in 1896 did not have such a vocabulary—one reason why even leading figures in the revival of literary Hebrew were often skeptical of the prospects of the revival of spoken Hebrew, or even rejected the very idea.

Following one of his visits to Palestine, Ahad Ha'am himself—one of the fathers of the modern Hebrew revival—wrote in 1901 of his skepticism regarding a revival of spoken Hebrew. "Hebrew speech," he admitted, "is fluent in the mouths of the youth so long as they speak of simple and common matters." But ask even the older students any slightly more complicated question, and "they begin to stutter [...] and seek aid in hand gestures and mimicry" (Ha'am 1901, pp. 1–3). True Hebrew speech, he concluded, was at best a matter for the distant future. Only a decade later, however, in the wake of another visit to Palestine, his estimation would change dramatically, and he would write that "when one comes to a Jewish colony, one is immediately struck by the recognition that it is saturated with a national Hebrew atmosphere. All aspects of life [...] are stamped with the stamp of Hebrew" (Ha'am 1912, p. 279). By the eve of World War I, spoken Hebrew, and a budding national culture that was founded on that language, had become a reality in Palestine.[6]

The existence of a Hebrew culture, its manifest influence on Jewish life both in Israel and beyond—an influence it began to exert at a very early stage in its development, and which is certainly palpable in the early twenty-first century—was all but inconceivable in the early twentieth century. In late 1925, the poet Haim Nahman Bialik lamented that "whatever the Jew creates in the Diaspora is always absorbed in the culture of others, it loses its [Jewish] identity" (Bialik 1959, p. 284). However, Bialik would have been hard-pressed to imagine that less than one hundred years later Israeli authors writing in Hebrew would be read around the world, translated into countless languages; that not only the Hebrew University of Jerusalem, at whose founding he spoke, but also a number of universities in Israel would be ranked among the important academic institutions in the world; that Israeli musicians would be exporting their sound both westward and eastward; that Israel would become an important exporter of cinema, television and theatrical works, both in original Hebrew-language versions and in linguistic and cultural translation.

Hardly an incidental outgrowth of the drive to establish a state, Hebrew language and culture—the formation of a Hebrew-speaking national entity in Palestine and later Israel—was the outgrowth of very self-conscious and deliberate efforts to create it. In a series of articles that appeared as the Zionist project in Palestine was still in its very early stages, Yosef Aharonowitz, editor of the Hebrew-language Labor-Zionist journal *Hapoel HaTzair* (which was then clearly emerging as an important voice in Hebrew letters), was critical of those voices that argued that Zionist funds ought to be used only for the most evident, material needs. "We are still in need of Millions for the redemption of the Land," these critics held, "and you come along and trouble yourselves with schools, newspapers, publishing houses and the like?" From a strictly material standpoint, some were arguing, and at a crucial moment when material needs in Palestine were acute, this was a waste of resources and energies.

Aharonowitz, however, was not convinced. Their position, he argued, was akin to suggesting that "our success is dependent on our raising a generation without learning, without knowledge and without manners." In fact, he stressed, "the question of culture in the Land of Israel serves neither to enhance the question of the Yishuv (the Zionist community in pre-state Palestine) nor to detract from it. Rather it is that very question in the sharpest relief" (Aharonowitz 1909, p. 3). A leader of the budding labor Zionism of Palestine (an ideological camp that would later emerge as the most dominant in pre-state Palestine and through the first three decades of statehood), Aharonowitz surely held the material needs of the Yishuv in high regard. In the end, however, it was culture that was to him the real question, the ultimate aim of the Zionist undertaking.

Aharonowitz was hardly alone. Even the individual seemingly most associated with the establishment of the state and with the centrality of statehood in Zionist history, David Ben-Gurion, would write, a few years after he had declared that state's independence, that "the establishment of the state does not mean that the vision has been fulfilled." If ambivalent about what he deemed the so-called Zionism of institutional life and of Jews who remained abroad, he remained clearly committed to what he deemed to be Zionism's true central purpose and meaning. The ultimate end of Zionism as he understood it, he stressed, was a messianic-prophetic vision, positioned at the meeting point of an ancient culture and longing for Zion on the one hand, and cultural revolution and social transformation on the other. "The miracle that has taken place in our generation," he explained, "is that the *vehicle* has been created for the fulfillment of the "redemptive vision" (Ben-Gurion 1998, pp. 45–49). That miraculous vehicle, of course, was the state itself. Vital, indispensable (indeed, miraculous)—but a vehicle rather than an *endziel* in itself.

Years before, in the wake of the Balfour Declaration of 1917, which provided the very first indication that a state may in fact come into being at some point in the future, another Labor leader (and Ben-Gurion's close friend) Berl Katznelson pointed to the conditions he considered necessary to make the future state mean-ingful. "Will the people invest its efforts in a national structure ruled by landlords?" he asked. Will they commit themselves to a structure in which "beneath the veil of 'national liberation' will be economic subjugation, in which gold will purchase all, in which the worker will labor under the whip of the taskmaster, and in which the stain of current culture—the deprivation of the worker, the enslavement of man—will flourish and thrive?" (Katznelson 1946–1950, p. 71). For Katznelson, the unprecedented Zionist achievement that was embodied in the Balfour Declaration and its promise of a national home was insignificant if it did not signify a human liberation which alone could make the national structure meaningful.

The principal impetus that fed the Zionist drive for cultural revolution was a sense that it was an existential requirement for Jewish life. But from the outset it emerged from more than a mere survival instinct, and contained within it more than a tactic for continued existence. In some sense, it could be argued that even the Zionist cultural revolution and renaissance was not alone the ultimate goal. In strains of Zionist thought that were far more widespread than often recognized, it too was often understood to have a further aim, which often took the form of secularized versions of the vision of the biblical prophets, a humanistic vision of a universal redemption of humankind. To be sure, not every conception of Zionism at all times shared this vision. But this utopian belief was a central axis of Zionist discourse that is reflected in an additional, very familiar divide within Zionism— the apparent conflict between the desire to be "a nation like any other nation," to "normalize" the Jewish people, on the one hand; and the claim to represent "a light unto the nations" on the other.

Zionism, in other words, was motivated by two seemingly conflicting (but often in fact converging) impetuses: on the one hand, a widespread diagnosis that held that the Jews, and Jewish existence were somehow "abnormal" inspired many Zionists to work toward what was often termed "normalization"—the transform- ation of the Jews into a "normal" people. On the other hand, many Zionists held that the social and human experiment of building a society virtually from scratch, arguably coupled with a lingering notion of Jewish chosenness and based in the notion that Judaism had already once bequeathed a moral heritage to much of the world through the Bible, would allow the new culture being created in Palestine to emerge as a beacon for others as well. There may, of course, be some hubris (or at least some potential for it) in the latter claim, but it was most fundamentally an expression of Zionism's understanding of itself as belonging to a far broader struggle for human liberation.

Additionally, it is also important to recognize that the conflict between the longing for so-called normalization and the striving for moral perfection is only an apparent one. They may have been in tension with one another, but they also very clearly coexisted within the thoughts of many key Zionist figures, thinkers, and writers. Indeed, one of Zionism's greatest strengths and defining characteristics lay, perhaps, in its ability to maintain these two impulses in productive tension with one another. It was possibly this tension that helped contribute to Zionism's ability to embrace self-criticism and often trenchant cultural critique.

Zionism and cultural–political–social criticism

The Zionist cultural project—the effort to create a new Hebrew culture—was the outgrowth of an often harsh critique of Jewish life and culture in the present— a deep pessimism as to the very prospects for a continued Jewish life in its present state. Indeed, critique and self-criticism would remain a central feature of Zionism throughout much of its history. This is a point worthy of some stress: The criticism that animated and motivated a great deal of Zionism was not a mere adornment, some more or less humorous manifestation of an ostensible Jewish contentiousness.

Criticism (of various kinds) was not only the starting point for Zionist diagnoses of what Zionists across the board deemed to be a Jewish malady, or anomaly. It was almost an ideal in Zionist thought and life, and certainly a quintessential compo- nent of what Zionism was and what it sought. One of the fundamental prerequisites for the transformation of Jewish life that Zionism sought was an open, often harsh, critique of the current state of Jewish life, culture, politics, leadership, and social structures. Different currents of thought within Zionism naturally laid stress on different aspects of the realities they sought to critique, diagnosed them in different ways, and chose to articulate their critiques in differing styles. But critique and criticism (including of Zionism itself) were an ever-present feature of Zionist life.

A polemical storm that erupted in 1910 surrounding the publication of a provocative article by author Yosef Haim Brenner (which came to be known as "the Brenner affair") is an excellent illustration of this centrality and near idealization of criticism. Although he touched on a number of sensitive and controversial issues, perhaps the deepest dismay in this piece by Brenner—an icon of the young labor-Zionist immigrants and frequently the *enfant terrible* of Hebrew letters—was caused by his effort to divorce the Jewish national revival in Palestine from any connection to Jewish religious tradition. "We free Jews," he wrote,

> have nothing whatsoever to do with Judaism, and yet we are nevertheless inside the collective no less than those who lay *tefillin* [phylacteries used by observant Jewish men in their daily prayers] and grow *tzitzis* [knotted fringes worn by religiously observant men on their clothing].
>
> *(Haver 1912, pp. 6–8)*

The many attacks and accusations that ensued were accompanied by a demand by Ahad Ha'am that the Odessa Committee (the central body of the *Hovevei Zion*, or "Lovers of Zion"—the Zionist organization that was established prior to Herzl's founding of the World Zionist Organization) halt its funding for the journal *Ha-Po'el ha-Tza'ir* (where Brenner's piece had appeared) until the entire editorial board was replaced. In response, a long list of writers and activists, including many who explicitly disavowed the contents of Brenner's article, insisted that the Zionist project in Palestine need not fear the expression of opinions, even when they may be harsh and unpleasant.

Even in the still very embryonic reality of a Hebrew Palestine, when Hebrew language and culture had little cause yet for self-confidence, Aharon David Gordon, himself a (very different) icon of labor Zionism, explained that although he disagreed with much of what Brenner had written, the expression of even such objectionable views as the ones in Brenner's piece was simply not a threat, but rather an indication of a vibrant cultural life. "In Palestine," he wrote, "a Jew does not need to constantly measure his national pulse every hour, for in this sense he is entirely healthy." In the place where a full national life was in the process of being created, according to Gordon, it had simply "never occurred to us that an individual's opinion could pose a threat of any kind to the wholeness of Jewry" (Gordon 1954, p. 44–50).[7] How much more is this the case, one might ask, from the perspective of the early twenty-first century, in a reality in which a well-established and thriving Hebrew culture exists within the context of a sovereign Jewish state?

Countless texts attest to the many areas of Jewish life, both in Palestine and in the Diaspora, that came in for often scathing appraisals that were deemed to be at the very heart of the Zionist cultural project. The focus might be on the bearers of culture and its sources: A participant in the seventh convention of the Labor-Zionist organization, "Ha-Po'el Ha-Tza'ir" in 1912 explained, for example, that the national culture that would eventually emerge would necessarily be the result of struggles over who would be its principal bearers. He was concerned that in recent times, the labor forces in Palestine had been derelict in their duties in this regard, and noted that "lately, given the neglect by the workers, many of the younger generation in the [First Aliya] colonies have become more zealous regarding Hebrew than the workers." It was of utmost importance, he argued, that "the principal bearers of culture" in Zionist Palestine be those who uphold the principles of democracy (as a member of the Labor-Zionist Ha-Po'el Ha-Tza'ir organization, to him this meant the forces of labor).[8]

One of the most powerful expressions of this notion of the importance of self-criticism and critique was written, once again, by Yosef Haim Brenner. In his well-known piece "Self-Criticism in Three Volumes," Brenner explained what he understood to be the most fundamental criterion for a healthy movement of national revival and cultural renaissance. "It is well known," he wrote,

> That self-evaluation is one of the conditions of higher consciousness— whether of the individual or of the collective. [...] once [individuals and human collectivities] progress from a primitive state and climb toward greater levels of the spirit, once they begin to be able to see the other, and relationships between the self and the other become more complex ... that is the point at which critique in general, and self-criticism in particular, become a necessity. It is a bad sign for any adult human being or for an ancient nation if they do not feel a need for true self-critique.
>
> *(Brenner 1914)*

As Brenner's commentary indicates (and one ought to remember Brenner's iconic status in this context), not only was self-criticism not absent from the project of constructing a national culture as it was taking shape (and later), but it was in fact seen as one of the forces necessary to the creation of that culture. To be sure, the phraseology and rhetoric of early twentieth-century Zionists in Palestine may today sound either inflated or excessively ornate, and certainly teeming with ideology in ways that to the more cynical ears of the early twenty-first century often sound naïve. At the same time, however, with a slight change in perspective, one might suggest that they expressed a daring and a boldness of vision which are, perhaps less fortunately, equally foreign to early twenty-first-century ears.

From the early twentieth to the early twenty-first century

Today, the divisions within Zionism, and those straining the fabric of Israeli society, are (at least apparently) focused less on competition over who will be the bearer of a national critique and the leader of the national culture. Although Israel remains home to a vibrant and vocal civil society, the political divisions in Israeli society seem at times to suffocate political discourse and to leave it flatter and more dichotomous than one might expect from so variegated a society. Much of Israel's increasingly polarized political discourse seems to take place between a camp that upholds the value of criticism (or a particular understanding of what "criticism" means), but rejects the purpose to which it was previously put—the anchoring of a robust national culture and another which rejects almost any critical commentary. In certain circles of what is today considered Israel's political "left," criticism remains a highly valued principle (although the term is often misunderstood, with analytical critique being confused—and replaced—with mere disparagement). Talk of the value of national culture, on the other hand, or of the nation itself, has been largely removed from the lexicon of legitimate discourse. The very word "Zionism" has become anathema to some.

At the opposite extreme, amongst the Israeli "right," the nation is celebrated, as is the word "Zionism"—indeed this camp often claims to speak in the name of Zionism. However, in some of these circles, criticism has come to be deemed a form of betrayal, and the kinds of criticism that in the past served as the basis for cultural generation, renewal and growth are increasingly being stifled. Through powerful representatives in government, as well as through non-governmental organizations whose power has grown through association with governmental figures, significant portions of the Israeli "right" (including those in the ruling coalition at the time of this writing) have in recent years taken significant legislative and other measures to place severe restrictions on the free and open critique that has long been a part of Zionism and Israeli life.

In all too many cases, by forsaking any claim to Zionism, the Israeli "left" has forsaken effective political and cultural debate, and has abandoned the very term "Zionism" to the abuse and distortions—or at the very least, to the extreme narrowing of its vision, scope and human aspirations—that it suffers at the hands of its would-be champions on the "right." There is, of course, a wide spectrum of legitimate interpretation of the Zionist past. But when such accusations are rooted in a growing global culture of post-truth, and when they become increasingly a part of the discourse of at least some of Israeli society, they become central to the question of what Zionism may be in the coming century. Criticism and critique, as I have argued above, have historically been quintessential components of Zionism, but they too can be fetishized and become ends in themselves. Here, it might be useful to consider Richard Rorty's commentary on of the critics of American society on the eve of the new century and at the dawn of the post-truth era. "National pride," Rorty writes,

> is to countries what self-respect is to individuals: a necessary condition for self-improvement. Too much national pride can produce bellicosity and imperialism, just as excessive self-respect can produce arrogance. But just as too little self-respect makes it difficult for a person to display moral courage, so insufficient national pride makes energetic and effective debate about national policy unlikely …
>
> … Those who hope to persuade a nation to exert itself need to remind their country of what it can take pride in as well as what it should be ashamed of. They must tell inspiring stories about episodes and figures in the nation's past—episodes and figures to which the country should remain true.
>
> *(1998, pp. 3–4)*

In the twenty-first century, Zionism's most pronounced challenges are those that have emerged from within itself. And if one of those challenges stems from the fact that a faction of Israeli society has adopted a critique that divorces itself from the kind of national pride that Rorty talks about, the greatest challenge is the fact that the more powerful segments of Israeli society today have committed themselves to a nationalism, or patriotism, that is devoid of criticism and critique. At its best, and at the core of its central currents, Zionism was among the remarkable human movements and humanistic ideas of the nineteenth and twentieth centuries. The primary tasks facing a Zionism of the twenty-first century is to contend with those ghosts from within that threaten to diminish, if not to annihilate, that ideal.

In much of popular discourse in and about Israel today, one must ostensibly choose between a "Zionism" that is devoid of critique or criticism, or a criticism of Israeli society that is free of, and rejects, Zionism. A central task of Zionism in the twenty-first century is to reclaim the inherent connection between the two and to rearticulate a Zionism that is not only open to critical thinking, but which places social, cultural, political criticism at its very heart. Here we might find one meeting point between the cultural and political goals of Zionism: Criticism, as this essay has argued, is an inherent part of what Zionism is. That includes—in fact demands—criticism of Israeli society, politics, culture, and certainly of particular policies implemented in these realms. At the same time, while this essay does not seek to demonstrate that criticism is necessarily an expression of anti-Zionism or certainly of anti-Semitism, it does sometimes cross that line. Some would-be criticism is manifestly an expression of anti-Semitism, now given a guise of acceptability under the transformative impact of Jewish statehood in a post-Holocaust world.

Consider, for example, some of the claims in M. Shahid Alam's *Israeli Exceptionalism—The Destabilizing Logic of Zionism*. Zionism, as Alam depicts it, was in its essence a twofold phenomenon: A form of racism based on a sense of Jewish racial superiority—Zionists, Alam writes, "did not lag behind the Western Gentiles in their conviction of racial superiority over people of color"—and an effort to enhance Jewish power (already greatly enhanced over the course of the nineteenth century, he writes) so as to ultimately be able to "press … Western military superiority into [the Zionists] service" (2009, p. 49). Lacking any true historical connection to Palestine, the Zionists' insistence on that land as the location for a Jewish state was based on their understanding that "a Jewish state in Palestine would advance their quest for power better than any alternative territory" (2009, p. 58). The book's historical distortions—some seemingly willful, others apparently the product of ignorance—include such formulations as the claim, for example, that Zionism's "*exclusionary* colonialism" (emphasis in the original) "could advance only by creating and promoting conflicts between the West and Islamicate" and that this was the fundamental logic that "has driven the Jewish state to deepen the conflict" (2009, p. 3).

Alam appears to be unclear as to whether he is studying Zionism or *The Protocols of the Elders of Zion*. To be sure, in its extreme (albeit subtly articulated) formulations, his may not be a typical book critical of Israel or Israeli policy. But it is an illustration of the ways in which fantasies of Jewish power that animated anti-Semitism have at times found their way into some of the rhetoric—including the would-be academic rhetoric—surrounding Zionism and Israel. Sadly, his is an extremism that seems to be an acceptable form of academic discourse today. Other, less extreme, formulations have entered the pantheon of academic claims regarding Zionism.

Edward Said, for example, in his "Zionism from the Standpoint of its Victims" (a problematic article which is nevertheless highly enough regarded as to have even spawned spin-offs) can make so bold a claim as his assertion that "Zionism *never* spoke of itself unambiguously as a Jewish liberation movement, but rather as a Jewish movement for colonial settlement in the Orient" (Said 1979, p. 23). In fact, virtually all Zionist writings (including the examples cited herein) speak of, elaborate on, explore, and problematize Zionism as a movement of Jewish liberation, whereas it would require painstaking research to locate a Zionist text that focuses on colonial settlement in the Orient. Even Herzl's *Der Judenstadt*, which purports to create a blueprint for colonization and settlement and to lay out concrete plans, focuses to a far greater extent on Herzl's diagnosis of anti-Semitism and on his consequent vision for a transformed Jewish life. Whatever claims may be made about Zionism and its approach to colonization, to the Arabs, to its relationships with empires and Empire, a rudimentary familiarity with Zionist thought (even a cursory perusal of Arthur Hertzberg's *The Zionist Idea*, for example) would show just how deeply problematic Said's claim is.

However, these are not Zionism's principal concerns. The rhetorical wars of which these are just minor examples are likely to continue in the twenty-first century. But whatever problem such accusations have posed to Zionism, it is the startling and unanticipated irony of their historic trajectory—the way in which some of Zionism's would-be representatives have been transforming the Jewish state that Zionism engendered into what its detractors have claimed it was all along—that remains the greatest challenge to Zionism in the twenty-first century. Figures within the current ruling government coalition, supported by a range of non-governmental organizations, have been working to engender a public discourse that delegitimizes criticism and open conversation and explicitly brands any critics as traitors. Leading political figures have launched legislative and other efforts to limit freedom of expression, and in other ways limit and stifle Israeli democracy.

Ironically, leading would-be defenders of Zionism in Israel have adopted the claim—once voiced by Israel's detractors rather than its would-be champions—that the state's Jewishness and its democratic character are in conflict, and they have consequently embarked on a range of efforts to limit its democratic character. An increasingly exclusionary vision of what Israel and the Jewishness of the state means has been promulgated by government and non-governmental actors. Policies and rhetoric designed to increasingly exclude Arabs and other minorities from the fabric of an Israeli democratic society (such as the effort to deny Arabic the status of an official language of the state—a status it has held since 1948) have become increasingly widespread. Not only do these phenomena threaten to undermine the achievements of Zionism (under the guise of Zionism itself), but perhaps more alarmingly, they represent a disquieting unconscious adoption of the very accusations made against Zionism and Israel, and a sadly unselfconscious campaign to produce an Israel that will in fact be in the image shaped by its detractors.

This essay began with a quote from Herzl that caught my attention as I walked down the exit hall at Ben-Gurion airport in January 2017—Zionism as an ideal of moral and spiritual perfection. It struck me in this context as sadly ironic that January 2017 was also the month in which the conviction of an Israeli Defense Force (IDF) soldier found to have shot and killed a gravely wounded Palestinian (wounded, to be sure, while attempting to stab other soldiers to death) elicited violence and threats against the military judges who had tried him, and who were now being cast as traitors; it was the month in which the Prime Minister and the Minister of Education, both of whom had expressed unquestionable support for the soldier (tacitly undermining the authority of his commanders who attempted to uphold ethical and chain-of-command standards and values previously deemed sacrosanct within the IDF itself) called immediately for a pardon for the accused killer. The Chief Justice of Israel's Supreme Court also came under attack in the same month for her defense of the military judges and of the rule of law. The previous months had seen government efforts to pass legislation bypassing Supreme Court rulings regarding settlements established on private Palestinian lands, coupled throughout with attacks on the court itself, which was lumped together with "leftists" and "traitors" of various stripes. All of this (and more) is undertaken in the name of a would-be Zionism, the meaning of which has now come to be unquestioning loyalty to government policy (assuming a government of a particular right-wing bent, of course: Twenty years earlier, it was the government itself, and its Prime Minister, Yitzhak Rabin who were being accused, by much the same cast of characters, as traitors—to the point, famously, of the political assassination of the Prime Minster himself).

Given the extent to which Zionism has been an embattled idea and Israel a discursively, diplomatically and militarily embattled state, the extent to which humanistic ideas and democratic principles and institutions have maintained central positions in Israeli life is striking and even surprising. Accusations against Zionism based in an Orwellian post-truth discourse (and to be clear—there are many charges that can be made in very legitimate terms) are disturbing for a range of reasons, but do not on their own pose a significant threat to Zionism in the twenty-first century. A state that is its own end and goal, a people that seeks isolation and self-ghettoization as opposed to becoming a part—indeed the beacon it once sought to become—of a human community of nations, are a state and a people that have betrayed the most central tenets of Zionism and some of its deepest and most ambitious goals.

Five years after the establishment of the state of Israel, its future president Zalman Shazar, wondered:

> Will we have the spiritual strength and flexibility to renew Zionist thought in our day, in light of the revolutionary changes that have taken place in the Diaspora and in Israel? ... Will we know how to reevaluate the place of the

Jewish people in the world, the place of the state in the life of the nation, and of the individual in the life of the nation, and to see them all in the light of this generation's vision of national redemption? Or are we doomed here too to [be stuck in] the particularism in which each group worships at its own shrine, neglecting the central temple? Will we continue to ignore the thoughts and aspirations of others, and consider them a priori to be rivals? The rebirth of collective Zionist thought can never grow from these self-ghettoizing monologues.

The greatest challenge for Zionism in the early twenty-first century is thus to wrest back its own ideals and vision, to expose the recasting of Zionism (by detractors and would-be champions alike) into an idea that is fundamentally ethnocentric, xenophobic, anti-democratic and self-ghettoizing as a betrayal of Zionism's core motivations and ideas. The central task of Zionism today, in the early twenty-first century, is to reconnect not only the link between Zionism and lively, probing criticism, but to reclaim the ends to which that critique was aimed: the creation of a vibrant Jewish-Hebrew culture that is one voice—a Jewish voice—in the universe of human culture, and the principal expression of the liberationist thrust that was Zionism's core. If Zionism is to have a life in the twenty-first century, it cannot come to be that which its detractors—and, today, its would-be leaders—claim it is. It must transcend those who would make it the equivalent of a xenophobic, exclusionary, racist militant chauvinism, and rediscover itself as the humanistic liberationist movement and idea that, in much of its manifestation historically, it has been.

Notes

1 See "Ben-Gurion Outlines Stand on Zionism; Sharett Criticizes U.S. Zionists," *Jewish Telegraphic Agency*, May 23, 1960. The institutional dilemmas of the Zionist bodies after 1948 are discussed further in Ronald W. Zweig, "Israel–Diaspora Relations in the Early Years of the State," in Laurence Silberstein, *New Perspectives on Israeli History* (New York: New York University Press, 1991), pp. 258–270.

2 Ben-Gurion makes this statement powerfully in the interview documented in the film "Ben-Gurion: an Epilogue." See also the discussion in Ariel Feldestein, *Ben-Gurion, Zionism and American Jewry: 1948–1963* (Routledge, 2006), pp. 159–166.

3 Shimoni, referring to Walter Laqueur's *History of Zionism*, in Shimoni, "Reformulations," 11.

4 Haskala, or the Jewish Enlightenment; various attempts at religious reform; the rise of orthodox Judaism as a response to reform and in an effort to preserve traditional Jewish society's ways of life, and others, were all attempts to maintain what these disparate currents each deemed the core of Judaism, while adapting it to the conditions of the modern world.

5 The new anti-Semitism, as some scholars have suggested, is one which bases itself less on race theory (which was prominent particularly in the late nineteenth and early twentieth centuries) and religious prejudice (which dates back much further, of course), but rather more on ideological and political hatreds. Among the most prominent advocates of the notion of a "new anti-semitism" are Alvin Rosenfeld—see, for example, his introduction

to *Deciphering the New Antisemitism* (Indiana University Press, 2015), pp. 1–4; and Bernard Lewis—see his "The New Anti-Semitism," in *The American Scholar* 75:1 (Winter, 2006), pp. 25–36.

6 For extensive discussion of the processes that helped make this happen, see Arieh Saposnik, *Becoming Hebrew: The Creation of a Jewish National Culture in Ottoman Palestine* (Oxford, 2008).

7 For full discussion of "the Brenner affair," which understands it primarily as a struggle for freedom of expression in the Yishuv and in Zionism, see Nurit Govrin, *"Me'ora Brenner": Ha-Ma'avak al Hofesh ha-Bitui* (Jerusalem, 1985).

8 "Be-Miflaga—Tamtzit ha-Vikuchim shel Asefatenu ha-Shevi'it," *Ha-Po'el ha-Tza'ir* 6: 8 (November 15, 1912), pp. 15–18.

References and further reading

Aharonowitz, Yosef. 1909. "Heichal ha-Kultura ha-Ivrit (Sof)." *Ha-Po'el ha-Tza'ir.* (2)17, p. 3.

Alam, M. Shahid. 2009. *Israeli Exceptionalism—The Destabilizing Logic of Zionism.* New York: Palgrave Macmillan, p. 49.

Beinart, Peter. 2012. *The Crisis of Zionism.* New York: Henry Holt, p. 161.

Ben-Gurion, David. 1998. "Zionism and Pseudo-Zionism," in Carol Diament (ed.), *Zionism: The Sequel.* New York: Haddasah Books, pp. 45–49.

Bialik, Haim Nahman. 1959. "Bialik on the Hebrew University," in Arthur Hertzberg, (ed.), *The Zionist Idea.* New York: Doubleday & Company and Herzl Press, 284 pp.

Brenner, Yosef Haim. 1914. "Ha'arachat Atzmenu bi-Sheloshet ha-Krachim." *Revivim.* 5.

Gordon, A.D. 1954. *Michtavim u-Reshimot.* Jerusalem, pp. 44–50.

Ha'am, Ahad. 1901. "Batei ha-Sefer be-Yafo." *Ha-Shilo'ah.* 7, pp. 1–3. March–April.

Ha'am, Ahad. 1912. "Sach Ha-Kol," *Ha-Shilo'ah.* 26, January–June, 279 pp.

Ha'am, Ahad. 1997. "The Jewish State and the Jewish Problem," in Arthur Hertzberg (ed.), *The Zionist Idea: A Historical Analysis and Reader.* Philadelphia, PA: Jewish Publication Society, pp. 262–269.

Haver (Brenner), Yosef. 1912. "Ba-Itonut u-va-Sifrut." *Ha-Po'el Ha-Tza'ir.* 4(3), pp. 6–8.

Herzl, Theodor. 1896. "The Jewish State (1896)," translated in Arthur Hertzberg (ed.), *The Zionist Idea.* New York: Atheneum, 209 pp.

Katznelson, Berl. 1946–1950. "Likrat ha-Yamim ha-Ba'im," in *Kitvei Berl Katznelson The Writings of Berl Katznelson.* Tel Aviv: Mapai/Davar Press, (I), 71 pp.

Rorty, Richard. 1998. *Achieving our Country: Leftist Thought in Twentieth-Century America.* Cambridge, MA: Harvard University Press, pp. 3–4.

Said, Edward. 1979. "Zionism from the Standpoint of its Victims." *Social Text.* 1, Winter, p. 23.

Shimoni, Gideon. 1995. "Reformulations of Zionist Ideology Since the Establishment of the State of Israel." *Studies in Contemporary Jewry.* 11, pp. 11–36.

PART I
The Israeli political system

2

ISRAELI DEMOCRACY UNDER STRESS

Itzhak Galnoor

Introduction

This overview of democracy in Israel is based on the assumption that the hidden, yet most important component in liberal democracies, is the unwritten contract between voters and elected officials, between citizens and leaders, according to which all sides will usually pursue shared objectives and at least adhere to the rules of the game. These rules include, among other things, the rule of law, the legality of government, and the possibility that all citizens will have equal rights and the opportunity to influence political action. These assumptions, considered naïve by ostensibly experienced people, are what largely determine the level of confidence in democracy itself, and thereby the firmness of the liberal democratic system. This firmness is predicated upon a broad and solid consensus about the rules of the game (free elections, majority rule, an independent judiciary, multiple parties, etc.) and the values inherent in these rules. These values are, first and foremost, equality (otherwise, why allow everyone to vote?) and freedom (only free people can exercise their rights). Taking stock after seventy years of its existence as a state, Israel's democratic trajectory invites critical analysis and an examination as to whether, and to what extent, the above rules of the game are followed.[1]

On March 17, 2015, Israeli voters elected a new Knesset. No less than twenty-five party lists competed for citizens' support and it was not initially clear which party would receive the most seats and who would be the next Prime Minister. After a fierce election campaign, ten parties passed the required threshold of 3.25% of the total votes required to be elected to the 120 seats in the Knesset. Turnout stood at 72 percent of eligible voters, about 5 percent more than the previous election, mainly because of increased participation among the Arab citizens in Israel. Generally, the elections proceeded without violence or interruption and the voters' free choice was safeguarded. Based on this recent democratic event, Israeli democracy could be described as functioning well, leaving little justification for the title of this essay, which alludes to a threat to, or an "interruption" in, Israel's democratic development. Additionally, Israeli democracy appears to be functioning well due to the maintenance of judicial independence, which does not hesitate to bring the high and mighty to justice, as demonstrated by the recent conviction of a former Prime Minister, Ehud Olmert, for corruption and with Prime Minister Binyamin Netanyahu currently under investigation by the police.

These facts notwithstanding, the purpose of this essay is to ask a different question: Why is it that while the institutional framework (which has remained mostly constant since the early days of the state) functions relatively well and the formal rules of the game have been generally observed, the values underlying them (e.g. minority rights) have not become axiomatic, and symptoms of anti-politics and anti-democracy are spreading?

Stated differently, most contemporary democracies face salient problems, such as the rise of populism, weak representation, rampant social media and "fake news," fear of immigration, alienation and quality of state services, amongst others. Similarly, many democracies face economic and social crises and growing gaps between the haves and the have-nots. However, there is a distinction between asking questions about the *procedures* and the *outcomes* of the democratic process and questioning the *value* of democracy itself. In Israel, both types of questions are present, and the latter seems to be growing in importance; that is, individuals, parties and groups are promoting their "competing" values to dilute, or even replace democracy. Most democracies have problems *within* themselves. Israel has problems with the *value of democracy* itself. The four main factors affecting and interrupting Israel's internal democratic development are as follows:

- The impact of the continuous occupation and the imperative of security considerations;
- The status of the Arab citizens within Israel;
- The growing socioeconomic gaps;
- The unresolved issue of state and religion.

These key factors will be explored throughout this essay, amongst other topics.

How long does it take to be democratically confident?

The experience of the twentieth century demonstrated that the more years of democracy a state accrues, the higher the probability that it will remain a democracy. What is the sequence of democratic development? One would assume that initially a society develops a strong collective belief in democratic values, above all freedom and equality, and then gradually moves on to instill democratic mechanisms to attain these values. However, research on democracy does not provide a clear answer as to what the sequence has actually constituted in the past. Historically, we find mixed paths: the gradual development of democracy in countries such as England, Sweden, and the United States; and the abrupt impos-ition of democracy upon countries such as Japan and Germany after World War II. Thus, democratic development can be a simultaneous, prolonged process based on the mutual nurturing of—and interaction between—commonly-held values and the rules of the game.

A related query, relevant to the Israeli situation, is: when does the fact that a country is a democracy become so self-evident that democratic norms are no longer contested? Based on the previous assumption that the more years a nation accumulates as a democracy (as per the experience of Western democracies), the higher its chances of remaining continuously democratic, the assumption can be posited that after plus/minus 100 years of continuous democracy, a country will remain democratic. Furthermore, most states have constitutions, but few have stable constitutions that have lasted for a century or more; those states that have retained constitutions on a long-term basis are all democracies.[2] Yet, the order of events—what leads to democratic and constitutional stability—is not clear: Perhaps a stable regime and well-established relations between state and society are what make a constitution stable, and not vice versa. For example, the relatively stable constitutions of Germany and Japan after 1945 demonstrate the importance of a constitution in a particular historical context.

Apparently, when the unwritten contract between society and politics becomes a norm, faith in the primacy of democracy also evolves, including its ability to con-tend with emergencies and crises. In short, a democratic political culture develops, which contains a "democratic soul" that guides the actions of individuals, groups, organizations and political institutions. The moral argument for democracy is that everyone has the right to shape one's own destiny; the practical argument is that a state that enjoys the trust of its citizens is much stronger, and an army of motivated citizens will better defend it than an army of mercenaries.

Israel: relevant background

In a comparative, global context, Israel can no longer be classed as an infant dem-ocracy. Democratic institutions existed in the Jewish community in Palestine in the pre-state period. The first Assembly of Representatives was elected in 1920, long before statehood. Since the establishment of the state in 1948, Israel has experienced a continuous democratic regime for seventy years, and including the pre-state era, for almost 100 years. Thus, one can say that democracy in Israel had a promising beginning, certainly compared with other democracies at that stage of development. In 1948, democracy was by and large taken for granted, and the Declaration of Independence is clearly a democratic text, even though the word "democracy" is not mentioned. Moreover, Israeli democracy managed to cope with major challenges. For instance, the pre-state rivalries between com-peting ideologically motivated political groups did not threaten the regime and were channeled to the elected parliament, the Knesset, thus establishing the legit-imacy of the political system; free elections were held continuously. Demonstrating the resilience of Israeli democracy, the elections of 1977 saw Mapai, the dominant party for many decades, ousted from power at the ballot box (the so-called "upheaval"), with the subsequent transition of power carried out smoothly, consensually and non-violently.

Needless to say, democracy in the first decades of the State of Israel was far from perfect. The first Prime Minister, David Ben-Gurion, often displayed centralizing tendencies and remained in power, on and off, until 1963. Politics at that time was almost entirely party-based, except for a few fields, for example security, the justice system, and higher education. The system was stable, because the new state institutions were inherited from the pre-state Yishuv period—a parliamentary system, a unicameral legislature, proportional elections, the centrality of political coalitions (with a dominant pivot party), a centralized national bureaucracy and weak local authorities. However, government at that time was not a dictatorship and certainly not a military regime, because civilian rule over the military was firmly established. Mapai, the ruling party, dominated politics, society and the economy. It could be blamed for curtailing participatory democracy, but it never achieved a majority in the Knesset and it was always forced to form coalitions in order to govern. In retrospect, Mapai was less dominant than the dominant parties in India, Japan and South Africa. Moreover, in the early sixties there were already indications of an evolution toward a less-dominated, less-organized democracy.

Levi Eshkol, who became Prime Minister in 1963, was much more of a civilian democratic leader than Ben-Gurion. He ended military rule over the Arab citizens of Israel, formed new alliances before the 1965 elections and was conciliatory toward his political rivals. Accordingly, Israel was entering a new phase of developing a more balanced, liberal democracy, with a legitimate political regime based on the first nine Basic Laws (1958–1988), which essentially codified the established political order. Despite the enormous changes in all fields, there have not been fundamental changes in the regime type itself since 1949, except for the direct election of mayors from 1975 and a short-lived experiment of direct elections of the prime minister (1996–2001), which is discussed in more detail below. At least until the late 1960s, the political system functioned, for better or worse, and was also quite stable, despite frequent crises. The political system could count on support from the broad consensus among the Jewish citizens until the 1970s: a sense of shared destiny, national-religious identity, Zionism and identification with the state (Galnoor 1982, pp. 79–110). However, both this consensus and the resulting support for democratic norms have been increasingly questioned.

Challenges to the democratic order

One might have expected the path of Israeli democracy to be marked by a progression from just observing the rules of the game to a stronger belief in democracy and its basic values. But this did not occur. The development of democracy in Israel was interrupted, and today this interruption is endangering the democratic rules of the game, including the rule of law.

In Israel, as in other states, the challenges of nation building hinder calm development and tip the balance of priorities from ensuring representation to strengthening governability. Furthermore, the long shadow of the Holocaust has been a powerful factor in making security considerations the top priority, sometimes at the expense of democratic norms. Other factors affecting Israeli democracy have been mass immigration, the challenge of creating a new nation, and the increasing presence of a nondemocratic, orthodox version of Judaism. Perhaps the strongest obstacle to a more normal development has been the security imperative, because of the recurring wars and continuous fight against terrorism. Further, since the 1980s, Israel has had frequent political turnovers in government, and in 1996, Prime Minister Yitzhak Rabin was murdered by a political extremist, because of his peace policy. Israel's uneven path of democratic development could be presented as follows: Whereas the formal rules of the game have been generally observed, the values underlying those rules (especially tolerance for opposing views and minority rights) have not become self-evident. Far from it.

Stocktaking: strengths of Israeli democracy

In general, basic democratic practices have been continuously observed in Israel: the existence of democratic institutions; regular and fair elections (twenty in seventy years, an average of an election every 3.5 years); and a real choice between many parties (an average of twelve in the Knesset). Finally, the principle of majority rule and coalition governments has functioned fairly well over the years, though lately this mechanism is increasingly under threat.

One of the major strengths of Israeli democracy has been the existence of an independent judicial system. The legal system in Israel has a history of producing judges who are not corrupt, and the Supreme Court has a right to oversee both Knesset legislation and the decisions of the executive branch. Official commissions of inquiry have repeatedly investigated the conduct of top decision makers during wars and other events, and many senior officeholders have been dismissed from office as a consequence of the commissions' recommendations. In addition, freedom of speech and expression are generally maintained and the media is free, although media ownership is increasingly concentrated in the hands of a few individuals. Additionally, the strength and importance of civil society and independent nonprofit organizations has been steadily growing. Despite the security burden and the influence of the military, Israel has never experienced a military regime in the state proper, as distinct from the occupied territories. Moreover, if we examine Israel according to Robert Dahl's list of institutional characteristics essential for a functioning democracy (an elected leadership; fair, free, and regularly held elections; an independent judiciary; freedom of expression; freedom of association; civil rights; and a professional civil service), Israel mostly fits the criteria. By conventional standards, Israel has been a continuous and stable democracy, particularly when compared to the other democracies established since 1945.

Stocktaking: weaknesses

However, democratic procedures are insufficient to secure liberal democratic hegemony. In order for a democracy to be stable and to flourish, the citizens must trust it and believe that it is both valuable and effective. The term "effective" is employed deliberately, because in the twentieth century, democracies won the war against nondemocratic regimes and outlasted almost all of them, demonstrating the utility of the democratic model. In Israel, however, opinion surveys indicate a weakened public support for democratic norms. According to the surveys of the Israel Democracy Institute, the aggregate, average figures for the years 2009–2013 are as follows:

For the following statements, there is a democratic (but gradually decreasing) majority:

- Support for democracy in general: 85 percent
- Support for freedom of expression: 75 percent
- Support for the right of all citizens to vote: 70 percent
- Support for equal rights for Arab citizens: 60 percent

For the following statements there is a small, or an absence of a, democratic majority:

- Support for limiting certain rights of orthodox Jews or Arab citizens: 55 percent
- Support the principle that the state should not be criticized publicly: 52 percent
- Support maintaining freedom of the press: 50 percent
- Support for the principle of preventing Arab citizens from participating in critical decisions regarding the future of the state: 86 percent

The picture regarding minority rights is even gloomier among young people, either because they are more truthful and less "politically correct" in their replies than their elders, or because they are less democratic. Israel's youth are also less likely to vote than their elders, suggesting dwindling trust in democratic instruments. The average turnout up to the elections in 1999 was approximately 82 percent. In 2001–2012, turnout decreased to 65 percent; and in 2013 and 2015 it rose to an average of 70 percent. These statistics paint a concerning picture for future public support for democracy in Israel.

Political life in Israel has always been turbulent and highly partisan. In Israel's multi-party system, the Knesset hosts an average of twelve parties at any given time. But, the new phenomenon is fragmentation. In the past, the largest party (either the left-of-center Labor or the right-of-center Likud) usually won approximately forty seats in the Knesset and could often form a relatively stable coalition. However, after the 2013 election, the biggest party—the Likud—won only twenty seats, and the unstable coalition headed by Binyamin Netanyahu, lasted only two years. After the 2015 elections, the biggest party—once more the Likud—won thirty seats (25 percent) in the Knesset and the coalition formed held only a one-seat majority of 61, though this later increased to 66.

TABLE 2.1 Trust in institutions in the 2000s (%)

	2003	2007	2011	2015
Supreme Court	70	58	69	62
IDF	83	73	86	85★
Knesset	51	32	52	35
Political parties	32	21	36	19
The government	55	30	51	36
The president	68	21★★	78	70
The media	49	44	52	36

★ In 2015, a wide disparity was recorded between the trust of Jewish and Arab citizens in the IDF—93% and 37%, respectively.

★★ The year 2007 was when the historical sexual offences of then-President Moshe Katsav were revealed, which may have affected public trust in institutions.

Source: Hermann, Tamar et al. 2015, pp. 85–89. Israeli Democracy Index. Reproduced with Permission from Israel Democracy Institute.

Democracies need institutions that not only function, but that inspire trust. The deterioration in institutional trustworthiness raises concerns about the strength of Israeli democracy. Do Israelis trust their institutions? Table 2.1 below shows that the non-elected, non-representative institutions enjoy greater trust than the Knesset, the government, and, in particular, the political parties. In addition, the decline of public trust in the media in Israel is worrisome.

The increasing levels of distrust indicated above dissuade citizens from participating in elections, reinforce the inclination to disparage the rule of law, and weaken democracy—all of which indeed occurred in Israel. Membership in parties used to be very high, but declined to an average of only 4 percent, before the 2013 and the 2015 elections. The flip side of the aversive sentiments toward politics and politicians is the growing support for authoritative mechanisms, which evokes longing for "strong leadership." Some Israeli legislators exacerbate this situation, by promoting nondemocratic legislation and proposals in the Knesset, such as bills violating the principle of equality, demanding loyalty oaths from citizens, discriminating against Arab citizens, limiting freedom of speech and opinion, restricting human rights organizations and attempting to reduce the independence of the Supreme Court.[3] Additionally, there exists another concern: without internalized democratic values, adherence to the rules of the game will continue to decline, including the rule of law and the rights of minorities, organizations and individuals. These legislative acts and proposals confirm the fear of nondemocratic exploitation of majority rule.

Direct elections of the Prime Minister (1996–2003): a lesson about the futility of political engineering

In Israel's parliamentary system, the Prime Minister and his government must pass a vote of confidence in the Knesset. Given the need for coalitions, the government is dependent on the support of the parties in the Knesset. Direct elections for the post of Prime Minister were first implemented in the 1996 election. The experiment failed—the law was first changed in 2001, and then in 2003 Israel reverted to the previous system entirely. The effects of this change can still be felt in both Israeli democracy and the political system as a whole. Simply stated: is it possible to strengthen the executive branch by changing the support base of the Prime Minister, that is, by giving him a personal mandate directly from the public, similar to that of presidential systems?

The law had historical origins, serving as an attempted remedy against public distrust and dissatisfaction in the status quo. In 1990, the second national unity government comprised of both Labor and Likud fell, after spending two years in political gridlock. Three months of political crisis were accompanied by widespread public protest: The public had lost its trust in the political leaders; demonstrations were held expressing revulsion at corruption and a desire for change in the political system. Thus, despite strong opposition from most Israeli political scientists,[4] the law mandating direct elections for the post of prime minister passed the Knesset in March 1992.[5]

Direct elections of prime ministers removed Israel from the family of parliamentary democracies, but also did not move it into the family of presidential democracies. The electoral system adopted was unique, as it combined some of the shortcomings of a parliamentary system with the shortcomings of a presidential system—a "presidential parliamentarism" (Hazan 1996, pp. 21–37). It was not a pure presidential system, because although the head of the executive branch was directly elected by the public, mutual dependence with the Knesset persisted. The Knesset could dismiss the Prime Minister or pass a vote of no-confidence in the government, while the Prime Minister had the power to dissolve the Knesset.

The result of direct elections

The objectives of the new law were to strengthen the power of the Prime Minister and the executive branch, weaken the bargaining power of the small parties, improve the quality of the political leadership and increase stability, while enhancing governability. In practice, however, the Prime Minister's role and effectiveness were weakened by the direct elections. The power bestowed upon the Prime Minister by direct election was only an illusion: the coalitions formed were fragile, and the governments became a revolving door for parties to enter, exit, and return again, thereby damaging the performance of the executive branch. Direct elections did not free the Prime Minister from the pitfalls of a coalition, or the difficulties of dealing with the demands of small parties. In practice, unstable coalition governments continued to be the norm, whilst winning election to the position of Prime Minister was not correlated with an increase in Knesset seats for the party of the victor. In fact, the voters "punished" the parties of the Prime Minister and diminished their power.

The tacit hope behind the adoption of direct elections was that the person chosen for Prime Minister would not be a party functionary or "politician," but a leader, a statesperson. Indeed, the first two prime ministers who won office via direct election (Binyamin Netanyahu and Ehud Barak) were relatively new faces and lacking in political experience. However, their terms in office were short, and neither was reelected. By contrast, Ariel Sharon, who also became prime minister through direct elections, was a seasoned political veteran. He was neither young, new, nor a media celebrity, yet he remained in power for five years until he was incapacitated by a stroke.

Direct elections did not enhance governability and increased stability—instead they reduced the power of the institution of the Prime Minister, disconnecting the officeholder from the political arena, which continued to be the Knesset, dominated by parties. Direct elections further reinforced a personality cult of the Prime Minister and the populist dimension of the political system as a whole. Making the Prime Minister directly accountable to the public did not boost democratic values, instead it undermined the collective responsibility of the government. The governments were unstable, as coalition membership frequently changed, and the Prime Minister repeatedly came up against resistance: in the Knesset, the coalition, the government, and ultimately the public.

Direct elections changed the party system. When direct elections were instituted in 1996, two relatively large parties held sway: The Likud and Labor together controlled some 65 percent of the Knesset seats after the 1988 and 1992 elections. Voting with two ballots—one for the Prime Minister and the other for the Knesset—inflated the mid-size and the small parties and deflated the power of the large parties. After two direct elections (1996 and 1999), the power of the two largest parties had diminished to a mere 38 percent (45 seats) in the Knesset (Kenig et al. 2004). In the 2015 elections, the two major parties together controlled only 42 percent of the vote (54 seats) in the Knesset. Thus, voting for a specific candidate for Prime Minister did not encourage voting for his or her party. Even after the abolition of direct elections, the party system remained weak and continued to be infiltrated by populist politicians and electoral trends.

The experiment with direct elections has significantly impacted Israeli democracy. Direct elections were instituted as a mechanism of direct democracy that aims to stimulate public participation. The assumption was that giving voters the opportunity to directly choose their prime minister, without the mediation of parties, would increase political participation. Proponents asserted that when citizens feel they have direct influence, they would want to exercise their democratic right to vote. Unlike the party list system, in which a Prime Minister is determined only after coalition negotiations, in direct elections the citizens decide on their prime minister. This assumption was proven incorrect, as the system did not increase voter turnout in Israel. The special election for prime minister—held in 2001—had the lowest turnout in history (62 percent). Moreover, Arab citizens largely boycotted these special elections, because they felt they had no suitable candidate, and could not express their preference for a party.

Lessons from the failure of direct elections in Israel

Rather than serve their purpose of increasing public trust and engagement in the political process, direct elections revealed the previously obscured complex web of relations between the democratic system and society. The experiment changed the system of governance in a way that was incompatible with Israel's social structure and political tradition. The main lesson learned was the need to be cautious of artificial transplants, because elements that work well elsewhere are not necessarily suitable for governance in other countries.[6]

When the head of the executive branch is elected by a majoritarian system, the winner takes all, even if the victory was by a slim margin (or an artificial majority). This is incompatible with Israeli political culture, which has been based on seeking consensus, inclusiveness, and a coalition government. Introducing a majoritarian component into the Israeli system was problematic, precisely because it gives a decisive victory to one side, creating absolute winners and losers. Direct elections in Israel, rather than fostering centrist politics, deepened the rifts between the diverse groups that comprised Israel society and placed democracy under further stress.

Direct elections, as well as party primaries (introduced to the Israeli political landscape in the past two decades), do not exist in most parliamentary systems. In Israel, these measures exacerbated the damage to parties as democratic representative bodies, and threatened to turn the Knesset into a shareholders' meeting of interest groups. In parliamentary democracies, parties operate in the constant tension between aggregating interests for the common good and representing particularistic interests. The cumulative total determines the long-term outcomes, and it is important for the scales to tip toward the good of all. Splitting the vote in direct elections threatened to tilt the balance in the wrong direction. The representatives in the Knesset emphasized their particularistic interests, leaving aside considerations about the common good. There is nothing wrong with adopting elements of direct democracy, if and only if these are adapted to the political culture and add a genuine (as opposed to populistic) channel for airing public preferences. With the Israeli experiment in direct elections, however, these conditions were not met. The period of direct election of the Prime Minister did not improve the capacity for making difficult decisions. On the contrary, it was increasingly more difficult to implement new policies in those years, because radical change required the broad support of the parliamentary coalition.

Presidential systems are not more stable than parliamentary systems; indeed, the opposite is true, if South America is considered. According to the aggregate political stability index published by the World Bank (which monitors democratic stability, constitutional changes, internal violence, etc.), the average positive score of thirty-three parliamentary systems was much higher than that of the twenty-seven presidential systems studied.[7] As noted, direct elections in Israel did not contribute to stability, partly because the Prime Minister and the Knesset claimed separate public legitimacy.

The failure of direct elections was an important reminder of the limitations on using the law to engineer governance. The image sold to the public was that of an elected "professional manager" (the Prime Minister) who would directly head the state and organize the affairs of state efficiently and without corruption, for the good of everyone. However, (good) politics is concerned with real needs, more than the so-called "rule of experts" advocated by the proponents of direct elections. The Israeli political system reflects the complexity of society, and any attempt to "organize it" must be cautious, reflective, and appropriate for the social fabric. The parties, social groups, the media, and coalitions are not superfluous "noise" in a democratic system, but serve important functions of mediation and interest aggregation. The effort to eliminate the legitimate mediators is not just futile, it puts democracy at risk.

Paradoxes and dilemmas

Diamond (1993) suggests four paradoxes of a democratic system. First, democracy literally means "rule by the people," but it depends, especially at the outset, on the behavior of the political elite; democracy requires broad and intensive participation by the citizens, but is very dependent on the commitment to democracy by a society's leaders (1993, pp. 21–43). In Israel's early years, despite the internal divisions and lack of a party with a Knesset majority, the level of public trust in the leadership was high. Were the leaders committed to democracy? By and large the answer is in the affirmative, at least as far as adherence to the democratic rules of the game were concerned. From this narrow perspective, democracy in Israel met Schumpeter's minimum requirements (1944): The role of citizens is to elect their leaders and allow them to govern, until the next election. Over the years, however, breaches emerged in relations between the citizens and their leaders, and it is doubtful that the current behavior of multiple politicians, notably those in power, is contributing to instilling democracy in Israel.

Second, democracy institutionalizes and regulates the struggle for power. But if the conflicts become too acute and society too divided, there is a danger of dissolving the shared framework, which leads to political instability. Democracy in Israel did institutionalize and regulate the internal power struggles, albeit at the expense of weaker groups in society. The political system was stable and had proven steering capacity, particularly in the area of security. Later, internal conflicts intensified, and today these conflicts continue to threaten the very capacity for shared political action.

Third, democratic regimes have an inherent internal tension: representativeness versus governance and steering capacity. Representativeness means that the citizen can influence the government and sometimes even be involved in the policymaking process; steering capacity requires the government to act not only according to the legitimate interests of individuals and groups, but also to mediate among interests and pursue the common good. That is, when the government turns the steering wheel, the entire ship must turn. Previously, the balance in Israel clearly tilted toward the requirements of governance and, despite the highly proportional electoral system, citizens' influence was strictly demarcated and exerted indirectly via powerful party intermediaries. However, democracy in Israel later became more representative because of new and diverse options available to citizens—especially through civil society organizations and new media channels—as well as more direct representativeness in the political parties. The prevailing assumption is that the scale tipped in favor of representativeness at the expense of governance, hence the attempts to strengthen the executive branch. Yet, as argued above, this assumption is rather misleading.

Finally, democracy is based on the ongoing renewable consent of the citizens to conditionally empower their representatives. The steadfastness of this consent depends on public legitimacy—an unwritten pact that is conditional, in part, on the government's effectiveness. Citizens expect the government to address security, social and economic problems and to enforce law and order. Consent and legitimacy depend on steering capacity, and sometimes this means that the representatives need to act decisively and face the judgment of the public only afterwards. This tension makes it difficult for democratic governments to make unpopular decisions, or to act on the basis of long-term considerations. In Israel, the crisis in the government's legitimacy looms as a tangible threat to democracy. Many Israeli citizens feel that the unwritten pact between state and society has been violated time and again and that they cannot trust the leaders' motives or the effectiveness of the government, even on security matters. This is expressed in a growing mood of "anti-politics"—frustration with, and revulsion over, the political system, and the loss of the previous Israeli passion to debate political issues. Thus, apathy among the citizens is a dangerous threat to the consolidation of democracy in contemporary Israel.

Threats to democracy in Israel

Compared to the list of strengths presented above, the democratic system in Israel also faces challenges that threaten to undermine its core values. In July 2018 the Knesset enacted a new Basic Law: Israel as the National Home of the Jewish People. The law gives priority to the Jewishness of the state and enables that to override clauses regarding democracy, downgrades the status of the Arab language in Israel, and sends a negative message about the status of non-Jews in the State of Israel. What are the advantages, if any, of such a formal legal declaration. The state has an official name—Israel; another Basic Law stipulates that the state is "Jewish and democratic." Thus, why add a caption—"a home for the Jewish people"—when in practice Israel is already such a home? Why change the so-called "balance" between "a Jewish and democratic state"? How much lack of confidence is revealed in such a legislative attempt that ignores the negative implications, not only for the Arab citizens, but for Israel's democracy in general?

The main threats to Israeli democracy derive from the inability to resolve four main challenges: the continuous occupation of the West Bank since 1967; the status of Arab citizens in Israel; the growing socioeconomic gaps between Israeli citizens; and the unresolved issue of balancing religion and state. Are these "wicked problems" inherently difficult to define, deeply disputed and perhaps impossible to resolve (Rittel and Webber 1973; Roberts 2000)? These problems have eroded the unwritten pact between state and citizens, according to which democratic leaders are elected to provide solutions, not just to contain or manage difficult problems. Leaving them as "open" issues tends to erode the moral infrastructure of democratic systems.

The problem of occupation

In addition to the arguments about the impossibility of limiting democracy to within the State of Israel only and not in the occupied territories, a democracy that—over the course of over fifty years—fails to address and solve the most important problem facing it loses trust. There is, of course, also a moral issue: Democracy requires popular belief in the justifiability of state actions. This is how democracies win wars. Since 1967, security in Israel has not improved, and all wars and military operations have been internally disputed. Even the excuse that "our rivals are not democratic" rings hollow, because vagueness surrounding the "decision not to decide" about the future of the occupied territories undermines trust in the efficacy of democracy.

Arab citizens in Israel

Arabs comprise about 20 percent of the Israeli population and, formally, they are equal citizens whose rights are protected by law. Despite lagging behind their Jewish counterparts overall, the standard of living of Arabs in Israel has improved considerably over the years. In practice, however, they continue to be largely alienated citizens, because the state grants obvious advantages to its Jewish citizens. In many respects, Israel is an ethnic (Jewish) democracy (Smooha 2002, p. 475), in which one-fifth of the population keeps asking whether there is a place for non-Jews in the state. An alienated minority is a moral issue and a danger to the strength of democracy. In the 2015 election, all Arab parties united into one "Joint List" with a new leader; concurrently Arab voter participation increased significantly and the party won 13 seats, making it the third largest in the Knesset. However, the Arab parties continue, in practice, to receive different treatment to their Jewish counterparts and are shut out of coalition negotiations. Thus, a group that continues to feel unfairly treated by society is liable to opt out of it. Democracy is therefore liable to become further limited and threatened from within by an alienated group of citizens that does not participate in elections, pay taxes, or even obey the law.

Growing socio-economic gaps

Is it possible to have a strong economy and a weak society? Theoretically, it is possible, and there are many democracies with deep social gaps. However, given the external threats, the continued existence of Israel depends on solidarity, not security. For many years, Israeli society enjoyed relative equality, but this has changed drastically in recent years; by the early 2000s, comparative inequality indices of democratic countries placed Israel as one of the most inequitable polities. This growing gap erodes citizens' trust in the political system, especially so since the gap has not been the result of globalization, as many claim, but rather a direct outcome of government policies, for instance, lowering direct taxation and giving other forms of preference to high income groups, or the continuous policy of privatization (Galnoor et al. 2015). The massive 2011 social protests against the high cost of living in Israel highlighted the existence of a link between the growing socioeconomic problem and the weakening of democracy. On the one hand, Israel's high-tech-based economy is among the most advanced in the world. On the other, the percentage of beneficiaries from economic growth has steadily decreased.

The problem of religion and state

Since 1948, the State of Israel has sought to preserve a balance between the demands of the powerful religious groups and the way of life of the majority, which is either secular or "traditional," that is, observant but not strictly religious. This balance has been largely eroded by religious groups (especially the settlers in the occupied territories) that consider their values to be "above" democracy. For instance, in a 2012 survey, a sample of the Jewish population was asked, "Which part of the definition 'a Jewish and democratic state' is more important for you?" The answers were: Jewish: 34 percent; democratic: 22 percent; both: 42 percent.[8] The above question implies a false choice, because democracy as such does not contradict any religious belief—unless one regards religious authority as being above the law of the state. The appearance of such a threat is a major obstacle to the development of Israel's democracy.

Conclusion

The combination of the four problems presented above (Israel's occupation, Arab citizens, growing socioeconomic gaps, and an unsteady balance between religion and state) has begun to erode both the moral and practical bases of democracy in Israel. The fact that they have remained open issues for a sustained period of time has contributed to undermining both democracy and citizens' lack of confidence in the advantages of democracy. The result has been a plethora of proposals to "strengthen" the state, by adding legal titles such as "Jewish democracy," "Zionist democracy," and most recently, "the national home of the Jewish people." Such additions *exclude* some groups, whereas the strength of democracy as a governing principle lies in its focus on *inclusion*.

   The futile attempt to strengthen the executive branch and its head (the direct elections for the position of Prime Minister) showed that other elements of the parliamentary system must be strengthened, particularly those that increase legitimacy and stability. Parliamentary systems in Israel function well, even though ongoing adjustments are needed, to help turn the gears of the legislative and executive branches, which partially interlock. Each branch has a purpose and a function of its own, and the tension between them gives the political system its dynamism and ability to be both representative and task-oriented. To strengthen "governability" one must hearken back to the wisdom of the main principle of the parliamentary system: strengthen the parliament, which itself empowers the executive branch.

Furthermore, the vacuum that developed in the Israeli political system accorded the Supreme Court a critical role in defending democracy, particularly in safeguarding the human rights that correspond to the new Basic Laws of 1992. To this category, we can add the determined and consistent battle of the law enforcement authorities against political and administrative corruption. Thus, the attacks of politicians against the oversight role of the Supreme Court represent a direct threat to democracy in Israel.

Based on the strengths described above, it remains possible—and is indeed an urgent priority—to restart the interrupted development of democracy, by emphasizing fundamental democratic values, as encapsulated by the apt phrase: "Human beings are born free and equal." Societies can escape dead ends, and Israeli society has proven in the past that it has this ability. It will require strengthening democratic education in schools, to build an enduring trust in democracy among young people.[9] The goal should be for individuals, and society at large, to learn that democracy does not contradict security, or religion, that it must safeguard minority rights, that it should strive to close social and economic gaps and invest in citizens' solidarity, and that it can coexist happily with all ideologies, beliefs, and identities.

Notes

1 Based on Itzhak Galnoor, "Israel: Interrupted Democratic Development?" *Turkish Policy Quarterly (TPQ)*, vol. 14, no. 1, May 2015, pp. 148–160; and on Itzhak Galnoor and Dana Blander, chapter 19, "Political Culture in Israel," in *Israel's Political System*, Am Oved, 2013 [Hebrew] and New York: Cambridge University Press, 2018.

2 Heading the list are Britain (an unwritten constitution), the United States (a constitution since 1787), Sweden (1807–1809), Holland and Norway (1814), Belgium (1831), New Zealand (1840, a Basic Law), Denmark (1849), Canada (1867, an unwritten constitution), Luxembourg (1868), Switzerland (1875), Australia (1900) and Finland (1919). These dates only mark milestones because constitutions by nature evolve and change. See Vernon Bogdanor (ed.), *Constitutions in Democratic Politics*, 1988; and the website of International Constitutional Law www.servat.unibe.ch/icl/.

3 Examples of laws and bills (2009–2015) that raise concern about non-democratic exploitation of majority rule. *General*: a proposal by a Kadima MK to subordinate democratic values to Israel being the nation-state of the Jewish people, and to lower the status of the Arabic language; the "Boycott Law," which allows for the suit of anyone who calls for a boycott of Israel—including areas under its control—without requiring that damages be proven, and allows for sanctions on NGOs calling for a boycott. *Curbing the High Court*: bills submitted by Likud MKs that would change the composition of the Judicial Appointments Committee in order to strengthen the hand of the justice minister on this committee, and hearing before the Knesset's Constitution Committee for candidates for the Supreme Court. *Loyalty and citizenship*: bills that would require a loyalty oath to Israel as a "Jewish, Zionist, and democratic state, and to its symbols and

values" as a condition for naturalized citizenship; stripping the citizenship of any person who acts against the Jewish people or Israel as the state of the Jewish people; mandating the playing of the national anthem at events in institutions of higher learning; allowing a special majority in the Knesset to impeach MKs (passed in 2016). *Restricting civil society*: a bill to amend the Defamation Law to permit libel suits against anyone who speaks ill of Israel or its entities—aimed primarily against organizations that publish information on rights violations by the IDF in the territories; a bill to tax organizations that receive donations from a foreign political entity; the Disclosure of Support from a Foreign Political Entity (Amendment) Law (enacted July 11, 2016). *Discrimination against women*: exclusion of women from public space—in the IDF, bus seating rules, on billboards and in publications, and in singing performances.

4 See, for example, Itzhak Galnoor, "A Rollercoaster," *Ha'aretz*, January 1, 1992. [Hebrew]
5 For a review of the legislative path of this law, see Gideon Alon, <u>Direct Election</u>, Tel Aviv: Bitan, 1995. [Hebrew]
6 Those who advocated for the change were partly aware of the adaptability problem, and therefore did not seek a full presidential system for Israel. Moreover, the failure of direct elections also suggests why a full presidential system may not work in Israeli democracy.
7 Political Stability in 61 Democracies (2005): www.worldbank.org/publicsector/.
8 Israel Democratic Institute (IDI), Democracy Index 2012.
9 Investment in reshaping the democratic political culture in Israel is much more important in my opinion than other suggested measures, such as a written constitution, or changing again the electoral system, or artificially further reducing the number of parties.

References and further reading

Alon, Gideon. 1995. *Direct Election*. Tel Aviv: Bitan. [Hebrew]
Asher, Arian and Michal Shamir (eds.). 2004. *The Elections in Israel 2003*. New Brunswick, NJ: Transaction, pp. 33–61.
Bogdanor, Vernon. 1988. *Constitutions in Democratic Politics*. Aldershot: Gower Publishing.
Crick, Bernard. 2002. *Democracy: A Very Short Introduction*. Oxford: Oxford University Press.
Diamond, Larry. 1993. "Democracy as a Paradox," in Ehud Sprinzak and Larry Diamond (eds.), *Israeli Democracy under Stress*. Boulder, CO: Lynne Rienner Publishers, pp. 21–43.
Galnoor, Itzhak. 1982. *Steering the Policy: Communication and Politics in Israel*. London: Sage.
Galnoor, Itzhak. 1992. "A Rollercoaster," *Ha'aretz*, January 1. [Hebrew]
Galnoor, Itzhak. 2015. "Israel: Interrupted Democratic Development?" *Turkish Policy Quarterly* (TPQ). 14(1), pp. 148–160.
Galnoor, Itzhak and Dana Blander. 2018 "Political Culture in Israel," in *Israel's Political System*. New York: Cambridge University Press.
Galnoor, Itzhak, Amir Paz-Fucks and Naomi Zion (eds.) 2015. *Privatization Policy in Israel*, The Van Leer Institute/Hakibbutz Hamehuchad [Hebrew]; English version to be published by Palgrave in 2018.
Hazan, Reuven. 1996. "Presidential Parliamentarism: Direct Popular Election of the Prime Minister, Israel's New Electoral and Political System." *Electoral Studies*. 15(1), February, pp. 21–37.
Hermann, Tamar, Ella Heller, Hanan Mozes, Kalman Neuman, Yuval Lebel, Gilad Be'ery. 2014. *The National-Religious Sector in Israel*. Jerusalem: Israel Democracy Institute.
Israel Democracy Institute (IDI). 2013. *Democracy Index*, 103 pp.
Kenig, Ofer, Gideon Rahat, and Reuven Hazan. 2004. "The Political Consequences of the Introduction and Repeal of the Direct Elections for the Prime Minister," in Asher Arian

and Michal Shamir (eds.), *The Elections in Israel—2003*. New Brunswick, NJ: Transaction Publishers, pp. 33–61.

Rittel, Horst and Melvin Webber. 1973. "Dilemmas in a General Theory of Planning." *Policy Sciences*. (4), pp. 155–169.

Roberts, Nancy C. 2000. "Wicked Problems and Networks Approaches to Resolutions." *The International Public Management Review*. 1(1), pp. 38–57.

Schumpeter, Joseph A. 1944. *Capitalism, Socialism and Democracy*. London: George Allen and Unwin.

Smooha, Sammy. 2002. "The Model of Ethnic Democracy: Israel as a Jewish and Democratic State." *Nations and Nationalism*. 8, pp. 472–491.

World Bank, "Political Stability in 61 Democracies (2005)": www1.worldbank.org/publicsector/indicators/htm

3

THE RISE OF THE ISRAELI RIGHT

Colin Shindler

Introduction

In March 2016, Sergeant Elor Azaria fired a bullet into the head of Abdel Fattah al-Sharif at close range. The Palestinian had attempted to carry out a knife attack in Hebron and was severely wounded when confronted by Israeli soldiers. While most of his colleagues believed that the danger from the disarmed Palestinian was over, Azaria apparently thought differently and acted on his own volition. A furious debate then opened up in Israel over whether Azaria had been justified or had acted recklessly. The IDF believed that he had made a professional error and he was soon charged with manslaughter and placed on trial. He was released in May 2018, having served just 9 months of an eighteen month sentence.

Avigdor Lieberman, leader of the right-wing Yisrael Beiteinu party, attended a pre-trial hearing while Naftali Bennett, leader of the national-religious HaBayit HaYehudi party, telephoned Azaria's parents to offer his support. This pushed Prime Minister Netanyahu into inviting Azaria's parents to visit his official residence. The Azaria case highlighted the deep fear of the Likud in being outmaneuvered by its rivals on the Israeli far-right. Netanyahu—and his Likud predecessors, Menachem Begin and Yitzhak Shamir—understood full well the threat from their right wing. They themselves had often adopted a right-wing radical position in order to attain a political objective.

The coalition between the Israeli center-right, the Likud and a plethora of far-right parties has been characteristic of all of Netanyahu's administrations. When right-of-center figures such as Ariel Sharon or parties such as Moledet have left Likud governments, Labor has often been willing to step into the breach. However, whatever the composition of this political solar system, the Likud has been at its center, radiating ideological energy since 1977, reflecting a rightward shift of Israeli public opinion.

While Menachem Begin astutely constructed the Likud from its genesis in the maximalist wing of Vladimir Jabotinsky's Revisionists, its components included disaffected members of the Zionist left. Moreover, it can be argued that several seminal figures of the Zionist right were influenced by the ideology of the European left. In the pre-state Yishuv of the 1920s, intellectuals associated with the broad left deserted the labor movement to join Jabotinsky's movement, where they constituted its maximalist wing. In the 1960s, Ben-Gurion broke with his own party, Mapai, to first form Rafi, then the State List, which became one of the founding component parties of the Likud. Throughout Zionist and Israeli history, there had often been moves from the left to the right—for ideological reasons, in response to personal rebukes, for opportunist motivations, for simply reading the mood of the Israeli public. Ironically the origins of the Israeli right lie in the ideological turmoil that permeated European Marxism at the beginning of the twentieth century.

The ideological crisis in Marxism

With the interment of Marx and Engels and the silencing of their voices, new interpretations of socialism emerged in order to meet the dictates of the fin de siècle political reality. These went beyond the realm of pure theory, beloved of political thinkers. Some left-wing thinkers now argued that bourgeois democracy and parliamentarianism could actually serve the interests of the proletariat and not be a distraction from revolutionary endeavor. The development of this new line of thought and its link to trends in society was noted by Ze'ev Sternhell, who claims that:

> Compulsory education, the spread of literacy in the countryside and the working class's slow but continuous acquisition of culture encouraged not the class consciousness of the proletariat but rather an increased consciousness of national identity. The creation of new strata of wage earners and the development of new tertiary activities proved the modernisation, contrary to all expectations, worked against socialism.
>
> *(Sternhell et al. 1994, p. 14)*

However, traditionalists totally rejected this analysis of an evolving situation: for them, it was heresy. While Karl Kautsky and Edouard Bernstein developed their opposing schools of thought, leftist nonconformists took note of the march of modernity and the advent of the technological revolution—and concluded that this necessitated the need for yet further revisionism. Orthodox Marxism, liberalism and the revolutionary traditions of the previous centuries were called into question. In France and Italy, under the influence of figures such as Georges Sorel and Arturo Labriola, revolutionary syndicalism made its appearance.

The Sorelians were the first revolutionaries of leftist origin to refuse to question ownership of private property, individual profit or the market economy. Sorel's philosophy highly influenced the Italian revolutionary syndicalists. A recent definition stated that:

> Syndicalism attempts to transform the trade union from a defensive institution concentrating on the protection of wages and hours into a vehicle for

the expansion of democracy beyond a disembodied parliamentary sphere removed from the realities of production.

(Schechter 2007)

Sorel was viewed as the thinker who would extricate socialism from its parliamentary quicksand. The emphasis that was placed upon the strike as a fundamental weapon of the proletariat was accompanied by Sorel's stress on the need for revolutionary violence. As he later moved away from Marxism, Sorel embraced anti-Semitism as an ingredient in opposing social-democratic values. On the eve of World War I, he wrote a series of articles, attacking Jewish capitalism and even rationalizing the blood libel. In its evolution from revolutionary syndicalism into national syndicalism, rationalism and individualism were rejected in favor of the nation. The nation would be above class. Indeed all classes would be participants in "the great fight against bourgeois and democratic decadence" (Sternhell et al. 1994, p. 27).

The genesis of revisionist Zionism

It was into this maelstrom of differing predictions for the twentieth century that the teenage Vladimir Jabotinsky was thrown shortly after his arrival in Rome, in the autumn of 1898. He had come from cosmopolitan, liberal Odessa, where Italian culture was widespread and favored. Indeed Odessa had been founded in 1794 as a southern St. Petersburg, in imitation of Naples. Jabotinsky felt very much at home in a Rome where many Jews were assimilated and in a liberal society whereby figures of Jewish origin such as Sidney Sonnino and Luigi Luzzati could reach the highest political office.

In his autobiographical *Story of My Life*, Jabotinsky famously recalled his lecturer at the University of Rome, Antonio Labriola, "the father of Italian Marxism" and regarded himself as "a follower" (Jabotinsky 2016, p. 52). For a few years, Labriola had worked with Georges Sorel, who wrote the preface to Labriola's *Essais sur la conception materialiste de l'histoire*. Yet it is also true that Jabotinsky knew about the works of Antonio Labriola's near-namesake Arturo Labriola, the so-called "father of Italian syndicalism," who was not mentioned in his autobiography. In two detailed articles for *Odesskie Novosti* shortly after his return to Russia, Jabotinsky wrote about Arturo Labriola and the background of revolutionary ideas in Italy.[1] Jabotinsky was clearly imbued with the political atmosphere of fin de siècle Rome while writing for the Odessa press. He justified Bakunin's warning against belief in the dictatorship of the proletariat at a literary evening and his interest in the writings of Peter Kropotkin, Pyotr Lavrov and Nikolai Mikhailovsky all drew the attention of the Odessa authorities to him. He had also written about Charlotte Corday—the assassin of Marat—and subsequently written a poem about her.

Jabotinsky also attracted the attention of the police through his close friendship with Vsevolod Lebedintsev, an old schoolmate and a member of the Social Revolutionaries. He was hanged in 1908 for his attempt to assassinate the Russian

Minister of Justice—he had threatened to blow himself up while carrying explosives (Geifman 2010). Lebedintsev and Jabotinsky shared a non-conformism that was common to many Russian intellectuals during this period of transition. Ironically, it was their love of Italian opera that led Jabotinsky to Zionism. It was the social revolutionary Lebedintsev who introduced him to the Zionist activist, Shlomo Saltzman during an intermission at the theatre.

Like the Italian revolutionary syndicalists, Jabotinsky found it difficult to believe in the wisdom of the masses and the ideal of a perfect future. The year 1903 proved to be a time when he was intellectually aimless—a period of literary stagnation, in which he questioned previously held convictions. It was a time of transition for many in Russia. For Jabotinsky, it was not just a reaction to the growing anti-Semitism, as exemplified by events such as the Kishinev pogrom, but almost a spiritual conversion to both Jewishness and Zionism. During the first decades of the twentieth century, Jabotinsky devoted time to study the nationalities question in European multinational states. He examined the works of writers such as Richard Charmatz and Georg Jellinek, but was clearly impressed by the works of Karl Renner. Jabotinsky wrote the introduction to the Russian language version of Renner's *Nation and State*. He was also attracted to Futurism, which Vladimir Mayakovsky and Velimir Khlebnikov promoted in Russia, but became a component later in emergent Italian fascism.

Jabotinsky was also fatalistic about the state of the world and often projected a Hobbesian outlook. In 1910, he wrote his well-known article, *Homo Homini Lupus* (Man is a Wolf to Man). In 1925, Jabotinsky formed the Revisionist Zionist movement, which was intended to pose an alternative pathway towards a state of the Jews and a return to Herzlian values. It did not recognize the first partition of Palestine by the British—that the East Bank had been lost to one of the scions of the Hashemite dynasty, Abdullah. It was also defined by the stagnation of the 1920s, after the high hopes unleashed by the Balfour Declaration proved premature, due to British vacillation. A frustrated Jabotinsky resigned several times from the Zionist Executive over the lack of progress, the extinguishing of hopes and the decline of Zionist dynamism. He recanted several times—and then finally exited at the beginning of 1923.

Abba Ahimeir and the maximalists

Jabotinsky was a charismatic leader, an intellectual with a command of languages and rhetoric, a liberal conservative who attracted multitudes of followers. A close aide later wrote:

> Beside the analytical, rational considerations which brought people to espouse the Revisionist cause, it had also attracted many who were drawn to it by temperament, either because of their inclination to assume extremist positions or because they were nonconformists by nature. Jabotinsky's own personality, uniting a first rate logical mind with the soul of a poet dissatisfied

with daily humdrum, reflected these two aspects. Many of my Revisionist co-workers shared both characteristics.

(Akzin 1989, p. 157)

The reaction of Jabotinsky to the October Revolution in Russia also drew many followers to his standard. Jabotinsky saw his newspapers in Odessa closed down, freedom of speech and expression curtailed and Russian cultural institutions emaciated by the Bolshevik authorities. In response, Jabotinsky moved gradually from a non-socialist position to an anti-socialist one. In 1925 he wrote *Basta*, in which he lamented the absence of the private sector—and that this course of events might well lead to fascism. In May 1927 he wrote *We, the Bourgeoisie*, which attacked "the cult of the proletariat." His point of reference was the national liberal revolutions of the nineteenth century, rather than the October revolution of the twentieth. This mindset was accentuated when the Polish Jewish middle class arrived in Palestine as part of the fourth aliyah. Their political milieu in Poland was undoubtedly anti-Soviet, due to bitter memories of being relegated to merely a geographical territory in the vast Tsarist Empire. In addition, Jabotinsky discovered during his visit to Poland in 1927 that many Jewish youth were enthusiastic Jewish nationalists.

In 1922, the first of numerous Soviet trials of Zionists took place. This was followed by both mass arrests and exile, as well as the granting of permission for many to leave for Palestine in 1924. When many of these new immigrants, often members of the pioneering Hapoel Hatzair, reached the Yishuv, they discovered adulatory attitudes towards the Soviet experiment amongst the labor Zionist elite. In contrast, these new immigrants argued—often from the familiarity of the inside of a Soviet prison—that they had experienced the reality of the USSR. During the next couple of years, many former socialists were attracted to Jabotinsky's Revisionists. This culminated in the appearance of three well-known labor intellectuals, Abba Ahimeir, Uri Zvi Greenberg and Yehoshua Hirsh Yeivin, at the Revisionist conference in Nahalat Yehuda, at the beginning of 1928. Abba Ahimeir even signed his articles "Aba Apostata" after the scholarly and reforming Roman Emperor, Julian II—'the Apostate'—who ruled between 361 and 363 AD and was personally more inclined towards a return to paganism away from the state religion of Christianity.

Yet there were clear differences between Jabotinsky and his new allies. By the late 1920s, Jabotinsky spoke in different voices to different audiences. His desire to cultivate Jewish youth through dramatic imagery often clashed with his commitment to parliamentarianism and negotiation with England. Such ambiguity could not be attributed to personalities such as Ahimeir, Yeivin and Greenberg, who soon constituted the leadership of the maximalist wing of the Revisionist movement. Ahimeir favored the rise of the national dictatorships—the regimes of Mussolini, Piłsudski and Atatürk. It was the persona of Lenin, the man who had made a revolution with few resources, rather than his social-democratic predecessor, Alexander Kerensky, which attracted Ahimeir's attention. Lenin argued that morality should be subordinated to politics—and not the other way around. While

Ahimeir rejected Bolshevism, he agreed with Lenin's trajectory—particularly his advocacy of "the path of violence, blood and personal sacrifice."

It was a short step to take for Ahimeir to express his appreciation for Italian fascism. In October 1928, Jabotinsky came to Palestine and Ahimeir welcomed him with an article entitled *On the Arrival of our Duce*,[2] in his series *From the Notebook of a Fascist*. In his next article he wrote: "our messiah will not arrive as a pauper on a donkey. He will come like all messiahs, riding a tank and bringing his commandments to his people." Yet Jabotinsky found this approach to be totally abhorrent and was privately scathing about such commentary. He had previously denigrated the idea of a "Duce," arguing that: "Buffaloes follow a leader. Civilized men have no leaders" (Jabotinsky 1926). However, Jabotinsky remained a figure of adoration for his young followers in Poland. While Jabotinsky wanted to encourage them to become involved in Zionism through radical rhetoric, he did not wish to push them into the arms of the Maximalists.

This ideological struggle reached its apogee at the fifth Revisionist conference in Vienna, in 1932. Ahimeir spoke about the emergence of a neo-Revisionism within Revisionist Zionism and compared it to the Jesuits who had "saved" Catholicism. In contrast, Jabotinsky looked back to the openness and liberalism of the Italy of his youth and exhibited great disdain for the absolute certainty of an age of ideology. He commented that "the dream of dictatorship" had become an epidemic amongst young people in general.

Jabotinsky, then in his early fifties, realized that he was losing influence amongst his young followers. For the rest of his life, until his death in 1940, Jabotinsky desperately attempted to bridge this growing gap through inspiring rhetoric, incendiary articles and dramatic gestures and proposals. As the storm clouds grew darker in Europe, his youthful followers began to follow a different path, whilst formally respecting Jabotinsky.

Ahimeir was more an intellectual than a political in-fighter. His many articles filled the pages of *Hazit Ha'am*, the periodical of the Maximalists. When Hitler was appointed Chancellor in January 1933, the Maximalists believed that the rise of German nationalism provided a lesson for all nationalist movements. Ahimeir's rejection of Soviet Communism came to the fore. In March 1933 he wrote: "Hitler has not yet treated us badly as Stalin has done … the anti-Semitic shell must be discarded, but not its anti-Marxist kernel."[3]

While Hitler's policies and brutal acts quickly disabused Ahimeir of his perception of the dynamism of this new German nationalism, Jabotinsky was not amused. He regarded the views of Ahimeir and others as "a stab in the back" and vehemently condemned anyone who followed this line as: "small-minded Jews," who "find favour before such a cruel tyrant."[4] Ahimeir's political star went into decline when he was falsely accused by the British of being involved in the murder of the labor Zionist leader, Haim Arlosoroff, in June 1933. When the case against him was dismissed through lack of evidence, the search of his apartment provided sufficient unpublished material to allow the British authorities to charge him with sedition.

Enter Menachem Begin

However, Ahimeir's stand drew the young Menachem Begin to the standard of the Maximalists. In 1933, Begin wrote *Betar and Its Message: A Letter to Jewish Parents*, in which he not only attacked the Zionist Left—"the red poison," but he was also disparaging about the state of Betar and claimed that its actions were non-revolutionary. This was an implicit criticism of Jabotinsky's philosophy. Begin also opposed any rapprochement with labor Zionism and the understandings which Jabotinsky and Ben-Gurion had arrived at during negotiations in London in 1934. Instead, he penned adulatory articles about Ahimeir and his philosophy of military Zionism.[5] The visits of such maximalists as Ahimeir and Uri Zvi Greenberg to Poland further influenced Begin and his generation while widening the gulf with Jabotinsky. In the post-Piłsudski era in Poland, Begin, like Ahimeir, argued for a revision of Revisionism. In early 1938, the Activist-Revisionist Front issued a manifesto that proclaimed a different path for the Zionist right. Begin was a prime mover in its publication. It stated:

> When it was founded and during the first years of its existence, Revisionism was understood by the Jewish masses, especially by the youth, as a revolutionary fighting movement, aiming at national liberation by means of uncompromising military action, both against the external enemy and against the internal traitors and unbelievers. However, in recent years Revisionism has restricted itself to the method of secret diplomacy, which we have mocked so much, in the direction of a completely pro-British orientation. The postulate of mass pressure on the external political factors has been completely forgotten. Within the Jewish people, the party executive has pursued an unceasing policy of seeking peace, thus ignoring the historic chances for a victorious crusade against liquidatory Zionism.

Begin demanded that the Revisionist movement should be completely restructured, "from the foundations upwards." It would no longer be a mass movement, but an elitist grouping, composed of a small unit of committed members who were ready for self-sacrifice.

When the inevitable altercation between Begin and Jabotinsky took place at the third conference of Betar in Warsaw in September 1938, these profound ideological differences were on public display. Jabotinsky condemned the approach of Begin since "conscience rules the world." He accused Begin of despair and fatalism. Jabotinsky felt that Begin's views were unworkable in the real world—a year before the outbreak of World War II. Jabotinsky remarked that there was no place in Betar for this kind of nonsense. Yet Jabotinsky's warnings fell on stony ground. The frustrated and discriminated nationalist Jewish youth of Poland in 1938 were now in no mood to accept Jabotinsky's long-held views. The confrontation marked the draining away of Jabotinsky's authority and his control over his acolytes. They saw Jabotinsky as the dreamer, the one who was out of touch. Israel Eldad (Scheib)—later one of the leaders of Lehi—was present and later commented:

On the morrow, we, the anguished, triumphed over him, the angel [Jabotinsky]. We, whose youth had not flowed to the beat of Pushkin and Lermontov, whose hearts did not bleed as his heart had bled for the cruelties of the Russian Revolution; we, who had no leisure between the First and Second World Wars to enjoy the melodies of Italy and its skies, who did not care whether the fascist regime was good or not, and did not understand, with our dry political analysis, why he refused to meet Mussolini; we, who were not from the generation of those who fought for the freedom of the citizen, for liberalism and parliamentary democracy, who did not grasp the secret of his sympathy for the democratic British regime and the freedom of the individual and respect for the individual in Britain itself. This was the psychological background to the argument and the struggle that went on at the conference on that day.[6]

Despite such remorse, the heirs of Maximalism had won the day: a key defining moment that shaped the rise of the modern Israeli right.

The schism in the Irgun

The Irgun Zvai Leumi had originally come into existence in 1931 as a result of the killings of Jews during the disturbances of 1929 and as a reaction to the British interpretation of such events, reflected in the Passfield White Paper. It was also known as "Haganah Bet" and gained the support of many other Zionist parties outside the broad labor Zionist movement. This did not include Jabotinsky, who kept his distance. Above all, the Irgun desired a stronger response to Arab attacks. With the outbreak of the Arab Revolt in 1936, there was a deep belief that "havlagah"—the official response of self-restraint and non-retaliation—was the wrong approach. The Irgun fragmented once more, with probably a quarter of its members returning to the Haganah. This left a more ideologically homogeneous nationalist Irgun, which Jabotinsky now agreed to lead. In 1937, after several changes of leadership, David Raziel took control supported by his close friend, Avraham Stern, a poet and classicist.

After the clash between Jabotinsky and Begin at the Warsaw Betar conference, the coalition of the Revisionists, Betar and the Irgun began to fragment. Betar moved away from the New Zionist Organization, the successor movement to the Revisionists, towards the Irgun and the doctrine of military Zionism. Begin's political star was in the ascendency in Betar while that of its leader, Aharon Propes, was in political decline. With the outbreak of World War II and the unexpected death of Jabotinsky in August 1940, differences within the Irgun became deeper and increasingly bitter. The Irgun collectively was unable to agree on its relationship to the British during the war against Nazism. Were they allies against Hitler or eternal enemies of Zionism? This dilemma affected many other national movements which opposed British colonialism—in Ireland, India and Egypt. A day after war had been declared between Germany and Britain, Jabotinsky aligned himself with the British—and did not remain neutral. This was not the case with Menachem Begin and Avraham Stern.

The split within the Irgun reached its apogee when its commander, David Raziel, supported Jabotinsky while Avraham Stern did not. Jewish national interests, Stern argued, were not the same as those of the British. Britain had declared war against Germany, not to save the Jews but to defend and protect its own position and security. Moreover, while Britain was fighting the Nazis, it was doing its utmost to bar the gates of salvation to millions of Jews trapped in Europe. In the summer of 1940 when Nazi Germany was conquering Europe and preparing for the invasion of Britain, Stern signed Communiqué 112. This was regarded as the genesis of the group that the British labeled "the Stern Gang," later known as Lehi. Stern believed that "the enemy of my enemy is my friend"—and approached the German Legation in Beirut in the mistaken belief that Hitler was a persecutor and not a liquidator, someone who could come to a political accommodation. Begin took a mid-way position between Jabotinsky and Stern, in that the enemy of my enemy was not automatically my friend. In 1940, he regarded the conflict as not "our war" and even after his arrival in Palestine in early 1942 argued against joining the British forces. Instead he advocated the formation of a Jewish army.

Begin's antipathy towards both the British and to the leading Zionist party, Mapai, hardened at the end of 1942, when the enormity of the Shoah was becoming clearer. His articles became more acerbic and his language more extreme. His declaration of the Revolt in 1944 against the British—while the war against Nazi Germany was still taking place—was to pre-empt the end of the five-year period of Jewish immigration as designated in the White Paper of 1939. While the permitted annual immigration figure of 15,000 Jews per annum was regarded as derisory, the Arabs of Palestine would have the final say on questions of immigration once this five-year period had terminated. The Revolt was also calculated to define a different type of Zionism—one which was in opposition to the beliefs, practices and policies of hegemonic labor Zionism and its non-socialist allies.

As Irgun commander, Begin made attempts to heal the rift in the right-wing camp. Lehi considered itself a post-Jabotinsky organization, dedicated to the assassination of British officials and Jewish informers in the image of the Russian Narodnaya Volya, the proto-socialist group which espoused revolutionary violence as a means of overthrowing the regime in Tsarist Russia. Begin instead viewed the Irgun as a Jewish army which did not harm civilians, but only attacked military targets. He therefore initially condemned the killings by Lehi of Lord Moyne in 1944 and of Count Bernadotte in 1948 during the war for Israel's independence. Yet there was also a personal animosity, with which the leaders of Lehi regarded Begin. Natan Yellin-Mor commented:

> Begin imagines himself standing on a high hill, carrying his utterances to those at its foot, whose eyes are uplifted to him. If they gaze at him with enthusiasm and admiration, he gives the one who so gazes a fatherly caress.
>
> *(Sofer 1988, p. 250)*

Yet Begin resisted the temptation to embark on a military path, once the state had been established. He resisted the exhortations to initiate a civil war in the aftermath of the sinking of the Irgun arms ship Altalena in June 1948 by the IDF and the killing of several of its members. Indeed, on the day after Ben-Gurion's declaration of independence, Begin spoke on Irgun radio. He invoked the heroes of the Zionist past, the murdered Jews of Europe, and placed the Irgun at the forefront of the struggle that "forced the (British) armies of occupation to evacuate the country and thus made possible the sovereignty and independence of the people of Israel in their homeland" (Begin 1948). Yet buried within the rhetoric was a pledge to take the parliamentary path, to convert the Irgun into a political movement, Tenu'at ha-Herut—the Herut (Freedom) movement. Begin ensured that Herut joined with neither the official Revisionists, nor the Fighters' party of Lehi for the first election in Israel in January 1949. This proved to be an astute decision, as the Revisionists were decimated and Lehi only won one seat. Nevertheless, Herut only won 14 seats out of 120, which was far below expectations.

On the other hand, most of Begin's rivals—Jabotinsky, Raziel, Stern—had been lowered into their graves. However, Begin emerged as the leader of a nationalist coalition, which quickly began to fragment. Herut lost almost half its seats in the second election in 1951, but recovered ground in the next election in 1955. It was due in part to Herut's uncompromising attitude in the Kastner affair. Its central figure was a member of Ben-Gurion's governing Mapai party and had been accused of saving his family and friends through negotiations with the Nazis in 1944, at the expense of Hungarian Jewry as a whole. During the Nazi occupation of Hungary, a special train had taken 1684 Jews to Switzerland, saving them from the death camps, whilst the rest of Hungarian Jewry was decimated by the Holocaust. Begin enabled the polarization of attitudes into an easy black and white explanation, and condemned any greyness of choice. Herut argued that Kastner should have called for an uprising, as took place in Warsaw, and raised questions about the moral integrity of Ben-Gurion's Mapai and whether they did enough to save Jews during the Shoah. One election poster read: "He [Kastner] votes for Mapai. You vote for Herut" (Shilon 2012, p. 180).

Another realignment of the left

Begin waited for allies to appear from the left, a tactic he had successfully employed in the past. During the 1950s, Begin assiduously cultivated the centrist General Zionists, but to no avail. By 1961, the General Zionists, now renamed the Liberals, were in a difficult position electorally. They had declined in each successive election since 1951 and were excluded from Ben-Gurion's government by prominent figures, who argued that it was now opportune to build an alliance of socialist and social-democratic parties—rather than with these representatives of the petty bourgeoisie. As Ben-Gurion had warned, this exclusion drew the Liberals closer to Begin and the forging of an electoral pact with Herut. This alliance ran as Gahal in the 1965 election.

Yet there were distinctive differences between the Liberals and Herut. Begin appreciated Jewish tradition while keeping a sharp political eye on the religious parties, who might prove to be future allies. The Liberals were more critical and demanded a reform of the religious establishment, whose record on corruption and rotten boroughs was less than perfect. Begin's rhetoric greatly appealed to the Israeli underclass, whilst the middle class, which endorsed private enterprise, looked traditionally to the Liberals. Moreover, the Liberals did not share Begin's animus towards West Germany and his opposition to the establishment of Israel–West Germany diplomatic relations.

By the early 1960s, Herut in general rarely mentioned any demands for seeking "the completeness of the Land." Moreover, there was no question of raising the reclamation of the East Bank in the agreement with the Liberals. However, the original ideology of Herut was never abandoned, but only relegated to the sanctum of innermost beliefs. In June 1966, Begin commented that it was "wholly inconceivable that any bit of the soil of the Land of Israel will be handed over to foreign rule" (Begin 1998, p. 126). Gahal won twenty-six seats in 1965, compared to a combined thirty-four for the Liberals and Herut in 1961. Even if the five seats of the breakaway Independent Liberals were taken into account, this was still several seats less than the 1961 total. Neither Herut nor the Liberals had benefitted. The new labor Alignment (Ma'arakh) of Mapai and Ahdut Ha'avodah had lost five seats. Even so, the Alignment—together with its allies in Mapam—could account for fifty-three seats, compared with Gahal's twenty-six.

Nevertheless, times were changing and many younger members of the Ma'arakh argued that the socialism of the pioneers did not match the realities of the 1960s. Moshe Dayan was already advocating the privatization of state land and a cessation of state funding to the traditional labor-controlled sector of Israeli society, whilst the respect shown to Ben-Gurion as the founder of the state was rapidly diminishing. While the election slogan in 1959 had been "Say Yes to the Old Man!" by the summer of 1965, few in Mapai were willing to agree. When Ben-Gurion finally challenged the serving Prime Minister, Levi Eshkol, he found that he could not displace him as he had done with Moshe Sharett, ten years before.

Ben-Gurion led his young acolytes—Peres, Dayan, Kollek, Herzog—into Rafi, the Israeli Workers' List—and into the political wilderness. In part it comprised those on the right of the party and those who were defined by Israel's security interests. Rafi attained a dismal ten seats in the 1965 election. The Mapai–Ahdut Ha'avodah alignment, on the other hand, had remained solid and secured forty-five seats, compared with a combined fifty in 1961. Rafi's exit left Mapai a more dovish party. This accentuated ideological differences with its partner, Yitzhak Tabenkin's Ahdut Ha'avodah, which was later not averse to colonizing the West Bank with socialist kibbutzim. Such developments provided new opportunities for Begin to expand his coalition of Herut and the Liberals. Indeed, in February 1966 Ben-Gurion surmised that there could now be cooperation on a number of issues with Begin's Gahal.

Gahal's poor performance in the 1965 elections was Begin's sixth as party leader. Even with the Liberals in tow, the number of seats fell far short of Mapai's total. In

1966, Begin was strongly challenged by his internal critics within Herut—yet he weathered the storm. His opponents, his Irgun comrades Shmuel Tamir and Gidi Paglin and his Revisionist rivals, Eliezer Shostak and Aryeh Altman, left Herut with Ehud Olmert to establish the Free Centre. It boasted four members of Knesset. The rebels had wished for a more flexible ideological approach than Begin was willing to permit and certainly did not wish to be hemmed in by a belief in an Israel encompassing both banks of the Jordan. They were also open to the prospect of partition. Even Jabotinsky's son, Eri, joined the Free Centre on the basis that Menachem Begin had distorted his father's legacy. These defections and a growing desire by the Liberals to break away from Herut placed Begin in a politically perilous position on the eve of the Six-Day War.

The run-up to the war prompted a lack of confidence in Israel's prime minister, Levi Eshkol, an impatience which arose while diplomatic options were being explored amidst broad subterranean moves afoot to reinstate Ben-Gurion. Many members of Mapai however strongly opposed Ben-Gurion's restoration. Instead, it was proposed that Rafi's Moshe Dayan should be appointed as Minister of Defense. Gahal, together with the National Religious Party (NRP), supported this move. After attempts to resist the entry of Rafi and Gahal, Eshkol invited representatives of the parties to join a wall-to-wall coalition.

The aftermath of the Six-Day War

With Israel's victory in only six days in June 1967, Begin finally achieved public recognition and respectability. He was a member of the government that had led the nation and overcome an unthinkable disaster. Begin entered government as minister without portfolio and subsequently appeared to withdraw from party politics, while cultivating the persona of an elder statesman. His ideological purpose in government was to rebut any suggestions to return any conquered territories—in particular, the West Bank—for peace. The war of 1967 had reversed the partition of 1947. The political status quo was now the retention of the territories. The conquest and occupation of the West Bank produced deeps rifts within all the parties: Mapai, Ahdut Ha'avodah, Rafi—and to a much lesser extent within Gahal and the NRP, whose ideological approach had always been geared towards a Greater Israel. Begin understood the debates and indeed splits within the parties as a once in a lifetime opportunity to create new alliances and expand Gahal.

In 1968, the Israeli Labor Party was established from a consolidation of Rafi, Ahdut Ha'avodah and Mapai. Nine out of the ten Rafi MKs and 60 per cent of Rafi members voted to return to Labor. Only Ben-Gurion denounced the idea of a return to the party whose predecessor he had founded; Rafi's rump established the State List with Ben-Gurion at its head. Moshe Dayan, who was now a member of Labor, promoted the linking of the territories economically to Israel and advocated the construction of four settlements next to Ramallah, Jenin, Nablus and Hebron. In 1969, he called for the introduction of Israeli law into the territories. Moreover, he argued that the traditional Labor formulation of "secure and agreed borders" should be replaced by "secure and strategic borders." Dayan and Peres from Rafi now represented Labor's right wing. These developments thus brought Gahal and the Labor right closer together.

Begin envisaged that Herut would be at the center of a coalition of orbiting outer parties, which included both disaffected members of Mapai, Ahdut Ha'avodah and Ben-Gurion's dwindling band of followers. Security hawks across the political spectrum argued that Israel should retain the West Bank for reasons of strategic depth. Religious Zionists believed that the conquest of locations that evoked a biblical resonance should be settled (Shindler 1991). Guided by rabbinical figures, such as the venerated Zvi Yehudah Kook, the outcome of the Six-Day War, it was argued, was a clear sign from God. The first settlement, Mehola, was established by the members of the religious youth movement, Bnei Akiva, in the northern West Bank and Jordan Valley as a security settlement. This demonstrated the convergence of interests between the security hawks and the religious right. Bnei Akiva was significantly affiliated to Hapoel Hamizrahi, which had actually voted in support of partition in 1947. The shift towards settlement thus reflected the changing attitudes in the national-religious public and leadership after 1967. Shortly after the end of the war, the Land of Israel Movement (LIM) published their manifesto. It stated:

> The whole of Eretz Israel is now in the hands of the Jewish people, and just as we are not allowed to give up the State of Israel so we are ordered to keep what we received there from Eretz Israel.
>
> *(Isaac 1976, p. 165)*

While many of the adherents of the right were natural signatories, luminaries from the old left such as Rachel Yanait-Ben-Zvi and Isser Harel also added their signatures. Yitzhak Zuckerman (Antek) and his wife, Zivia Lubetkin, leaders of the Warsaw Ghetto uprising, with a background in the labor Zionist movement, also backed the document.

Leaders of the literary intelligentsia, which usually supported labor Zionism, were represented by prominent figures, such as the poet Natan Alterman and the Nobel Prize winner, Shai Agnon. Such unlikely bedfellows would have been unthinkable a few years earlier, but the Land of Israel Movement provided a socializing mechanism, which facilitated dialogue between past enemies (Shindler 2015).

There was also the desire to return to settlements, from which Jews had been ousted in the past—Hebron (1929) and Gush Etzion (1948)—and above all, to be able to live close to the Western Wall and the Temple Mount in Jerusalem. Moshe Levinger and Eliezer Waldman, both followers of Zvi Yehuda Kook, hired rooms at the Park hotel in Hebron for the Passover festival in 1968—and refused to leave, even at the request of the city's military governor. The slow fragmentation of Labor due to ideological dissonance within it, the rift between the old guard in the NRP and its radical youth and the broad drift to the right of Ben-Gurion's followers all assisted in enlarging Begin's catchment area of authority.

Unlike Jabotinsky, the traditionalist Begin understood the world of Judaism. He was capable of "drawing on religious concepts and modalities of thought that have undergone a process of secularization" (Naor 2005). Begin shrewdly cultivated the disaffected. For example, the Supreme Court ruled in 1970 that a Jew was someone who defined himself as a Jew. In a subsequent Knesset debate, Begin argued there had never been a distinction between nation and religion in Jewish history. Non-orthodox Jews, he said, wished "to humiliate and insult religious law." Begin was also lucky. He pulled Gahal out of government in 1970 and therefore avoided the opprobrium hurled at Labor for the debacle of the Yom Kippur war in 1973.

Noted military figures, such as Ezer Weizmann and Ariel Sharon, joined his political camp—laying the foundations for the formation of the Likud in 1973. The Likud also included the Herut dissidents of the Free Centre. As the Right coalesced, the Left disintegrated. The reaction to the Yom Kippur War and the high number of casualties catalyzed a move from the left to the right within the Israeli public. The Mizrahim (mainly Jews originating from Mediterranean and Middle Eastern countries), the young and the Israeli underclass, deserted Labor and flocked to Begin's standard in the 1973 election. Begin was now perceived as a founding father of the state. Even with Yitzhak Rabin at the helm, Labor looked jaded. Scandal followed upon scandal and the coup de grâce was the discovery of a joint foreign bank account—a technical offence according to Israeli law—operated by Rabin's wife.

In the 1977 election, Labor's vote was split by the establishment of the newly formed, center-left Democratic Movement for Change—and Menachem Begin emerged as the victor at his ninth attempt to be Prime Minister, at the age of 64. Begin soon cemented his relationship with Dayan by offering him the Ministry of Foreign Affairs, while the NRP was given—for the first time—the Ministry of Internal Affairs, a ministry which was not concerned with purely religious affairs.

Prospects and challenges

In 1949, Herut had won 14 seats. By 1977, the Herut core in the Likud had actually not fared much better, but the Likud coalition of parties proved to be remarkably successful, propelling the Herut movement to power. The Camp David agreement in 1979 between Israel and Egypt was hailed by many commentators worldwide, but the disillusionment within Herut and the Israeli right in general precipitated a schism that gave rise to the far-right. It spawned parties such as Tehiya, Tsomet and Moledet in the 1980s, which found a ready-made constituency—often amongst the growing number of West Bank settlers. Within the Likud itself, opponents of the leadership found it advantageous to adopt a position of right-wing populism. Outside the Likud, far-right parties campaigned to attract sympathetic Likud members and voters to their standards. Begin, and his successors in the Likud leadership—Yitzhak Shamir and Binyamin Netanyahu—all devised strategies to prevent an erosion of support and a movement to the far-right.

Even during the interregnums of Rabin and Sharon, the Likud proved to be a central staple component of government. Moreover, the split in 2004, where sitting

Prime Minister Ariel Sharon left the Likud to found the new, centrist Kadima, proved to be just a setback, rather than the end of the road for the Likud. The collapse of the Oslo peace process, the rise of Islamism, the threat of Iranian nuclear weapons, the disarray in the aftermath of the Arab Spring, the Syrian Civil War—all these events moved the Israeli electorate to the right, in the belief that the right—rather than the left—would protect them from instability and uncertainty. Sharon was seen as the bulwark against the suicide bombers of Hamas and Islamic Jihad during the first years of the twenty-first century. The desire for security and stability trumped all other considerations, including opposition to the expansion of the West Bank settlements—a fundamental ideological belief of the Likud.

In the 2015 elections, the Likud victory proved both opinion polls and political commentators completely wrong in their predictions. Moreover, it suggested a reversal of the schism in 1979, in that there was a drift of votes from the far-right back to the Likud. The left in 2015—primarily represented by the Zionist Union, Meretz and Yesh Atid—had shrunk to forty seats, far short of the blocking majority of sixty-one Knesset seats that would have been required. The far-right—HaBayit HaYehudi and Yisrael Beiteinu—together with the increasingly right-wing, ultra-orthodox parties—Shas and United Torah Judaism—accounted for twenty-seven seats. The far-right and the center-right Likud accounted for sixty-seven seats—and if the centrist Kulanu is added, this increases to seventy seven. While violence reigns in the Islamic and Arab worlds, there is little appetite for change amongst the Israeli electorate. Netanyahu, although unloved, is seen as the guarantor of security during adverse times. There is, therefore, little opportunity for a political resurrection of the Israeli left, while the storm rages outside Israel's borders. Thus, the Israeli right remains the dominant, hegemonic force in Israeli politics, having completed its journey from obscurity to the Prime Minister's office.

Notes

1 *Odesskie Novosti*, 19 July 1901, 8 August 1901.
2 *Doar Hayom*, 10 October 1928.
3 Abba Ahimeir, *Hazit Ha'am*, 31 March 1933.
4 Vladimir Jabotinsky, Letter to the Editors of *Hazit Ha'am*, 17 May 1933, *Igrot 1932–1933*, Tel Aviv 2006.
5 Menachem Begin, *Unzer Welt*, 9 August 1935.
6 Protocols of the Third World Conference of Betar (Bucharest, 1940), p. 88, Jabotinsky Institute Archives.

References and further reading

Akzin, Benjamin. 1989. *Mi-Rigah li-Yerushalayim*. Jerusalem: The Library of the World Zionist Organization, pp. 157.
Begin, Menachem. 1948. "The State of Israel has Arisen." *Herut*. 15 May.
Begin, Menachem. 1998. "Address to the Herut and Liberal Centers," *Hayom* June 28 1966 in Sasson Sofer (ed.), *Begin: An Anatomy of Leadership*. Oxford: Blackwell Publishers, 126 pp.

Geifman, Anna. 2010. *Death Orders: The Vanguard of Modern Terrorism in Revolutionary Russia.* New York: Praeger, 104 pp.

Isaac, Rael Jean. 1976. *Israel Divided: Ideological Politics in the Jewish State.* Baltimore, MD: The Johns Hopkins University Press, 165 pp.

Jabotinsky, Vladimir. 1926. "Zionist Fascism." *The Zionist*, 25 June.

Jabotinsky, Vladimir. 2006. Letters to the Editors of *Hazit Ha'am*, May 17, 1933, *Igrot 1932–1933.* Jerusalem: Mekhon Z'aboṭinsḳi be-Yiśra'el : ha-Sifriyah ha-Tsiyonit 'al-yad ha-Histadrut ha-Tsiyonit ha-'olamit.

Jabotinsky, Vladimir. 2016. *Story of My Life.* Brian Horowitz and Leonid Katsis (eds.). Detroit, MI: Wayne State University Press, 52 pp.

Naor, Arye. 2005. "Hawks' Beaks, Doves' Feathers: Likud Prime Ministers between Ideology and Reality." *Israel Studies.* 19(3), Fall.

Schechter, Darrow. 2007. *The History of the Left from Marx to the Present.* London: Bloomsbury Publishing PLC, 108 pp.

Shilon, Avi. 2012. *Menachem Begin: A Life.* New Haven, CT: Yale University Press, 180 pp.

Shindler, Colin. 1991. *Ploughshares into Swords? Israelis and Jews in the Shadow of the Intifada.* London: I. B. Tauris, pp. 64–65.

Shindler, Colin. 2015. *The Rise of the Israeli Right: From Odessa to Hebron.* London: Cambridge University Press, pp. 281–282.

Sofer, Sasson. 1988. *Begin: An Anatomy of Leadership.* Oxford: Blackwell Publishers, 250 pp.

Sternhell, Ze'ev, Mario Sznajder and Maia Asheri. 1994. *The Birth of Fascist Ideology: From Cultural Rebellion to Political Revolution.* Princeton, NJ: Princeton University Press, p. 47.

4

POLITICAL PARTIES AND PARLIAMENTARY POLITICS

Reuven Y. Hazan and Chen Friedberg

Introduction

This essay examines the political parties that mediate between state and society, scrutinizing their socio-political functions in Israel's democratic political institutions. First, there is a brief history of Israeli electoral politics. Second, the main rifts that divide Israeli society and create distinct political parties and blocs are delineated. The focus then shifts to parliamentary politics in Israel, examining— amongst other issues—how the lack of a codified constitution affects the electoral and political systems. This essay then concludes by pointing out a disparity within Israeli politics and society: that despite the declining influence of "traditional" parties, long-established political groups continue to hold the balance of power within the Knesset and the executive.

Israel's evolving party system

Since the 1930s—long before the state was established—and up to the 1970s, Israel had a dominant party system (Hazan 1998). That is, one party, the center-left Labor Party, was significantly larger than any other party, although it never won an absolute majority of the parliamentary seats. Labor captured the pivotal position at the center of the political map—there was no majority to its left or to its right and thus no coalition government could be established without it. This gave Labor the power to choose its coalition partners, and to hold onto the key positions in government: the post of prime minister and the ministries of defense, finance, and foreign affairs. Labor also held a majority of Knesset members within the coalition and a majority of cabinet ministers within the government, which allowed it to advance its policies. During that era, although Israel had a multi-party coalition government, Labor's hold on power was somewhat similar to that of a majority party in a two-party system (Medding 2000).

Labor's first loss, in the 1977 elections, signified the end of the dominant party system. The demise of Labor's dominance shifted the party system toward a bipolar multi-party configuration, based on center-left and center-right party alliances. In the new bipolar multi-party system, two large parties—Labor and Likud—competed with each other for the leading position, although both were always short of an absolute majority, while the smaller parties behaved as "satellites" to one of the larger ones, creating two almost equally-sized blocs of parties. This structure was clearly more competitive than the earlier phase of Labor dominance that characterized the early years of statehood. From the mid-1970s and until the end of the twentieth century, most governments were led by the right-of-center Likud, but Israel also had two Labor-led governments and two unity governments—a "grand coalition" comprised of both Labor and Likud, along with some of their respective satellite parties.

The first sixteen years of the twenty-first century began with a unity government and continued with a Likud victory in 2003; the party then split in 2005 and suffered its worst election defeat ever in the 2006 elections. Yet the year 2009 engendered a Likud resurgence, as the party founded a new coalition government after elections; subsequently, the Likud has maintained this position of power, winning two more elections. Labor, the formerly dominant party, continued its decline: in 2009, it dropped to being the fourth largest party, but also managed to recapture second place in 2015, despite losing the election. There have been repeated attempts since the 1970s to establish a centrist party, but these attempts largely failed until 2003, when the centrist Shinui became the third largest party in Israel. In 2006, Israel saw, for the first time, a centrist party—Kadima—win more seats than any other party, leading to the formation of the first Israeli government that was not led by Labor or the Likud. By 2013, Kadima had collapsed, but the formation of the Yesh Atid and Movement parties by Yair Lapid and Tzipi Livni respectively, ensured the political center retains parliamentary influence. Similarly, the 2015 elections saw the Kulanu Party become the latest centrist political party in the Knesset, demonstrating the proliferation of "center parties." However, no one party or ideology was truly hegemonic throughout this volatile era. Conversely, one clear, constant trend had been the decline of the political parties as the main actors in Israeli politics, together with the growth of personalized politics and the impact of non-party actors.

The party system after the most recent 2015 elections is represented in a two-dimensional map in Figure 4.1. These two dimensions are the two most important social cleavages in Israeli society, unlike the dominant socioeconomic dimension that defines party politics in other democracies. The main issue that determines electoral preferences in Israel is that of the parties' stances on matters of security, running from the dovish ("Land for Peace") on the left to the hawkish ("Greater Israel") on the right. The second dimension is that of religion, which runs from the most ultra-orthodox (haredi) on top to the most secular on bottom. These two dimensions also delineate the coalition potential of each party. The size of each party circle is based on the number of seats it won in the elections.

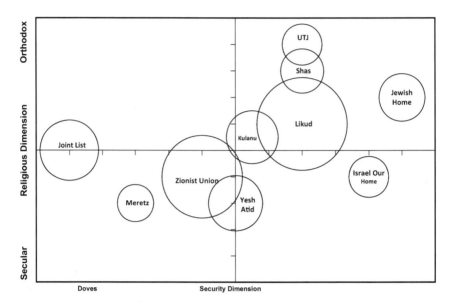

FIGURE 4.1 The Israeli Party Map in 2015

Source: Gideon Rahat, Reuven Y. Hazan & Pazit Ben-Nun Bloom, *Representation* 2016 Vol. 52, #1, pp. 99–117, "Stable Blocs and Multiple Identities: The 2015 Elections in Israel," copyright © 2016 McDougall Trust, London, reprinted by permission of Taylor & Francis Ltd, www.tandfonline.com on behalf of McDougall Trust, London.

The social basis of party politics

Israeli politics in general, and the party system in particular, can be described as a microcosm of the main social tensions that influence, and are influenced by, the political positions prominent in the body politic, outside of the Knesset. That is, among Israel's political parties we find representatives of a plethora of perspectives, spanning religious and secular, communalists and individualists, hawks and doves, socialists and capitalists, all reflecting the many compromises and clashes in the arena of party politics.

The institutional order manages these conflicts, allowing the opposing sides to debate—harshly at times, but still within the democratic rules of the game in the electoral, party and legislative arenas. Within the party system, the most severe conflicts are between supporters of hawkish and dovish approaches to questions of security, and between supporters of a secular state and advocates of an enhanced role for religion in the public sphere. These key cleavages, which often define Israeli party politics, are examined in greater depth below.

Throughout democratic polities, electoral and societal cleavages abound; many democracies share similar rifts within their electorates (Lijphart et al. 2000). In Israeli society, at least six unique, central cleavages exist that find expression in politics through the political parties. This chapter will subsequently examine each of these key cleavages, which are delineated below in order of political saliency:

1.   The security-based ideological cleavage
2.   The religious–secular Jewish divide
3.   The Jewish–Arab rift
4.   The Ashkenazi–Mizrahi ethnic split
5.   The socioeconomic cleavage
6.   The new immigrant–veteran immigrant and native Israeli division

The ideological-security cleavage

Until 1967, the main ideological cleavage in Israel was similar to that in most other countries—a socialist left, versus a capitalist right. However, the "Six-Day War" of 1967 changed everything, ensuring the debate on foreign affairs and security rose to predominance. The focus of this debate was—and continues to be—the fate of the territories that were captured in the conflict, especially the West Bank and Gaza Strip, which have an indigenous population of Palestinians. On one side of the debate, the so-called doves support a "land-for-peace" compromise with the Arab countries and the Palestinians. They justify this stand as moral (such as the right of the Palestinians to self-determination), as strategic (Israel is a tiny country, surrounded by over twenty Arab states, and cannot live by the sword forever), and as a demographic interest of Israel (the Israeli Arabs and Palestinians together will be a majority if Israel annexes the territories, ensuring Israel is no longer a Jewish state).

On the other side of the debate, the so-called hawks support the idea of "Greater Israel" and policies that would strengthen the hold of Israel throughout all these territories, such as the building and development of settlements. Hawks justify this stand as historical-religious (the land of biblical Israel), as strategic (only resolute steadfastness can convince a hostile Arab world that Israel is resilient), and based on security interests (the territories are an important buffer zone, allowing Israel to better defend itself, whilst a hostile Palestinian state would threaten Israel's existence).

This divide constitutes the main, salient cleavage in contemporary Israeli politics, and it influences voting more than any other cleavage. The potential of parties to come together to form a government is defined first and foremost by their stance on this issue. The ideological doves–hawks cleavage is affiliated with other cleavages, but they do not overlap. For example: religious Jews tend to be hawkish; Arabs are mainly dovish. Nevertheless, Russian immigrants are mainly secular but mostly hawkish, demonstrating that secular publics can also hold hawkish views on questions of security.

The religious–secular cleavage

The most prominent religious rift in Israel is within the Jewish majority, which makes up approximately 80 percent of Israel's population. This cleavage is therefore intra-religious and is based on the question of religious versus secular beliefs and observance within Judaism. This intra-Jewish rift permeates throughout Israeli society and politics, affecting everything from an individual's daily routine to differing worldviews and party affiliation.

Yet this cleavage is not a dichotomy: a large group within Jewish society places itself in between the secular and the ultra-orthodox. This group is labeled "traditional" and includes people who practice some, but not all, of the religious Jewish customs. Yet the rift between the secular and the ultra-orthodox is wide. Most ultra-orthodox Jews voluntarily live in separate communities or neighborhoods, the men attend separate religious schools, most do not serve in the military (although it is compulsory for secular Jews, the ultra-orthodox receive an exemption), and do not work, preferring to dedicate themselves to religious studies). Thus, ultra-orthodox Jews are often insulated from the outside world; arguably, the principal interaction point between this sector and the broader society to which it belongs is within the political arena. It is important to also distinguish between national-religious and ultra-orthodox Jews. National-religious Jews serve in the military, work for their livelihood, and attend universities; they are thus relatively integrated into Israeli society. The secular–religious rift is therefore a continuum, with four points of reference. At one pole are the ultra-orthodox, followed by national-religious Jews; the religious "center" of Israel contains traditional Jews, whilst secular Jews represent the opposing pole to the ultra-orthodox.

This cleavage has multiple political expressions. The ultra-orthodox parties represent religious interests exclusively, but the predominant national-religious party in the Knesset advocates both religious and security policies. There are moderate hawkish and dovish parties that appeal to traditional Jews, but there are extremist parties on both ends of the security dimension that support a separation between religion and state. Moreover, the territorial-security issue has come to largely overlap with the religious issue. That is, whilst there are exceptions to this rule, the strength of religious beliefs and observance is positively and strongly correlated with hawkish stands, while secular Jews generally lean toward dovish positions.

The Jewish–Arab cleavage

The rift between the Jewish majority and the Israeli-Arab minority is probably the deepest and sharpest one in Israeli society. Although the Arab minority has Israeli citizenship—unlike the Palestinians in the territories captured in 1967—the memory of the armed struggle between these two communities before and at the time of the establishment of Israel, the subsequent military administration imposed on this community by Israel (1949–1966), and the persistent bias of the Jewish-dominated state against the Israeli Arabs, whether practically or symbolically, helps sustain their separate identity. Most Jews and Arabs live in separate cities, towns, and villages. Even in "mixed" cities, such as Haifa, most live in separate neighborhoods. Almost all Jews and Arabs are educated in separate school systems, and most Arabs are not drafted into compulsory military service. Meeting points between these two groups do exist—at universities and colleges, as consumers and in the workplace—but these are quite limited and come relatively late in life. Intermarriage is rare, and is seen in a negative light by both communities. The result is an almost dichotomous rift, which is also found in the political arena.

Many Jews, and the Jewish-dominated state institutions, are suspicious of the Arab minority and question its loyalty to the state. This is largely because this minority within Israel is framed and frames itself as part of the large, Arab majority in the region, which Israeli Jews perceive as hostile. In addition, Israeli Arabs often identify themselves as constituting part of the larger Palestinian nation, increasing their alienation from Jewish-Israeli society. Nevertheless, Israeli Arabs are frequently perceived with suspicion by the Palestinians in the occupied territories and elsewhere, and by the Arab countries in the area (Al-Haj 2004).

Despite these hurdles, Jews and Arabs in Israel have managed to coexist. Over time, the Arab community has increased its involvement in many fields, such as education, health, and business. In absolute terms, Israeli Arabs live in better conditions than most of the Arabs in the Middle East. Yet the gap between them and the Jewish population endures, and is a sign of persistent inequality.

In political terms, the Arabs have tended to favor more radical parties, such as the Israeli Communist Party. Until the late 1970s, many Arabs voted for "Zionist" parties, mainly those on the left that espoused dovish positions and included a few Arab representatives on their electoral lists. By the 1990s, however, the majority of the Arab vote shifted to the more "authentic" Arab parties that stressed Arab, Palestinian, and Muslim identities.

The Ashkenazi–Mizrahi cleavage

Jews immigrated to Israel from all over the world. Once in Israel, many preserved their previous ethnic identities in one form or another. These identities have to do with their historical experience and cultural background as Jews in the particular country they came from. The main distinction is between Ashkenazi Jews, whose origins are in Europe and America, and Mizrahi Jews, whose origins are in Asia (mainly Middle Eastern countries) and North Africa. Different cultural-religious traditions developed in these regions and have often been maintained by these communities in Israel.

The elite group within the Zionist movement and in the local Jewish community in the British Mandate of Palestine (since the 1920s) was mainly Ashkenazi; most Mizrahi Jews came to Israel after the establishment of the state in 1948, much later than the Ashkenazi pioneers. The concept of Zionism was often perceived differently by these two divergent groups. The Ashkenazi Jews perceived it as an ideology—an active, modern, national revolution versus the traditional-religious, passive, communal past—and they were mainly secular and socialist. Among the Mizrahi Jews, Zionism was seen as a continuation, and even fulfillment, of religious tradition, of which the return to Zion was an integral part (Dowty 1998).

This cleavage is significant, but not particularly deep—especially in comparison to the Jewish–Arab and the secular–religious cleavages. Indeed, Ashkenazi and Mizrahi Jews live side by side, go to the same schools, serve in the same military units and study in the same universities. Except for the ultra-orthodox community, where there still exists an extreme separation between Ashkenazi and Mizrahi Jews in educational systems and in marriage, there is no significant separation. The rate of Ashkenazi–Mizrahi intermarriage is around 25 percent and rising. The Mizrahi "late-comers" have integrated well into Israeli society in general and in various elites, particularly the political one, Mizrahi Jews enjoy a proportional share of representation. Though a gap between Mizrahi and Ashkenazi Jews still persists in higher education and economic prosperity, the cleavage is not dichotomous because the two identities are now significantly mixed. This ensures that many Jews born in the contemporary State of Israel have both Ashkenazi and Mizrahi roots.

The Socioeconomic cleavage

After 1967, security issues supplanted socioeconomic status as the main cleavage defining the ideological divides between Israeli political parties. The socio-economic cleavage has been unable to regain its dominant position in politics, because of several factors. Among Jews, the economically disadvantaged tend to vote for right-wing hawkish parties and the more affluent tend to vote for left-wing dovish parties—underlining that voting is driven predominantly by security concerns—due to a series of factors such as country or origin, time of arrival in Israel and treatment by the governing Labor party, among others. The two groups that have the highest percentage of low-income members, the Israeli Arabs and the ultra-orthodox Jews, vote for opposing parties on the dominant security dimension. In short, the differences between the dovish and hawkish parties on the socio-economic dimension have become blurred over time. The socioeconomic cleavage had thus become mediated by other, more prominent cleavages (Horowitz and Lissak 1989).

On several occasions, Israeli political parties have attempted to re-emphasize the significance of the socioeconomic cleavage, with little long-term success. Significant changes, however, could be seen after massive social protests during the summer of 2011, when the socioeconomic cleavage returned to help frame political preferences, influencing both the elections and the party system in a significant manner. Young Israeli adults, who felt they lacked economic and social opportunities for advancement, primarily led the social protests. Specifically, young Israelis claimed that the liberalization of Israel's economy in the 1980s contributed to a substantial increase in the standard of living of their parents' generation, but now impeded similar increases for their generation. Shalev (2012) claims that between 2005 and 2010, the proportional income of the typical Israeli-Jewish working family dropped dramatically, while the rising cost of housing made this erosion of income an even more significant problem. However, the social protests did not constitute a struggle of the poor against the rich, but rather of frustrated parts of the eroding middle class against the state. The two poorest social groups in Israel, the Arabs and the ultra-orthodox, largely did not take part in the protests.

Eschewing the traditional security cleavage, the social protests and the parties and interest groups spawned by the movement attempted to remain apolitical and consensus-based. The socioeconomic grievances that erupted demonstrated that many Israelis prioritize domestic issues, despite the continued salience of pressing security issues. The elections of 2013 and 2015 each brought a new domestically focused political party into the Israeli political arena (Yesh Atid in 2013 and Kulanu in 2015), and each in turn became an essential part of the government, while other parties increased their focus on socioeconomic issues during their campaigns. However, the dominance of the security cleavage remains evident, since the predominant governing party after both elections remained the Likud, which focused its campaign mainly on the security issue.

The new immigrants versus the veteran immigrants and native Israelis cleavage

Due to the relatively young age of the country, and the fact that it has grown more than tenfold in population in almost seven decades, most Jews are either immigrants or first- and second-generation Israelis. However, there is a rift that runs between veterans and newcomers. The most politically significant rift is between veteran immigrants and natives on the one side, and the large group of new immigrants from the former Soviet Union on the other side. This large group of over one million people immigrated to Israel at the beginning of the 1990s, after the collapse of the Soviet Union, and now make up approximately 20 percent of Israeli society. Arriving in such unprecedented numbers allowed them to preserve their language and culture; there are Russian newspapers, magazines, a TV channel, theater, and specialty shops that offer everything from books in Russian to imported food.

Since 1996, this wave of immigration has been represented by new parties and within the established parties, new immigrant-focused sub-groups were created; Israel's main parties have frequently placed immigrants from the former Soviet Union on their candidate lists. Starting with only a handful of seats in the late 1990s, the main immigrant party—Yisrael Beitenu—became the third largest party in Israel in 2009. However, not all of its voters nor its representatives are immigrants from the former Soviet Union, which signifies an attempt to widen the party's appeal and draw support from other parts of the electorate. However, the party subsequently declined in the 2013 and 2015 elections. That Yisrael Beitenu sought to widen its appeal, whilst its electoral fortunes declined, indicates that within a single generation, this wave of immigration successfully integrated into Israeli society, at least politically. The same cannot be said for the much smaller group of Jewish immigrants from Ethiopia, who have had a considerably more challenging absorption process and who—representing less than 1 percent of the Israeli population— have had minimal political impact as a group.

The Israeli parties and party system

From party monopoly to party decline

The previous section delineated the main rifts that divide Israeli society politically and create distinct political parties. Subsequently, this essay will now examine political parties: the organizations that mediate between the society and the state, whose function it is to bring social identities and interests into the democratic political institutions.

Political parties were the central actors both in the pre-state period and during the first few decades after independence. They were the dominant, maybe even the exclusive, mediators between state and society (Galnoor 1982; Horowitz and Lissak 1989). As such, they can be described as classic mass parties. They had a wide membership base that was estimated at more than one-quarter of the population. They had affiliated youth movements, sport clubs, newspapers, and magazines. Even health care associations and banks were linked and identified with them. Over time, however, the parties lost their dominant status as the mediators between state and society. Other channels of communication between the citizen and the state became available with the development of the mass media, the consolidation of a more autonomous civil society, and the "judicialization" of politics. More recently, the personalization of politics (Rahat and Sheafer 2007) means that citizens and lobbyists can approach individual politicians, regardless of their political affiliation, with their demands and grievances.

The decline of parties in Israel has been dramatic. Standard indicators such as party membership, electoral volatility, voting for the main parties, and trust in and identification with political parties, all point to a sharp drop (Kenig and Knafelman 2013). This decline is also evident when examining parties from a functional perspective: parties now share the functions of communication, interest representation and aggregation with other political actors (such as civil society groups). Political parties have lost their monopoly status as focal points for identity and they have a decreasing impact on the policy direction of government, even though they still hold a monopoly on the election of representatives to public office.

Party blocs and social cleavages

The Knesset—Israel's parliament—often plays host to a multitude of parties at the same time, sometimes even more than a dozen. However, most of them belong to one of a handful of "camps," which overlap or correspond with long-established societal cleavages. Belonging to these camps reflects a party's ideology and, in many cases, a social identity. Most Israeli voters will not stray from their camp, but they do swing from one party to another within a camp, especially when one party is more likely to be in the coalition that will be formed after the elections. The social cleavages described above are thus the basis for the classification of the parties represented in the Knesset into the following five political camps: dovish-left, hawkish-right, socioeconomic-center, religious, and Arab.

The most prominent member of the dovish or left camp was, and continues to be, Labor (and its predecessor Mapai), which dominated pre-state and state politics until 1977. The left includes parties with socialist and social-democratic ideologies and/or parties with dovish perceptions (especially since 1967). After the 2013 and 2015 elections, the parties in this camp were the Labor/Zionist Union and the smaller, more left-wing Meretz.

The right includes parties that rejected the dominant socialist ideology (before 1967) and also parties that hold hawkish stands (mainly since 1967). Prominent in this camp is the Likud, which has established itself as the leading force in Israeli politics since 1977. In the last two elections this camp included the Jewish Home, a religious, significantly hawkish party, and Yisrael Beitenu, an extremely hawkish yet secular party, whose support is largely concentrated amongst Russian immigrant voters.

The electoral base of the center changed dramatically in the aftermath of the 2011 social protests. Previously, the center used to be defined as a "third way" between the dovish and the hawkish camps. Since 2011, the center has largely been defined by its focus on domestic socioeconomic policies, in response to the shifting concerns of its core voters. In 2013, the new Yesh Atid party was the primary centrist party, and in 2015, a new centrist party, Kulanu, competed with Yesh Atid for the centrist vote.

The religious camp includes those parties that represent ultra-orthodox identities and interests. In the past, these parties positioned themselves in the middle of the party spectrum, but since 1977 they have leaned further to the right and prefer both to support and join right-wing governments. However, when the left has achieved the necessary majority to create a government, the ultra-orthodox have readily joined the coalition, in exchange for promoting their particular interests. The two ultra-orthodox parties are distinguished by their cultural background— Shas purports to represent the Mizrahi (Sephardi) religious community and United Torah Judaism (UTJ) is overwhelmingly Ashkenazi in demographic composition.

The Arab camp is primarily composed of political parties, whose voters and representatives are largely Israeli Arabs. Since the 1980s, these include different ideological and cultural streams, such as Arab-nationalist and Muslim. All the primary Arab parties hold non-Zionist, and even anti-Zionist, stances and as a result, none of their members have ever participated in any Israeli government. In 2013 there were three small Arab parties represented in the Knesset—Hadash, Balad, and Ra'am/Ta'al—but in the 2015 elections these parties united, under the label of the Joint List.

None of the five camps described above has a majority in the population or in politics. If the Arabs are added to the dovish parties, two groups continue to lack a majority. The same is usually true for the ultra-orthodox and the hawkish party groups, ensuring that cross-party cooperation has to include multiple parties, across divergent and sometimes opposing ideological groups.

Table 4.1 presents a classification of the political parties in Israel, based on the social cleavage that dominates their identity. Some cleavages divide between two

TABLE 4.1 Social cleavages and political parties in Israel

Social Cleavage	Political Parties in 2015 (2013 in parentheses)
Security	Doves: Zionist Union (Labor), Meretz, Joint List (Balad, Hadash, Ra'am/Ta'al)
	Hawks: Likud, Jewish Home, Israel Our Home
Religion	Religious: UTJ, Shas, Jewish Home
	Secular: Meretz, Hadash, Yesh Atid, Israel Our Home
Jewish–Arab	Arab: Joint List (Balad, Hadash, Ra'am/Ta'al)
	Jewish: Likud, Zionist Union (Labor), Yesh Atid, Kulanu, Jewish Home, Shas, UTJ, Israel Our Home, Meretz
Ashkenazi–Mizrahi	Ashkenazi: UTJ
	Mizrahi: Shas
Socio-economic	Yesh Atid, Kulanu
Immigrants	Israel Our Home

opposing poles, such as the main security cleavage between doves and hawks, or the religious cleavage between ultra-orthodox and secular, while other cleavages create political parties to advance their interests without an "opposing" pole, such as the socioeconomic or immigrant cleavages.

Parliamentary politics

The "constitutional" setting

The 1947 United Nations resolution that called for the establishment of Israel explicitly recommended that the new state adopt a constitution. Several drafts of a constitution were written and discussed in various forums, and Israel's first elections, in 1949, were for the Constituent Assembly that was entrusted with producing a constitution. Yet deliberations in the elected assembly did not result in a codified constitutional document, but rather in a political compromise resolution. The assembly instructed one of its committees to prepare a draft constitution, built chapter by chapter, in such a way that each would constitute a separate "Basic Law," later to be combined into a constitution and presented to the parliament, once the committee completed its work. The Constituent Assembly also symbolically changed its name to the First Knesset, which means that all subsequent parliaments elected in Israel have held both legislative and constitution-making powers.

Today, Israel is one of the few democracies without a codified constitution, as is also the case in the United Kingdom and New Zealand. Nevertheless, Israel has rules that define the political power structure, the authority of the branches of government, the interaction between them and their relations with the public. These rules are found in several Basic Laws passed by the parliament over the years and interpreted by court decisions.

The electoral system and the branches of government

Israel has free, fair, and open democratic elections, in which every citizen has the right both to elect and to be elected. Yet, Israel does pose a few limitations on the right to be elected, as do other democracies. From independence and until the 1980s, any party could run and no parties were banned. However, in 1965, the Central Elections Committee refused to allow the Socialist List to participate in elections, because it ruled that the party was comprised of members of an illegal movement that denied the right of Israel to exist. The Supreme Court, which automatically reviews every decision by the Central Elections Committee to ban a party, refused to repeal this decision in a majority verdict.

By the 1980s things had changed, and after the election of Kach, an extreme right-wing, racist party, to the Knesset in 1984, laws to limit eligibility were adopted. The law now determines that a party, as well as a single candidate, cannot run if its actions, expressly or by implication, include the negation of the existence of the State of Israel as a Jewish and democratic state, incitement to racism, or support of violent struggle against the state. Since the 1980s, only Kach was disqualified from participation in the elections. Other parties have been disqualified by the Central Elections Committee, but the Supreme Court has reversed these decisions. In short, Israeli democracy and elections allow many voices to be heard.

The 120 members of the Knesset are elected through a closed-list (parties present ordered lists of candidates and voters can choose only between parties) proportional representation system (parties win a share of seats relative to their share of the vote) in a single nation-wide constituency (Israel has one district; it is not divided into electoral constituencies). The electoral system for the Knesset was changed only slightly since the first elections: the threshold was increased to 1 percent (valid since the 1951 elections), to 1.5 percent (1992), 2 percent (2006) and most recently to 3.25 percent (2015). In the 2015 elections, approximately 137,000 votes were needed to pass the legal threshold of 3.25 percent, and the "price" of each seat was slightly more than 35,000 votes.

The Israeli electoral system is, therefore, highly representative, allowing for authentic expressions of the various social interests, ideologies, and identities that compose the mosaic of Israeli society. Simultaneously, the electoral system has been criticized for allowing an excess number of political parties to enter the Knesset, making the governing process more difficult. Interest aggregation is therefore mainly conducted not within parties but between them, in the Knesset and even within the coalition government (Rahat and Hazan 2005). The Israeli electoral system has thus been described as "hyper-representative" (Shugart 2001). The electoral system has also been accused of being too party-centered: a closed-list countrywide system, in which voters cast only a party ballot for a list of candidates, does not result in sufficient accountability of the elected representatives to the voters. This is why electoral reform has always been, and continues to be, a salient issue in Israeli politics. In 1996, a major electoral reform was implemented, creating a separately and directly elected Prime Minister, but its goals of strengthening the main parties were not met and it was abolished by the 2003 elections (Hazan 1996; Kenig et al. 2005).

Israeli citizens do not need to pre-register in order to take part in elections; they are automatically signed up to the voter registry. However, they must be physically present in Israel on election day, since there are no absentee or early ballots. Taking into account the fact that a sizeable number of Israeli citizens either live, conduct business, or vacation abroad, the approximately 80 percent turnout that has been recorded in elections throughout the second half of the twentieth century is therefore significantly high. At the beginning of the twenty-first century, there was a sharp decline in electoral turnout to below 70 percent, but this trend has been partially righted since a record low in 2006, with turnout reaching 73.5 percent in 2015.

The relatively low levels of Israeli-Arab turnout since the 1960s—which is comparatively lower than the Jewish turnout, especially taking into consideration the fact that a smaller percentage of Arabs live, work, or travel abroad—demonstrates that many feel alienated from the state and its institutions. This interpretation is supported by the fact that when it comes to local government elections, the Arab turnout is much higher. That is, Israeli Arabs do participate in the democratic process, but they participate more when they think that their vote will have an impact on policymaking in general and on their lives in particular.

Systematic studies of voter behavior based on surveys are available for Israel since 1969. These studies stress the importance of the politics of social identity in Israeli voting behavior. National, communal, and religious factors significantly explain voting patterns in Israeli elections: Arabs are likely to vote for the non-Zionist parties, Jews for the Zionist ones; Ashkenazi Jews are more likely to vote for the left, Mizrahi Jews for the right; new immigrants from Russia lean to the secular right, secular veteran Jews to the left; religious Jews almost exclusively vote for the right and the religious parties.

Israel is a parliamentary democracy. The executive emerges from the Knesset based on a majority coalition and it needs the Knesset's continuous support in order to survive its full tenure in office. As of 2018, Israel has formally had thirty-four coalition governments (Table 4.2). While twenty of them—almost 60 percent—were established following elections, the rest were formed during a Knesset term. Some of the latter were due to the resignation of the Prime Minister, which officially requires the formation of a new government even if exactly the same parties reestablish it. For instance, Israel's first Prime Minister—David Ben-Gurion—resigned several times in order to discipline his government, only to return with a similar governing coalition. Government turnovers also stem from other causes, such as the death of the Prime Minister during his term (as was the case with Levi Eshkol and Yitzhak Rabin). Interestingly, the only time when a government was ousted in a vote of no-confidence, the ejected Prime Minister (Yitzhak Shamir) succeeded in reestablishing a coalition government under his leadership. In the first seventy years of the State of Israel, there were twenty parliamentary elections; this means that on average, the Knesset term lasts almost three and a half years, relatively close to its complete term of office.

TABLE 4.2 Israeli coalition governments 1949–2015*

Period	Knesset	Gov't	Prime Minister (Party)	# Parties	# MKs	Size of PM's Party (% of coalition)
03/1949–11/1950	1	1	David Ben-Gurion (Mapai)	5	73	46 (63%)
11/1950–10/1951		2	David Ben-Gurion (Mapai)	5	73	46 (63%)
10/1951–12/1952	2	3	David Ben-Gurion (Mapai)	8	65	45 (69%)
12/1952–10/1954		4	David Ben-Gurion (Mapai)	9	89	45 (50%)
10/1954–06/1955		5	Moshe Sharet (Mapai)	9	91	45 (49%)
06/1955–11/1955		6	Moshe Sharet (Mapai)	6	68	45 (66%)
11/1955–01/1958	3	7	David Ben-Gurion (Mapai)	8	80	40 (50%)
01/1958–12/1959		8	David Ben-Gurion (Mapai)	8	80	40 (50%)
12/1959–11/1961	4	9	David Ben-Gurion (Mapai)	9	92	47 (51%)
11/1961–06/1963	5	10	David Ben-Gurion (Mapai)	6	68	42 (61%)
06/1963–12/1964		11	Levi Eshkol (Mapai)	6	68	42 (61%)
12/1964–01/1966		12	Levi Eshkol (Mapai)	6	67	42 (62%)
01/1966–03/1969	6	13	Levi Eshkol (Labor)	7	75	45 (60%)
03/1969–12/1969		14	Golda Meir (Labor)	7	104	45 (43%)
12/1969–03/1974	7	15	Golda Meir (Labor)	6	102	56 (55%)
03/1974–06/1974	8	16	Golda Meir (Labor)	3	68	51 (75%)
06/1974–06/1977		17	Yitzhak Rabin (Labor)	3	61	51 (83%)
06/1977–08/1981	9	18	Menachem Begin (Likud)	5	62	43 (69%)
08/1981–10/1983	10	19	Menachem Begin (Likud)	4	61	48 (78%)
10/1983–09/1984		20	Yitzhak Shamir (Likud)	6	62	48 (77%)
09/1984–10/1986	11	21	Shimon Peres (Labor)	8	97	44 (45%)
10/1986–12/1988		22	Yitzhak Shamir (Likud)	7	96	41 (42%)
12/1988–06/1990	12	23	Yitzhak Shamir (Likud)	6	97	40 (41%)
06/1990–07/1992		24	Yitzhak Shamir (Likud)	8	65	40 (61%)

(continued)

TABLE 4.2 (Cont.)

Period	Knesset	Gov't	Prime Minister (Party)	# Parties	# MKs	Size of PM's Party (% of coalition)
07/1992–11/1995	13	25	Yitzhak Rabin (Labor)	3	62	44 (70%)
11/1995–06/1996		26	Shimon Peres (Labor)	3	59	44 (74%)
06/1996–07/1999	14	27	Binyamin Netanyahu (Likud)	6	66	32 (48%)
07/1999–03/2001	15	28	Ehud Barak (Labor)	7	75	26 (34%)
03/2001–02/2003		29	Ariel Sharon (Likud)	7	80	19 (23%)
02/2003–05/2006	16	30	Ariel Sharon (Likud)	5	68	38 (55%)
05/2006–03/2009	17	31	Ehud Olmert (Kadima)	4	67	29 (43%)
03/2009–03/2013	18	32	Binyamin Netanyahu (Likud)	5	69	27 (39%)
03/2013–05/2015	19	33	Binyamin Netanyahu (Likud)	5	68	31 (45%)
05/2015–	20	34	Binyamin Netanyahu (Likud)	5	61	30 (49%)

* The table indicates the number of coalition parties and members on the day the government was sworn in, it does not address any changes made in the composition of the coalition during the government's term in office.

Sources: Knesset websites: www.knesset.gov.il/faction/heb/FactionGovernment.asp and www.knesset.gov.il/govt/heb/GovtByNumber.asp;

Parties in the parliamentary arena

As in other democracies, in Israel the PPG (parliamentary party group) is made up of those representatives elected to the Knesset, and it comprises the legislative arm of the party. A single PPG can represent one party or several parties that decide to run together, in which case a joint list of candidates is presented to the voters. Since the Israeli voters elect closed lists in a nation-wide district, not single candidates in small districts, the PPGs play a significant role in the activity of the Israeli parliament. They are responsible for the formation of the government, they are the basis of legislative activity, and they are accorded both rights and privileges by the Knesset.

The Knesset's Rules of Procedure grant the PPGs exclusive powers. For example, the PPGs have complete control over the nomination of MKs (Members of Knesset) to the committees—the workhorse of any democratic legislature. Committee members are selected according to the principle of proportionality, based on the PPG's size in the Knesset. The PPGs are also granted the right to change or remove their committee members at will (Hazan 2001). While the majority of the coalition in the plenary must be replicated in each committee, ten out of the twelve permanent committee chairs are allocated to the PPGs in the governing coalition. The remaining two committee chairs are allocated to the opposition PPGs—one (by law) is the State Control Committee and the other (by custom) is the Economic Affairs Committee. Moreover, the quotas for both debating private members bills and submitting motions for the agenda are allocated to the PPGs based on their relative size, and only PPGs can submit motions of no-confidence.

Strong party discipline and cohesion has traditionally characterized the parties in the Knesset (Rahat 2007). However, the weakening of the parties due to domestic reasons—such as the adoption of primaries by some parties as the method of candidate selection, and to international trends—such as personalization, has loosened party cohesion to a limited extent. Knesset members from both the coalition and the opposition occasionally vote against their party position, or abstain from voting, but an examination of the voting patterns in the plenary shows that the levels of party cohesion in Israel (based on the Rice Index) are still relatively high compared to other democracies. The decline of party discipline can be detected not in the overt voting patterns of MKs, but rather in latent forms, such as MKs giving statements to the media that contradict the party's position (Hazan 2014).

The Knesset Law (1994) allows PPGs to split. However, a split is considered to be legal—meaning that those MKs who break from their PPG will still be entitled to all the parliamentary and financial privileges—only if a minimum of one-third of the MKs split from their parent PPG. If a single Knesset member abandons his PPG, they are considered a "dissenter" and severe sanctions are levied against them—they cannot join another PPG, cannot serve as a minister or a deputy minister, are denied public funding and the opportunity to run in the next elections as a candidate of a PPG that was represented in the outgoing Knesset. In short, to be denied recognition as part of a PPG is to be quite powerless in the Israeli parliament.

Political parties in Israel primarily operate according to two laws: The Party Finance Law (1973) and The Parties Law (1992). The first law regulates the ongoing expenses of the parties as well as their election expenses. It determines that parties are entitled to public funding according to their relative size in the Knesset, and that they are allowed to receive limited private donations. The State Comptroller (chosen by the Knesset) enforces this law and oversees the financing of the parties. After every election, the State Comptroller publishes a detailed report on each party and imposes a penalty on those who violated the rules. Comparatively speaking, the policy of funding political parties in Israel is very different than in most established democracies. Israel places severe restrictions on parties regarding the recruitment of private donations, but as compensation, gives them generous public funding. In fact, the public funding allocated to parties for election purposes in Israel is the highest in the world, while the amount of private donations allowed is amongst the lowest (Ben-Bassat and Dahan 2014).

The Parties Law changed the legal status of the political parties in Israel, defined how they were to be managed, the operation of their internal institutions and the terms for accepting members. However, the law does not force internal democracy on the parties, or include instructions for how each party will choose its candidates. Particular importance, both legal and public, is placed on the Party Registrar, who is responsible for the registration of political parties and for the supervision over their actions according to the Parties Law.

The PPGs—the legislative arm of the political parties—are the key players in the Knesset. As such, the legislature grants them significant formal powers, which are anchored in several laws and in the Knesset's Rules of Procedure. However, as strong as the parties inside the legislative arena might be, in the social arena they were weakened dramatically over the years due to institutional (the consequences of the unsuccessful electoral reforms in the 1990s) and cultural (personalization, reduced trust in elected officials) processes that are more comparative in nature than unique to the Israeli case.

Conclusion: prospects and challenges

The State of Israel was established by mass parties and, at least until the 1960s, it was referred to as a "parties' state" (Akzin 1955). These strong, ideological, well-organized parties—first and foremost Mapai/Labor—controlled other governmental organs such as the bureaucracy, the local authorities and the national institutions. They also exercised major influence over the education system, housing, and employment, and provided their members with social, cultural, educational, and even economic support. Since the 1970s, the Israeli parties began to lose power (corresponding to a process occurring in most established democracies) and became what they are today—a mix of cadre, catch-all, cartel, and post-cartel sectarian parties (Yishai 2001). Several processes contributed to this: the development of the mass media, which reduced the citizens' dependence on parties; the growing mistrust of the political system by the Israeli public, particularly the wariness of the political parties; the liberalization of the socioeconomic arenas; the reforms in the electoral system, which reduced the size of the major parties dramatically; and the judicialization and personalization of politics.

The contemporary Israeli party system is composed of both old parties, with roots going back to the pre-state era of the British Mandate of Palestine, and (relatively) new parties, continuously being established since the foundation of the state. Both party types still represent the Israeli "tribes" or cleavages quite well, contributing to the legitimacy of the political system. Some, however, argue that the parties represent Israeli society too well, nourishing socio-political sub-cultures that with the passing of time now have less rather than more in common.

The processes described in this essay show that the influence of the political parties in the political system have weakened. This decline is even more evident in the social sphere, where parties still represent distinct social cleavages but at the same time they have also become more connected to the state than to civil society. Interestingly, the parties have managed to maintain their position in the highly institutionalized legislative arena. This apparent contradiction might help explain the increasing calls for electoral and political reform in Israel, emanating mainly from civil society but also from within the political system itself. The continued existence of such a disparity within, and between, Israeli politics and society could potentially endanger the still fragile nature and infrastructure of Israel's democracy if it is overlooked as Israeli politics continues to develop.

References and further reading

Akzin, Benjamin. 1955. "The Role of Parties in Israel Democracy." *Journal of Democracy.* 17(4), pp. 507–545.

Al-Haj, Majid. 2004. "The Status of Palestinians in Israel: A Double Periphery in an Ethnonational State," in A. Dowty (ed.), *Critical Issues in Israeli Society.* Westport, CT: Praeger, pp. 109–126.

Arian, Asher. 2005. *Politics in Israel: The Second Republic.* 2nd edn. Washington, DC: CQ Press.

Barnett, Michael (ed). 1996. *Israel in Comparative Perspective: Challenging the Conventional Wisdom.* Albany, NY: State University of New York Press.

Ben-Bassat, Avi and Momi Dahan. 2014. *Reforms, Politics, and Corruption.* Jerusalem: Israel Democracy Institute [Hebrew]

Dowty, Alan. 1998. *The Jewish State: A Century Later.* Berkeley, CA: University of California Press.

Galnoor, Itzhak. 1982. *Steering the Polity.* London: Sage.

Galnoor, Itzhak and D. Blander. 2013. *The Political System of Israel.* Tel Aviv: Am Oved [Hebrew]

Hazan, Reuven Y. 1996. "Presidential Parliamentarism: Direct Popular Election of the Prime Minister, Israel's New Electoral and Political System." *Electoral Studies.* 15(1), pp. 21–37.

Hazan, Reuven Y. 1998. "Party System Change in Israel, 1948–1998: A Conceptual and Theoretical Border-stretching of Europe?" in P. Pennings and J.-E. Lane (eds.), *Comparing Party System Change.* London: Routledge, pp. 151–166.

Hazan, Reuven Y. 2001. *Reforming Parliamentary Committees: Israel in Comparative Perspective.* Columbus, OH: Ohio State University Press.

Hazan, Reuven Y. 2014. "Candidate Selection: Implications and Challenges for Legislative Research," in S. Martin, T. Saalfeld and K.W. Strøm (eds.), *Oxford Handbook of Legislative Studies.* Oxford: Oxford University Press, pp. 213–230.

Horowitz, Dan and Moshe Lissak. 1989. *Trouble in Utopia: The Overburdened Polity of Israel*. Albany, NY: State University of New York Press.

Kenig, Ofer and Anna Knafelman. 2013. "The Decline of the Large Aggregative Parties," in Gideon Rahat, Shlomit Barnea, Chen Friedberg and Ofer Kenig (eds.), *Reforming Israel's Political System*. Tel Aviv and Jerusalem: Am Oved and the Israel Democracy Institute, pp. 145–183 [Hebrew]

Kenig, Ofer, Gideon Rahat and Reuven Y. Hazan. 2005. "The Political Consequences of the Introduction and the Repeal of the Direct Elections for the Prime Minister," in Asher Arian and Michal Shamir (eds.), *The Elections in Israel 2003*. New York: Transaction Books, pp. 33–61.

Levi-Faur, David, Gabriel Sheffer and David Vogel (eds.). 1999. *Israel: Dynamics of Change and Continuity*. London: Frank Cass.

Lijphart, Arend, Peter Bowman and Reuven Hazan. "Party Systems and Issue Dimensions: Israel and Thirty-Five Other Old and New Democracies Compared," in Reuven Hazan and Moshe Maor (eds.), *Parties, Elections and Cleavages: Israel in Comparative and Theoretical Perspective*. London: Frank Cass, pp. 29–51.

Mahler, Gregory S. 2016. *Politics and Government in Israel: The Maturation of a Modern State*. 3rd edn. Lanham, MD: Rowman & Littlefield.

Medding, Peter. 2000. "From Government by Party to Government Despite Party," in Reuven.Y. Hazan and Moshe Maor (eds.), *Parties, Elections and Cleavages: Israel in Comparative and Theoretical Perspective*. London: Frank Cass, pp. 172–208.

Rahat, Gideon. 2007. "Determinants of Party Cohesion: Evidence from the Case of the Israeli Parliament." *Parliamentary Affairs*. 60(2), pp. 279–296.

Rahat, Gideon and Reuven Y. Hazan. 2005. "Israel: The Politics of an Extreme Electoral System," in M. Gallagher and P. Mitchell (eds.), *The Politics of Electoral Systems*. Oxford: Oxford University Press, pp. 333–351.

Rahat, Gideon and Tamir Sheafer. 2007. "The Personalization(s) of Politics: Israel 1949–2003." *Political Communication*. 24(1), pp. 65–80.

Shafir, Gershon and Yoav Peled. 2002. *Being Israeli: The Dynamics of Multiple Citizenship*. Cambridge: Cambridge University Press.

Shalev, Michael. 2012. "The Economic Background of the Social Protest of Summer 2011," in Dan Ben-David (ed.), *State of the Nation Report: Society, Economy and Policy in Israel 2011–2012*. Jerusalem: Taub Center for Social Policy Studies in Israel, pp. 161–220.

Shapira, Anita. 2014. *Israel: A History*. Waltham, MA: Brandeis University Press.

Shugart, Matthew. 2001. "'Extreme' Electoral Systems and the Appeal of the Mixed-Member Alternative," in Matthew Shugart and Martin P. Wattenberg (eds.), *Mixed-Member Electoral Systems: The Best of Both Worlds?* Oxford: Oxford University Press, pp. 25–51.

Yishai, Yael. 2001. "Bringing Society Back In: Post-cartel Parties in Israel." *Party Politics*. 7(6), pp. 667–687.

5

EXTRA-PARLIAMENTARY POLITICS

The settlement movement's success story

Eitan Y. Alimi

The settlement movement is one of the most (if not *the* most) influential social movements the State of Israel has ever known. In slightly over a decade of political activism, the consolidated movement managed to become a central cultural, social, and political power, amassing a considerable influence over policymakers and public opinion. Strategically combining institutional and non-institutional politics, the movement has made headway into society, the army, and the political system, and managed to sustain itself, despite major challenges and setbacks, for several decades now. Irrespective of changes in Israeli policies and coalitions, there has been a steady rise in both number of settlements, legal and illegal outposts, and their population—arguably the most central pillar of its agenda.[1]

This essay has two purposes: First, to examine the sources of the movement's success, through an analysis that combines three central fields of interaction—within the movement, between the movement and the political establishment, and between the movement and the military[2]—during its incipient stage (1967 and 1973), as well as during the first decade of operation. Such a multi-pronged analytical approach provides a comprehensive understanding of the movement's unparalleled success in and of itself and in comparison to other social movements in the Israeli political landscape, a research agenda that has been surprisingly lacking in existing studies.

The second purpose of this essay is to assess these sources of success in light of the most serious and meaningful challenge the movement has faced since its emergence—the Disengagement Plan from the Gaza Strip and northern West Bank of 2005 (also known as the Gaza Pullout)—by pointing out meaningful patterns and trends in each of the three aforementioned fields of interaction. The worrisome expansion of two related phenomena to the growth of the settlement movement has increasingly featured in Israeli political discourse—the ultra-radical Hilltop Youth and extreme acts of "Price Tag" violence. Given the challenges these issues embody, both in terms of upholding law and order and deeper questions as to the legitimacy of the Israeli political system and regional stability, the value of an assessment of the settlement movement, however illustrative and suggestive is apparent.

Three points of clarification are in order. First, as much as this chapter follows others in treating the June 1967 "Six-Day" War as a critical juncture or transformative event in the sense of exacerbating "specific and systematically explicable transformation and re-articulations of the cultural and social structures that were already in operation before the event" (McAdam and Sewell 2001, p. 102),[3] it is important to avoid an overemphasis on those transformed structures to the point of neglecting the role of social forces. Second, while the analysis that follows respects the influence of ideas and values on social and political processes, it nevertheless walks along interactive lines, namely, how cultural and ideational templates gain and lose saliency in the context of social interactions. Third, in trying to assess the sources of the movements' success in the post-Gaza Pullout period based on developments taking place more than a generation earlier, I make no claim that no change unfolded in the social and political contexts in which the movement has been operating. I do maintain, however, that these changes are essentially changes *in* those fields of interaction rather than changes *of* them, thus allowing for a sober and cautious extrapolation to be made.

The rise and growth of the settlement Movement

Scholars generally agree that the results of the Six-Day War have had transformative effects on almost every aspect of the Israeli State and society. Like other transformative events, the Israeli military occupation of the Disputed Territories has had a path-dependent-like effect, acting as a catalyst in resurfacing and channeling specific issues and processes in various aspects and dimensions of the Israeli polity, domestically as well as internationally. The unexpected Israeli takeover of the West Bank and Gaza Strip exacerbated meaningful processes in various arenas, of which three are of primary concern to this essay: the development of the settlement movement and its missionary-like political activism; the configuration of relations between the movement and the political environment; and the movement's increased involvement in the Israeli military.

Intra-movement features and dynamics

Between 1967 and 1973, settlement-oriented political activism was sporadic, with initiatives taken by a variety of social forces, between which there was little, mostly ad hoc coordination, with no overarching organizational framework. The first settlement initiative, for example, took place only one week following the UN-imposed cease-fire, consisting of Zionist-left-wing Achdut Ha'avoda Kibbutz members, who settled Marom Golan in the Golan Heights with only a belated and somewhat half-hearted involvement of activists from other groups and political streams (Demant 1988). Several weeks later, however, a second settlement initiative taken by members of the Jewish orthodox National Religious Party (NRP) "youth circle," aimed at renewing Jewish presence in the 1948 conquered religious kibbutz of Kfar Etzion, already demonstrated the multi-sectoral nature of the movement's social bases.

I'm here Chanan Porat (a graduate of the orthodox Jewish learning center, the Mercaz HaRav Yeshiva) who headed the group, there were other soon-to-be influential figures (religious as well as secular) of the broader movement, including: Rabbi Moshe Levinger, Aharon Amir and Elyakin Haetzni. Indeed, the group constituted more than just a handful of activists. The broadening circle of participants was visible already in early 1968, during the first stage of a new settlement initiative in Hebron. When a small group of activists approached the military governor of the Palestinian-populated city of Hebron, asking authorization to celebrate the Jewish holiday of Passover in the City Park Hotel, they were quickly joined by dozens of supporters. Many of the participants in the Passover Seder, totaling sixty, came from the Greater Land of Israel Movement (HaTenu'ah Lema'an Eretz Yisrael Hashlemah) which was comprised of former politicians, reserve generals, and intellectuals. Formed in September 1967, that movement consisted of members whose ideology was known as "territorial maximalism," whereby they claimed the Jewish right to sovereignty over the whole territory of Eretz Yisrael (originally encompassing all of Mandatory Palestine) (Sprinzak 1991).

The various social forces that became part of the settlement movement and the different ideological currents they represented were essential to the decision to expand settlement activity to the Samaria region of the West Bank, alongside the decision to form the settlement pressure group Gush Emunim (Bloc of the Faithful—hereinafter: the Bloc). The decision to expand settlement activity was made in mid-1973 by two Hebron settlers, Beni Katzover and Menachem Felix, leading them to form a new settlement nucleus: Elon Moreh (the biblical name for Nablus). In the face of a mild public response to the founding of Kiryat Arba in 1968, and a failure to attract new residents, it was hoped that settling Samaria would generate the expected enthusiasm and support (Zertal and Eldar 2004).[4] As plans to move into Hawara, a Palestinian village adjacent to Nablus, were made, the depth and scope of the movement's social bases was demonstrated once again, when activists from almost all social and political forces flocked into the deserted Syrian city of Kuneitra to establish the Keshet settlement in the Golan Heights, in late May 1974 (Rubinstein 1982).

Precipitating both settlement initiatives was the formation of the Bloc, in February 1974. Among those who participated in the founding meeting were several graduates of Mercaz HaRav Yeshiva, representatives from Greater Land of Israel Movement and from the Golan Heights settlement of Marom Golan, a representative of the orthodox religious Bnei Akiva youth movement world secretariat, and two National Religious Party members. Several principles came out from this and other subsequent meetings, two of which are central to the argument developed herein. First, the movement would be a trans-party movement, with no party affiliation. Second, the movement should be as broad-base as possible, all-Israeli and cross-national, aimed at re-elevating and reviving the broken spirit of the people of

Israel who were in a state of despair, had lost their way, and turned to non-religious nihilism.

Beginning June 1974, those principles were translated into deeds, as was first and most emphatically demonstrated in the campaign to settle Hawara. In the face of lingering governmental approval, the nucleus—accompanied by the influential Rabbi Tzvi Yehuda Kook, several members of the Knesset, including representatives of NRP and approximately one hundred settler activists, set foot in Hawara. Throughout the eight attempts to settle what later came to be called Kaddumim, the Gush Emunim movement fully demonstrated its mobilizing potential and resources, as well as the widespread public support it enjoyed. What enabled the organizing of the almost eighteen-month-long protest campaign and subsequent activities was related to important organizational developments, some of which reflected the broad-base and society-wide appeal and aspiration of the movement. It was not only a matter of dividing labor in order to raise funds or to effectively orchestrate the numerous protest activities, but there was also a need to form recruitment committees, development outreach committees in charge of establishing branches in major cities and a public activity committee responsible for giving house talks as well as public talks in synagogues throughout the country (Shafat 1995).

Indeed, one of the most central features of the settlement movement, even during its early stages, was its heterogenic composition. Gush Emunim not only enjoyed the support of various cross-sectional groups regardless of age, ethnicity, socioeconomic status, life style or political affiliation, but a variety of organizations actually became an integral part of the broadening movement. This unique feature of heterogeneity was clearly demonstrated during the struggle over settling Samaria, when individuals and groups from almost all possible parts of the social and polit-ical spectrum came to participate, express solidarity, or even provide meals for the activists. Though not free of tension and occasional rifts, the idea of "communal settlement" (*Yishuv Kehilati*) epitomized not only the idea of attracting as many people as possible regardless of religious, economic, social or political background, but also the idea of accommodating the different styles of ideological outlooks of the various movement group members (Newman 1985; Sprinzak 1991).

However, not all groups and organizations that could have been considered part of the settlement movement shared this conception and strategy of cross-sectoralism, or were interested in "settling in the hearts" of all Israelis (Feige 2009). Some, as was the case with Rabbi Meir Kahane's Jewish Defense League (later renamed Kach) and with Gershon Solomon's Temple Mount Loyalists, cared little about social inte-gration, moderation or pragmatism in rhetoric and deeds. For most of the time period covered by this study and into the mid-to-late 1980s, it is revealing that as part of the predominant conception and strategy of cross-sectoral alliance building and its related social integration, groups like Kach and Temple Mount Loyalists were seen as "unwanted children," to use Della Porta and Tarrow's term (1986), not only by the Israeli establishment but also by the settlement movement.

Between movement and political environment: "cherished children"

What kind of transformations and rearticulations of the Israeli cultural and social structures did the results of the June 1967 War emphasize? What were the precise effects of these processes on the settlement movement's strategy and consequently its bargaining position vis-à-vis the Israeli political environment, from which the movement was able to generate input into decision-making and thus shape the political process? With some exceptions (most notably the full annexation of East Jerusalem), the only policy the government was capable of pursuing was that of "decision of indecision": postponing a clear-cut decision with regard to the newly-captured territories' future status. Officially, this policy meant a willingness to use the territories as a bargaining chip for peace, if a genuine Arab initiative were to surface. Practically, as it soon became clear that no such Arab initiative was on the horizon, this policy entailed a willingness to extend the temporality of the Israeli hold over the territories. Essentially, this "ongoing temporality" reflected the deep division among Israeli policymakers—representing different elites and constituencies—over the territorial fulfillment of Zionism.

Despite some overlap, three sets of justifications for maintaining control over the territories can be identified. For some policymakers, the wave of national sentiments and public euphoria made it politically unwise to speak in favor of returning the territories, prompting them to maintain or strengthen their political standing through alignment with the mood of the general public. For others, the justification was security considerations, according to which Israel should create "facts on the ground" by settling Jews in strategic areas that would, in the short-run, act as security buffer zones and, in the long run, be included in any possible future peace negotiation with Arab states. For others still, the justification for maintaining a hold over the territories was essentially a religious-ideological issue, according to which the State of Israel—as the state of the Jewish People—has moral and historical rights over them.

This combination of political considerations not only provided impressive, cross-party support for the policy of settlement, but also combined to create the necessary space for action, essential for the rise of settlement-driven political activism. From the vantage point of the settlers, this favorable political context distilled and shaped the prospects for—and strategy of—contentious collective action. True, accumulating power within NRP was unquestionably valuable, given the proportional representation of the Israeli political system, a feature that granted the relatively small religious parties disproportionate political influence. This was especially true, given the gradual weakening of the ruling Labor Alignment Party and concomitantly gradual strengthening of its main competitor, the right-of-center Likud. Yet, as much as a better positioning within NRP was important for the settlement movement, focusing solely on NRP ministers and members of Knesset would reveal only part of the process by which the movement managed to acquire such a strong political leverage.

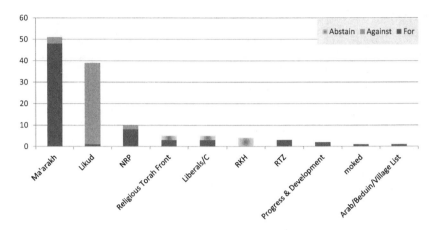

FIGURE 5.1 Israel–Egypt interim agreement and territorial withdrawals (09/03/75)

Source: Knesset Chronicles.[5]

To better understand this process, it is important to first acknowledge the fact that the combination of considerations for maintaining a hold over the territories captured in 1967 transcends party lines. Data on the Knesset vote that approved the US-led interim agreement with Egypt in 1975 (Figure 5.1), which saw limited Israeli territorial concessions within the Sinai Peninsula, reveals that the majority of NRP members of the Knesset voted in line with Rabin's Labor-led Government, while potential political allies of the movement were found in various parties including Likud, Labor (HaMa'arakh) and the ultra-orthodox parties.

Equally meaningful was the strategic efforts of leaders of the movement to secure political allies, which helps explain the strong political bargaining position the movement managed to gain. Movement leaders made conscious attempts to frame and justify their demands in such a way that would resonate with the political interests and values of as many members of government as possible, and made sure to buttress these efforts relationally, by establishing contacts and ties either directly or with the help of brokers. Thus, if during the attempts to settle Kfar Etzion, settlers aligned their sentimental-historical claims with security justifications, during the attempts to settle Hebron, the security justification was infused with a Jewish religious narrative, charged with a sense of vengeance. Because the Cave of the Patriarchs, which lies in the center of Hebron, had always been regarded as the most sacred religious site for Jews in the West Bank, settling at the heart of Palestinian population was seen as a redeeming act, which served to "[honor] the people of Israel, depriving the 1929 murderers and their successors of victory, and ensuring safety to the region and the entirety of Israel" (Feige 2002, pp. 105–108). In both settlement initiatives, what turned out to be of considerable importance was the brokering role played not only by politicians in connecting movement leaders and the government, but also the involvement of people who had personal relations with power-holders (Krovim La'Malkhut), as was the case with Israeli poet and territorial maximalist Natan Alterman and his friendship with Defense Minister Moshe Dayan (Shiloah 1989).

In retrospect, what was perceived at first as a setback to the realization of the campaign to settle Samaria—the 1973 Yom Kippur War between Israel, Egypt, and Syria—turned out to be significant in facilitating an even more favorable shift in the structure of political opportunity for the settlement movement. The critical impact of the Yom Kippur War significantly exacerbated the weakening of the Labor Party, internally as well as externally. There is little doubt that the misconduct and scandalous unfolding of the war, the public criticism of the failings of the political and military leaderships and the intensifying internal struggles within Labor—all combined to facilitate the success of the engagement-like strategy and skills of the settlement movement leadership. Between 1974 and 1977, and despite Prime Minister Rabin's harsh position and occasional statements that the government would not cave in to the pressure exerted on it by the settlers, the movement managed to have its way, gradually establishing several settlements throughout the Samaria region of the West Bank.

Finally, further adding to the favorable political conditions which the settlement movement enjoyed and on which it kept capitalizing, was the gradual, yet consistent, strengthening of the Likud, particularly party leader Menachem Begin's growing role as valuable political ally. Relying on the increase in his party's share of representation in the Knesset, Begin managed to form a majority of members of the Knesset that not only thwarted an initiative from within Rabin's government to evict the settlers from the military base of Kaddum by force, but Begin was also behind the Cabinet decision of April 17, 1977 to establish a new settlement called Kaddumim. As noted by Weisburd (1989), this majority included fifteen members of the religious parties, some of whom were also members of the Cabinet, and seven Labor members that favored territorial maximalism.[6] In the May 1977 national elections, the value of Begin as a political ally became formalized and maximized to the fullest, following the rise to power of Likud. For members of the movement, who saw themselves as a major factor behind the downfall of Labor, it was perceived as a glorious moment, given the ideological affinity between the movement and their new all-powerful benefactor.

Between movement and security forces: complementing symbiosis

Given that the Israeli Defense Force (IDF) has never been free of politics, coupled with the fact it had become the sovereign power in the West Bank and Gaza Strip, it is not surprising that part of the sources of the settlement movement's success was the nature of its interaction with the IDF. Of particular relevance is the interaction between the IDF and the Religious Zionist (RZ) public. This is so for two reasons. First, in broad perspective, religious Zionist settler groups have long become the most central and influential force within the settlement movement.

Second, interaction with the IDF has taken a unique form and content—the Arrangement Yeshivah (Yeshivat Hesder)[7]—which, although having existed for more than a decade earlier, went through meaningful changes following 1967 and took on distinctive features in the settlements. The analysis below follows and employs distinctions made by Israeli sociologist Baruch Kimmerling between the boundaries of conscription, which relates to who will and who will not be drafted, and according to which criteria, and the service framework, which relates to "who will serve in what type of unit, the duration of the service, and how it will serve military and other aims, at times extending to redefinition of the army goals and methods" (Kimmerling 1979, pp. 23–24).

The boundaries of military conscription

From the vantage point of youth members of the religious Zionist public, exemption from, or deferment of, military service has never been considered a meaningful option and military service was and still is, seen as obligatory, no less than pursuit of Jewish learning is seen as obligatory (Cohen 1993). Complementarily, on the part of heads of the state and the IDF, for both security and societal considerations, it was vital to look for ways that would facilitate that integration of religious Zionist youth within the framework of the military. Despite preliminary accommodations of the IDF (e.g. adherence to the specific Jewish dietary regulations [*Kashrut*] in IDF kitchens), once enlisted, many religious Zionist graduates experienced profound challenges to their self-identity and to their ability to observe religious duties.

In the early 1950s, a small group of Yeshiva students called Gahelet (Hebrew for ember) secretly decided to reformulate their conscription to the army in a way that their service would combine vocational Torah training. This initiative would, in six years' time, develop into a formal *Hesder* (Hebrew for arrangement) between the Yeshivot rabbis and the IDF, which would include, for example, agreements regarding length or locus of the service (e.g. alternate terms of service with Yeshiva study, and eligibility for a restricted range of military units, respectively). Moreover, the unique nature of this framework is also expressed in the fact that *Hesder* soldiers are not only enlisted en masse, but they are also not separated from the non-military institutions, with which they were previously affiliated. For example, rabbis are allowed to visit their students in respective bases, and Hesder conscripts are allowed to address their rabbis whenever in need of guidance and advice.

The convergence of interests of religious Zionist rabbis and activists on the one hand, and of the IDF on the other, took on an accelerated pace following 1967, prompting an extended set of accommodations and adjustments, as well as an increase in the number of Arrangement Yeshivot cohorts. The IDF's interest to populate its ranks with highly motivated conscripts who, in turn, sought influential positions through which to achieve greater public standing, led to additional forms of adjustments, such as formulating a special oath for religious Zionist conscripts (Levy 2007). Thus, it was no coincidence that, given the IDF's acute need for quality manpower, Minister of Defense—Shimon Peres—approached the head of the *Hesder* Committee in the wake of the Yom Kippur War and asked him to work to increase the number of enlisted Yeshiva students.[8]

Ever since the establishment in 1965 of *Hesder*, the number of Yeshivot was steadily on the rise, with a consistently growing number located in the territories occupied by Israel in 1967.[9] It is estimated that by 1996, there were twenty-six operating Yeshivot, with 4,600 graduates per year, which constituted approximately 15 percent to 20 percent of the total RZ sector conscripts. Following the Six-Day War, what initially was an isolated instance of alternative religious-army accommodation quickly assumed the status of a norm, with ever-growing numbers of religious Zionist youngsters enlisted through one of the existing special frameworks. Thus, the *Hesder* system set the basis for a far-reaching set of accommodations for religious Zionist yeshiva conscripts, leading to subsequent attempts to shape the framework of military service.

The framework of the military service

The lack of clear separation between army, state and society, and the similar lack of clear separation between the military and the political echelons (Levy 2007; Peri 2006), are two powerful structural conditions that facilitated RZ leaders and activists' attempts in shaping the content of the military service. Shortly after the 1967 War, senior officers within the IDF realized that the political echelon welcomed the presence of Jewish settlers in the territories and, in fact, that the IDF should consider the settlers as valuable allies. Regardless of the specific impetus behind it, it became clear that a unique alliance, endorsed by the government, had developed between settlers and the IDF, setting the stage for meaningful changes in the nature of interactions between both. In fact, it was Moshe Dayan, as Minister of Defense, who in 1968 instructed the IDF to house the Hebron group of settlers in the military governor's compound in the city and—as became known only later—to arm and train them.

With the takeover of the territories and the rapidly increasing number of Jewish settlements, it became abundantly clear that the tasks assigned to the IDF dramatically expanded in scope. The new system which was established, the Area Defense System (ADS), was transposed from the pre-state period, when the establishment of frontier settlements infused national-political goals and security needs. The ADS was based on the principle that all isolated settlements should be engaging in routine security tasks, but should also be capable of defending themselves independently, or deterring military attacks and invasions until the army was free to handle the attackers (Gal-Or 1990). Thus, those settlements were provided with their own armed personnel, and became part of the overall defense system, designed to complement the IDF's tasks. Essentially, this situation amounted to an increasingly influential positioning for the movement's leaders, allowing them to shape the goals and methods of their constituents' military service.

The complementing symbiosis between the IDF and the movement leadership was further shaped by a meaningful change in the ADS, specifically the development of ADS battalions. In the context of the traumatic evacuation of Yamit in the northern Sinai in 1982 as part of the Israeli–Egyptian peace treaty, and the controversial first Lebanon War (1982–1985) which polarized Israeli public opinion, Chief of Staff Rafael Eitan decided to minimize the presence of the IDF throughout the territories, and instead sought to assign the policing and routine security tasks to local settlement-based units. In practical terms, this change ensured that the ADS battalions were solely responsible for routine security not only inside settlements, but also throughout the West Bank and Gaza Strip. Second, ADS battalions were and are staffed mainly by soldiers who actually live in the settlements. Third, the growing security value of the ADS battalions and the expanding presence of the Jewish population throughout the territories has led to a greater demand on the part of settlers to be actively involved in shaping IDF policy for the territories. Since the early 1980s, a security committee of the ADS battalions has routinely informed the IDF of various emerging needs and demands and—as of 1982— following a ruling by then-Defense Minister Ariel Sharon, representatives of the committee have participated in IDF high command operational meetings.

The success of the settlement movement: an assessment of recent trends and implications

The development of the interactive-relational patterns highlighted in the above sections continued beyond the timeframe analyzed, and thus the sources of the movement's success have continued to consolidate. Even though Gush Emunim ceased to exist as an organization during the mid-1980s, its resonance as a vision to pursue through the numerous organizations, forums, and mobilizing structures (some of which became semi-institutional) that the movement managed to form and sustain over the years remained. Similarly, the settlement movement and political system witnessed a change in the structure of relations: increasing numbers of movement figures entered the political system, either into existing parties or into newly formed parties. This enabled the movement to secure and stabilize its political bargaining position, which withstood not only the unity governments of the 1980s, but also the most challenging obstacle to the settlement agenda, namely, Rabin-led ruling coalition of 1992–1995. Finally, concerning settler movement– IDF relations, changes in the boundaries of conscription and the framework of the military service, most notably the formation of *Mekhinot Kedam Tzeva'iot*[10] (Hebrew for pre-conscription religious colleges), which was implemented in the late 1980s, have in fact tightened the symbiotic relations between the settlement movement and the IDF.

Perhaps nowhere was the power of the movement more readily and emphatically apparent—revealing the sources of its success—than when facing its most formidable challenge ever: the Gaza Disengagement Plan. Between August 15, 2005 and September 22, 2005, Israeli security forces ended the almost four-decade-long Jewish presence in the Gaza Strip—organized in twenty-one settlements, most of which were known as *Gush Katif* (Hebrew for harvest block)—also dismantling four settlements located at the northern part of the West Bank, forcefully evacu-ating a total of 9,280 settlers. Never before had the movement been forced to face such an unprecedented challenge to its settlement agenda, expressed not only in the sheer fact of dismantling existing settlements and forceful evacuation of settlers, but also the magnitude and scope of the plan.

Despite the eventual failure to stop the plan from materializing, the almost 18-month-long protest campaign demonstrated the unparalleled powers of the movement. The continued resilience of the movement was illustrated by their ability to mobilize tens of thousands of activists and supporters in a variety of insti-tutional and extra-institutional orchestrated protest events, alongside an impres-sive management of cooperation among more than twenty different groups and organizations. Equally, this can be seen by the various measures that senior officers within both the IDF and the police took to accommodate the needs and requests of the movement leadership and rank-and-file members, alongside the enduring support of various elements of the Israeli public for the settlers. Critically, the settle-ment movement demonstrated its power through an impactful series of political initiatives, including legislative motions, votes of no-confidence, internal-party ref-erenda, ministerial resignations and party walk-outs from the coalition. Indeed, the Knesset was forced to vote on a public referendum regarding the disengagement, an unprecedented legislative move in Israeli history (Alimi 2016).[11]

On initial inspection, the immediate aftermath of the Gaza Pullout saw no earth-shattering repercussions. Yet, as it slowly became clear, an increasing number of settler groups, some pre-existing and some newly developing, began to exacer-bate secessionist trends of settler youth, by illicitly occupying hilltops throughout the West Bank, and propelling the development of a new coercive strategy of con-tention by settler activists known as Price Tag. The first meaningful expression of these combined developments took place during the early morning hours of February 1, 2006, in Amona—an unauthorized outpost, built in 1995, near the West Bank crown-settlement, Ofra. The anti-settlement group Peace Now successfully petitioned the Israeli High Court of Justice from July 2005 to remove the outpost, leading to a government declaration of its intention to follow the Court's ruling from November 2005. The special police force sent to Amona during the early morning hours of February 1, 2006, to uphold the dismantling of nine permanent housing units, faced determined opposition by settler activists who had entrenched themselves in Amona.

The most prevalent account for the events in Amona in particular, and to the increasingly worsening violent trends more generally, suggests that Amona was a redemptive violent reaction meant to "erase the disgrace of the Gaza Pullout" on the part of the bitter and alienated settler public (Sheleg 2007; Pedahzur and Perliger 2009; Roth 2014). While it would be wrong to disregard the influence of the widespread sense of betrayal and alienation on the part of many of the settler public and, more generally, the RZ population, this kind of explanation hides more than it reveals. If we accept the maxim of Arendt (1970) that increased use of vio-lence is usually an indication of the weakening of power, then a more nuanced and valid account is found in an examination (however brief) of those sources of movement's power.

The most immediately salient trend surfacing in the wake of the 2005 pullout regarded intense competition for power among the various movement organizations, reflecting deepening social and ideological polarizations within the settlement movement itself. These intra-movement dynamics of cooperation and conflict existed throughout the years, in fact as early as the incipient stages of the movement, and yet they took on a much deeper and consequential tone in the wake of the 2005 pullout. Despite earnest attempts on the part of the pragmatic movement organizations—most centrally the YESHA Council[12]—to preserve its status and power, it became increasingly clear that growing numbers of more radical groups refused to accept its preferred agenda of remaining an integral part of state and society. The legitimacy and authority crisis experienced by the pragmatic leadership (political and spiritual alike) was already felt during the run-up to the Amona events, expressed in grass-roots organizations, for example, *Ha-Lev Ha-Yehudi* (the Jewish Heart) and *Homesh Tekhila* (Homesh First) that acted unilaterally and were central to the development of subsequent violent acts. Baruch Marzel, one of the most notorious ultra-radical settler leaders, provided the following account to YESHA Council's deteriorating status after the pullout, in an interview this author conducted with him in mid-2009:

> The truth is that no one considers them leadership … they have no mandate. YESHA Council begs "Homesh Tekhila" to cooperate, but we refuse … we don't fight them and don't work with them, nor trust them. They can do nothing. These days there are "Ha-Lev Ha-Yehudi", "Komemiyut" … and more organizations … as well as action cells and committees in each Judea and Samaria settlement that are separated from and act independently of YESHA Council, and this began after the expulsion.

This trend has direct implications for the deepening polarization between the movement and the broader, mostly secular Israeli public. Challenges to the old maxim regarding the importance and value of "settling in the hearts" of all Israelis resurfaced, this time with greater intensity. Those challenges have been seriously undermining the attempts by the pragmatic wing of the leadership of the settler movement to promote initiatives seeking greater engagement between the movement and Israel's secular public. Beginning in 2007, those initiatives included greater representation of the secular settler population within the council's institutions, as part of broader institutional democratization, as well as the growing recognition of the need to strengthen ties between the settler world and the general public. It is probably too early to tell whether those initiatives have been successful. What is beyond doubt, however, is the unwillingness of the ultra-radical grassroots groups to follow suit, thereby threatening to undermine this initiative. This is exemplified by the increasing instances of so-called "Price Tag" violence against anyone who is perceived as hostile to the settlement project, including the YESHA Council. All this unquestionably shapes—and is shaped by—the interaction between the settler movement and the IDF.

Targeting IDF property, as well as soldiers and officers, has played second fiddle to attacks on Palestinians. The unprecedented, and central, role of the IDF in the Gaza Pullout gave rise to deepening tensions, and at times animosity between the settler movement and the IDF, fueling a shift from a complementary symbiosis to a competing, at times conflicting, one. This process, which has occasionally led to violent clashes, is indicative not only of the intense intra-movement competition, but also reflects the weakening of the bargaining position, and the declining influence of the settler movement within the IDF. Despite the fact that this process was halted, temporarily, during some of the recent military operations and wars, due to a shared sense of responsibility and fate, it has not affected the overall pattern of a breakdown of coordination and trust between both sides.

Indeed, the weeks before the Amona mayhem of February 2006 witnessed several instances of violence against soldiers and military outposts. This trend reappeared with greater intensity and severity, threatening to become a defining feature of the relationship between both sides. A powerful example took place in December 2008, after Hilltop Youth activists took over a Palestinian-owned house in Hebron, which became known as *Beit Ha-Meriva* (The house of Quarrel). Facing pending eviction, Daniela Weiss, a leading figure in the Hilltop Youth, established an operational headquarter to counter the imminent eviction, declaring defiantly that the YESHA Council will not be allowed to participate in those meetings, and that unlike previous instances, this time settlers would not be willing to comply with the eviction order. The forceful eviction of hundreds of settlers resulted in the injury of twenty people on both sides, whilst the Price Tag operations in nearby Palestinian villages continued after the evacuation had been completed. Thus, there is little wonder why heads of the IDF (often jointly with the Ministry of Defense) have been considering ways to tighten supervision on settlers' freedom of action (e.g. restrictions on open-fire regulations) and to punish settler leaders and institutions that engage in or call for unlawful violent behavior, insubordination, and incitement to mutiny (e.g. shutting down or withholding state financial support from Hesder Yeshivot).

Finally, even though interaction between the movement and the political establishment suggests a less clear-cut trend—due to a recent strengthening of the movement's bargaining position—it is nonetheless possible to argue that the movement faces an unfavorable political opportunity structure that hampers its ability to generate meaningful and consequential input into the Israeli political process. This is the case most centrally because the movement no longer enjoys a cross-party, diverse array of political allies. The settlement movement's political base—previously the National Religious Party but currently HaBayit HaYehudi (the Jewish Home), led by Naftali Bennett—lacks the maneuvering space and pivotal role it used to have in the past between Labor and Likud, and does not yet have a sufficient amount of the votes to constitute a serious competitor to the Likud as a ruling party.

Indeed, as early as November 2005, and soon after Prime Minister Ariel Sharon formed the centrist Kadima Party, it became clear that the movement was losing ground in terms of its political bargaining position. Sharon's Kadima attracted many former Likud members and Likud under its new leader—Binyamin Netanyahu—acted systematically and successfully to diminish the political power of hardcore pro-movement forces within it. Additionally, the fragmentation inside the RZ political camp itself hampered any chance for meaningful achievements. For a brief moment, and especially after three years of a Kadima-led, pro-unilateral withdrawal coalition and a resolutely anti-settlements and outposts cabinet, the 2009 national elections and their immediate aftermath brought some rays of hope. Yet it soon became clear that, despite the dramatic strengthening of the right (i.e. the Likud and Ha-Ichud Ha-Leumi [Hebrew for National Union]), and the rise to power of Netanyahu, the translation of the potential for shaping policy to actual and meaningful policy change was partial at best. This combination of structural and perceptual gaps between expectations and capabilities, which continues to the present and involves chronic inconsistency in terms of governmental settlement-related policy, has been pushing growing number of settlers into the Hilltop youth ranks, with increasing signs of a war mentality between settler activists and state authorities.

The chapter is based in part on research funded by the Levi Eshkol Center, and the Cherrick Center of the Hebrew University, Jerusalem, and assisted by Gaya Polat, Liora Norwich, Alon Burstein, Efrat Daskal, and Adi Livni.

Notes

1 See Alimi and Hirsch-hoefler (2012); Hazan and Rahat (2010); Lustick (1988); Pedahzur (2012); Sprinzak (1991); Weisburd (1989); Zertal and Eldar (2004).
2 An analysis of pre-June 1967 stages of the fields of interaction examined here is beyond the scope of this chapter. These topics have been well studied and documented by Aran (1986), Cohen (1998), Cohen (1993), Schwartz (2009), to name only a few.
3 Needless to say, the distinction I make here among the three fields is analytical. Also, my focus on these fields and less on others (e.g. settlers and Palestinians) reflects, in the main, length considerations.
4 The plan to settle near Nablus was thwarted by the Yom Kippur War of October 1973. As will be argued, however, the Yom Kippur war turned out to be decisive in shaping the political conditions favorable for the expansion of settlement activity.
5 Special thanks go to Gideon Rahat for providing me with the original data.
6 It is noteworthy that the support of those Labor members of the Knesset rested on the formal endorsement of the Labor settlement movement and the socialist camp (i.e. the Unified Kibbutz, Union of Groups and Kibbutzim, the National Kibbutz and the Cooperative Settlement Movement), taking shape at the Ein Vered Conference (the Greater Land of Israel Loyalist Circle of the Labor Movement) in 1975.
7 Hesder is an Israeli yeshiva program which combines advanced Talmudic studies with military service in the Israel Defense Forces, usually within a Religious Zionist framework.
8 *Yediot Ahronot* (October 17, 1974).

9 Of the nine HesderYeshivot established during the first decade following the 1967 War, seven were established in the Territories.

10 *Mekhinot* students defer their military service for a year, which they spend in efforts to strengthen their religious affiliations. Thereafter, graduates of this framework generally enlist in elite fighting formations.

11 Several passages in this section borrow from Alimi (2013).

12 The Yesha Council is an umbrella organization of municipal councils of Jewish settlements in the West Bank (and formerly in the Gaza Strip), known by the Hebrew acronymYesha.

References and further reading

Alimi, Eitan Y. 2013. *Between Engagement and Disengagement Politics:The Settlers' Struggle against the Disengagement Plan and its Consequences.* Tel Aviv: Resling. [Hebrew]

Alimi, Eitan Y. 2016. "The Relational Context of Radicalization:The Case of Jewish Settler Contention before and after the Gaza Pullout." *Political Studies.* 64(4), pp. 910–929.

Alimi, Eitan Y. and Hirsch-Hoefler, Sivan. 2012. "Structure of Political Opportunities and Threats, and Movement-Countermovement Interaction in Segmented Composite Regimes." *Comparative Politics.* (41), pp. 331–349.

Aran, Gideon. 1986. "From Religious Zionism to Zionist Religion: The Roots of Gush Emunim." *Studies in Contemporary Jewry.* (2), pp. 116–143.

Arendt, Hannah. 1970. *On Violence.* Orlando, FL: Harcourt, Inc.

Cohen, Asher. 1998. *The Prayer Shawl and the Flag: Religious Zionism and the Vision of a Torah State in Israel's Formative Years.* Jerusalem:Yad Izhak Ben-Zvi. [Hebrew]

Cohen, Stuart A. 1993. "The HesderYeshivot in Israel:A Church–State Military Arrangement." *Journal of Church and State.* 35(1), pp. 113–130.

Della Porta, Donatella and Sidney Tarrow. 1986. "Unwanted Children: Political Violence and the Cycle of Protest in Italy, 1966–1973." *European Journal of Political Research.* (14), pp. 607–632.

Demant, Peter R. 1988. *Ploughshares into Swords: Israeli Settlement Policy in the Occupied Territories, 1967–1977.* PhD Dissertation. The Hebrew University.

Feige, Michael. 2002. *One Space, Two Places: Gush Emunim, Peace Now and the Construction of Israeli Space.* Jerusalem:The Hebrew University Magnes Press. [Hebrew]

Feige, Michael. 2009. Settling in the Hearts - Jewish Fundamentalism in the Occupied Territories. Detroit, Michigan:Wayne State University Press.

Gal-Or, Naomi. 1990. *The Jewish Underground: Our Terrorism.* Tel Aviv: Hakibbutz Hameuchad. [Hebrew]

Hazan, Reuven and Gidi Rahat. 2010. "Israeli Political Parties and Settlements," in Cheryl A. Rubenberg (ed.), *Encyclopedia of the Israeli–Palestinian Conflict.* Boulder, CO: Lynne Rienner Publishers.

Kimmerling, Baruch. 1979. "Determination of the Boundaries and Frameworks of Conscription: Two Dimensions of Civil–Military Relations in Israel." *Studies in Comparative International Development.* 14(1), pp. 22–41.

Levy, Yagil. 2007. "The Embedded Military: Why did the IDF Perform Effectively in Executing the Disengagement Plan?" *Security Studies.* 16(3), pp. 382–408.

Lustick, Ian S. 1988. *For the Land and the Lord.* New York: Council on Foreign Relations.

McAdam, Doug and William H. Sewell, Jr. 2001. "It's About Time: Temporality in the Study of Social Movements and Revolutions," in R.R. Aminzade, J.A. Goldstone, D. McAdam,

E.J. Perry, W.H. Sewell Jr., S. Tarrow, and C. Tilly (eds.), *Silence and Voice in the Study of Contentious Politics*. Cambridge: Cambridge University Press, pp. 89–125.

Newman, David. 1985. *The Impact of Gush Emunim*. London: Croom Helm.

Pedahzur, Ami. 2012. *The Triumph of Israel's Radical Right*. New York: Oxford University Press.

Pedahzur, Ami and Arie Perliger. 2009. *Jewish Terrorism in Israel*. New York: Columbia University Press.

Peri, Yoram. 2006. *Generals in the Cabinet Room: How the Military Shapes Israeli Policy*. Washington, DC: United States Institute of Peace Press.

Roth, Anat. 2014. *Not at any Cost—From Gush Katif to Amona: The Story Behind the Struggle over the Land of Israel*. Tel Aviv: Miskal—Yedioth Ahronoth Books and Chemed Books. [Hebrew]

Rubinstein, Danny. 1982. *On the Lord's Side: Gush Emunim*. Tel Aviv: Hakibbutz Hameuchad. [Hebrew]

Schwartz, Dov. 2009. *Religious-Zionism: History and Ideology*. Boston, MA: Academic Studies Press.

Shafat, Gershon. 1995. *Gush Emunim: The Story Behind the Scenes*. Beit El: Shafran, Dvir. [Hebrew]

Sheleg, Yair. 2007. *The Political and Social Ramifications of Evacuating Settlements in Judea, Samaria, and the Gaza Strip—Disengagement 2005 as a Test Case*. Jerusalem: Israeli Democracy Institute Press. [Hebrew]

Shiloah, Zvi. 1989. *The Guilt of Jerusalem*. Tel Aviv: Karni. [Hebrew]

Sprinzak, Ehud. 1991. *The Ascendance of Israel's Radical Right*. New York and Oxford: Oxford University Press.

Weisburd, David. 1989. *Jewish Settler Violence: Deviance as Social Reaction*. University Park, PA: The Pennsylvania State University Press.

Zertal, Idith and Eldar Akiva. 2009. *Lords of the Land: The Settlers and the State of Israel 1967–2004*. New York: Nation Books.

PART II
Issues in Israeli society

6

THE ISRAELI ECONOMY

Success as the new normal

Pinchas Landau

Introduction

This essay seeks to trace the extraordinary metamorphosis which, over the course of two decades, has seen the Israeli economy move from being weak and marginal to being strong and, in many respects, a global powerhouse. On the basis of key macro-economic metrics used to assess national economies, there can be no doubt that in the decade since the Great Financial Crisis (GFC) of 2007–2009, the Israeli economy has been one of the top performers among the developed countries. From a longer-term perspective, the very fact that the Israeli economy is now firmly entrenched in the "developed economy" category—let alone in its top echelon—is a testimony to how far it has come. Examining the economy through a more short-term lens, the striking feature is the consistency and resilience of the main positive trends, in contrast to the volatility or outright weakness displayed by many veteran, developed economies.

Despite the positive data and trends, some analysts have chosen to highlight the negative aspects—whether trends or new developments—within the overall Israeli economic performance. Elements of this critique are discussed in this essay and their relative strength—even, in some cases, continued validity—are considered. In general, it may be said that some of the most deeply-entrenched sources of concern regarding the macro-economy and the socio-economy around the turn of the century have been reversed, rendered harmless or at least mitigated. Conversely, some challenges already "on the agenda" ten or twenty years ago continue to pose problems—or have even been aggravated—while entirely new ones have emerged, some of them stemming from the economy's overall success. The analysis presented here will argue that the main achievements in the macro-economic sphere are real rather than artificial, sustainable rather than ephemeral and are likely to be expanded further in the coming decade. These achievements provide the basis and will generate the resources that will enable the very real and substantial challenges facing a small, open economy in a volatile regional and global environment to be addressed and either resolved or at least contained.

This essay uses 1996 as a starting point, because twenty years is a sufficient period of time to provide perspective on all the key developments and to identify the forces at work in the Israeli economy. Admittedly, that starting point—whether labeled "1996" specifically, or "the mid-1990s"—is somewhat artificial. The more accepted and more "correct" date would be July 1, 1985, when the Economic Stabilization Program (ESP) was enacted. That event marks the true watershed in Israeli economic history, not only between the period of gradual descent into hyperinflation and the subsequent period of the gradual achievement of monetary and fiscal stability, but also—far more fundamentally—between the era of a socialist/statist, centrally run economy, to one increasingly open to market forces and integrated into the global economy. Yet, precisely because a comparison between 1985 and 2018 is so extreme, it is of little value to an effort in understanding the Israeli economy today. It is, indeed, essential to know, understand and appreciate what happened in 1985 and the years that followed. However, that period of upheaval was largely over by 1996, whilst this essay concentrates on the last two decades of Israeli economic developments.

In the mid-1990s, the efforts of the Israeli state and society were directed toward two endeavors, both of which were fraught with major risks, but each of which had the potential to stimulate enormous positive changes in all areas of national life. These were the peace process with the Palestinians and the absorption of a wave of mass immigration from the countries known by then as "FSU"—the former Soviet Union—which included, Ukraine, Belarus, the Baltic and Caucasian successor states, the "stans" and, of course, Russia itself. By 1996, the peace process was in trouble: its Israeli architects, Yitzhak Rabin and Shimon Peres had been, respectively, assassinated in November 1995 and defeated in an election in May 1996. The "Russian immigration," as it was called, already numbered over 650,000 persons (the country's total population in 1989, when the wave began, was only 4.5 million) and was slackening. Consequently, its immediate impact on the economy was turning from strongly positive to mildly negative—while its phenomenal long-term impact was only dimly discernible and hence not widely understood. The focus, therefore, was on the immediate issues of immigrant absorption—what Israel needed to do for the immigrants, rather than what the immigrants could and would do for Israel.

Thus, Israel's macro-economic situation in 1996 displayed an inconclusive combination of dominant features. Economic growth was still strong, with GDP rising 6 percent in 1996, but was showing a clear downward trend (to an average rate of below 4 percent in 1997–1999), as the scale of immigration declined and with it both the level of new construction underway and the number of new entrants into the labor force. Meanwhile, the budget deficit was very high, as the government continued to fund major spending programs needed to absorb the immigrants into Israeli society. This large deficit was feeding a stubbornly high inflation rate, which was still in double digits at a time when the developed world was adopting the "Maastricht standards" that set a standard of 2 percent annual inflation and a current budget deficit: GDP ratio of 3 percent. Furthermore—and despite outstanding success in facilitating the rapid integration of working-age immigrants into the labor force—the underlying fact remained that the overall rate of labor force participation, at 53.6 percent, was extremely low by the standards of advanced economies.[1]

In the critical external sector, Israel's trade deficit and overall current account deficit were, in the mid-1990s, exceptionally large in terms of GDP, again reflecting the huge investments and spending necessitated by immigrant absorption. The large external deficit and high domestic inflation translated into a chronically weak currency, which generated higher prices and perpetuated the inflationary cycle. This ensured that the outlook was problematic, at the least, in the short term, whilst the longer-term prospects were more positive, but mixed. Fast forward to 2016[2] and the macro-economic summary reads as follows (see Figure 6.1):

Economic growth reached 4 percent in 2016, well above the 3.25 percent average rate recorded in 2012–2015. Yet, both these figures were far superior to the levels achieved by most developed economies in the current decade (the preliminary estimate for 2017 GDP growth is 3 percent).

The budget deficit for 2016—as for 2015 (and, by initial estimates, for 2017)—was around 2 percent of GDP and thus below the planned level in each of those years, reflecting strong revenue inflows, coupled with a continued spending discipline. As a result, Israel's ratio of government debt to GDP has fallen consistently and, at below 60 percent in 2017, is far lower than that of most developed economies. Inflation is running at around zero, although outright deflation has been avoided.

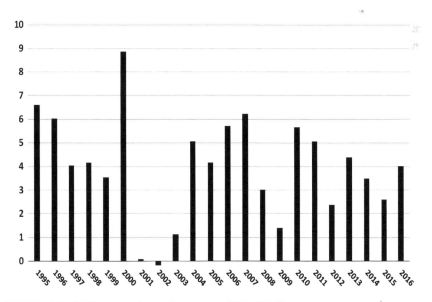

FIGURE 6.1 GDP, annual change in percent, 1995–2016[3]

Furthermore, since 2003, Israel has run a surplus on its current account, which has gradually increased to levels equivalent to 3–4 percent of GDP. As a result, the country has ceased to be a net debtor internationally and is, instead, a large and growing creditor nation. These factors have made the Israeli shekel one of the strongest currencies in the world in the last decade. In the domestic economy, the labor force has seen consistent progress since 2003: unemployment has fallen to record low levels, employment has steadily risen, as has the participation rate. Real wages have risen every year since the end of the Great Financial Crisis in 2009, at first slowly, but more rapidly in recent years.

Thus, the outlook for the Israeli economy is positive in both the short and long term. Challenges are numerous and, in some cases, significant—but the ability to address and resolve them clearly exists. The question that inevitably arises from these comparative snapshots is—what happened? How has the superior economic performance represented by the dry statistics been achieved?

What happened? Explaining the Israeli economic turnaround

The first—and the simplest—part of the answer to "what happened?" is gleaned by reviewing the key developments in the country's economy over this twenty-year period. The excesses and distortions that accumulated during the immigration-driven boom of 1990–1996 led inevitably to a slowdown, in the latter years of the decade. This strongly cyclical pattern had characterized the Israeli and pre-state Mandatory Palestinian economy throughout the twentieth century.[4] While the 1990s saw this cycle at work again, a key element was absent: in contrast to the length and strength of the boom, when the slowdown came it proved less severe than in previous iterations, because of a highly significant structural change in the economy. Israel's burgeoning "hi-tech" sector had evolved to the point where it was an important participant in the global tech boom of the 1990s and its exponential growth partially offset the weakness in the domestic economy.

The potential of high-tech to create an entirely new paradigm for high-value-added economic growth was quickly appreciated. However, this proved to be a mixed blessing, because it created a "dual economy" which featured both a very fast-growing but still small high-tech sector paying high wages to a narrow segment of the labor force, alongside the still-dominant "old economy" sectors and the bloated public sector, which were characterized by low added-value and paid low wages to the bulk of the labor force. But this embryonic socioeconomic problem was quickly overshadowed by the abrupt outbreak of a major crisis which, because of its multi-faceted nature, can be seen as a "triple whammy." This crisis sent the economy into its longest and deepest-ever recession, in which GDP declined for ten successive quarters, from the final quarter of 2000 through the first quarter of 2003.[5] The three blows that descended on the Israeli economy came from different directions and it was their cumulative effect that explains the severity of the recession.

First, beginning in the spring of 2000, came the "tech-wreck"—the collapse of the internet bubble and of the Nasdaq share market, where most of the new Israeli hi-tech companies had been floated during the 1990s. This proved to be the most spectacular crash to date of the "new economy," causing funding for new ventures to dry up and most of the existing start-up companies to close, along with quite a few established ones: nothing in the hi-tech sectors remained unscathed. Second, October 2000 saw the Second Intifada break out. The initial wave of clashes between Palestinian youths and Israeli security forces quickly metastasized into a systematic campaign of suicide bombings directed against civilians, with public transport, restaurants, shops and other public places the main targets. The economic impact was devastating, as tourism collapsed and general consumer activity shriveled, with consequent heavy job losses, causing unemployment to rise to double-digit levels by 2003. Finally, in 2001–2002, a general global recession—distinct from the slump in the tech sectors—hurt Israel's non-technology export sectors. The result was that, for the first time in Israeli history, the domestic economy and the external sector plunged in tandem, dragging the economy remorselessly down.

Only in 2003 did a tentative turnaround begin, as the battered domestic economy began to emerge from the intifada, while exports responded to the renewal of global growth. The shake-out in the tech sector continued into 2004 and even thereafter, the scale of the damage wrought on technology investors and companies was so great that the recovery process was long and gradual. Thus, in the years prior to the GFC of 2007–2009, while the Israeli economy benefited from, and participated in, the global economic boom, it was still deeply scarred and only slowly emerging from the trauma it had undergone in the opening years of the twenty-first century.

Yet the years of crisis and recession had been put to good use.[6] The years 2002–2005 marked the most intense and prolonged period of structural reform that the Israeli economy had ever undergone. These reforms included a fundamental restructuring of the tax system; completing the restructuring and recapitalization of the pension system (begun in 1995); capital market reforms that, together with the pension reforms, gave rise to a vibrant corporate bond market and modernized the government bond market; revamping the regulation of the financial sector, in particular of the banks, by imposing strong constraints on corporate lending (following the collapse of several small banks and heavy losses for the big banks in 2001–2002); and a large-scale privatization of state-owned companies.

The reforms were essential in their own right and laid the basis for the prolonged period of economic expansion, which began in 2003 and has continued through the present. As an added, unexpected bonus, they would also enable the Israeli financial system largely to avoid the problems that gutted the American and European banks in the GFC. Of course, the scale and severity of the GFC was such that no country could be unaffected. However, Israel suffered relatively mild symptoms of economic stagnation: only in the months immediately following the post-Lehman Brothers collapse—late 2008 and early 2009—was there a sharp slowdown in economic activity, primarily in the external sector. This stemmed from the disruption of normal trade finance activity and was countered by timely measures by Israeli government ministries and agencies. The domestic economy was largely unaffected because, fortunately, the global crisis did not last long enough for its negative impact to filter through into what was a healthy economic organism.

Thus by the second half of 2009, the Israeli economy was growing rapidly again and, spurred by the stimulatory impact of the policies initiated in America, China and elsewhere, it was able to regain rates of GDP growth of over 5 percent per annum in 2010–2011. However, in the new, post-crisis environment of very low growth in the developed economies, these rates proved unsustainable and, beginning in late 2011, they began to decline. Furthermore, whereas in the years leading up to and following the GFC, Israel's economic growth had been export-led, after 2011 it was the domestic economy that took the pivotal role. Private consumption and, to a lesser extent, investment contributed most of the (lower) growth that the economy managed in 2012–2015.

However, expectations of continued weakness were confounded, with growth rising back to 4 percent in 2016 and remaining robust in 2017. Consumption remained a key factor, with an unprecedented boom in vehicle imports—by both households and businesses—as well as in consumption of services, notably foreign vacations. Although cheap credit helped fuel this spending spree, it was underpinned by a sharp and ongoing rise in real disposable income, thanks to the collapse of energy and other commodity prices in 2014–2015. The consumer boom was directed largely at imported goods and services, but the impact on the current account surplus was limited, thanks to renewed rapid growth in service exports. Meanwhile, exports of goods have stagnated during the last five years, as key export sectors and companies—the chemicals sector centered around the Israel Chemicals Group and the pharma sector, dominated by Teva Pharmaceuticals—have been hit by crises in their global sectors, aggravated by their own strategic blunders at the corporate level.

This review of the economy's path over the last twenty years, whilst making clear that it was not a straight line but rather contained ups, downs and diversions along the way, only provides the "what" and "when" of what happened, with some hints as to the "why." It still does not explain how the Israeli economy has come to consistently out-perform expectations, especially in recent years. The "three pillars" on which the Israeli economy rests—and from which it gains its strength and sustainability—will subsequently examined in full below.

The three pillars

It is possible to identify three separate components that contributed to this long-term success, each essential in its own way. One relates to the external sector, one to the domestic economy and one, behind the scenes and facilitating both of the other pillars, relates to the government sector.

A: From chronic deficit to chronic surplus

The greatest and most dramatic change in the Israeli economy over the last twenty years is its move from running a chronic deficit on trade and the wider balance of payments—making it reliant on foreign borrowing and aid to finance this deficit—to running a "chronic" surplus and thereby becoming a net lender internationally.

Most older Israelis, who grew up in an economic environment characterized by permanent deficits and frequent crises have, perhaps understandably, great difficulty in accepting and internalizing the idea that their country, which they had grown up knowing to be poor and needy, is now prosperous and economically independent. Foreigners, fed by a mainstream media which has systematically missed, or at least ignored, the Israeli macro-economic metamorphosis, are largely unaware of the new realities, let alone of their wider implications. Such foreign awareness as exists is encapsulated in the description of Israel as the "start-up nation." This relates to the remarkable fact that Israel has become one of the most entrepreneurial and innovative cultures in the world: the number of start-up companies Israel spawns is not only world-leading in relative terms, but even in absolute terms this small country ranks ahead of many large, developed economies. Yet the start-up sector is as much a sociological and cultural phenomenon as it is an economic one. What has facilitated Israel's macro-economic metamorphosis is the global shift from an industrial economic structure, to a technological one in which human capital is far more important than physical, or even financial, capital.

The single data series that, more than any other, encapsulates the change in the Israeli economy over the past twenty years is the balance of trade in services. Israel's trade in goods has always been in deficit, because of the need to buy raw materials—from oil to grains to metals—as well as most consumer goods. Meanwhile, until the late 1990s, trade in services was a minor adjunct to trade in goods, in which the small volume of trade in services—tourism, shipping, etc.—generated an unimportant outcome, usually a marginal deficit. However, the growth of software exports—the primary service product of the post-industrial age—together with Israel's "production line" of start-up companies typically sold at an early stage of their development, has created an entirely new paradigm. Software and other technology-oriented service products, notably R&D and consultancy, are lumped together in the data under the nondescript title of "other services," but they have grown to far overshadow the traditional service sectors of tourism, transportation and finance.

The huge expansion of these kinds of service exports has generated a large and growing surplus in trade in services (see Figure 6.2). This surplus has, in the course of the period under review, come to first equal and eventually to exceed the deficit in trade in goods—marking a fundamental switch in the status and prospects of the entire Israeli economy.

In addition to the growing surplus from trade in services and the ongoing, but variable, deficit from trade in goods, the other main components of the current account have also grown over time. In particular, primary income—meaning the inbound stream of income stemming from labor (wages) and capital (interest and dividends) generated by Israeli personnel and financial assets overseas, less the income generated by the growing phalanx of foreign workers in Israel and of foreign financial investment in Israel—has been consistently negative, as the outflow

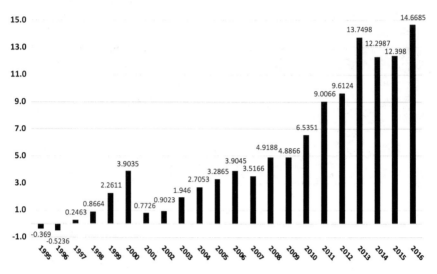

FIGURE 6.2 Balance of trade in services, 1995–2016, US$bn

Source: Compiled by Author.

has grown much faster than the inflow. Conversely, secondary income, mainly uni-lateral transfers, has been consistently positive, thanks to US aid (75 percent of it recycled via purchases of American-made weapons and equipment, which are included in imports of goods) and the monetary support of Diaspora Jewry to the Israeli government and to Israeli educational, medical and other social institutions.[7]

The sum of the deficits and surpluses of these four items—trade in goods, trade in services, primary income and secondary income—comprises the current account, and it is this which has moved so decisively from negative to positive, as shown in Figure 6.3.

However, while the dominant force behind this trend has been service exports, another point demands mention, because it, too, represents a critical and permanent improvement in Israel's external position. In March 2013, the large offshore natural gas field, Tamar, began production. Although Tamar was not the first Israeli natural gas field to be found, developed and brought into production, nor the largest—Leviathan, discovered in 2010, is far larger—the arrival of Tamar marked a mile-stone in the macro-economic history of the country. It has allowed a significant sum to be permanently sliced off Israel's energy bill—the cost of importing the country's oil, gas, coal and other energy sources, but this is only a "downpayment" in a process that, whilst proving longer than had been imagined, will eventually lead to Israel becoming a net energy exporter and thus achieving a surplus on its trade account.

These goals, long regarded as inconceivable, will be achieved when the Leviathan field is brought into production. This is currently scheduled to begin happening in late 2019 but, despite significant progress during 2016–2017 on all fronts—political,

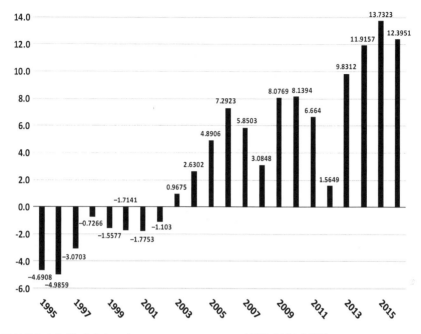

FIGURE 6.3 Deficit/surplus on current account, 1995–2016, US$bn

Source: Compiled by Author.

regulatory, financial, and commercial—there are still major issues for the Leviathan project to overcome before it can realize its enormous potential. It is therefore entirely possible that the full impact of Leviathan on the economy will not be felt until the late 2020s.

B: The poster boy of the Washington Consensus

Although government policies have been instrumental in nurturing the Israeli high-tech sectors over several decades, government cannot take the main credit for the emergence of Israel as a leading global player in many key technology sectors. As for the more recent development of an Israeli energy sector, the role of government has been mixed at best. Two main charges must be laid at the door of Israeli governments across the years in this context: the failure to more enthusiastically promote oil and gas exploration throughout the country's history, but especially in the period since 1990; and, more recently, the serial blundering and general confusion that delayed the development of Leviathan after its discovery and thereby delayed further exploration and, most likely, additional discoveries.

Proponents of free markets will see these examples as excellent illustrations of what governments should and should not do: it should avoid seeking to "pick winners," whether sectors or specific corporations, instead working proactively to create an environment in which winners—entrepreneurs, companies and sectors—can emerge and thrive. That is because any specific successes or failures a government may attain in these efforts, important though they may be, are marginal compared to the role of government in creating and overseeing the country's general economic environment. In this area of macro-economic management, the data points to a very clear conclusion—that the record of Israeli governments over the last twenty years has been extremely positive.

The success of macro-economic policies in this period is dramatic in absolute terms, but it is especially remarkable in two relative contexts. First, the achievement of a period of unbroken economic expansion since 2003, against a background of fiscal and monetary stability and a steadily improving external position, is little short of stunning in the context of Israel's own history—in particular the disastrous failures of macro-economic policy and management in the "lost decade" from 1973–1985, when the budget deficit ran out of control, the economy descended into hyperinflation, the banking system engaged in a spectacular cycle of boom and bust and the external deficit ballooned to the point where national bankruptcy loomed.

Second, the achievements of the last decade in the areas of fiscal restraint and consolidation, labor force expansion, financial sector stability, as well as growing external surpluses, stand in glaring contrast to the negative trends in most developed economies during and after the Great Financial Crisis and the Great Recession. Indeed, if the performance of the developed economies in the post-GFC period is measured using the Maastricht criteria,[8] in the area of fiscal management—especially current budget deficits and the ratio of government debt to GDP—most countries deviated significantly from target levels. Israel, on the other hand, has consistently met the budget deficit target and has recently reached and surpassed the debt/GDP target. In short, in terms of the set of policies known as "the Washington Consensus" that form the bedrock of "neo-liberal economics," Israel could easily serve as the "poster boy" example of a country that has successfully applied them and greatly benefited as a result.

The obvious question is—how did this happen? How did the former deficit junkie become a reformed character and the country, in which all but one of its banks were "bad" in 1986, become the one in which none went bad in 2008 or subsequently? The technical answers may be found in the nitty-gritty of specific measures and detailed policies. But the fundamental answer lies in the area of political economy: the emergence, during the 1990s and early years of this century, of a broad consensus across Israel's numerous and variegated political parties regarding the main principles that should govern economic policy.

The consensus dictates that monetary policy be conducted by an independent central bank within a framework of inflation targeting and a freely floating exchange rate; that fiscal policy be anchored in a framework of clear deficit targets and spending caps; that government divest itself of ownership and control of businesses; and that banks and other financial institutions be subject to a supervisory regime sufficiently onerous to ensure that they never again threaten the stability and functioning of the wider economy. All of these principles have, over the years, been subjected to pressures, tinkered with and sometimes crudely altered—especially the spending caps and deficit targets. But from a long-term perspective, they have been respected and largely adhered to. The single major exception, at the height of the recession-driven, fiscal crisis of 2002, resulted in such severe disruptions in both the domestic and external economy[9] and generated such trauma among both politicians and civil servants, that its longer-term legacy was to greatly strengthen institutional commitments to the policy framework.

C: The revolution in the domestic socio-economy

The emergence in the late 1990s of a "dual economy" structure, in which a small but highly-dynamic "new economy" coexisted with a much larger, much more inefficient and hence poorer "old economy," has already been noted. That structure remains very much in evidence today. Yet developments within the larger, poorer, "old economy" over the last two decades have been no less dramatic—and arguably have been even more important for the country—than those in the "cutting-edge" sectors that comprise the "new economy."

By the turn of the century, it was apparent to most economists and many lay observers that key trends then at work in the "old economy" were so pernicious that, if left to develop undisturbed, they represented an existential threat to the economy and, by extension, to the country itself. The trends in question were socioeconomic in nature. They related to the rapid demographic changes that were then beginning to become evident, whereby two hitherto marginal demographic groups were displaying phenomenally rapid growth. These were the ultra-orthodox ("Haredi") Jewish population and the Israeli-Arab population.

The Haredim had, by the end of the century, grown from a fringe group to one that comprised some 5–8 percent of the total population, depending how it was defined and measured. Its most prominent economic characteristic was that most of its male adults did not join the labor force, instead remaining in full-time religious educational frameworks. Haredi females, on the other hand, did work, but were also engaged in bearing and raising large families—7 to 8 children was standard and more were commonplace—and also had low educational qualifications, albeit better than their male counterparts.

"Israeli-Arabs" were a much larger group, comprising between 15 and 18 percent of the total population, if all the sub-groups—including Christian, Druze and other religious and ethnic communities—are included. The economic problem within this diverse community was similar to that of the Haredim, namely low labor force participation rates, but with reversed gender roles: the non-participation was concentrated among females, rather than males, with both sexes characterized by low educational levels. In terms of demographics, Israeli-Arab birth rates had been declining for decades, although they were still considerably higher than those of the overall Jewish population. However, Bedouin Arabs, most of whom live in the country's southern region, were achieving very high birth rates, via polygamous family structures.

The rapid population growth of these groups was considerably facilitated by the relentless expansion of welfare payments, primarily—but by no means solely—child allowances. The increase in welfare payments reflected two unconnected developments, in different spheres. In the fiscal context, defense spending had been on a downward trajectory since the mid-1980s, while the total government budget expanded rapidly in the 1990s, thanks to rapid GDP growth—so that extra resources were available within the budget. Meanwhile, in the political sphere, the Haredi political parties had assumed the role of kingmakers at the governmental level, because neither of the two main political blocs—the right-wing parties led by Likud and the left-wing parties led by Labor—could achieve a majority in the Knesset without their support. Haredi parties therefore offered their support to both political blocs at divergent moments, in return for a steady expansion of the budgets—in local government, education, welfare, and religious affairs—that fed their institutions and thus, directly or indirectly, supported their constituencies.[10]

By the turn of the century, commentators and politicians from both sides of the political spectrum were concerned that, within fifteen to twenty years at most, the budget would collapse under the weight of the welfare spending being imposed upon it. Nevertheless, political exigencies prevented any reversal of the trends and, on the contrary, consistently exacerbated the problem. However, the severe recession of the early years of the century brought matters to a head far earlier than had been predicted—and the imminence of budgetary collapse in 2002 turned structural reforms that had hitherto seemed politically impossible, into an urgent and existential requirement. Emerging victorious in the 2003 Knesset election, Likud leader Ariel Sharon excluded the Haredi parties from power for the first time in a generation, replacing them in the coalition government with an overtly anti-Haredi, pro-reform, middle-class protest party led by Yosef "Tommy" Lapid.[11] Sharon appointed Binyamin Netanyahu as Finance Minister and, acting together, these two rivals pushed through the sweeping social and economic reforms that changed the direction of the Israeli economy.

Netanyahu took the axe to the forest of welfare programs that had sprung up over the previous fifteen years, with particularly swinging cuts made in child allowances. Indeed, so fierce were these measures that, several years later, Sharon's successor Ehud Olmert admitted they had been applied too aggressively and mitigated some of them—albeit without changing the direction of the restructuring they were driving within the Israeli socio-economy. The impact is visible first and foremost in the labor market. Beginning in 2003, when the economy began recovering from the recession, and continuing until 2015, not only did unemployment rates steadily decline, but employment levels consistently rose. As a result, the labor force participation rate—the Achilles heel of the Israeli economy in 2000—has risen to levels that are now above those of the US and are approaching the EU average (see Figure 6.4).

The rise in participation rates reflects in particular the upheaval in Haredi society, in which the downtrend on male employment has been sharply reversed, while female employment rates have also risen. A similar phenomenon is underway

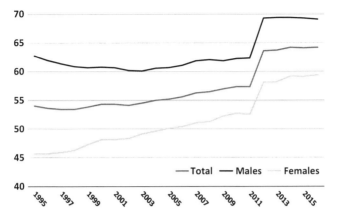

FIGURE 6.4 Labor force participation rate, population aged 15+, 1995–2016[12]

Source: Compiled by Author.

in Israeli-Arab society, albeit to a lesser extent. However, these changes are still very much in their infancy. To the "stick" of welfare cuts and the reduction of special sectoral budgets has been added the "carrot" of a growing panoply of government programs, often delivered via specialized NGOs, designed to close the educational gaps between the marginal and mainstream populations, as well as to alter societal norms by promoting training and employment. The process underway is thus a generational undertaking, which has already sparked a fundamental transformation in the expectations of young Haredim and Israeli-Arabs. The threat posed by the negative trends of the 1990s has been eliminated and a much more positive set of trends is emerging. These, however, will require considerable further nurturing and encouragement if they are to achieve their full potential.

Real problems versus bogeymen

The fact that Israel has become an ongoing economic success story does not mean that the country has no serious economic or socioeconomic challenges. In fact, there are numerous problems—some stubborn survivors from earlier years, others the products of the years of prosperity. Among the latter, an economic issue that has come to the fore in recent years is that of the strength of the shekel against almost all other currencies, leading to the claim that the Israeli currency has become "overvalued." This assertion is contentious, because professional economists disagree over how best to define and then measure the amorphous concept of "overvaluation." Yet this is a matter of potentially great importance: a country with a "chronic" current account surplus must expect to have a strong currency—and must learn to live with it. On the other hand, if the shekel is "excessively" strong and hence "overvalued," the clear implication is that a policy response is required. However, what that response might or should be is by no means obvious; rather, it is open to dispute.

Of much greater importance to the general public, and hence a socio-political issue as much as an economic one, is the high cost of living in Israel. Here, too, the existence of this phenomenon is quite easy to demonstrate on an objective basis—but not so its causes, and hence the desired policy response. The general consensus among economists—although by no means the unanimous view—is that the high level of retail prices in many sectors reflects these sectors' monopolistic or oligopolistic structures and the lack of competition that either caused, or at least resulted from, these structures. Yet even if this diagnosis is valid, the standard treatment prescribed for such economic illnesses is not always applicable in the Israeli context (for example, opening up sectors to foreign competition presupposes the willingness of foreign players to enter the Israeli market), or it may be blocked by political or commercial interests.

But the most vexing problem generated by prosperity is its inherently unequal nature, which causes income and wealth distribution to become ever more skewed. This feature is especially apparent in the Israeli context, where great wealth is being produced by a small and largely self-contained section of the population, which works in and around the technology sectors, while the bulk of the population falls steadily further behind. While by no means a uniquely Israeli problem, this is a more severe concern in Israel than in most developed economies, because of the now-entrenched feature of the "dual economy." Redistributive taxation can ameliorate this problem, but raising taxes carries the risk that firms and entrepreneurs may emigrate to lower-tax countries. A more fundamental approach would be to encourage and facilitate access to the "upper-tier" of the dual economy on the part of a broader cross-section of the population, in socioeconomic, ethnic and religious terms. This is being pursued in a range of government policies, notably including education but, by its very nature, will only make an impact over the medium to long term.

Another problem, now widespread in the developed world, is that of very low rates of productivity growth. In Israel, this issue is undoubtedly linked to the "dual economy" problem, but another, more positive factor is also at work—the rise in labor force participation. The expansion of employment, driven by the changes in Haredi and Israeli-Arab workforce patterns noted above, has brought into the labor force many unskilled people, with low or no formal qualifications. This quantitative gain has brought with it a qualitative decline, which has had a negative impact on productivity. However, as these new entrants are absorbed into the economy, their productivity may be expected to rise—while those coming after them will better prepare themselves, prior to their own entry into the job market.

There are also several issues which are widely perceived, in the media and hence among the general public, as serious problems—but which are not so. Either they are not serious, or they are not problems at all, at least in the context in which they are set. The most prominent such issue is the so-called "housing crisis." Once the hyperbolic rhetoric surrounding this topic is stripped away, it transpires that the problem—as far as the public is concerned—is that the prices of apartments and houses have jumped sharply since 2007 (see Figure 6.5). In national terms, house

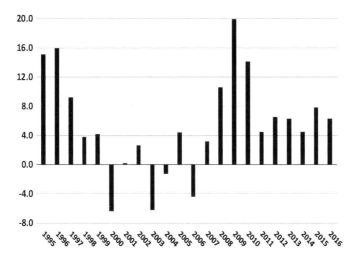

FIGURE 6.5 Prices of owner-occupied homes, annual percentage change, 1995–2016
Source: Compiled by Author.

prices have risen by some 130 percent, while in specific areas the rise has been far greater. The fact that successive governments have promised to end, or even reverse, this trend but have failed to do so despite all their efforts, has made housing into the leading socio-political issue, surpassing even that of the high cost of living.

The underlying problems of the housing sector, which encompass the ownership of land, its designation (as agricultural, residential, etc.) and the legal and bureaucratic procedures involved in changing that designation and in planning and construction, as well as the backward construction methods in use, are all well known and have for decades proven exceptionally resistant to change. Yet these problems, which are all too real, have not prevented the number of housing starts per annum from rising by two-thirds and the area under construction by almost 90 percent from the nadir reached in 2004. These basic facts prove that the rise in prices has not been caused solely, or even primarily, by shortage of supply.

Rather, there has been a tremendous upsurge in demand, beyond the quantity stemming from the formation of new households and from established households "moving up the housing ladder." This extra demand represents a financial phenomenon. The era of near-zero interest rates and very low returns from conventional safe investments, such as government bonds, has driven many Israelis to invest in the residential housing market, where they identify the double opportunity of an income stream from rent and the prospect of capital gains as apartment values rise.

Although the scale of the problem has been mitigated by a series of regulatory moves by the Bank of Israel—aimed at making large mortgages hard to obtain—and fiscal moves by the Treasury, which have reduced the tax advantage of investing in real estate, prices have continued to rise. Nevertheless, their rate of increase has slowed sharply in 2016–2017, probably reflecting the sharp rise in mortgage lending rates. Looking ahead, the global trend toward higher interest rates may presage a hike in domestic rates for the first time in many years and this, together with the cumulative impact of the measures noted above, should weaken the underlying rationale for investing in housing and lead to a new equilibrium in the residential market.

Other threats often cited with regard to the economy have failed to make a significant impact. Thus the "BDS" (boycott, divest and sanctions) movement, which has developed in recent years in Europe and North America and which urges governments, corporations and households to cut their economic and business links with Israel, has had no discernible impact in these areas. The movement's potency, if at all, is concentrated in the academic and cultural spheres. The impact of the Israel–Palestinian dispute has also been negligible in Israeli economic and commercial activity. Furthermore, as the focus of Israeli trade and investment flows shifts from west to east and the importance of Europe as a trading partner declines, the "linkage" between the Palestinian issue, in the widest sense, and investment and commercial decisions made by governments and companies will likely fade further.

Finally, with regard to the wider Israeli–Arab conflict and its impact on Israel: immediately on Israel's creation, all the Arab countries imposed a boycott on Israel that encompassed not just Israeli companies and products, but also foreign companies that traded with or invested in Israel. This was a significant negative factor in the first decades after independence. However, the boycott was largely discontinued in the 1990s—under US pressure on the Arab countries—enabling closer links between Israel and countries such as China, Japan and India, which had hitherto felt constrained by it. But only in the current century, have trade and investment ties with Gulf Arab states begun to emerge from the shadows and even these tenuous links, as well as those with Egypt and Jordan which have formal peace treaties with Israel, remain fragile and limited. Furthermore, the general absence of intra-regional trade, even between the Arab countries themselves, suggests that even if the political issues were somehow overcome, the economic and commercial consequences of a political settlement would be quite limited.

Future trends

"Even paranoids can have real enemies," Henry Kissinger supposedly said about Israel in the 1970s, and even highly successful economies can have real concerns—especially in the volatile and dangerous global economic environment of the twenty-first century. Israel's chief concerns for the future are not, as is widely assumed, overseas—in the areas of national security or geopolitical alignments. Rather, they are domestic and relate to social, economic and socioeconomic issues.

That social and economic issues are being linked, both in the diagnosis of problems and in proposed solutions, is a positive sign. It reflects an understanding that simplistic, populist pseudo-solutions will not achieve the desired results—only a long-term approach that encompasses all aspects of a given issue will do so. Thus, with regard to the vexed question of Israel's unsatisfactory levels of educational achievement in key subjects such as math and English, there is a systemic understanding that this is a critical long-term issue for the economy, as well as a social problem. Israel will not be able to maintain its standing as a center of technological innovation and scientific research without a high-quality educational system that equips students with know-ledge and skills and enables them to develop their talents.

The prominence of education in policy formulation is itself good news. Even better news is that the need to raise educational standards is not—or not only—a government-led, top-down initiative. The link between educational standards and achievements and between income levels and widening gaps in income and wealth has been identified and internalized by all sections of Israeli society. Nowhere is this more apparent than among the young Israeli-Arabs and Haredim, where a new and far more proactive approach is taking hold. This finds expression in twin demands, one addressed to the governmental system that these sectors receive at least their fair share of educational resources (buildings, teachers, materials), while the second is directed inwards to the specific society and culture, that it utilize these resources to prepare itself for full participation in the Israeli labor market and, by extension, in the wider society.

Education is thus the key front within a wider struggle to move from a culture of passive dependence that fosters marginalization and poverty, to one of proactive self-advancement that aspires to join the societal mainstream and achieve its income levels and living standards. Educational standards also feature prominently in any discussion of how to improve the very low rate of productivity growth noted above. However, the problem of low productivity is part and parcel of the "dual economy" that has developed over the last generation. The hi-tech sectors are characterized by productivity levels that are above the OECD average, while the productivity of the economy as a whole languishes at low rankings in international comparisons. One obvious way to address this problem is by expanding the hi-tech sector. But the greater and equally essential challenge is to raise the productivity of the rest of the economy, which in any scenario will remain the employer of the bulk of the workforce. Here, the focus must be on micro-economic issues—such as legal and regulatory reforms that remove barriers to entry and hence to competition.

Yet economic reforms are political initiatives and the reformist drive that was so prominent a feature of Israeli public life in the first decade of this century has largely faded in the second. Prolonged prosperity tends to create an indulgent atmosphere in which disruptive reforms are unwelcome—but that makes them more, rather than less necessary. Sooner or later, the public mood will change to support—or even demand—a new wave of reforms, which may have a different ideological underpinning than the previous wave. When those circumstances are in place, there are two main reasons for believing that the problems outlined above— as well as others—will be successfully resolved. The first stems from their being domestic socioeconomic issues, the solutions to which must be found domestically and do not require the involvement of external parties. These issues are the subject of debate between opposing views, but the Israeli record demonstrates that once a strong government charts a clear policy direction, it is able to execute it. Yet mustering the will to define and pursue a policy agenda, although the sine qua non for progress, may not be sufficient.

The second enabling factor is that Israel has the means to translate domestic goals, once defined, into reality. The resources needed include a large, vocal, and increasingly well-educated younger generation, which Israel's positive demographic structure, unique among developed countries, has created. The other key resource is the availability of adequate financing, without which even the best plans cannot succeed. On this score, too, Israel is well-endowed. Indeed, there is reason to expect further improvement in the country's fiscal position, particularly due to the royalties and taxes expected to flow to the government's coffers from the offshore gas fields; when Leviathan is accessed, this flow will be multiplied. Future governments should therefore be in the enviable position of being able to readily fund the investments in human and physical capital that they deem desirable.

A virtuous circle is thus attainable, whereby large and growing population groups previously regarded as marginal are mainstreamed into the labor force, while this quantitative increase is coupled with a qualitative upgrading of the labor force as whole, enabling the "new economy" sectors to retain and enhance their global standing. This will ensure that Israel continues to generate current account surpluses and strengthen its external financial position. Meanwhile, the continued development of offshore energy resources will eliminate the trade deficit, further increasing the current account surplus—and also generating the fiscal revenues to finance the investments needed in education, infrastructure, health, and housing. None of the links in this chain are in any way guaranteed, nor can they be taken for granted. Yet they all already exist and are at work. All that is necessary to achieve continued and enhanced success is more of the same.

Notes

1 This figure is misleading, as explained in Note 12; a more realistic figure would be around 58 percent—but even that was very low on a comparative basis.
2 The availability of data for part of 2017 would vary from one data series to another and would also be subject to the frequent and often significant revisions common to macro-economic data—especially in Israel.
3 Note on sources: all the data presented in the tables/figures included in this essay are produced by the author and are taken directly from official sources: the Central Bureau of Statistics, the Bank of Israel and the Ministry of Finance.
4 Each wave of immigration triggered a construction-driven boom in the domestic economy. The boom sucked in imports needed for both investment (construction) and consumption, while the extra spending necessitated by immigrant absorption caused the government's budget deficit to balloon. The financial strains generated by swollen deficits in both foreign trade and the state budget would force the government to "apply the brakes"—and the resultant slowdown would spiral into a full-fledged recession.
5 This was what the data published at that time showed, using the then-accepted methodology for calculating GDP. These data formed the basis on which the governments of the time made their policy decisions and, it is fair to say, accurately reflected the way most Israelis experienced that period. Many years later, the GDP data going back to the

mid-1990s were revised upwards, in line with new methods of measuring output, especially of technology-oriented sectors; given the large and growing share of high-tech in the Israeli economy, Israel was one of the major beneficiaries of this change.

6 The expression "never waste a good crisis," which was introduced into American political and economic parlance by Ram Emanuel, Barack Obama's first Chief of Staff at the White House, had its source in the senior echelon of Israel's Ministry of Finance, which had learnt this lesson the hard way back in the eighties and applied it with striking success in the "noughties."

7 This summary of the trends in primary and secondary income is valid for the period under discussion. However, there are growing indications that it will become much less so going forward. The deficit in primary income is set to shrink, thanks to the rapid growth in Israel's net overseas financial assets, which turned positive (assets exceeding liabilities) for the first time only in 2016, but by September 2017 amounted to $135bn. The increase in net income from this growing pool of overseas assets has been constrained by the very low, zero and even negative interest rates in the capital markets of developed countries since the GFC. Now that interest rates have begun to rise, this constraint will weaken and the income flow from Israel's overseas financial assets will expand accordingly. Conversely, the positive trend in secondary income will be eroded by the ongoing decline in German reparations payments (as Holocaust survivors dwindle), in the net size of unilateral transfers via donations etc.—and, possibly, by future reductions in US aid. Many of these emerging trends can be identified, albeit in an embryonic state, in the data on Israel's financial account for 2016–2017.

8 These were used in the 1990s to determine the suitability of national economies to join the embryonic European Monetary Union [the euro].

9 These disruptions included a plunge in the shekel's value to record low levels, the consequent doubling of interest rates in six weeks—all against a background of a rapidly-increasing budget deficit and fierce public disagreements between senior policymakers.

10 These increased budgets were not exclusive to the Haredi parties and constituencies but applied to all, or most, other groups; the criteria for child allowances, as a critical example, were universal.

11 A veteran journalist and a neophyte politician. His son, Yair Lapid, also quit a highly successful media career a decade later, to found and lead Yesh Atid, now the leading opposition party.

12 The abrupt increase portrayed in Figure 6.4 as occurring in 2012 is the result of a methodological change, imposed on the Israeli Central Bureau of Statistics by the OECD, to bring the Israeli data into line with internationally accepted norms. The implication, therefore, is that the pre-2012 Israeli data should be some 5 percent or so higher than the rate depicted in the Figure. However, the crucial feature remains unchanged—the existence of a slow and steady improvement, underway since 2003.

Further reading

Bank of Israel. Bank of Israel Annual Report 2016. www.boi.org.il/en/NewsAndPublications/RegularPublications/Pages/DochBankIsrael2016.aspx

Ben-Bassat, Avi. 2002. "The Israeli Economy 1985–1998," in *Government Intervention to Market Economics.* Cambridge, MA: MIT Press.

Braude, Kobi, Zviya Erdman, and Merav Shemesh. 2011. "Israel and the Global Crisis, 2007–09." Zvi Eckstein, Stanley Fischer and Karnit Flug (eds.), Jerusalem: Bank of Israel. www.boi.org.il/deptdata/mehkar/crisis/crisis_2007_2009_eng.pdf.

Cuckierman, Alex. "The Conquest of Israeli Inflation and Current Policy Dilemmas." *Center for Economic Policy Research*. Policy paper DO10955.

IMF.org. Israel: 2017 Article IV Consultation. www.imf.org/en/Publications/CR/Issues/2017/03/28/Israel-2017-Article-IV-Consultation-Press-Release-Staff-Report-and-Statement-by-the-44769

Katz, Yaakov. 2017. *The Weapon Wizards: How Israel Became a High-Tech Military Superpower*. New York: Martin's Press.

Leiderman, Leonardo. 1993. *Inflation and Disinflation: The Israeli Experiment*. Chicago, IL: University of Chicago Press.

Razin, Assaf. 2018. *Israel and the World Economy: The Power of Globalization*. Cambridge, MA: The MIT Press.

Rivlin, Paul. 2010. *The Israeli Economy from the Foundation of the State through the 21st Century*. Cambridge: Cambridge University Press.

———. 2016. "Stabilization and Liberalization in the Israeli Economy," in *Handbook of Research on Comparative Economic Development Perspectives on Europe and the MENA Region*. eds. M. Mustafa Erdoğdu and Bryan Christiansen. Hershey, PA: IGI Global.

Rosenberg, David. (forthcoming in 2018.) *Israel's Technology Economy: Origins and Impact 2018*.

Senor, Dan, and Saul Singer. 2011. *Start-up Nation: The Story of Israel's Economic Miracle* Reprint Edition. New York: Twelve.

Taub Center for Social Policy Studies.

———. Economic Survey of Israel 2016. www.oecd.org/israel/economic-survey-israel.htm

———. A Macroeconomic Picture of the Economy in 2017. http://taubcenter.org.il/a-macroeconomic-picture-of-the-economy-in-2017/

———. Why Does the Start-Up Nation Still Have Low Productivity?. http://taubcenter.org.il/why-is-productivity-so-low-in-the-start-up-nation/.

7

MULTICULTURALISM AND IDENTITY POLITICS

Rebecca B. Kook

> Multiculturalism is not just about living apart but also about living together.
> —*M. Karayanni, 2007, p. 54*

Introduction

The national project, of which the state of Israel is a sterling example, is a political idea that posits that culture and cultural identity should be the basis of political sovereignty and political legitimacy. Indeed Zionism, the national movement of the Jewish people, was premised on the assumption that the Jews, as a cultural-national group, are deserving of a political state of their own, on the basis of their cultural identity as a nation. In its capacity as a national movement, therefore, one of the primary aims of Zionism was not merely to act towards attaining the territory necessary for national self-determination, but to act towards cohering the Jewish people into a cultural and political nation. In the political sensibility of late nineteenth-century and early twentieth-century politics, this involved an active, mobilizatory project of incorporating cultural difference into a coherent, unified nation. The idea that the success of the national project was dependent on this incorporating—and assimilating—spirit was adopted by the founding fathers of the Israeli state and characterized Israeli politics and society, well into the first three or even four decades of its early political history. Within this political worldview, plurality of identities is something that nationalism seeks to overcome, not to celebrate.

Multiculturalism, on the other hand, celebrates cultural diversity. Within the multicultural worldview, cultural diversity is not to be overcome—but to be recognized and supported. The public and political recognition of cultural identity is believed to be critical to the well-being of the members of the diverse groups, to reduce inter-group conflict and therefore to contribute towards the long-term stability of the polity. If nationalism is premised on the existence of a mobilizing, dominant *core*, then multiculturalism posits the autonomy of minority cultures and identities within a society whose core strives for the support of diversity rather than its assimilation. In the eyes of many observers, multiculturalism has replaced nation building both as an empirical description as well as a normative ethos in Israeli society (Yonah 2007).

Israeli society is, and has always been, culturally diverse. Even at the apex of the nation-building period, it constituted a rich and vibrant mosaic of different languages, religions, ethnicities, and nationalities. However, Israel, at the turn of the twenty-first century, is a far cry from the pioneering, collectivist and mobilized society that it was in its early years; the unifying spirit of nation building has been replaced by a strong spirit of individualism, and with it—the demands for cultural recognition and a multicultural paradigm have grown strong. Moreover, the passing of the nation-building project and the rise of individualism has rendered Israel, in the eyes of many, without a unifying core. Lacking this core, diversity has been replaced by fragmentation, and the spirit of "engathering" by a network of polarized and antagonistic groups.

Contemporary Israeli society can be seen as a society wrought with anxiety over this polarization. In January 2016, then President Reuven Rivlin, made a speech to the Israeli parliament in which he made the following observation:

> Every day I meet citizens from different sectors within Israeli society. Religious, orthodox, secular, Arabs. There is much that separates them. However, I am continually surprised to discover that they share a common sentiment. All of them, with no exception, think of themselves as a persecuted minority, whose identity and values are subject to constant threat from other groups.
>
> *(President Reuven Rivlin, January 2016)*

According to Rivlin, up until recently Israel was constituted by a dominant "secular and Zionist" majority/core, that coexisted peacefully with three minorities: the Palestinian-Arabs, the Jewish ultra-orthodox; and the national-religious. This has been replaced by what he calls "the New Israeli Order"; an order in which there is no dominant majority and where each minority is more or less equal in its size to each other. Israel today is a society of minorities—Secular Jews, Arabs, National Religious and Ultra-Orthodox; distinct and separate, occupying segregated spaces, schools, courts, and media. Inter-group competition is salient, with the "tribes" vying amongst each other for ownership over Israeli society.

Indeed, Israel today embodies a paradox: on the one hand, it is a culturally, ethnically and religiously diverse society which recognizes its diversity through a multitude of multicultural mechanisms, ranging from a proportional electoral system, through language rights, distinct educational systems, and autonomous religious courts. However, these mechanisms of cultural recognition are ineffective at facilitating the co-existence of diversity. As Rivlin pointed out, Israeli society is a polarized society. Secular Jews feel imposed upon by orthodox Jews; Arabs feel marginalized by the Jews; and orthodox Jews feel threatened by the pervasive secularity of non-observant Jews.

How is it that, in an immigrant society—which seemingly accommodates cultural difference with a variety of mechanisms including language, education and religious autonomy—there is such a pervasive sense of victimization and polarization? In this essay I argue that the polarization that seems to characterize Israeli society results not from a lack of multicultural mechanisms, but rather from the lack of a shared or common core; or, in other words, deep disagreement on *what it is to be an Israeli*. Not only do the different groups within Israeli society lack a shared understanding of this concept, they are deeply conflicted as to what it should be. Should Israel be a religious polity, or a secular and democratic one? Should Israel be a national society, or perhaps a bi-national one? Effective multicultural mechanisms are impossible to implement in diverse societies that lack even the most basic agreement on what constitutes the whole.

The essay is composed of three sections. In the first section, I present a brief discussion of the basic concepts of multiculturalism, with the aim of employing them in my analysis of Israeli society. In the second section, I discuss the main cultural groups in Israeli society, focusing on the different mechanisms developed by the Israeli polity to recognize and acknowledge their identity. In the third and final section, I discuss the different conceptions of what it is to be an Israeli and suggest possible ways in which to move forward.

On multiculturalism

In their article on "Liberalism and the Right to Culture," Margalit and Halbertal open with the following sentence: "Human beings have a right to culture—not just any culture, but their own. The right to culture has far-reaching implications for the liberal conception of the state" (Margalit and Halbertal 1994, p. 492). Contemporary multiculturalism proceeds from this very basic assumption and asserts that *given* the right to culture, states, including liberal states, have a political as well as an ethical obligation to enable individual members of that state to exercise that right.

Most democratic states recognize this right to culture, but they negotiate cultural difference in vastly different ways and with vastly different outcomes. While there are varieties of approaches to multiculturalism, any serious multicultural framework provides some version of group rights. A group right is different from an individual right in a number of significant ways. First, it is a collective right, granted not to individuals but to groups; second, it is selective, that is, it is granted to some groups and not to others, and finally, it demands that the state take active measures to ensure the provision of those rights, such as the provision of resources (Pinto 2015). This final characteristic is particularly significant since the failure to provide these measures can often result in an ineffective or problematic implementation of the right.

Hence, the first issue to consider when we consider group rights is the extent to which the state is prepared to commit itself in the active provision of such rights. However, even if the state is ready and willing, given that group rights are most usually granted in the context of *multiple* groups, there are numerous difficulties that can arise that have to do with the relationship between the different groups, and with the different relationships between the groups and the state.

Menachem Mautner, in his discussion of multiculturalism in Israel, points to one particular difficulty which arises when there are significant differences *between* the groups in terms of their preference for regime type, political culture and the nature of the legal system. This difficulty is the existence of different types of images, or imaginaries, of the desired society and polity. Given the fact that the image of Israeli society shared by orthodox Jews is significantly different from that shared by secular Jews, and that the ideal image of Israeli society maintained by most Palestinians in Israel is vastly different from that held by most Jews—both secular and religious—the ability of any multicultural mechanism to reduce conflict and facilitate co-existence is significantly weakened and the potential for conflict is high (Mautner 2008).

Multicultural diversity in Israeli society

Israel—as almost all societies—is a culturally diverse one. The dominant cultural difference is between the Jewish citizens of the state, who constitute 82.7 percent of the general population, and the members of the Arab-Palestinian minority, who number 17.3 percent of the population and who are non-Jewish.[1] However, neither the Jewish majority nor the Palestinian minority are monolithic groups. While the primary, shared language of the Palestinian minority is Arabic, this group is religiously diverse: 85 percent of Arab-Palestinians in Israel are Muslim, 7.5 percent Christian and the remaining 8 percent are Druze. Similarly, while the Jewish majority, on the whole, share the same language—Hebrew—and are officially members of the same religion, members of this group differ significantly in terms of degrees (or shades) of religiosity and in terms of ethnicity: 43 percent of the Jewish majority define themselves as secular, 23 percent define themselves as traditional, 12 percent as very traditional and 9.5 percent as ultra-orthodox.

In terms of ethnicity, ethnic origin in Israel is based on the country of origin of the individuals themselves, or their ancestors. In 2015, close to half of the Jewish majority in Israel self-identified as being of Ashkenazi (i.e. European) origin; 37.6 percent as Mizrahi (from North Africa or the Middle East); 7.6 percent as both; and 6.3 percent as neither.[2] Data from 2016 pointed to the existence of close to 985,000 immigrants from the former Soviet Union, and 139,000 from Ethiopia. In addition, since the 1990s, Israel has been home to a growing, non-Jewish migrant worker population, and there are today close to 250,000 documented and undocumented labor migrants and asylum seekers. Finally, there are two and a half million Palestinians who live under Israeli military control in the West Bank and the Gaza Strip. These two latter groups are not Israeli citizens and are therefore beyond the purview of this study.

Israel's complex set of policies designed to accommodate its diverse groups of citizens emerged out of a need (and desire) to negotiate between the two pillars of

Israel's national identity: On the one hand—a Jewish nation-state, whose main raison d'etat is to provide the Jewish majority with a mechanism of self-determination, and whose identity is therefore implicitly linked to the cultural identity of the Jewish majority. At the same time, Israel is a democratic polity, committed to providing all of its citizens with equal rights and opportunities—regardless of religion, language or nationality. This delicate balancing act has produced a myriad of different cultural mechanisms that do not really fit together in a coherent paradigm and constitute a rather eclectic mixture of group rights, minority privileges, and assimilatory policies, implemented alongside diversity programs.

While some of these policies have been successful in producing a balance between autonomy and stability, many of them have served to exacerbate the fragmentation and heighten the sense of alienation within and between the divergent sectors within Israeli society. It is to a discussion of these state policies that this essay will now turn. It should be noted, however, that any discussion of multiculturalism in Israel is incomplete without analyzing the diversity of Jewish ethnicity, the labor migrants and asylum seekers, and of course the Palestinians in the West Bank and Gaza Strip. However, this analysis focuses on those cultural accommodations that are part of official state policy. Given that Israel has designed such accommodations only for the Jewish majority and the Palestinian minority—the analysis in this essay focuses solely on them.

The accommodation of Jewish identity in the Israeli state

Israel is one of the few democratic nation-states whose ethnic identity is officially and legally constituted by the state. The identity of Israel as a Jewish state is clearly stated in Israel's declaration of Independence, and reiterated in a number of key pieces of legislation. Thus, while most discussions of multiculturalism focus on accommodations to *minority* cultures, because of the very central place that Jewish ethnic identity plays in the Israeli polity, any discussion of cultural accommodations in Israel must include—and begin—with an examination of the ways in which the state accommodates the majority culture and how these accommodations impact on the fabric of the polity.

The starting point of this discussion is the very simple, yet crucial, fact that Judaism constitutes a wholistic identity and confers upon its members both a national/cultural identity as well as a religious identity. In Israel, therefore, membership in the Jewish religion implies membership in the Jewish nationality. This is a critical characteristic and forms the basis of the fundamental difference between the Israeli nation-state and other democratic nation-states: membership in the main national group of the state is predicated upon membership in or affiliation with the Jewish religion, and hence *with a particular group within Israeli society*. Indeed, this has led Yiftachel to describe Israel not as a democracy, but as an ethnocracy (Yiftachel 1999, pp. 364–390). Hence, the myriad ways in which nation-states privilege the "state nationality"[3]—in its incorporating national symbols, and in its general commitment to this nation's self-realization—in

Israel are limited to one group only (albeit a majority group). Finally, because of the overlap between Jewish religion and Jewish nationality, the fact that the state is heavily involved in the management of Jewish nationality confers privileged status on the Jewish community in Israel, in respect to other, non-Jewish communities.

This is, therefore, the first dimension of the cultural-national accommodation of the Jewish identity in Israel—*in its capacity as a nation and not a religion.* The ethno-cultural Jewish character of the state is manifested in many aspects of the Israeli polity. These include the privileged status of Hebrew over Arabic—though both are recognized official languages; the distribution of land and the privileging of Jewish ownership over non-Jewish ownership; the use of Jewish symbols in the public sphere—including the national anthem, the flag, the state-symbol and the fact that the day of rest and public holidays are based on the Jewish calendar; the official goal of the public education system, which is to "foster and nurture the history of the Jewish people—its values, norms and culture." And finally, perhaps most critically, in the immigration policy of the state, clearly exemplified in the Law of Return, which states that all Jews, by virtue of their Jewish identity, are eligible for citizenship in the State of Israel.

In its capacity as a religion, the Jewish character of Israel manifests itself first and foremost in a lack of separation between the state and religious institutions. Thus, the second way in which the Jewish "group" is accommodated is in its capacity as a religious group—and not a national group. However, while Judaism is a diverse mosaic of different shades of religiosity—of religious custom and religious lifestyle—within Israel, privileged status is conferred on the orthodox variant of belief only. This is done through the institution of the Chief Rabbinate, which is in charge of supervising the implementation of religious laws and customs. Thus, ironically, in the state whose raison d'etre was to secure Jewish national existence, the majority variants of non-orthodox Jewish belief in the world today—Reform and Conservative—are officially not recognized. The explanation for this lies in the historical domination of Jewish orthodoxy in pre-State politics both within the Zionist movement, and later in the State of Israel.

As mentioned above, the Jewish population in Israel is divided in terms of degrees of religiosity. Amongst the over 50 percent of Israel's population who define themselves as non-secular, two groups stand out: the Haredim (ultra-orthodox), literally translated into "those who stand in fear of God" and who constitute a small minority (9.5 percent of the Jewish population) and the "national-religious"—who are religiously orthodox, but differ from the ultra-orthodox in a number of ways—both in terms of religious observance and in terms of ideological belief, and who constitute close to 25 percent of the Jewish population of Israel. Ultra-orthodox Judaism refers to a collective identity expressed in a strict and uniform dress code, extremely strict modesty codes for women, concentration in homogeneous neighborhoods, and a rigid rejection of secular education and all forms of secular media. Any contact with secular lifestyles is often seen by more rigid ultra-orthodox groups as threatening and sinful. The national-religious, while orthodox in their custom, are integrated into the mainstream of Israeli society and coexist with great ease alongside their secular compatriots (Lehmann 2012, pp. 1029–1043).

In terms of ideological beliefs, while individuals identifying with these groups tend to reject the idea of a secular state and believe in the ideal of a state that would ultimately be ruled according to the Torah, the ultra-orthodox are openly hostile to the Zionist project, seeing it as defying the notion of the messianic redemption. In accordance with this theological and ideological division, Israel has developed a number of different types of mechanisms aimed at accommodating members of the ultra-orthodox group. These can be divided into two categories: those that incorporate and accommodate all members of the Jewish religion in Israel, and those that target only the ultra-orthodox group.

The origin of these accommodations is in an agreement signed by Israel's first Prime Minister, David Ben-Gurion and the representatives of the religious parties in 1947, commonly known as the "status quo" agreement. This name reflected the idea that it *preserved* the arrangements previously existing under the pre-state British Mandate and inherited from the Ottoman Empire. According to these arrangements, the different religious communities were allowed to operate their own legal systems in the sphere of personal status law. The agreements and the arrangements that put the status quo in place can be seen as quintessential multicultural mechanisms, as they were negotiated between the two sides, with an understanding of the difference between the religious and secular communities on the one hand, and the need for both communities to find an arrangement that would allow them to coexist on the other.

The agreement has four main clauses: the first concerns issues of personal status and confers total authority to the religious courts in these issues, and thereby establishes the authority of the Israeli rabbinate over marriages and divorces of all Jews in Israel. The second clause determines Saturday as the official rest day in the public sphere (hence laying the basis for the prohibition of public transport and the operation of businesses on the Sabbath). The third clause refers to the demand to maintain religious dietary laws in all public kitchens, and the final one grants the religious groups the right to maintain "an autonomous" educational system (Lehmann 2012, pp. 1029–1043). While the justification for these clauses is to enable orthodox Jews to freely practice their religion, in essence the three clauses serve to impose religious practice on non-observant Jews and the general population at large.

The last clause of the agreement resulted in the creation of two religious orthodox educational tracts; the first, which is called Mamlachti Dati (state religious), mainly serving the national-religious population. It is funded by the state, and its curriculum, hiring, and pedagogy is regulated by the Ministry of Education. The second track is ultra-orthodox, is also funded by the state, but is totally autonomous in its curriculum decisions, its hiring practices and in its pedagogy. In these schools, there is almost no teaching of so-called "secular" subjects such as science, math and English. In 2015, 61.2 percent of Israeli youth studied in regular (secular) public schools, 21.4 percent studied in national-religious public schools; and the remaining 17.4 percent studied in ultra-orthodox schools.

The final accommodation accorded to the orthodox group as part of the status quo agreement concerns military service. Three arrangements have developed over the years. The first is complete exemption from army service, granted to orthodox youth who can prove that they are studying in an institution of religious learning (Yeshiva); the second is the development of a special military track that allows religious study alongside military service; and the final one is the exemption of religious women from military service. The first arrangement is highly contentious in contemporary Israeli society, as the number of exemptions in this category have risen dramatically over the years, resulting in an inherently unequal universal conscription policy.

The cultural and religious accommodation of the Palestinian minority

In their identity, the Palestinian minority in Israel constitute the most intense challenge to the identity of the state and hence to its complex system of cultural accommodations. First and foremost, at 17.3 percent of the citizen population at large, Palestinian citizens of Israel are identified in all official documents and registers as a national minority and are referred to in their national identity cards and passports as members of the Arab nationality.[4] Second, Palestinian citizens of Israel constitute the largest non-Jewish minority in terms of religion; the majority are Muslims, with small Christian and Druze populations. Finally, members of the Palestinian minority are Arabic speakers, and hence are also a linguistic minority in a predominantly Hebrew-speaking society. Hence the Palestinian minority is at one and the same time a national, religious, and linguistic minority, and embodies three overlapping cleavage lines (Kook 2002).

Given Israel's official identity as a Jewish state, and the consequent intense and pervasive commitment to the self-realization of the Jewish nation, the ability of members of the Palestinian minority to freely exercise their cultural identity is significantly constrained. Moreover, the conjunction of their minority status and their (increasing) self-identification as Palestinians has led to significant discrimination on many dimensions. Indeed, despite their official citizenship status, the relationship between the state and the Palestinian minority has been an unresolved source of tension and conflict. For many of Israel's Jewish citizens, as for its leaders, it is difficult to disentangle the identity and interests of this citizen minority, from those of the larger Palestinian nation, with whom Israel has been involved in an often-violent, ethno-national conflict over sovereignty and territory since its establishment. Hence, the relationship between this minority and the state is ambivalent and ambiguous: the identity of individuals belonging to the Palestinian minority often straddles between being citizens and bearers of democratic rights in a non-liberal democratic state, and being members of a minority and "enemy" nation.

Palestinian citizens of Israel are eligible for the rights and legal protections provided for by the democratic system in Israel. They have recourse to the Israeli legal and judicial system, they vote in local and national elections, and are represented by

Arab political parties in the national parliament and in local government.[5] However, there are many ways in which members of the Palestinian minority are treated unequally. Some of that inequality is a function of their identity as non-Jews in a Jewish state. Eligibility for land ownership and property rights in large portions of the territory of the state, alongside "homeland" immigration rights, for example, are the exclusive rights of Jews.

In addition, there exists deep inequality in government budget allocation in most areas—including education, welfare, and health. Thus, despite changes over the years, the Palestinian minority in Israel is considered both a marginalized and discriminated minority and viewed by many Jewish Israelis with suspicion. In a 2015 survey conducted by the Israel Democracy Institute, close to 70 percent of the Israeli population felt that relations between the Jews and Arabs in Israel are the most polarized amongst all different groups; close to 60 percent of the Jewish population opposed the inclusion of Palestinian political parties in ruling coalitions and close to 40 percent of Israeli Jews were unwilling to have Arabs as their neighbors. Nonetheless, despite their marginalized status in Israeli society, the Palestinian minority collectively is afforded a number of cultural accommodations, whose official purpose is to allow this group to exercise their own cultural/religious/national identity, within a society that is committed to the majority culture.

Group rights of the Palestinian minority

The Palestinian minority is afforded a certain degree of cultural autonomy in three areas: language, religion, and education. In addition, members of the minority are de facto exempt from compulsory military service, though they are permitted to volunteer. While the first three mechanisms constitute significant cultural rights, and if properly implemented go a long way to both maintain and preserve minority cultures, two issues prevent their full implementation. The first is the fact that their implementation is often inconsistent and lacking. This is particularly evident, as demonstrated below, in the case of language rights. The second issue involves the control over the design and extent of the rights themselves. As illustrated in the previous section, the collective accommodations awarded to the ultra-orthodox Jews were granted by the state through a process of negotiation with the leadership of the minority itself; in the case of the Palestinian minority, accommodations were imposed upon them in a series of one-sided decisions, taken by the Jewish Israeli leadership. Hence, they are more likely to produce a feeling of *control* than recognition. The final "right"—exemption from military service—is less of a right and more of a designation accorded to the minority by the state.

Israel recognizes two official languages: Hebrew and Arabic. The right to their own language—Arabic—accorded to the Palestinian minority, is legally based in legislation inherited by the Israeli legal system from the British Mandate. The law dictates that the state needs to ensure that its citizens are able to "converse" with state offices in their own language—specifically, in Arabic and in Hebrew. The law focuses both on the need for citizens to be able to freely approach the state and be understood, as well as the need for the state to communicate its proclamations in the language spoken by its citizens. The commonly accepted implications of this law are that Arabic speaking citizens be free to use Arabic in their communication with government offices and with the legal system. Lacking any explicit reference to the preservation and value of culture, most legal scholars have pointed out that the language rights for the Arab minority are presented as the individual liberal right to language and the right to equality and not as a specific group right. Moreover, the law is barely implemented in mixed cities and in most government-run offices, with Arabic speakers clearly disadvantaged. Finally, given that Hebrew is the main language of commerce, higher education and the media, and that Israeli society is not a bi-lingual but rather a uni-lingual society—the ability of the minority to truly exercise this right to language is severely curtailed (Pinto 2009, pp. 26–52).

In terms of education, a separate educational track was established for the Palestinian minority, in which the language of instruction is Arabic. In these schools, Hebrew is taught as a second language. The schools are public, fully funded by the state, and under the supervision of the Ministry of Education. As opposed to the implementation of the language rights, implementation of the separate educational system for Israel's Arabic speaking citizens is pervasive; indeed, up until the reform instituted in 1970, members of the Arab minority were unable to attend Hebrew-language schools. The system covers both primary and secondary schools. Parallel to the state-sponsored Arabic language schools, the state permits and funds a separate private educational system, which services mainly Christian Arabs and is run primarily through the church system (Al-Haj 2002).

While educational rights are seen as a main vehicle for the self-expression of minority identity, the language of instruction is only one component of an independent educational system; the determining of curricula is the other, and is no less significant. In Israel, the curricula of the Arabic language schools mirrors the curricula of the Jewish educational tract and is determined by committees, with minimal or no input from the minority itself. The school curricula does not incorporate Arabic literature, Palestinian history or Palestinian traditions, and is commonly seen, by members of the minority, as a means of the majority culture to further inculcate the dominant culture and history and not as a means of preserving and maintaining the minority culture.

The religious rights accorded to the minority reflect a very similar paradigm. These rights are embedded legally in the Ottoman milet system inherited by the state of Israel, whereby issues of personal status—for example, marriage, divorce, burial, birth—are under the exclusive jurisdiction of the separate Muslim, Christian and Jewish religious courts. As is the case with the Jews, the authority of the religious courts is imposed upon the non-religious population, affording secular Palestinian citizens of Israel with no avenue for civil divorce or marriage. This has particularly difficult implications for women, whose status under Muslim law is significantly curtailed (Karayanni 2007).

To conclude, while the Palestinian minority are seemingly accorded group rights and hence by implication are accorded the status of a national minority—the negligible implementation alongside the lack of control by the minority itself render these rights only partially effective in maintaining and preserving the minority culture. Indeed, it could be argued that they succeed in isolating and excluding the minority even further.

Discussion and conclusion

Having provided an overview of the main multicultural accommodations that Israel has developed vis-à-vis the Jewish majority and the Palestinian minority over the years, this essay now returns to its point of departure. What is the goal of multicultural accommodation, and why should states accommodate cultural difference? The self-evident goal of any multicultural accommodation is to provide what has come to be seen as a basic right: the right of groups to exercise their own culture freely, and fully. However, implicit within this goal is the growing understanding that the long-term stability of culturally diverse societies is dependent today upon a certain degree of multicultural accommodation. In short: that the ability of groups to live *together* is dependent upon the proper and just recognition of their *difference*. Hence, multiculturalism has two goals: the first is the well-being of the group, and the second is the well-being of the larger society. So the first question to address in this closing section is: does Israel's matrix of cultural accommodation policies contribute to the well-being of the different groups within the state? Have they facilitated the groups' ability to exercise their own culture freely and fully?

The group that has benefitted the most by cultural and national accommodations provided by Israel is undoubtedly the Jewish majority group. The reality of Jewish sovereignty, its impact on national symbols, immigration policy, distribution of land, the development of the Hebrew language and culture, all of these have undoubtedly enabled the Jewish nation to express its cultural identity freely and, some would argue, fully. However, the price paid for this achievement has been dear. First, because of the reluctance of Israel to distinguish between religion and nationality, and Israel's heavy commitment to managing religion, growing numbers of Israel's secular Jewish population feel that the religious identity of the state is dominating its more secular national identity, and that the accommodations made to the ultra-orthodox Jewish group have given them the power to increasingly impose norms of behavior and cultural values that are anathema to the other essentially secular and liberal-minded members. Hence, increasingly it is difficult to extricate the secular-cultural Jewish identity from the state-sponsored Jewish religious identity.

The second price is the growing understanding by the Jewish members of society, that the maintenance of a Jewish national state which supports an exclusively Jewish national identity is potentially exclusionary of members of the other, non-Jewish groups—specifically, the non-Jewish Palestinian minority. The growing anti-pluralist legislation, passed by right-wing parties since the 18th Israeli Knesset, is testimony to the fragile nature of democratic equality in such a national and political context (Ozacky-Lazar and Jabareen 2016).[6] Widespread recognition (and growing support) of the decline of the democratic dimension of Israeli society is evident on many dimensions of Israeli public life.

Nonetheless, while the cultural accommodations have been at least partially successful for the cultural expression of members of the Jewish majority, they have been almost singularly *ineffective* in their impact on the Palestinian minority. The status of Arabic is inferior to that of Hebrew and it is not realistically possible to conduct a full life in Arabic alone; the schools are underfunded compared to their Jewish counterparts and the curriculum does not reflect the national culture; the exemption from army service often serves to marginalize the minority even further when seeking employment, housing and education benefits. And finally, in terms of religious autonomy, the fact that personal status issues are under the exclusive jurisdiction of religious courts, and that Israel has not adopted a civil institute of marriage and divorce that one can opt out to, undermines the idea that the realm of religious autonomy contributes to the free and open expression of cultural identity.

Thus, the answer to the question of whether Israeli policies benefit minority groups sadly seems to be—no, not really. The accommodations have indeed benefited parts of the Jewish majority, but have failed in their ability to enhance the freedom and self-realization of the Palestinian minority as well as that of large parts of the Jewish majority. So this essay now turns to the second question: have the cultural accommodations contributed to the peaceful co-existence of the different groups and hence to the long-term stability of the society as a whole?

To answer this question, one must return to President Rivlin's "Speech of the Tribes." In his speech Rivlin noted that over time, and particularly since the decline of the hegemonic (albeit exclusionary) core of Israeli society constituted by the Labor movement, the population in Israel has grown to include four more or less equal groups lacking a dominant core; each one feeling victimized by the other. Survey and opinion data confirm this sorry situation, with increasingly high numbers of Israelis testifying to their declining levels of identification with Israelis outside of their own group. This is evident both in relations between secular and religious Jews, and between Jews and Palestinians. Herein lies the tremendous conundrum of Israeli society: the implementation of multicultural accommodations—most critically language and educational rights for the Palestinian minority and religious autonomy and control for the ultra-orthodox group—have served not to diminish conflict between the groups and facilitate stability, but in fact the opposite: to enhance suspicion and hostility and most critically, to fuel a shared sense of victimhood and persecution. Israeli diversity has transformed into fragmentation.

Nevertheless, Israel's predicament is not unique. One of the most fundamental and common problems facing multicultural societies is how to keep the society together. In other words: How do we prevent multicultural mechanisms from transforming into mechanisms of separation and domination? The growing intensity surrounding independence referenda in Canada, Spain and Great Britain are testimony to what Will Kymlicka (2000) has called the "slippery slope" of cultural rights. And if this slope is a slippery one in societies such as those mentioned above, where the answer to our first question was affirmative—then how much more slippery is that slope in Israel where the answer to our first question was largely negative, when the cultural rights granted do not even really satisfy the *internal* needs of the group members.

One of the solutions that theorists have provided to this problem is the strengthening of a sphere or concept of shared citizenship, which implies that citizens in a society are bound together not merely by the fact that they hold the same passport and vote in the same elections. Instead, diverse groups should be encouraged to share a certain sense of common identity that allows them to tolerate the presence and rights of others, and to acknowledge the legitimacy of those requests. Lacking these very basic assumptions, the provision of group rights and different degrees of autonomy can give rise to hostility, a sense of victimhood and competition. Within societies that lack this kind of common base, the dangers of limited rights and autonomy seem to far outweigh the benefits.

In Israel, as Yoav Peled wrote so presciently nearly three decades ago, there is not one shared citizenship regime, but three, divided along the ethno-religious lines (Peled 1992, pp. 432–443). Similarly, as many other observers have noted, the groups within Israeli society are separated not merely by different identities, but by different imaginaries of what Israeli society should be. The problems facing a shared conception of citizenship in Israel are multiple, but at their core there are two. The first is the deep disagreement among some members of the Jewish group as to the definition of Jewish statehood: should Israel be a religious state, or a fundamentally secular one with a separation of religious and political institutions and hence the ability to forge a secular public sphere? The second deep disagreement exists among some members of the Palestinian group and those of the Jewish group as to the definition of the national collective: should it continue to be defined as a Jewish state, dedicated first and foremost to the well-being of the Jewish nation, or should it be defined as a bi-national state? Hence, three imaginaries exist within Israeli society, polarized and distinct from one another: the first of Israel as a religious state; the second of Israel as a bi-national state; and the third of a liberal Jewish state.

Perhaps the solution for Israel's future lies in examining its past. During Israel's first decade of statehood, when everything was new, and reality—though dire— seemed somehow full of possibility, a number of political movements, from both the left and the right of the political map, forwarded the idea that Israel be constituted not as the nation-state of the *Jewish* nation but of the *Israeli* nation. The idea was not that Israel would disavow its commitment to the re-birth of the Jewish people, but that Israel would foster a shared national identity that would be able to coexist alongside the diversity inherent in Israeli society. This would promote an Israeli national identity that would incorporate, but not negate, the diverse religious, ethnic and even national identities that constituted Israeli society.

An Israeli nationality would provide citizens not merely with an Israeli passport and I.D. number, but with a shared and equal attachment to the national project; a realm of citizenship that would allow Muslims, Christians, Jews—secular and religious—western and eastern—to partake in a common culture. Thus, a distinctly Israeli identity could ensure that Israel's national identity therefore be distinguished from its religious identity, allowing for a significant basis of shared values. This national identity would be secular and liberal, while also able to incorporate and not negate diversity of beliefs and identities.

In 2010, the Israeli Supreme Court denied an appeal by an organization called "I am Israeli" to allow their members to register, in the official state registrar, as members of the Israeli nationality. The majority opinion stated that as of yet, no such nationality has developed. Indeed today, close to seventy years after the creation of the Israeli state, Israel refuses to recognize the official existence of an Israeli nationality, distinct from the Jewish nationality. Ultimately, the recognition of, and support for the idea of an inclusive Israeli national identity offers one possible way out of the conundrum described above, by allowing Israelis of different shades not only to live apart, but also to harbor the possibility of living together.

Notes

1 Within the larger "Jewish" population I count the 4 percent of Israel's population who are non-Arab non-Jews—mainly immigrants from the FSU who managed to gain citizenship through the Law of Return but are not Jewish according to religious law. Hence while they are not Jewish according to their religion, they are Jewish by nationality. Unless otherwise noted, the statistics I bring in this essay are based on the Social Survey conducted by the Israeli Central Bureau of Statistics, 2015.
2 This data is from the Israeli Democracy Index 2015 published by the Israel Democracy Institute.
3 I use the term "state-nationality" to refer to that nation for whom the state, in legal terms, exists. In most democratic nation-states the state-nationality overlaps with the body of citizens; in Israel, it does not but is defined by membership in the Jewish group.
4 Up until 1999 the Israeli identification cards, required of all Israeli citizens over the age of 16 to carry at all times, identified citizens on the basis of nationality, with the Jewish citizens designated as members of the Jewish nationality, and the minority Palestinians as members of the Arab nationality.
5 In the 2015 elections the four Palestinian parties merged into one joint party and won thirteen seats in the Israeli parliament, making them the third largest party in power.
6 After this book went to press, in the summer of 2018, the Israeli parliament passed the "Nation-State Law" aimed to entrench Israel's Jewish identity in a basic law. The law makes no mention or acknowledgment of the status of the non-Jewish minorities. Widespread protest amongst the non-Jewish minority - particularly the Druze members – erupted.

References and further reading

Al-Haj, Majid. 2002. "Multiculturalism in Deeply Divided Societies: The Israeli Case." *International Journal of Intercultural Relations.* 26(2), pp. 169–183.
Karayanni, Michael Mousa. 2007. "Multiculture Me no More! On Multicultural Qualifications and the Palestinian-Arab Minority of Israel." *Diogenes.* 54(3), pp. 39–58.
Kook, Rebecca B. 2002. *The Logic of Democratic Exclusion: African Americans in the United States and Palestinian Citizens in Israel.* Lanham, MD: Lexington Books.
Kymlicka, Will. 2000. *Multicultural Citizenship: A Liberal Theory of Minority Rights.* Oxford: Clarendon Press.

Lehmann, David. 2012. "Israel: State Management of Religion Or Religious Management of the State?" *Citizenship Studies.* 16(8), pp. 1029–1043.

Margalit, Avishai and Moshe Halbertal. 1994. "Liberalism and the Right to Culture." *Social Research.* 61(3), pp. 491–510.

Mautner, Menachem. 2008. *Law and Culture in Israel at the Threshold of the Twenty-First Century.* Tel Aviv: Am Oved Publishers Ltd.

Ozacky-Lazar, Sarah and Yousef Jabareen (eds.) 2016. *Conditional Citizenship: On Citizenship, Equality and Offensive Legislation.* Tel Aviv: Pardes Publishers.

Peled, Yoav. 1992. "Ethnic Democracy and the Legal Construction of Citizenship: Arab Citizens of the Jewish State." *American Political Science Review.* 86(2), pp. 432–443.

Pinto, Meital. 2009. "Who is Afraid of Language Rights in Israel?" in Avi Sagi and Ohad Nachtomy (eds.), *The Multicultural Challenge in Israel.* Boston, MA: Academic Studies Press, pp. 26–52.

Pinto, Meital. 2015. "The Absence of the Right to Culture of Minorities Within Minorities in Israel: A Tale of a Cultural Dissent Case." *Laws.* 4(3), pp. 579–601.

Yiftachel, Oren. 1999. "'Ethnocracy': The Politics of Judaizing Israel/Palestine." *Constellations.* 6(3), pp. 364–390.

Yonah, Yossi. 2007. *In Virtue of Difference: The Multicultural Project in Israel.* Jerusalem: Hakibbutz Hameuchad Publishing House.

8

RELIGION AND STATE

Ofer Zalzberg

Historical background

Israel's religious challenges, initially concentrated and mostly limited to Erase small, distinct communities, have increased in scope and gravity over the years. Against this backdrop of the growing centrality of religion-related disagreements, Israel's fundamental religious challenges have become salient for all its citizens, touching directly on the country's social contract and dividing the country. As Israelis confront these challenges, they will have to provide answers to the secular public's crisis of identity and to the incongruence between Jewish law (halacha) and concepts of modern sovereignty. Simultaneously, Israeli society is undergoing a fundamental demographic change, affecting public perceptions concerning the proper interplay of religion and state. The purpose of this essay is to describe the current questions facing the relationship between religion and state in Israel, whilst examining the divergent paths Israel may pursue in addressing these challenges.

During the early years of Israel's existence, the challenge of state building and of absorbing successive waves of new immigrants meant that religious challenges received scant attention from the public or from policymakers. Concurrently, the religious challenges that did exist were focused on two relatively small and uniform religious minorities within a hegemonic secular majority: the ultra-orthodox population, composed of highly conservative non-Zionist groups, and the national-religious population, who identified with Zionism. Strongly rejecting modern secular culture, the ultra-orthodox leaders contented themselves primarily with demanding autonomy for themselves, thereby isolating their community from the Israeli mainstream. By contrast, until the "Yom Kippur War" of October 1973, the national-religious Jewish leaders and community largely integrated into mainstream Israeli society, still unmarked by the proactive political messianism that would later become more hegemonic within this sector of Israeli society.

The broader tension between civil law and Jewish religious law (halacha) was addressed primarily by the so-called "status quo" shaped by Israel's first Prime Minister, David Ben-Gurion in 1947. The agreement sought to reassure the international community that the new State of Israel would not be a theocracy, whilst also demonstrating to the ultra-orthodox leadership that Israel will not abandon Jewish tradition. The status quo agreement was designed to mitigate some of the concerns of the ultra-orthodox leadership, thereby removing the potential threat of this community refusing to support the establishment of a Jewish state. Enshrined in a letter from Ben-Gurion to the ultra-orthodox leadership, the status quo contained various provisions: that the legal day of rest would be Shabbat (Friday night to Saturday night); family law—notably personal status issues such as marriage, divorce, burials, and Conversations—would be congruent with Jewish law (halacha), government-supported institutions will have kosher kitchens and the ultra-orthodox community would have autonomy over its educational institutions.

In practice, Israel addressed the question of family law by continuing the Ottoman *milet* ("religious community") system, in which law was personal, depending on the confessional community one belongs to, rather than applying a single law to all citizens within the state's borders. This meant that the Chief Rabbinate and Rabbinic Courts, the Churches and the Sharia Courts had sole control over family law. In sum, the state formally respected traditional law while granting individuals freedom within it. For instance, though public transport would cease for the duration of Shabbat, private citizens would be free to drive their own cars.

This arrangement entailed some significant compromises. On the one hand, the absence of public transport on Shabbat disproportionately affects poorer private citizens, who do not own cars. Many Israeli citizens were and are unable to marry and divorce in Israel, particularly those forbidden to marry by orthodox Jewish law, such as inter-faith couples and same-sex couples (Halperin-Kaddari 2015).[1] On the other hand, Israel's religious leaders were no less offended by what they saw as their complicity in many violations of Jewish religious law in the public sphere. And yet, Israeli secular and ultra-orthodox elites chose to tolerate these compromises for many years: not only because they had more pressing concerns, but also because they perceived the other group as a temporary phenomenon. Ultra-orthodox leaders tended to view secular Jews as destined to return to Jewish traditions and thus disappear from the stage of history. Likewise, secular Zionist leaders saw ultra-orthodox Jews as a remnant of an archaic past, destined to shed their strict traditions and integrate into modern Israeli society in due course.

Religious non-Jewish minorities—primarily Muslims, Christians and Druze—enjoyed a degree of autonomy, thanks to the continuation of the Ottoman milet system, but this came at a price. In the context of the 1948 Israeli War of Independence, Muslim religious institutions were intentionally weakened by the emerging state. The local institutions and vast land estates of the Waqf—an Islamic trust—were nationalized and their decisions on issues extending beyond family law required explicit state approval. Nevertheless, the Muslim religious institutions retains significant influence over Muslim Israeli citizens. Indeed, secular-minded

Muslims, Christians and Druze—as well as Israeli Jews—are constrained by the religious monopoly over life cycle events such as marriage and divorce.

Though not insignificant in size, religious Jews in the new state were clearly a minority, thus limiting their ambitions. In the Knesset, each Jewish religious community had its own political parties—the modern orthodox National Religious Party routinely held around 10 percent of the available seats in the Knesset, whereas the smaller, ultra-orthodox parties, such as Agudat Israel and Poalei Agudat Israel, held together roughly 5 percent of Knesset seats. Facing a dominant secular majority, the religious groups were content with the status quo and primarily sought autonomy. Their leaders signed Israel's Declaration of Independence in spite of its explicit egalitarian sections, such as the premise that: "[Israel] will ensure complete equality of social and political rights to all its inhabitants irrespective of religion, race or sex."

By 1953, schools within the state education sector were comprised of four currents: state-run secular schools, state-run national-religious schools, independent government-recognized ultra-orthodox schools and Arab schools. Fundamental theological and halachic reservations regarding non-Jewish citizens and secular Jews were muted because these were seen as a necessary evil; these reservations therefore did not become a major issue, due to the weakness of these religious minorities and the existential necessity felt by Israel's leadership in the early days of statehood to commit to the international community and abide by democratic norms. The waiver Ben-Gurion granted to 400 ultra-orthodox pupils from military draft, so that they could dedicate themselves to Torah study, was a symbolic exception in light of the recent holocaust that threatened to annihilate Torah study. Ben-Guron did not expect or predict that in 1977, Prime Minister Menachem Begin would extend an de-facto exemption to all of the rapidly growing Ultra-Orthodox public, who wished to dedicate themselves to Torah study.

Israel's religious challenges experienced a major shift in the 1970s and 1980s, in reaction to developments in the Israeli–Arab conflict. The June 1967 and October 1973 wars generated a theological earthquake in religious Zionism. The dramatic victory, leading to Israeli control over much of the historic Jewish homeland in the "Six-Day War" of June 1967, and the ensuing sense of near-defeat in October 1973, made the teachings of Rabbi Zvi Yehuda Kook (1891–1982), son of the first Ashkenazi Chief Rabbi of the pre-1948 Jewish community in Mandatory Palestine, much more appealing. Kook claimed that Jews should proactively strive to achieve full redemption, which will come only when the entire People of Israel live in the entire Land of Israel, under full Jewish sovereignty.

Kook's doctrine taught that settlement construction in the West Bank, also known as Judea and Samaria—the historic core of the biblical Jewish Kingdoms— forms an intrinsic part of advancement toward the third and final redemption for the Jewish people. Moreover, settlements would eventually prevent further military losses, providing security for the State of Israel. Politically, the ideological core of this new movement coalesced around Gush Emunim (Bloc of the Faithful), an extra-parliamentary, national-religious movement promoting Israeli sovereignty the Sinai Peninsula, the Golan Heights, West Bank and Gaza Strip, by settling

Israeli civilians in these areas. Whilst Gush Emunim sought to transform the culture and perceptions of the Israeli body politic, the movement met greater success in affecting policy, rather than fundamentally changing civil society. It convinced Israeli governments, of both left-wing and right-wing persuasions, to support settlement growth: by 1990 there were approximately 81,900 settlers in the West Bank (excluding East Jerusalem). However, settlement growth was primarily the product of security-centered concerns, rather than theological-messianic principles. The limited traction of religious principles was reflected in party politics, where national-religious voters remained isolated within small National Religious Party, which was committed to act in accordance with the Torah.

In parallel, ultra-orthodox party politics grew stronger and yet more fragmented politically as a result of a combination of factors: the growing size of the ultra-orthodox population, the political mobilization of Jews from Middle Eastern countries and the exclusion of Sephardic representatives from the Ashkenazi-dominated Agudat Hatora party. In 1984, Rabbi Ovadia Yosef (1920–2013) founded Shas, a party bringing together Sephardi Jews of different degrees of observance, seeking to address discrimination of this population by Ashkenazi elites—both secular and religious. Winning support from non ultra-orthodox constituencies, who sought to correct these historical wrongs, Shas was increasingly successful at the ballot box. By the early 1990s, it was established wisdom that the ultra-orthodox parties were the kingmakers of Israeli politics.

Following elections in Israel, the president of the state (a non-partisan role) consults all parties represented in the Knesset, acting on their recommendations to grant one party the right to attempt to found a coalition. Since Israeli politics is divided relatively equally, along the left–right lines pertaining to policy regarding the Israeli–Palestinian conflict, ultra-orthodox parties with narrower sectorial interests often serve as the decisive factor in a president's nomination. In the 1999 Knesset elections, Shas held seventeen out of the 120 Knesset seats, ensuring that ultra-orthodoxy reached an unprecedented peak in its political power. In response, Israel's secular public mobilized around the same issues, but with radically different outlooks, under the banner of the leftist social-democratic Meretz and the centrist liberal Shinui. The ultra-orthodox parties and their secular opponents began an "electoral tango"—a tit-for-tat escalatory dynamic—which led to their respective gains at the ballot box and to an increasingly polarized public discourse.

Indeed, as a result of this underlying tension, secular–religious conflicts have become more common and more political. Liberals and ultra-orthodox activists vociferously demonstrated for and against the opening of Jerusalem's Bar Ilan Road, a major throughway in a majority ultra-orthodox area, on Shabbat (the so-called "Shabbat Battles"). Secular and religious Israeli Zionists demanded an end to the exemption from military service for ultra-orthodox Jewish seminary students, while ultra-orthodox parties conditioned their political support on its continuation. LGBT rights activists paraded in Tel Aviv, while ultra-orthodox activists demonstrated against same-sex relations. The status of women generated tensions, over issues as diverse as separate sidewalks for women and men in highly conservative areas of ultra-orthodox areas of Jerusalem, segregated seating on bus lines which mainly serve ultra-orthodox passengers and allowing orthodox soldiers to leave the room, when a female singer would perform. These tensions increased as Israeli society undergoes a changing of elites: a shift from the center-left Mapai's so-called Melting Pot policy—assimilating Jewish immigrants into socialist, secular Zionism while suppressing their original cultures—to religious Zionism's attempts to fashion Israeli society in its own image.

The late national-religious journalist, Bambi Sheleg—a sharp observer of Israeli society and politics—argued the kernel of Israel's dysfunctional foreign and domestic policies is rooted in the failure of these two elites to address the basic denial underlying their thinking (Sheleg 2005). Mapai's left-wing or liberal successors, Sheleg argued, are focused on self-realization and on importing Western practices and norms, "even when these are irrelevant to a young and vulnerable Israel" and have "a drastic deficit in commitment to the spiritual and cultural future of the [Jewish] people." The same trends of opting for particular identity over cosmopolitan attitudes could be seen elsewhere in the West: for example, in the 2016 British vote to leave the European Union. In contrast, Kook's adherents, Sheleg claimed, have an overdose of Jewish commitments. They are therefore blind to the existence and rights of non-Jews, feel solely responsible for the spiritual and cultural future of the Jewish people and believe that the entire Jewish people will and should look exactly like them. It is these dual challenges which Israeli leaders and Israeli society—both religious and secular—need to address.

The central religious challenges today

The most dramatic change in the manner Israeli society addresses its religious challenges occurred during the 1990s, creating a dissonant conversation about state and religion that continues to this day. As the Cold War ended with a US victory, Israel opened up to globalization in an unprecedented scope: imports and exports spiked, Western norms became central in the intra-Israeli conversation and legislators emulated international—particularly Western—laws. The controversy over these processes was somewhat stifled by tensions over the concurrent Oslo peace process with the Palestinians. Yet peacemaking was perceived as part of the project of opening Israel up to the world, by accepting international norms and shedding parts of Israel's historical homeland and Jewish traditions. These changes were not limited to one side of the political spectrum: what now defined the political left and right in Israel was support, or opposition, to the two-state solution.

The public conversation in Israel polarized, reflecting an identity crisis in Israeli society. The crisis related to differences over peacemaking, but was no less a reflection of a general crisis in the Western world, as the cosmopolitan secularization thesis (the notion that religion will decline in the modern industrialized era) collapsed and particularist identities, often grounded in religion, returned to the public and political spheres. Against this backdrop, two competing camps have emerged: a secular-liberal camp, which sees itself as responsible for the democratic dimension of the expression a "Jewish and Democratic state," and as defender of humanist and liberal values which empower individual autonomy; and a camp which sees itself as charged with ensuring Jewish continuity and the particular needs of the Jewish people, with a stronger association with Jewish religion and culture and a collectivist moral worldview.

The tensions between the two camps are divided between two layers. The first layer focuses on the practices of individuals and communities, particularly the state's administration of religious services like marriage, divorce, burial and conversion, as well as regulations and funding for providing synagogues, Kosher food and ritual baths. The second layer focuses on the state's national Jewish character and the manners in which it can be realized within the state. These include the passing of the controversial Jewish nation-state law, which defines Israel as the nation-state of the Jewish people (downgrading of collective rights for the Arab minority); the Conversion law, which defines not only who is Jewish but what is Jewishness; the struggles over the rites and practices permitted at sacred sites, most notably the Western Wall; the specific contestation over the Temple Mount, which lies within the tension between realizing Jewish sovereignty over it and shifting towards radical messianism and loss of political realism; and the question of the attitude towards the Arab minority, in terms of the rights of its members collectively and as individuals.

The secular crisis of identity

For the secular-liberal camp, increased exposure to the West made the pre-existing religious–secular contradictions both more flagrant and offensive. Additionally, the dynamics of the Israeli–Palestinian conflict contributed to societal divisions. The terror attacks during the Oslo process, the failure of the Camp David talks, the ensuing Second Intifada and the Israeli withdrawal from the Gaza Strip pushed the entire Israeli body politic to the right. This was the case not only in terms of skepticism regarding a peace agreement with the Palestinians, but increasingly also with respect to preferring Jewish identity over cosmopolitanism. With territorial compromise appearing increasingly irrelevant, left and right became defined by the question of being first and foremost Israeli or Jewish.

However, Israeli Jews became gradually exposed to the fact that their leaders had no easy answer as to what it means to be Jewish, when steering a modern sovereign state. The minimalist national secular reply—ensuring a Jewish majority—failed to satisfy a non-religious public experiencing a crisis as to what being Jewish actually is. Secular, national Jewish identity failed to placate a public once satisfied with this paradigm. Confronted with the challenges of growing exposure to the west, the intensification of globalization, an increasing sense of existential threat as a result of the violent escalation of the Israeli–Palestinian conflict and statements by Israel's own leaders about the many existential threats faced by the state, led to a new public search for a collective identity (Ram 2009). The crisis of secular identity in Israel also emanated from non-Israeli factors, corresponding with the resurgence of religion in the Middle East and beyond.

In short, the answers of religious and national elites to the identity crisis facing the Israeli public were deemed largely irrelevant by most secular Jews. The center of gravity of secular Zionists—of both the Labor and the Revisionist strands—moved from national dedication to self-realization. Instead of perceiving "success" to constitute dedicating one's life to politics or to a military career, secular Israelis increasingly turned to making innovative contributions to Israel's groundbreaking start-up companies and the idea of Israel as the Start-up Nation (Senor and Singer 2009). The increasing global awareness of many in the secular Zionist camp led its members to pursue international business activities and to move to leading academic and research institutions worldwide. Thus, the Western focus on self-realization and civic identities provided secular Zionists with an answer to the growing dissonance between a universalistic worldview and an increasingly ethno-centrist society.

The answer of Israel's ultra-orthodox to the crisis of modernity was primarily focused around increased isolation in closed communities, thereby protecting Jewish identity from global influences; thus, this group had scant input in most areas of policymaking. By contrast, secular ultra-nationalism, led by right-wing politicians like Avigdor Lieberman, ascended after the Second Intifada, thanks to the simplistic answer it provided to the crisis of identity. This simplistic answer came in the form of an enemy: an approach of self-definition based on the exclusive message of "we are the ones who are against the Arabs." National-religious politicians failed repeatedly to convince the public that their thinking was sufficiently in line with modernity—both in terms of its strong empowerment of the individual and of the contemporary state system and its constraints—and it was only recently, when led by the successful, globally-minded businessman, Naftali Bennett, that their popularity reached other, non-religious parts of society (Herman et al. 2014).[2]

Despite the crisis of identity and security, most secular Jews continued following their own respective elites and voting for them. The main phenomenon appearing in reaction to the crisis of identity was the Jewish Renewal sector: organizations and communities offering paths to connect to Jewish identity in a variety of ways (Newberg 2013).[3] These activities enable secular Zionist Jews to reclaim Jewish diasporic texts and resources without becoming religious and to renew interest in contemporary Hebrew culture. The early Zionist revolution came with a rupture from tradition. Breaking away from the politically passive religious state of mind that often characterized Diaspora Judaism—most emblematically Europe's ultra-orthodox communities—was probably necessary for Zionism's success. But it came at a cost: hostility toward the traditional texts, which came to sanctify political passivity. In contrast, the Jewish Renewal phenomenon seeks to overcome the hostility and reassert ownership of tradition. Limited so far to tens of thousands of Israeli Jews, the nascent phenomenon raises the cardinal question: can cultural nationalism address the identity crisis of secular ethnic nationalism? This will depend primarily on whether cultural engagement will be limited to the individual realm, or if it can become a motivating collective force. It is with the latter in mind that the renowned Israeli author Yochi Brandes named this phenomenon "the Second Zionist Revolution."

By contrast, the masorti (traditional) public, a major constituent of Israeli society composed primarily of Jews from Islamic countries, has been historically characterized by more flexibility toward Jewish law. Self-defining masorti Jews often oscillate between periods in which they would be more or less observant of Jewish law and selective with respect to the parts of it they opt to respect or ignore (Yadgar 2011). Moreover, the masorti public is divided by those who self-define as traditional-secular (masorti-hiloni) and those who define themselves as traditional-religious (masorti-dati). The former largely corresponds with the category that sociologist Nissim Leon coined "gray Mizrachiut": un-emphasized, un-ideological and focused on individualized social mobility. This phenomenon has grown in size since the late 1970s, as a result of increasing social mobilization among the Sephardi population. Their main sources of inspiration for the traditional-secular population are inherited parental customs. While this is true also of the traditional-religious, the latter group also seeks to abide by rabbinic guidance and is often more strict in observance. Opinion polling in 2012 suggested that the traditional public is divided between roughly two-thirds that are traditional-secular and one-third that is traditional-religious (Central Bureau of Statistics 2012).

Halachic incongruence with modern sovereignty

Concurrent to the crises affecting the secular population, Israel's religious leaders face no less serious challenges of their own. Exposure to the west increased a sense of threat to Jewish continuity felt by the religious public—that Hollywood, McDonalds and the internet would inundate and replace Jewish culture and tradition, eroding long-held conservative family values, while international institutions and law would override their Jewish equivalents. The so-called Constitutional Revolution, which occurred in the early 1990s, threatened the same camp who saw liberalizing constitutional changes as demonstrative of increasing systematic preference for individual rights over collective identity and for Western-inspired Israeli law to override Jewish law. During this period, the Israeli Supreme Court granted two new basic laws dealing with human rights a supra-legal status: Basic Law: Human Dignity, and Freedom and Basic Law: Freedom of Occupation. These laws, for example, to a ruling in 1992, where the Supreme Court decided to allow the import of pork, in spite of Israel's kosher laws. For a public viewing the halacha as the kernel of Jewish persistence and as reflective of the divine, these transformations were considered a major threat, with most reacting by seeking to rigidly preserve the halacha as it is, rather than adapting Jewish tradition to changing circumstances.

This intransigent attitude only made it more difficult for religious leaders to adapt the halacha to the challenges of life in modern Israel. The halacha was created by rabbis during centuries in which Jews lived in communities under foreign rule: it is presently not adapted to exercising Jewish sovereignty. To the extent that the Rabbis can draw on pre-halachic periods for inspiration about Jewish sovereignty during biblical times, they find decisions and patterns of behavior that were relevant for pre-modern times. Copying and pasting them to today's reality is highly challenging. For example, the controversial public letter of 2011 signed by dozens of primarily national-religious rabbis, forbids selling and renting houses to Arabs, clashing with the modern concept of citizenship and the norm of equality in a democratic state. Moreover, Jewish decision-making during the last two millennia was guided by the halacha, which was created when rabbis had power only over their own relatively uniform Jewish community. But the conditions of sovereignty in modern Israel are such that decisions affect four specific groups: Jews of various kinds within Israel, non-Jews in Israel, Jews outside Israel and non-Jews near Israel. Unlike community rabbis in Yemen and Poland, the halacha therefore has to confront new challenges, without precedent in Jewish history.

First, Jewish society is much more diverse, not least due to the prevalence of atheism and secularism, posing a challenge to those seeing the halacha as a framework to ensure Jewish continuity and to pass on divine truths. Second, roughly a fifth of Israel's population is non-Jewish, defying pre-modern Jewish notions, which limit citizenship, property ownership and collective rights to the single dominant ethnicity. Third, world Jewry is influenced by Israeli decisions, because both non-Jews and Jews often identify Israel with Jewishness. Concepts like negating the diaspora are challenged by a world in which the State of Israel needs the support of Jews who live outside its borders. Fourth, the presence of millions of Palestinians between the Jordan River and the Mediterranean Sea forces rabbis to struggle with dramatic halachic, theological and eschatological questions. What individual and collective rights should be accorded to non-Jews under Jewish sovereignty? Under which conditions, if any, can territorial concessions be religiously correct? How can Israel address the tension between the messianic aspirations of building a Third Temple and the mundane, complex geopolitical realities of the modern world?

Unable to address these conceptual lacunae, religious Zionist political activists repeatedly failed in securing Gush Emunim's redemptory objectives. For the ideological core of Israel's national-religious public, the most evident failure was the inability of the national-religious parties to prevent the 2005 Gaza Disengagement. When Prime Minister Ariel Sharon brought the decision to uproot 8,000 primarily national-religious settlers from Gaza to a vote at the cabinet, he fired ministers from coalition parties who opposed the decision. Subsequently, a significant number of activists within the religious right changed strategy, shifting away from the sectorial national-religious parties to the governing, more mainstream Likud party, registering national-religious voters as members of the Likud. By 2013, this strategy bore fruit, as pro-settlement cliques acquired roughly a third of the votes within the party institutions, such as in primaries (International Crisis Group 2013).[4] Because there are no powerful blocs with opposite agendas within the Likud (e.g. pro-two states or favoring separation of religion from the state) national-religious mobilization strongly colored the party's entire agenda in Rabbi Kook's colors. Because of a national, dramatic decline in party membership across the board, the entryism of the religious right was made even more significant, increasing this group's power.

In contrast, ultra-orthodox politics has been affected primarily by the rapid rise of ultra-orthodox independent media and growing internet usage within the community. Having lost their near-monopoly of information over their constituents, ultra-orthodox politicians found themselves repeatedly embarrassed. In September 2016, a coalition crisis was born after a report in an ultra-orthodox news website exposed work on Shabbat at the Haifa Port. Driven by pressure from their previously complacent public, the reaction of the ultra-orthodox political elite was profound and inflexible, going beyond the de facto compromises the very same politicians agreed to behind the scenes.

The changing demographic composition of society

With secular–religious and Jewish–Arab tensions mounting, and long-term trends suggesting that Israel is undergoing fundamental changes, Israel's President— Reuven Rivlin—responded to these trends in 2015 with a seminal presidential speech. In his "Four Tribes Speech," Rivlin argued that Israelis have no choice but to craft "a new Israeli order": a new social contract. Rivlin based his speech on analysis of data of first grade classes in 2018, that indicates Israeli society is undergoing a far-reaching, demographic transformation: from having a clear, firmly secular Zionist majority and a few minority groups, to the future status quo of no clear majority or minority groups.[5] Children in each of the four tribes are educated to have a dramatically different outlook regarding fundamental values and the character of the State of Israel, leading Rivlin to ask: "Will this be a secular, liberal state, Jewish and democratic? Will it be a state based on Jewish religious law? Or a religious democratic state? Will it be a state of all its citizens, of all its national ethnic groups?" Whereas Zionism was the shared ideology, with military service constituting the melting pot of traditional Israeli society, in the emerging reality based on demographics in first grade classes, less than half of the population explicitly defines itself as Zionist, or serves in the army.[6] The future remains hard to predict, not least because Israeli society is undergoing deep parallel processes of both religionization and secularization (Ben Porat 2013).

But the status quo can no longer be taken for granted, and religious answers to the question of what constitutes "Israeliness" are markedly different from secular ones. The central religious challenge today therefore concerns the state's entire identity and is decisive for its future. The main religious challenge of contemporary Israel is weaving a social contract, which compromises as minimally as possible both individual autonomy and Jewish continuity, satisfying the competing demands of as many stakeholders as possible. The challenge is particularly complex, because it has to be addressed in the context of the changing of elites in Israel and the decline of traditional power brokers.

Future options

Within contemporary Israel, competing normative visions of the future coalesce around three distinct, broad options. The first is an Israel, in which a conservative interpretation of the halacha is the lynchpin. In such an Israel, Knesset legislation will increasingly reflect religious law. Religion will gradually be taught in secular schools—and Jewishness will be defined around loyalty to the Torah. Steadily, the public sphere will come to be governed by the halacha. Encouraged by demographic trends, namely the growing numbers of ultra-orthodox and national-religious Jews, the growing de facto acceptance of Zionism among the ultra-orthodox, and the increasing conservatism in parts of the national-religious public, which seeks to shield itself from globalization, advocates come primarily from the national-ultra-orthodox communities. In the absence of major adaptations of the halacha to the condition of modern sovereignty, such a transformation will violate human rights in many ways, most notably with respect to the non-Jewish and secular population of Israel. In the 2015 elections, the most prominent advocate of this scenario was the Yachad ["Together" in Hebrew] party, led by a coalition of nationalist ultra-orthodox and socially conservative national-religious politicians. That the party failed to cross the electoral threshold suggests this vision currently lacks a critical mass of support.

The second option is an Israel in which there is a further separation of state and religion than the current status quo. Among the practical demands of advocates of this approach are civil weddings in town halls, abolishing (or diluting) the Chief Rabbinate and the operation of public transport regularly on Shabbat. Finding encouragement in Supreme Court rulings and support from US Jewry, liberal advocates promote a future in which liberal democratic elements of the state's character would take precedence over its Jewishness. Religious advocates of this approach, often US-born, tend to emphasize the US model, arguing separation would allow religion to prosper. Secular advocates, usually of European origins, tend to focus on the French model, seeking to limit religious practice to the private sphere. Such a reality would force ultra-orthodox and national-religious Jews to maintain genealogical lists in order to ensure they do not marry Israeli citizens who are classed as non-Jews according to their definition of the halacha. In the absence of major changes in the priority liberals accord to Jewish continuity, in such a reality secular life will become increasingly distant from Jewish identity in the sense of daily personal practices. The leftist Meretz and some elements of the Arab Joint List are the main advocates for this scenario.

The third approach consists of an Israel which embraces a plurality of ways of being Jewish. Advocates of such a hybrid model call on the state to recognize and allocate resources to different Jewish currents. They work to complement the Chief Rabbinate with a civil marriage track, while promoting multiple public spheres—halachic, free and hybrid; for example, a public swimming pool would operate at different times, according to these different norms. In such a scenario, Jewishness will be defined as national in the broadest sense of the word, including both religious and cultural realizations of identity. This reality, too, has manifestations across Israel as different towns have in effect embraced one of these three models: the public sphere in Tel Aviv is essentially secular, in nearby Bnei Barak it is conservative-halachic and in Rehovot a hybrid reality exists, with an ultra-orthodox mayor ensuring the public swimming pool is open on Saturday while the selling of tickets takes place only on weekdays; during the week there are both separate and mixed bathing times for women and men. No political parties promote this from the outset, but many engage in similar post-facto compromises. Individual MKs from the Jewish Renewal sector and the liberal wings of the national-religious and ultra-orthodox populations, affiliated primarily with centrist parties like Yesh Atid, Kulanu and Am Shalem—where secular and religious politicians sit together—stand out in promoting such a scenario as desirable pluralism, rather than accepting it post-facto as a reality. Such a scenario is thought to be particularly appealing to the Masorti community, who balance individual autonomy and respect for Jewish tradition.

The determining factors for the weaving of a new social contract

Three principal factors will determine how Israel would address the religious challenges it faces. The first is the ongoing evolution of secular attitudes: will uncompromising liberalism or post-secular liberalism gain the upper hand? Will secular Israelis embrace an attitude allowing religious expressions and practice in the public sphere? Will secular Jews focus exclusively on the self, their own community and universal solidarity, or will they also demonstrate commitment to Jewish cultural continuity? Will secular Jews teach seminal texts of diasporic Judaism and will they do so employing religious-halachic teachings, or secular-cultural ones?

The second factor is the adaptation of the halacha, in the midst of a crisis of rabbinic authority. Will rabbinic leaders adapt the halacha to the unprecedented reality and challenges of modern Jewish sovereignty? Will religious communities be chiefly guided by illiberal rabbinic guidance, or by liberal rabbinic guidance? Will Israel witness the decline of rabbinic guidance altogether? On these issues two trends are central: the fragmentation of the rabbinic establishment and the receding importance of rabbinic guidance for many religious Jewish Israelis.

The fragmentation of the rabbinic establishment is increasingly salient in both the national-religious and ultra-orthodox communities. Since Rabbi Zvi Kook passed away, religious Zionism shifted away from a single rabbinic authority to several competing ones. Equally, ultra-orthodoxy no longer possesses a clear Gdol Hador—a rabbi recognized as the greatest sage of the generation. Following the death of Rabbi Eliyashiv in 2012, the Ashkenazi Lithuanian community split into two political parties: Degel Hatorah and Bnei Torah—competing with each other in municipal elections. Similarly, the Sephardic ultra-orthodox Shas party witnessed a split on the eve of the 2013 national elections, with Shas's former chairperson Eli Yishai departing with several prominent rabbis to found the Yachad party. Though Yachad failed to cross the electoral threshold, it attracted many voters from Shas and posed a major blow to its purportedly irrefutable religious credentials. Religious fragmentation means halachic change is both easier and more difficult. Change is easier because it is no longer clear to observant people what God actually "thinks" or, figuratively speaking, how God would vote, making it easier for individuals to pursue a different path than rabbinic guidance suggests. In such cases,

individuals often decide based on substantive considerations, as opposed to theoretical principled-theological ones. Yet halachic change is also made more difficult,
because rabbis feel vulnerable when making decisions, for which others would
criticize them as misreading the divine will. Many rabbis therefore argue it would
take a new *gdol hador* for truly significant rulings to be issued. If in the past a Prime
Minister seeking religious legitimacy to a decision needed to secure the support
only of the national-religious and ultra-orthodox *gdol hador*, today he or she needs
to engage with over twenty prominent rabbis.

The decline in deference to rabbinic authority (*da'at torah*)[7]—or rather the
increase in individual autonomy—is salient in both the national-religious and
the ultra-orthodox populations. Rabbi Yuval Sherlow estimates that two-thirds
of Israel's national-religious population seeks rabbinic guidance only on the most
obviously religious issues (e.g. Kosher food), but by and large not on political or
societal questions. Indeed, religious activism in which the activists themselves
decide what is the correct reading of the halacha is increasingly prevalent. For
example, there exists today two significant nonprofit religious LGBT organizations:
the *Kashrut Kehilatit* initiative allows restaurant and café owners to publicize themselves as halachically kosher in the absence of explicit authorization from the Chief
Rabbinate, or indeed any rabbi. In parallel, some of Israel's foremost scholars of
ultra-orthodoxy point to a decline in *da'at torah*, which leads to the democratization of the rabbinic leadership (Brown 2011). Due to the decreasing importance
and power of the rabbinic leadership, non-rabbinic religious leaders increasingly
shoulder the burden of leading the religious population.

The third decisive factor relates to the structuring of society, particularly the
secular–religious divide. The more government policies will promote both separate
and shared spaces for the secular and observant populations, the less this cleavage
will be characterized by an all or nothing dynamic, and vice versa. Investing heavily
therefore in the consolidation or creation of such distinct spheres—secular-liberal,
conservative-halachic and hybrid—will allow people who cannot or do not want
to share a space with those with whom they face a radical disagreement to have an
alternative to all out confrontation. Concretely this would mean, for example, that
financing ultra-orthodox cities should be a priority, in order to decrease the probability of highly tense conflicts in hybrid cities. If illiberal, ultra-orthodox Israelis
will have no residential solutions in such spaces, they will look for solutions elsewhere, creating conflict with other sectors in society. This principle holds equally
for other groups.

It is premature to state with certainty what kind of future Israel will emerge
with. But so far, it appears that the limited ability of secular leaders to propose
political solutions that also address the needs of the religious population leaves
the debate dominated by religious leaders. Simultaneously, the crisis of the rabbinic leadership suggests that religious politicians—conservative and progressive
alike—will be the ones shaping reality. In the near future, the high level of secular–
religious polarization suggests a trajectory in which changes will occur only gradually, addressing symptom by symptom, with the sequencing driven by crises and

the compromises made chiefly by progressive and conservative religious politicians. It is within these sub-optimal conditions that Israel has to address its central religious challenge today: finding a new equilibrium for the state's entire identity and weaving a new social contract, which compromises as minimally as possible both individual autonomy and Jewish continuity.

Notes

1   Israel allows for Common-law marriage and recognizes civic weddings conducted abroad. By decreasing the plight these measures in effect strengthen the religious monopoly over marriage and divorce. More than 10 per cent of the couples registering as married in Israel do so after being married abroad (Halperin-Kaddari 2015).
2   While only 10 percent of Israel's Jews self-define as "religious" in Israel's Central Bureau of Statistics poll, findings from a 2014 comprehensive poll were that at least 22 percent of Israel's Jewish population consider it "belongs to the national religious sector" (Hermann et al. 2014).
3   The most salient are pluralistic Batei Midrash and Jewish cultural ceremonies of life (circumcision, bar mitzvahs, weddings, burials, etc.) and holidays.
4   The groups numbered some 20,000 of the 120,000 Likud members and while only half of the general membership actually participates in the votes, some 90 percent of the national religious groups participate in them.
5   In 1990, the distribution was 52 percent secular Zionist, 16 percent national religious, 9 percent ultra orthodox and 23 percent Arab. First grade composition in 2018 is 38 percent secular Zionist, 15 percent national religious, 22 percent ultra orthodox and 25 percent Arab.
6   President Reuven Rivlin, Address to the 15th Annual Herzliya Conference, 7 June 2015. Available at www.president.gov.il/English/ThePresident/Speeches/Pages/news_070615_ 01.aspx.
7   *Da'at Torah* (Knowledge of the Torah) is a concept in Haredi Judaism according to which Jews should seek the input of rabbinic scholars not just on matters of Jewish law, but on all important life matters, on the grounds that knowledge of the Torah aids everything in life.

References and further reading

Ben Porat, Guy. 2013. *Between State and Synagogue: The Secularization of Contemporary Israel.* Cambridge: Cambridge University Press.
Brown, Benjamin. 2011. *Toward Democratization in the Haredi Leadership? The Doctrine of Da'at Torah at the Turn of the Twentieth and Twenty-First Centuries.* Jerusalem: Israel Democracy Institute.
Central Bureau of Statistics. 2012. The Social Survey, Israel: 2009–2010, Statistilite 124, April, p. 3. Available at www.cbs.gov.il/statistical/seker-chevrati-e124.pdf.
Halperin-Kaddari, Ruth. 2015. "Civil Marriage in Israel." *Identities: Journal of Jewish Culture and Identity.* 6, pp. 101–126.
Hermann, Tamar, Ella Heller, Hanan Mozes, Kalman Neuman, Yuval Lebel and Gilad Be'ery. 2014. *The National-Religious Sector in Israel.* Jerusalem: Israel Democracy Institute.
International Crisis Group. 2013. "Leap of Faith: Israel's National Religious and the Israeli– Palestinian Conflict." *Middle East Report.* 147. November 21.
Israel Democracy Institute, Policy Paper 89. April 2011. [Hebrew]

Israel Democracy Institute, 2014, p. 23. [Hebrew]

Newberg, Adina. 2013. "Elu v Elu: Towards integration of Identity and Multiple Narratives in the Jewish Renewal Sector and Beyond." *International Journal of Jewish Education Research (IJJER)*. 5–6, pp. 231–278.

Ram, Haggai. 2009. *Iranophobia: The Logic of an Israeli Obsession*. Stanford, CA: Stanford University Press.

Senor, Dan and Saul Singer. 2009. *Start-up Nation: The Story of Israel's Economic Miracle*. New York: Twelve.

Sheleg, Bambi. Between Two Denials, *Ma'ariv*, 2 October 2005.

Yadgar, Yaacov. 2011. *Secularism and Religion in Jewish Israeli Politics: Traditionists and Modernity*. London: Routledge.

9

EMERGING ELITES AND NEW POLITICAL IDEAS AMONGST PALESTINIANS IN ISRAEL

Amal Jamal

Arab-Palestinian society in Israel is characterized by a high degree of internal divergence within its social, political, and cultural spheres, in addition to an ongoing, deep structural transformation. In recent decades, after a long period of coping with a political defeat and a profound social crisis, a new type of political thought has begun to emerge within Arab-Palestinian society. This new political thought reflects the political will and imagination of an emerging new elite, striving to not only win recognition of its role, but also transform the entire political reality in which it lives.

The new political imagination seeks the creation of a political reality that extends far beyond the goal of normalizing the existence of Arab-Palestinian society in the Israeli state. It challenges Israel's exclusive identity as the state of the Jewish people, which is translated into policies of uprooting, marginalizing and oppressing Palestinians. The Palestinian-Arab elite, whilst being excluded from the Israeli power structure, still manages to add the colors of its unwanted identity into the Israeli collage. It forces the Jewish majority to either listen or react in manners that reveal the true character of the Israeli state, as not only illiberal, but mainly dominated by a sophisticated differential racializing ideology, which is based on segregation and a regime of preferentialism. Since the overwhelming majority of Israeli policies within the political and socioeconomic sphere are exclusively dictated by its Jewish majority, the emerging Arab elite has tried to expose the manipulations of democratic procedures by the Jewish majority, who promote policies that go against basic democratic principles, such as the protection of basic rights of indigenous-national minorities, as defined by various international conventions (Kymlicka 2008).

Israeli state institutions maintain that the views of the Arab-Palestinian public are different from those presented by the emerging elite. These institutional arguments form part of a constant campaign to delegitimize the latter, but simultaneously demonstrate that the official policies of domination—employed by the State since

1948—have not undermined the ability of the Palestinian citizens to voice the violation of their basic rights, even when they have been unable to take part in the decision-making process that determines their lives.

This essay argues that the Arab-Palestinian elite that has emerged in Israel in recent decades is, indeed, representative of the emancipatory political spirit, dominant in Palestinian society in Israel—a fact evident in its socioeconomic, regional, sectarian and ideological diversity. Simultaneously, the emerging Palestinian elite in Israel is not homogeneous; it is more representative of the oppositional consciousness of its constituent community. The factions within it are a consequence of a unique set of old and new social traits and ideologies, such as Palestinianness, indigenousness, Arabism and Islamism. These common ideological sources do not prevent the competition over power positions vis-à-vis state policies. Concurrently, the state tolerates the struggle against it to some degree, thereby containing it and legitimizing itself, as tolerant and open for change. The first signs of the emerging elite can be traced as far back as the 1980s, but it was not until the 1990s that the distinct characteristics of this elite truly emerged.

The emerging Palestinian elite in Israel has no choice but to operate from within the state's structure. This limits its ability to maneuver, forcing it to adapt to specific patterns of behavior, especially in the last three decades, when new legislation, the last of which is the nation-state law, began introducing new conditions for its participation in the political arena. As a consequence, this elite is constantly forced to fight for its existence and legitimacy.

For the purpose of theorizing this specific case, it is necessary to frame it within a structured model, as theorized, albeit slightly differently by Pierre Bourdieu (1977) and Anthony Giddens (1984). Both scholars recognized a long time ago the need to bridge the gap between structural analytic paradigms, such as the class or elitist ones, and individualistic models of society, such as rational choice or behavioral theories. They also sought to bridge the relationship between practical, economic aspects of social activity—which were limited to political economy—and cultural and symbolic aspects, which were delimited within cultural studies.

Both scholars have demonstrated that political life is created within a structure, which sets limits on the political players within it. However, the players act as agents, who seek to overcome the limitations of the structure and promote their interests, thus reshaping the structure according to their own interests and needs. Hence, according to Bourdieu (1977), the social structure is both structuring and being structured at the same time; Giddens iterated the importance of structuration as the reflection of the social process (1984). The need to reflect on the mutual implications between the structure's constraints and the agents acting as part of this structure—while also transforming it—has been theorized by other scholars from different theoretical traditions, prominent of which are Étienne Balibar (2011) and Nancy Fraser (1997). Both scholars have demonstrated the importance of dynamic analyses of the socio-political arena as a vehicle to better understand the complexities of power struggle and competition (Balibar 2002).

The defiant Palestinian elite, aware of the constraints imposed by the Israeli political and ideological structure, seeks to be creative and flexible; it is gaining experience in manipulating the structure of opportunities whenever possible, mobilizing internal resources for resistance and re-framing its struggle against the hegemonic majority in order to pull the ethical veil away from the true face of the Jewish exclusive and oppressive hegemony. These efforts are reflected in the affirmation of universal values of equality and freedom and the insistence on the principle of "part-taking" and on the transformation of the current Israeli "distribution of the sensible," as Jacques Rancière has defined it (Rancière 2004). Aware of its own weaknesses and inability to control the structure within which it acts, the Palestinian elite nevertheless exposes the Israeli political system for what it really is, whilst also forcing it to listen to the demands and utterances of the Arab elite. Thereby, this elite manages to expropriate the sovereignty of the sovereign Jewish majority and expose its unnatural hegemony. This art of politics is reflected in various forms, but due to the spatial constraints, this essay will be limited to exploring the "vision documents" published by various segments of this elite in the last decade.

Socio-demographic transformations in the Arab elites in Israel

Since the *Nakba of 1948*, which demolished the political, financial, and cultural Palestinian elite in the territories that became the State of Israel, the number of educated people, intellectuals, and professionals has been constantly on the rise (Jamal and Bsoul 2014). The Palestinian leadership in Israel went through several extreme transformations, but only some of them will be presented here. During the first few decades after the establishment of the State of Israel, the depleted state of the Arab leadership was a direct result of the *Nakba*. The vast majority of the political, financial, and cultural Palestinian elite vanished in 1948 (Sa'di and Abu-Lughod 2007). Any leader who was involved in some way in opposing the Zionist movement was deported, and those who remained were closely monitored by the Israeli security forces (Cohen 2006; Pappe 2006) Zureik, 2016.

Additionally, second- and third-rate leaders who stayed in Israel had to submit to the new rules as dictated by the state (Lustick 1980). The military regime imposed on the Arab population after the war resulted in severe limitations on freedom of speech, freedom of movement, and the freedom of assembly of the Arab public, and, in practice, prevented any real political mobilization (Bäuml 2007). In the meantime, as part of their efforts to enhance their control over Arab society, the Israeli authorities began nurturing young and ambitious members of the more dominant clans that remained in Israel (in many cases, these were clans that had previously been marginalized in Palestinian society), who were willing to cooperate with the state in exchange for Knesset seats or other positions of power (Lustick 1980). These individuals would then constitute the members of the Arab political lists affiliated with the Jewish Mapai party (which will later become the Labor Party), which was consistently the largest party in the Knesset, up until the late 1970s.

Hence, most of the members of the post-1948 Arab leadership were traditional leaders, who based their power on religious and family ties, held a utilitarian worldview, and submitted to the state's dictate without posing any challenge. Most of the leaders of these Arab parties did not even have a basic level of formal education (Jamal 2006); many of them had only graduated from elementary school. Some were members of larger clans, while others managed to garner the support of influential clans, which offered them the social backing needed in order to compete against their opponents. Others still accepted blindly the state's dictates, and in return provided services that other leaders could not, or would not provide, such as paved roads, connecting houses to the electric grid or the water supply network, etc.

The only two movements that were not supported by the Israeli government during these early years were *Al-Ard*, which demanded the establishment of a Palestinian state based on the UN 1947 Partition Plan, and the Israeli Communist Party (Kaufman 1997). Similar to their counterparts in the Mapai-affiliated political lists, the leaders of these two movements were also relatively young and at the outset of their political careers, but in contrast to other Arab leaders their level of education was higher, and they displayed greater independence (Jamal 2006). The leaders of *Al-Ard* were mainly the decedents of Palestinian families that had been displaced and deprived of their main sources of income and social power, due to Israel's policy of land expropriation and the present absentee legal and judicial philosophy. Some of them were members of lower-middle-class families, which had strong national consciousness, and viewed Israel as a pure colonial project, clashing with the basic interests of the Palestinian people. The leaders of *Al-Ard* were more educated than the average leaders in the Arab community. They were directly connected to the pre-1948 national leadership, but with a more realistic worldview and a greater understanding of the asymmetry of power vis-à-vis the Zionist movement. Concurrently, they recognized the inherent incongruity of the Zionist movement with the basic aspirations of the Palestinian people and the Arab nation.

The Arab leaders of the Israeli Communist Party were also young, but more educated than the leaders of Mapai's Arab political lists. Mostly in their 20s, they had been part of the Palestinian Communist Party before 1948. Due to their support of the UN Partition Plan of 1947, and the empathy of some of them showed to the creation of a Jewish state in the face of the Arab attacks, they were either granted permission to stay, or allowed to return from their areas of refuge to their places of residence, despite their criticism of government policies (Ghanem 2001; Kaufman 1997). The senior party leaders were mostly members of the Greek Orthodox Christian community, including notable figures such as Emile Habibi, Tawfik Toubi, Emile Touma, Saliba Khamis, Nimer Murkus and others. Loyal to their Marxist-Leninist ideology, the party leaders viewed Jewish Palestinian relations mostly in terms of a class struggle, and their criticism of the state's discriminating policy against Palestinian citizens focused mainly on class exploitation.

Communist Arab leaders supported the establishment of a Palestinian state, demanded the return of the Palestinian refugees to their original homes, and objected to the state's land expropriation policies (Jamal 2010). At the same time, they also recognized the right of the State of Israel to exist and the legitimacy of

Jewish immigration to Israel, and spoke of Jewish–Arab camaraderie in a struggle against the discriminatory state's policies (Ghanem 2001). The Arab leaders of the Communist party were persecuted for protecting Arab interests and raising particularly sensitive issues, such as the status of refugees, the continuation of the military regime, and land expropriation (Bäuml 2007).

Comparatively, today's Arab elites are decidedly more educated, and their members come from a more diverse educational background. Recent decades have seen the emergence of a large group of Arab intellectuals specializing in a variety of fields and disciplines. Contemporary Palestinian-Arab society includes experts in fields such as: medicine, pharmaceutics, engineering, law, social work, science, and behavioral science. One of the key features of this group is that their training was not exclusively from the Israeli education system, but also of other educational institutions in Eastern and Western Europe, as well as in the United States. The process started with student missions to Soviet states, arranged by the Communist Party, and continued with various students receiving their medical and law education in European countries (such as Italy and Germany), and graduate degrees in the United States.

The rising level of education among the Arab elite resulted in better professional skills, while also initiating a process of cultural and political awakening, and the rise of political expectations. This rise was reflected in the growing mobility of Arab intellectuals, as well as a growing involvement in civil society issues, such as trying to infiltrate the Israeli labor market and fight against the government's exclusionary policies in services and social integration. Another result was a rising level of education among the political leadership, which directly impacted on its self-perception and behavioral patterns in the political and social realms.

In the past, the achievements of Palestinian students within Israeli educational institutions were significantly below average. Yet, according to statistical data, the numbers of Arab students and academics is constantly on the rise (Al-Haj 2003). In the academic year 1956–1957, there were forty-six Arab students in Israel, an overall 0.6 percent of the entire student population. By 1979–1980, there were 1,634 Arab students—about 3 percent of the student population. Between 1988 and 1998, the number of Arab students had risen from 6.7 percent to 8.7 percent. In 1998–1999, there were 7,903 Arab students—7.1 percent of the entire student population in Israel (Manna 2008). According to the Central Bureau of Statistics, in 2004–2005, there were 9,967 Arab students, compared with 7,200 in 2000–2001. The number of Arab college students was 2,000 in the year 1999–2000, and 4,553 in 2004–2005. In 2004, the number of Arabs with sixteen or more years of education was 94,486—a testimony to the fast-paced growth of the Arab academic and professional elite.

This data clearly shows a significant rise in the number of Arab students studying in Israeli higher education institutions, yet the rate of growth remains low when compared to the overall Arab population in Israel. The numbers of students studying for graduate degrees are even lower, though they are also constantly on the rise. In 2007–2008, 6.4 percent of the master's degree students and 3.5 percent of the doctorate degree students in Israel were Arabs. In 2008–2009, the rates were 6.5 percent and 3.7 percent, respectively; in 2009–2010—6.9 percent and 4 percent; in 2010–2011—8.2 percent and 4.4 percent; in 2011–2012—9 percent and 4.4 percent; and in 2012–2013—9.2 percent and 4.9 percent. These changes reflect a slow but significant growth in the number of Arab citizens who received higher education, developed a career, and translated their education into a higher level of income, compared to their parents. These graduates represent an important human resource contributing to the creation of an educated Arab middle class—a class that is developing expectations for a better socioeconomic reality.

Only a small group of Arab academics has been appointed to positions in Israeli academic institutions, but they have made significant contributions to the development of the academic discourse on issues related to the status of the Arab population in Israel, especially in respect to policy and human rights. Arab academic staff members, although a few in number, have succeeded in introducing the rights of Arab citizens into the academic and political debate in Israel, as well as in various international forums. They are joined in those efforts by a large group of Arab professionals, particularly lawyers and human rights activists, who are active in NGOs in Israel and abroad (Jamal 2017). The Arab academics and professionals are at the forefront of the Arab public, searching for ways to promote its civil, political, financial, and cultural rights. Gradually, they create the moral, legal, and political foundations for the demand of full integration of the Arab citizens into the policy-making processes in Israel and particularly the realization of their right for effective representation in the institutions that determine their future (Jamal 2011).

An examination of elected Arab officials, particularly in the Knesset, reveals vast changes within this group as well. The number of academics among this small group of elites is constantly growing, and these academics are slowly but tenaciously changing the political orientation of the leadership, affecting its modes of operation versus the state, and their own patterns of political mobility. Until 1981, most of the Arab Knesset members—particularly those connected with the Labor party—were not educated. Out of the seventy Arab Knesset members between the years 1949 and 1984, only seven possessed an undergraduate education, and nineteen of them had never received any formal education.

In comparison, since 1984 and until the 19th Knesset (elected in 2013), eighty out of the eighty-nine Knesset members had at least an undergraduate degree, and the rate of graduate-degree recipients has been growing in recent years. Five of the Arab representatives in the 19th Knesset had a PhD, one had an MA, and four had a BA degree. This data reflects a qualitative change in the intellectual qualities of the political leadership of the Arab-Palestinian elite. Although this sharp trend does not accurately represent local leadership in Arab municipalities, significant change is also taking place at a local level, despite the fact that the educated leadership still often relies on family ties.

Historically—outside of the institutional political sphere—many young Arabs with leadership skills looked for paths to social mobility that were not dependent on the state, and directed their attention to the CSO sphere. The first organizations that were established in the mid-1970s focused on providing services for the Arab public in areas neglected by the State. According to a survey I conducted among ninety-seven activists in twenty CSOs in the year 2010, the average age of the activists was 34. Additionally, 75 percent of the activists had an academic degree; 16 percent studied in non-academic institutions, and 9 percent had no tertiary education. When analyzing the educational characteristics of 159 board members in twenty Arab national CSOs, I found that their level of education was particularly high: 2 percent were professors, 12 percent had a PhD, 19 percent had an MA degree, 49 percent had a BA, and 10 percent had higher education diplomas. Sixty percent of the board members studied in higher education institutions (HEIs) in Israel, and 12 percent studied in Europe or in the United States.

This data reveals the intense involvement of a significant number of intellectuals in civil society organizations (CSOs), a field that has undergone a tremendous development in recent years (Jamal 2017). When I interviewed a representative sample of leaders in those CSOs, I discovered that they perceived civil society as a sphere that allowed them to address some of the needs of Arab society that were not met by the State, thereby both protesting against governmental policy and mobilizing against it. They regarded their work as oppositional civic activism—dictated by formal rules—whilst also being able to challenge the rules of the game, empowering Arab citizens vis-à-vis discriminatory and disempowering state practices.

Unlike the previous generation of leaders, who were nurtured and sometimes even chosen by the Israeli establishment, the younger generation had to fight to establish their status in society and the state's formal institutions. This was the case for many of the prominent leaders who influence the social and political reality of Arab-Palestinian society in Israel. The prominent presence of second-generation Palestinians, who are the focus of this essay, facilitates the continuous development of young leadership that seeks to capture influential positions within society and the economy. The technological development in the fields of communication and information over recent decades has created greater social mobility, which has been allowing young leaders to develop their reputations and influence consciousness using the new information technologies (Jamal 2014b). The new generation of leaders is gaining increasing influence, though their power is not yet backed by formal authority or an official position.

Young leaders offer a significant contribution to consciousness shaping, although the organizational manifestation of their power has yet to be fully felt. Online activism and the use of new media for political mobility and social protest were often found to be extremely important tools. The best example is the protest against the Prawer Plan, a governmental zoning plan that aimed to gather all Bedouins, living in unrecognized villages in the Negev area, into existing towns or newly established ones. The mobilization of youth against the plan, which empowered the local population and led them to intensify their resistance, forced the government to seek alternative ways to reach its goals. The governmental reaction to the massive mobilization against the plan, a change that isn't characteristic of government policies against the Arab population, reflected the sophisticated forms of mobilization emerging among young Arab leaders. The latter managed to unveil the real intentions behind the modernization discourse utilized by governmental agencies and demonstrate that they are not only aware of the hidden agenda of the government, but also their ability to force the government to react so it reveals its true character.

Socio-political transformations and new political thought

It would be difficult to argue that there is a single organized and coherent political philosophy and doctrine within the Arab-Palestinian society in Israel. The best documentation in this aspect would have been the political platforms of Arab parties, which compete with each other for the vote of the Arab electorate; yet, those platforms cannot be seen as accurately representing the positions of the Arab-Palestinian public in Israel. This is due to the fact that the Arab parties draft their platforms according to the Israeli election laws, which make it very difficult for Arabs to present a coherent, organized, and complete political platform, particularly in light of the legal limitations of the last years.

The Israeli election laws, for example, limit the ability of Arab parties to act against the Jewish and Zionist nature of the State, forcing Arab parties to blur their position concerning their regional political vision. Thus, the platforms of Arab parties have not included alternative political models, such as a "bi-national state," or "a state of all its citizens," although those ideas are quite common among the Arab political elite. Furthermore, the platforms of Arab parties do not represent the extra-parliamentary political movements, despite the wide public support enjoyed by some of them, such as the Northern Branch of the Islamic Movement in Israel, which was outlawed by the Israeli Minister of Defense, along with its CSOs and media institutions, in November 2015.

In order to reflect the key elements in Arab political thought in Israel, we must look for representative writings or documents that reflect the political ideals accepted by the majority or the entire public. Additionally, we must pay attention to the writings and documentation of leaders and intellectuals, in an attempt to find the common denominators of political thought, despite the danger of reductionism or over-generalization. In the face of the political situation and the election laws, we can find a justification, albeit partial, for viewing manifestos as a reliable source of information concerning the key elements of Arab-Palestinian political thought in Israel (Ozacky-Lazar and Kabha 2008).

There are three distinctive types of manifestos. The first type comprises the "Vision Documents" published by various groups of political leaders and intellectuals, most of them secular, in the years 2006–2007. These include the Vision Document published by the National Committee for the Heads of the Arab Local Municipalities (2006), the Democratic Constitution presented by Adallah (2007), and the Haifa Declaration published by Mada Al-Carmel (2007). These works are the result of a comprehensive intellectual effort, which included all of the political factions in Arab society, except for the Northern Branch of the Islamic Movement.

Their ideas represent the mainstream political thought in Arab-Palestinian society in Israel, even if those ideas were initiated by leaders and intellectuals with no official representative role. Notwithstanding the criticism against the initiators of these documents, the vision documents represent the common conceptual ideas accepted by most of the Arab political parties, including the pragmatic southern branch of the Islamic Movement.

The second type of document is the "autarkic society" model presented by Sheikh Raed Salah, leader of the northern branch of the Islamic Movement, as part of his religious and ideological thought. The idea of an autarkic society was presented in response to the signs of weakness in Arab-Palestinian society, particularly in its dealings with the policy of the Israeli government after October 2000 and the Second Palestinian Intifada. An autarkic society means establishing organizations and institutions that can provide the daily needs of society. These organizations must be differentiated from the state institutions, which use the partial services provided by them to enhance the dependency of Arab-Palestinian society on the state. The idea is based on an all-inclusive Islamic worldview, including commerce, manufacturing, consuming, and banking methods, etc. The third type of documents is exemplified by the manifesto introduced by the southern branch of the Islamic Movement, which was ratified as its official manifesto on 26 January, 2018. This document is composed of six sections, starting with defining the movement and its vision and ending with presenting the principles, values, goals and mechanism of action of the movement. This document is a mixture of theological, political, cultural, and social discourse that locates the Islamic movement at the center of the universe.

It is not possible to delve into all three types in this context. Therefore, a few major ideas will be presented, in order to demonstrate the main thesis of this chapter; namely that the emerging new political elite in Arab-Palestinian society in Israel is introducing new challenging political thought that has a major impact on the relationship between the state and the indigenous Palestinian minority.

All the documents described above include many sub-sections, starting with a discussion of the ideal society and ending with a political-social manifesto, or an informal constitution. Similar to vision documents in other case studies, the ones under discussion also reflect the political desire and ambition to change reality (Sargent 2008). They reflect the dissatisfaction of their authors with the existing reality, while undermining it and offering potentially preferable options. The vision documents discussed are formative texts, which are reflective of the spirit of the era and thereby enable access to the collective mind of the society in which they are published.

The first common and most central feature of all types of documents published in the last decade is the fact that they represent oppositional consciousness, revolting against the dominant circumstances and seeking to achieve liberation from the conditions which Palestinians are still experiencing as a result of the Palestinian Nakba in 1948. All these documents voice a political dissatisfaction with the political reality of submission to a sovereign power that excludes Palestinians from defining their way of life and the rules of collective conduct, according to which their lives are determined. All the documents seek emancipation, through asserting the right of Palestinians to have rights. They reflect the philosophy of "part-taking" asserted as a fundamental element in democratic politics and in defining sovereignty, in a reality completely hijacked by a Jewish majority that neglects and ignores how this reality has come about. As such they not only question the identity of the sovereign, but also seek to transform the reality in order to become an integral part of the sovereign power in the entire space of Israel–Palestine.

Collectively these documents present a firm ontological disposition that locates Palestinians in Israel as part and parcel of the Palestinian people and assert the natural rights of the Palestinian people over its homeland, which has been colonized by a foreign settler movement. The documents explicate the deep and long-lasting conflict between the oppressed Palestinian people who were and are still being uprooted from its homeland by the settler-colonial Zionist movement and the Israeli state, bearing witness to the wrongdoings of the latter. The language of the documents may differ on the conceptualizations utilized to describe the reality in which the Palestinians in Israel live, nonetheless most of them narrate the chain of wrongdoings conducted by the Israeli state and demand corrective justice. As such they form an ethical critique cf Zionism, which differs from how the latter is conceived by the majority of Jews in Israel and elsewhere. Furthermore, all documents reject the asymmetrical power relations between the Jewish majority and the Palestinians, whether citizens or inhabitants of the Palestinian areas occupied by Israel in 1967, and seek equity in determining the future of the land. This rejection is based on the Israeli policies of the last decades, which seek to blur the differentiation between Israel within the green line and the Palestinian areas occupied in 1967.

The similarities in the ontological reading of the circumstances under which Palestinians live does not necessarily mean a full agreement on the language used in order to describe this reality. The discourse of the vision documents of 2006–2007 is primarily of a liberal-secular, sovereign and modernist political entity that conceptualizes itself and its environment based on the political and legal language of international law and agreements. In contrast, the language of both documents of the two branches of the Islamic movement is theological, according to which Islamic values and norms are the ones that determine the nature of the Islamic society and the relationships within it, and set its priorities when it comes to its relationship with its broader environment. The theological language dominating both documents differs when it comes to coping with the hegemonic political and cultural reality.

Whereas all secular vision documents and the manifesto of the southern branch of the Islamic movement choose a political discourse based on democratic, peaceful and tolerant values and practices, the northern branch of the Islamic movement emphasizes a religious language that is based on clear eschatological hierarchical theology. Furthermore, the secular vision documents and the manifesto of the southern branch of the Islamic movement tend to be pragmatic in dealing with the given political and cultural reality and therefore the movement operates from within the Israeli electoral system, seeking to transform it from within. In contrast, the autarkic society document advocates an alternative path outside of the Israeli national electoral system, despite the decision to operate from within the municipal system. The autarkic society document emphasizes an Islamic religious paradigm that serves as the foundation for the establishment of Islamic organizations, such as schools, hospitals, markets, professional unions, and banks. The idea is to establish an autonomous organizational and financial network, which provides services in all areas of life, thus creating a protective layer around the in-group members, avoiding dependency on the state institutions.

When it comes to internal affairs, the secular vision documents present an ideological array tending toward liberalism and democracy, which competes with the rising power of religion and the Islamic Movement for dictating the way of life in Arab towns and villages in Israel. Whenever the documents refer to authentic social values, they are written from a secular-liberal point of view. This paradigm dominates the moral and social ethical imagination prevalent in the documents, which strive to instill them in the ideal future society.

In contrast, when it comes to documents affiliated with both branches of the Islamic movement, the social and cultural ideals dominating both documents are religious and theological. These reflect the growing religionization of Arab-Palestinian society. They reject the social-cultural model presented in the secular vision documents and introduce a more conservative civilizational model, based on Quranic and Sharia values and laws. Notwithstanding this overlap between the documents of the two branches of the Islamic movement, they deeply differ when it comes not only to the pragmatics of politics but also when it comes to the relationship between Islamic and democratic values. The manifesto of the southern branch is loaded with concepts and ideas that reconcile democracy with Islamic conceptualizations of society and the state. Despite the fact that the final sovereignty is given to the divine authority and its manifestations on earth—the prophet, the Quran and the Suna—the manifesto leaves much to be decided for the community, based on open and participatory deliberations. The autarkic society presented by the leader of the northern branch is much stricter on patriarchal social values and is very committed to hierarchical political authority.

The vision documents of 2006–2007 and the manifesto of the southern branch of the Islamic movement reflect the constructive ambivalence or intentional hybridity that is commonly found in the political platforms of Arab parties in dealing with the complex relationship between national and civil affiliation. Since the nationality and citizenship of Arab-Palestinian Israeli citizens are uncorrelated, or even contrasting, these citizens have to make a constant effort to overcome their double marginality, or their "state of siege" (Suleiman 2002; Rabinowitz 1997). These documents represent a tenacious effort not only for a better self-positioning within the existing structure of opportunities in the Israeli and Palestinian reality, but also its complete transformation in ways that normalize the political, economic, and cultural life of the Palestinian community in Israel. This struggle for better self-positioning finds evidence in the idea of a "double consciousness," or an "in-between" hybridity, which is translated into a constant movement between the two sides of the conflict to the extent that both are transformed (Bhabha 2004). These documents make clear that the Israeli and Palestinian affiliations of the Arab-Palestinians in Israel are not symmetrical: while the Palestinian one is national and cultural, the Israeli identity is predominantly legal and instrumental.

As such, the documents are a clear reflection of a strong tendency among the Palestinian minority in Israel to establish the self as a political subject, with unique interests derived from its position in the tensed interim space between state and nation. The documents represent a political subject combining their Palestinian past, nationality and culture, with their Israeli reality and existence. They reflect the development of a collective double and unique political consciousness, which is expressed in the slogan of the National Democratic Assembly (Balad): "National identity and full citizenship," in the demand for peace and equality presented by Hadash (The Democratic Front for Peace and Equality) or in the constructive language utilized by the southern branch of the Islamic movement, which seeks reconciliation between its theological vision and the daily political reality.

In contrast, the idea of the autarkic society is inherently religious, by which religion should dictate the behavior patterns of the followers and delineate a clear hierarchy of authority between religious leaders and the rest of the community. These ideas include, among other things, the distribution of property according to Islamic principles, which hinders the idea of civil equality; it also encourages polygamy, as a practice that can assist Arab-Palestinian society to overcome its challenges, both in the demographic and cultural aspects. Accordingly, polygamy, which compromises female equality, allows society to enhance demographic growth in a way that will increase the Palestinian population in Israel and change the current demographic status quo.

All vision documents present an alternative spacio-temporal paradigm to that of the Zionist movement and thereby reject the efforts made by the state of Israel to differentiate between different groups of Palestinians, based on its own interests. The documents highlight the Palestinian national and cultural spacio-temporality, according to which the land of Palestine is the homeland of the Palestinian people, who have been living in it for centuries and have established their cultural and traditional way of life in deep connection with the land. The historical narrative presented in the documents creates an inherent link between the Palestinian dwelling in the lands of Palestine as an existentially-significant experience, and the historical truth, which relies on a unique perception of time and history.

Thus, this historical narrative turns Zionism into an act of self-enforcement, not only over the physical sphere, but also over history and its temporality. According to all the documents, Zionism is not perceived as a "real" legitimate national movement; instead it is a settler-colonial movement that transformed the entire landscape of Palestine and its people. This position, reiterated differently in the different documents, is based on the perception that the connection between Jews and Palestine does not rely on an authentic connection between dwelling and existential, temporal being. The basic evidence of this unauthenticity is that fact that the immigration of Jews to Palestine was accompanied by the imposition of new concepts of time and space, and thus reflects an inherent self-estrangement, manifested in the behavior of the Israeli-Jewish society.

According to the documents, the best proof of the authentic connection between Palestinians and the land of Palestine is the Palestinians who live in the heart of the land, despite the uprooting policies of the Zionist movement. Therefore, the imagined physical and temporal sphere of Palestine is essentially Palestinian, despite the presence of millions of Jews. This latter fact is addressed on the pragmatic level, only after the principle pillars of Palestinian national and civilizational imagination is established.

Accordingly, the documents recognize the fact that Zionism has presented new and challenging parameters to the physical, temporal, and existential space in which Palestinians dwell. They argue that these parameters must be addressed, and thus appear in the documents as practical circumventional conditions. However, these parameters are unacceptable in principle and therefore cannot form the valuational foundations and conceptual tools by which the reconciliation between Jews and Palestinians is negotiated. All documents express a positive moral standing towards the Jewish presence in Palestine and show much understanding towards the rights that should be guaranteed for Jews in the land, but simultaneously reject the main pillars of the Zionist narrative, especially the exclusive right of Jews over the land, the expansionist nature of settling it, and the ethnic majoritarian system by which decisions are legitimated in the Israeli control system.

On the practical level, the differences between the Zionist and the Palestinian narratives entail major moral and ethical implications. While the documents offer an ethical and humane statement, they do not remain loyal to the practical implications derived from the historical paradigm presented in them; rather, based on the historical human truth created after 1948, they offer a compromise, as the only viable moral option. Thus, they offer a deep and honest acceptance of the Jewish existence in Israel, but not to the Zionist ideology and its motifs as a theological paradigm that justifies this existence, nor to the political establishment, created based on the Zionist ideology, which denies them their historical rights in their own homeland.

At this point, the distinction between the borders of the state and the boundaries of the homeland becomes clearer. The Arab-Palestinians in Israel see the entire territory of Palestine as their homeland. Thus, any acceptance of a political solution resulting in its partition is nothing but a political solution, and does not relinquish their historical bond with Palestine as a whole. This position is reflected in the rise of the indigenousness discourse in Arab-Palestinian political thought in recent decades, which is very well established in the Haifa Declaration and the Manifesto of the southern branch of the Islamic movement. This discourse grants moral and historical priority for the Palestinians over the disputed lands. Hence, a vivid discourse has been developing in recent years, concerning the one-state solution as the best institutional solution that can solve the Palestinian problem, without reneging on the national rights of Jews in Israel. This position reflects an attempt to resist the fragmentation of the Palestinian people, which started with the idea of Partition in 1947. In this solution, Israeli Jews will retain their self-determination. However, their rights within a single, democratic state, will not undermine the corresponding claims of Palestinians.

By way of conclusion

This essay illustrates that we cannot understand the emergence of new ideological conceptions in Arab-Palestinian society in Israel without tying these trends to the development of new elites in recent decades. Higher levels of education and standards of living among the ever-growing Arab middle class allowed the allocation of human and monetary resources toward political, civil, and social activities, amplifying the struggle for dominance between various ideas. The higher level of education among the key officials in political, social, and cultural Arab-Palestinian organizations in Israel brought on an evident development in the level of political awareness and thought.

Notwithstanding these developments, the higher level of education has also brought harsher internal ideological disputes. The forming and crystallizing of ideologies underline the disputes between them, even when there is a wide consensus concerning the end goal of the struggle—national rights and complete civil equality—and the means to achieve them in the entire land of Palestine. The ideological disputes are reflected in organizations and movements, leading to internal struggles between parties and people, as reflected in the number of vision documents analyzed in this chapter.

The ideological conflict between the various fragments of the emerging Arab-Palestinian elite reflects both a personal and organizational struggle, which makes it a serious challenge to create coalitions based on shared values. The organizational and ideological divergence in this elite creates competition between the different factions over resources, perceptions, and cultural symbols. The socioeconomic differentiation among the dominant Arab elite is balanced by the different sources of power of the various parts of these elite. While the elite are more and more representative of the social structure with its different aspects, there is a struggle over ideological, financial, and political power resources. This struggle often amplifies the internal fragmentation and the inability to meet the expectations of the Arab public, particularly when considering the ongoing struggle against the state's discriminating policies.

The isolation of the dogmatic faction of the Islamic Movement and the struggle between the Communist and the nationalist factions underline the ideological disputes within Arab political activity, but they do not prevent necessary collaborations designed to promote the common interests of the Arab-Palestinian public. The struggle between the visionaries of the various factions is sometimes reflected in criticism against the activity and plans of the High Follow-Up Committee for Arab Citizens of Israel, which represents one of the greatest achievements of the Arab leadership since the creation of the post-1948 reality. Yet, despite the ideological differences and the fragmentary policies of the Israeli state, the leadership of the various segments of Palestinian society still manage to form pragmatic agreements utilized to achieve shared political and civil goals. The creation of the Joint List before the 20th Knesset election and the ambivalent position taken by the leaders of the northern branch of the Islamic Movement toward the legitimacy of Arab citizens participating in the elections for the Knesset, which was designed to further strengthen the Joint List, illustrate the ability of the Arab leadership to overcome some of the differences when needed. Furthermore, the energies invested in preserving the Joint List and the empathy shown by all factions toward the northern branch of the Islamic movement, after it was declared illegal in November 2015, reflects the bridging and bonding efforts made by all components of the leadership. This unity has engendered a common strategy and vision for determining the values and institutional setting according to which the Arab-Palestinians out to live.

Indeed, the unification of the Arab parliamentary parties under one joint list is an important change in this aspect. One should not ignore the fact that this change was imposed by the political system and the raising of the electoral threshold, and thus cannot be seen as solely reflecting a fundamental change in the behavior and activity patterns of the Arab political elite. The struggle over the composition of the candidate list and the personalization of the political representation reflect the fragile nature of this union, although it does represent an important transformation compared to the partisan fragmentation and ideological struggle that characterized the three previous decades. Time will tell if and how the parties continue to work together in the long run, and how they will translate this unification into a common political project.

Looking ahead to the new generation—the new media generation—one wonders how things will develop in the future. The new generation of leaders, who are the third generation after the *Nakbah*, bring new patterns of social mobility and new patterns of communication between them and the public. The new patterns of communication make it difficult to predict future developments. In light of the regional instability and the weakness of the Palestinian leadership in the West Bank and Gaza, and particularly in light of the conflict between the Palestinian National Authority and Hamas, it appears that the Israeli political arena and the struggle for civil rights, and particularly for equality and against discrimination and marginalization, is becoming the main sphere in which the Arab leadership operate safely (Jamal 2014a). The unification of the Arab parties is an important step in the process of transferring the authority from the present generation of leaders to the next. The question that is yet to be answered is if, and in what way, the political tradition of the current leadership and its political thought will shape the next generation of leaders, or if this generation will be able to utilize the communication tools and their culture of deliberation to create new political fronts, which will be able to deal better with the challenges presented by the state, particularly in light of the growing nationalistic radicalism and blunt racism in Israeli society.

References and further reading

Abd Al-Fatah, A. 2013. *The crisis of conflict resolution and the one-state horizons.* Available at: www.arabs48.com/?mod=articles&ID=64371. [Arabic]

Abu rabia-Queder, Sarab. 2008. *Excluded and Loved: Educated Bedouin Women's Life Stories.* Jerusalem: Magness. [Hebrew]

Adallah. 2007. *The Democratic Constitution.* Available at: www.adalah.org/uploads/oldfiles/ Public/files/democratic_constitution-english.pdf.

Al-Haj, Majid. 1993. "The Impact of the Intifada on Arabs in Israel: The Case of Double Periphery," in Akiba Cohen and Gadi Wolfsfeld (eds.), *Framing the Intifada: Media and People.* Norwood, NJ: Ablex, pp. 64–75.

Al-Haj, Majid. 2003. "Higher Education among the Arabs in Israel: Formal Policy between Empowerment and Control." *Higher Education Policy.* 16, pp. 351–368.

Anderson, Benedict. 1983. *Imagined Communities: Reflections on the Origin and Spread of Nationalism.* London: Verso.

Balibar, Étienne. 2002. "Three Concepts of Politics," in *Politics and the Other Scene.* London: Verso.

Balibar, Étienne. 2011. "Structure: Method or Subversion of the Social Sciences?" *Radical Philosophy,* (165).

Bäuml, Yair. 2007. *A Blue and White Shadow: The Israeli Establishment's Policy and Actions Among its Arab Citizens: The Formative Years: 1958–1968.* Haifa: Pardes. [Hebrew]

Bhabha, Homi. 2004. "The Other Question: Stereotype, Discrimination and the Discourse of Colonialism," in *The Location of Culture.* London/ New York: Routledge, pp. 66–92.

Bishara, Azmi. 2010. *On the Arabian Question: Introduction to Arabian Democratic Manifesto.* Beirut: Center for Arab Unity Studies. [Arabic]

Bourdieu, Pierre. 1977. *An Outline of a Theory of Practice.* Translated by Richard Nice. London: Cambridge University Press.

Central Bureau of Statistics. 2001. *The Arab Population in Israel* (*Statistilite* 27).

Chatterjee, Partha. 1993. *The Nation and its Fragments: Colonial and Postcolonial Histories.* Princeton, NJ: Princeton University Press.

Cohen, Hillel. 2006. *Good Arabs: The Israeli Security Services and the Israeli Arabs.* Jerusalem: Keter. [Hebrew]

Du Bois, William E.B. 1903. *The Souls of Black Folk: Essays and Sketches.* Chicago, IL: A.C. McClurg & Co.

Fanon, Frantz. 2008. *Black Skin, White Masks.* Translated by Richard Philcox. Grove Press: New York.

Fraser, Nancy. 1997. *Justice Interruptus: Critical Reflections on the 'Postsocialist' Condition.* London: Routledge.

Ghanem, As'ad. 2001. *The Palestinian-Arab Minority in Israel, 1948–2000: A Political Study.* New York: State University of New York Press.

Giddens, Anthony. 1984. *The Constitution of Society: Outline of the Theory of Structuration.* Cambridge: Polity Press.

Haider, Aziz. 2017. "Introduction," in *Political Aspects in the Life of Palestinians in Israel.* Jerusalem: Van Leer, pp. 4–17.

Havemann, Paul (ed.) 1999. *Indigenous Peoples Rights in Australia, Canada and New Zealand.* Oxford: Oxford University Press.

Heidegger, M. 1977. "Building, Dwelling, Thinking," in D.F. Krell (ed.), *Basic Writings: From Being and Time (1927) to the Task of Thinking (1964).* New York: Harper and Row, pp. 323–339.

Jabareen, R. 2007. *In support of our leader Shawqi Khatib—say no to the Future Vision Documents distortion.* Available at: www.aljabha.org/?i=24751. [Arabic]

Jamal, Amal. 2006. "The Arab Leadership in Israel: Ascendance and Fragmentation." *Journal of Palestine Studies.* 35(2), pp. 6–22.

Jamal, Amal. 2008a. "On the Hardships of the Race-tainted Era," in Y. Shenhav and Y. Yona (eds.), *Racism in Israel.* Tel Aviv and Jerusalem: The Van Leer Institute and ha-Kibutz ha-Meuhad, pp. 348–380. [Hebrew]

Jamal, Amal. 2008b. "The Counter-hegemonic Role of Civil Society: Palestinian-Arab NGO's in Israel." *Citizenship Studies.* 12(3), 283–306.

Jamal, Amal. 2009. "The Contradictions of State–Minority Relations in Israel: The Search for Clarifications." *Constellations.* 16(3), pp. 493–508.

Jamal, Amal. 2010. *Mechanisms for the Creation of Quiet Arabs.* Nazareth: I'lam. [Arabic]

Jamal, Amal. 2011. *Arab Minority Nationalism in Israel: The Politics of Indigeneity.* London: Routledge.

Jamal, Amal. 2012. "Shared Sovereignty as Default: National Conflicts and Differential Solutions." *The Public Sphere.* 6, pp. 42–74. [Hebrew]

Jamal, Amal. 2014a. "The Fluidity of the Political Lexicon of Palestinians in Israel in Face of the Arab Spring." *Eretz Aheret.* 69.

Jamal, Amal. 2014b. Digital Communality, Online Intimacy and the Changing Patterns of Social Engagement. Available at: www.ilam-center.org/he/article.aspx?id=265. [Hebrew]

Jamal, Amal. 2017. "Rising Elites and Political Thought Among Palestinians in Israel," in *Political Aspects in the Life of Palestinians in Israel.* Jerusalem: Van Leer, pp. 19–51.

Jamal, Amal and Samah Bsoul. 2014. *The Palestinian Nakba in the Israeli Public Sphere: Formations of Denial and Responsibility.* Nazareth: I'lam.

Kaufman, Ilana. 1997. *Arab National Communism in the Jewish State.* Gainesville, FL: University Press of Florida.

Khatib, Kamal. 2011. *The Green Erosion Continues.* Available at: http://kamal-khateb.com/?p=969. [Arabic]

Kymlicka, Will. 2008. "The Internationalization of Minority Rights." *International Journal of Constitutional Law.* 6(1), pp. 1–32.

Lustick, Ian. 1980. *Arabs in the Jewish State: A Study in the Effective Control of a Minority Population.* Austin, TX and London: University of Texas Press.

Mada Al-Carmel. 2007. The Haifa Declaration. Available at: http://mada-research.org/en/files/2007/09/haifaenglish.pdf/.

Manna, Adel. 2008. *Arab Society in Israel: Populations, Society, Economy (2).* Jerusalem and Tel Aviv: The Van Leer Institute and ha-Kibutz ha-Meuhad. [Hebrew]

National Committee for the Heads of the Arab Local Authorities (2006). *The Future Vision of the Palestinian Arabs in Israel.* Available at: http://tinyurl.com/9n7q4ck.

Ozacky-Lazar, S. and Kabha, M. (eds.) 2008. *Between Vision and Reality: The Vision Papers of the Arabs in Israel, 2006–2007.* Jerusalem: The Citizens' Accord Forum. [Hebrew]

Pappe, Ilan. 2006. *The Ethnic Cleansing of Palestine.* Oxford: Oneworld.

Rabinowitz, Dan. 1997. *Overlooking Nazareth: The Ethnography of Exclusion in Galilee.* Cambridge: Cambridge University Press.

Rabinowitz, Dan and Abu-Baker, Khawla. 2002. *The Upright Generation.* Jerusalem: Keter. [Hebrew]

Rancière, Jacques. 2004. *The Politics of Aesthetics.* London/New York: Continuum.

Sa'di, Ahmad and Abu-Lughod, Lila (eds.) 2007. *Nakba: Palestine, 1948, and the Claims of Memory.* New York: Columbia University Press.

Salah, R. 2007. "The Follow-up Committee—Where To?" *Sawt al-Haq wa-al-Huriyya,* February 2. [Arabic]

Sargent, Lyman Tower. 2008. "Ideology and Utopia: Karl Mannheim and Paul Ricoeur." *Journal of Political Ideology*. 13(3), pp. 263–273.

Suleiman, Ramzi. 2002. "Minority Self-Categorization: The Case of the Palestinians in Israel." *Peace and Conflict: Journal of Peace Psychology*. 8(1), pp. 31–46.

Tal, Avriham. 2006. "This is a Declaration of War." *Haaretz*, December 8, 2006. [Hebrew]

Unger, Roberto Mangabeira. 1987. *False Necessity: Anti-necessitarian Social Theory in the Service of Radical Democracy*. Cambridge: Cambridge University Press.

Zubeidat, A. 2006. The Current and Future Blindness of Israelis. *Hadith al-Nass*, December 22. [Arabic]

Zureik, Elia. 1979. *The Palestinians in Israel: A Study in Internal Colonialism*. London: Routledge and Kegan Paul.

Zureik, Elia. 2016 Israel's Colonial Project in Palestine: Brutal Pursuit. Oxon: Routledge.

10

POLITICAL REPRESENTATION OF WOMEN AND GENDER (IN)EQUALITY

Reut Itzkovitch-Malka

Introduction

The story of women in Israeli society—their status, representation and rights—is replete with contradictions and anomalies. On the one hand, women were granted, albeit, not without a struggle, the right to vote and to serve in the representative institutions of pre-state Israel as early as 1920. In the 1970s, Israel had a female Prime Minister, which was rather unusual at the time. This, alongside the myth of the pioneering and fighting women, the Kibbutzim and their (supposedly) egalitarian ideology, the compulsory conscription of women into the IDF, and the Declaration of Independence, which stated that Israel would be a democratic state without differences of religion, race and gender, created a *myth of gender equality* (Herzog 2004).

Nonetheless, despite the fact that women have been active participants in the public sphere since the pre-state era, their power has been consistently constrained (Chazan 2011). This is true across the political, social, economic, and culture spheres. Female legislators constitute a record number in today's Knesset, (32 out of a 120 Members of Knesset in the 20th Knesset are women) yet there is still a long way to go to achieve equal representation. Female professors are underrepresented among Israeli academic faculty across the board, despite the fact that female students (of undergraduate, as well as graduate, degrees) outnumber their male counterparts; women earn lower wages compared to men in the same profession and with the same qualifications, despite the fact that women make up for almost half the workforce. Additionally, women continue to suffer from domestic violence and sexual harassment, despite noteworthy progress made in terms of legislation and public discourse.

The result of this two-faced situation was that women, who often did not feel discriminated against or misrepresented, did not stand up to protest against such wrongs for many years. Since women were supposedly considered to be equal citizens and believed to enjoy the same rights as men, there was no need for them to develop a different political agenda or to adopt different political behavioral patterns to those of men. This undermined the basis for feminist collective action and masked the true gender inequality in Israeli society.

As demonstrated by the variety of issues raised in the opening paragraph of this essay, there are multiple angles to the issue of women in Israeli society. This essay will focus on the representation of women in formal politics, since representation brings with it significant implications, extending beyond the boundaries of the political arena. The significance of focusing on women's representation in formal politics presents itself in three forms. First, the representation of women in the political institutions can serve as a mirror, reflecting and illuminating women's status in other realms of society. Though there is no perfect correlation between women's political power and their status in other arenas, some inference can be deduced regarding the latter by studying the former.[1]

Second, the analysis of women's participation and representation in formal politics opens a window for the discussion of issues that are relevant for women and their status in Israeli society in general, and not just in politics. As such, this chapter will examine different cultural, sociological and contextual issues affecting women, such as their social roles and prospects for entering the political world.

Third, and most importantly, the representation of women in political institutions not only reflects their status in society, but also helps to shape and model it. This is because the equal representation of women in politics in general, and in parliament in particular, is consistent with the values of equality and justice, grants legitimacy to the democratic-liberal regime, and helps inculcate a view of women as citizens of equal standing with men. That is, since parliament is not just any institution, but *the* representative institution in any democratic regime, the issue of gender equality in the legislative chamber is magnified, as it has a symbolic importance extending above and beyond the institution itself. Moreover, the political representative institutions exert a substantial amount of influence over the construction and implementation of social policy. Indeed, it has been argued that women bring something different to politics than their male counterparts by providing a voice for underrepresented groups and values, ensuring that their representation is critical to enhancing the status of women in society.

The essay will proceed as follows. First, it will outline the contours of women's representation in Israeli formal politics: the Knesset and the cabinet, as well as political institutions in the local arena. Subsequently, data regarding the assignment of governmental portfolios to female cabinet members and the assignment of parliamentary committees to female Knesset members will be presented. Following this descriptive snapshot, this essay will address women's substantive representation, asking what it is that Israeli women do once they enter parliament and whether and how they promote gender equality. Finally, this essay will discuss the unique Israeli political and social context, delineating the plethora of effects this context may have on women's participation and representation in politics, as well as in other realms of society. Thus, this essay will address issues such as the predominance of national security in Israeli politics and society; the political culture and social tradition; and the unique ties between women and demography in contemporary Israel.

Descriptive female representation in Israeli politics

When the state of Israel was established in 1948, it was seen as natural for women to be entitled to vote in elections for all representative institutions, as well as to run for office. The predominance of these perceptions is often presented as a testimony to the impressive societal role played by Israeli women, even in the 1940s and 1950s. Strengthening this view is the fact that in the first decade since its establishment, Israel possessed what was then considered a comparatively high percentage of female legislators in its parliament. In 1958, Israel was ranked 4th in the world in terms of its descriptive representation for women. Eleven women served as Members of the Knesset (MKs), representing 9.2 percent of all Knesset members; only Sweden, Finland and the Netherlands had a higher ratio of women representatives (Brichta 1975). This placed Israel as a world leader in terms of women's political representation and helped sustain the above-mentioned myth of gender equality.

However, this perspective overlooks two important facts. First, it ignores the significant struggle fought by women during the pre-state period (the time of the "Yishuv") to win suffrage and eligibility. Such rights were not handed to women on a silver platter; on the contrary, women waged a prolonged battle in order to achieve them, a battle which is only seldom mentioned in Israeli historical discourse (Fogiel-Bijaoui 1992). Second, what started off with a bang ended with a whimper: the representation of women in the Israeli parliament did not continue to rise as it did in other countries, and Israel was soon comparatively left behind. In 2016, Israel was ranked 56th globally for women's parliamentary representation (IPU 2016), demonstrating that the initial, promising signs towards a trend of equal representation proved illusory.

Women in the Knesset and in government

The patterns of female representation in the Knesset can be divided into three phases (see Figure 10.1 below). In the state's first decade, which includes the first three Knesset terms (1949–1959), the proportion of female MKs remained stable and, as noted, rather high in comparative terms. Then, for four decades, until 1999, there was a decline in the number of female legislators, ranging from a low of seven (1988) to a peak of eleven (1992). However, in the last seven Knesset terms, there has been a substantial increase in the number of female MKs, with their proportion steadily growing in each term (with the exception of the 2006 elections). As of 2016, notwithstanding any subsequent developments, thirty-two women (27 percent of the legislature) serve in the 20th Knesset.[2] This is the largest number of female MKs since the establishment of the state, reflecting the trend of improvement in female representation, which has been particularly evident in the last two decades.

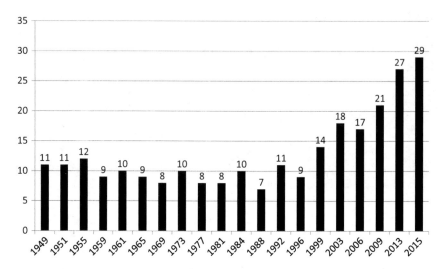

FIGURE 10.1 The number of female Knesset Members (each figure represents female representation on the date the Knesset was installed)

Source: Shapira et al. (2016).

While this overall trend is impressive, it is not uniform across all parties represented in the Knesset. Existing research shows that female representation tends to be higher in parties with a socialist or social-democratic tradition or in post-materialist parties; in contrast, it tends to be particularly low in extreme right parties (Reynolds 1999; Kittilson 2011). Examining the political origins of women elected to the Knesset shows that, until 2003, most female MKs indeed belonged to left-wing parties. Moreover, until 1996, even when the Israeli political right held most of the seats in the Knesset, it never presented more than three female MKs simultaneously. Thus, left-wing parties were mainly responsible for the representation of women in the Knesset.

However, since 2003, the left wing of the political map can no longer claim the lion's share of female MKs. For example, out of the twenty-nine women who entered the Knesset after the 2015 elections, thirteen were affiliated with left-wing parties, nine belonged to right-wing parties and seven came from center parties. In the 19th Knesset, this trend was even more evident: only eight out of twenty-seven women who entered the Knesset after the 2013 elections were affiliated with left-wing parties; ten belonged to right-wing parties and nine came from center parties. It is possible to explain this change by highlighting the growing number of female MKs in some right-wing parties (particularly the Likud and Yisrael Beytenu), as well as by the significant decline in the electoral power and cumulative Knesset representation of left-wing parties.

The division between the political left and right in Israel, which is based mostly on the respective party's position on matters of peace and security, is not the most meaningful indicator of the party's position on issues of women's representation. Instead, it appears that the more prominent social rift is that between the religious and the secular sectors within Israel. This rift divides Israeli society into two communities, which differ from one another on the question of women and their participation in the public sphere. These divisions are also reflected in the political system, creating a parliament in which parties that refrain from placing women in their candidate lists operate alongside parties where the presence of women is natural and well-accepted. That is, while some Israeli parties deliberately exclude women, others see women's participation in the political arena as an important democratic principle (Shapira et al. 2016).

Since 1996, there has been an increase in the parliamentary power of parties that exclude women, compared to prior periods. This phenomenon, which is mostly evident in the strengthening of the orthodox Jewish religious parties (Shas and United Torah Judaism) and the Islamic Arab parties, which also exclude women, shrinks the pool of seats available for women. Nevertheless, this did not harm cumulative female representation in the Knesset. On the contrary, despite the decrease in the number of seats available for women, there has been a marked increase in their political representation. Thus, the increase in women's representation among the parties that do not exclude them is even more prominent than it appears in the statistics. For example, after the elections to the 19th Knesset (2013), the proportion of female legislators among secular parties was 28 percent (twenty-seven out of ninety-eight seats won by secular parties), as opposed to 22.5 percent representation when calculated out of the total seats in the house. In other words, due to the unique political constellation in the Israeli parliament, some parties compensate for other parties' lack of female representation.

Notwithstanding the increase in the representation of women in the Israeli legislature and its importance, a similar increase did not occur in the executive. Though there has been a slight improvement in women's representation in the Israeli cabinet, the situation is far from satisfactory. In the first twenty-five years of Israeli governments (1949–1974) there was only one woman around the cabinet table, the same woman who eventually became Prime Minister: Golda Meir. From Meir's retirement from political life in 1974, up until 1983, the cabinet was completely devoid of female representation.[3] In the period between 1983 and 1992, the cabinet had either just one female minister or none at all. The rise to power of the Israeli center-left in 1992 created a precedent: the government included, for the first time, two female ministers. Subsequently, the first government of the Likud's Ariel Sharon, which was sworn in in March 2001, created another precedent: three women served in the government. However, since the Sharon administration was a very large government (which included at its peak thirty ministers), the relative proportion of women among all the ministers was only 10 percent.

The 33rd government (sworn in on March 2013) continued the upward trend and included four women out of twenty-two cabinet ministers on the day it was sworn in. That is, women comprised 18 percent of all ministers, a rather low percentage, and yet this was an all-time record in terms of the representation of women in Israeli governments. In the 34th government, after the entrance of the Yisrael Beytenu party into Prime Minister Binyamin Netanyahu's government, there are four women in the government at the time of writing, comprising 13 percent of its total ministers. This situation is particularly bleak in light of the global trend of greater female presence in cabinets and leadership roles. In many democracies, the proportion of women in the government often exceeds their proportion in the parliament (see, for example, recent governments in Norway, Sweden, Finland, France, Spain, and Austria). The situation in Israel is very different from this pattern, where the percentage of women in government is significantly lower than their percentage in the Knesset.

This picture of acute inequality, as demonstrated by the slim proportion of women among the total number of ministers, is further validated by examining the importance of the ministerial portfolios assigned to women. According to existing literature, even when women are appointed to serve in government roles around the world, it is rare that they are given high-profile portfolios. Usually they are assigned to the less important, lower-profile ones (Krook and O'Brien 2012; Druckman and Warwick 2005). Israel is no different in this regard, with women being assigned, in line with existing gender-based stereotypes, to head ministries which address "soft," "care-giving" policy issues, or those which primarily concern the private, rather than public, sphere, such as social assistance, health, education, and welfare. Never has a female politician been appointed as the Minister of Defense or the Minister of Finance, two of the most important ministries in Israel. Furthermore, the absence of women from the Ministry of Defense is even seen as "natural" to many members of the Israeli public, given the predominance of the male-dominated security discourse in Israeli politics, an issue discussed subsequently in this chapter.

A similar gendered hierarchy is also apparent in the committee assignment of female MKs. Here too, it is possible to point at salient differences between men and women, with women being assigned, in much larger proportions, membership in those Knesset committees which deal with policy issues considered "feminine," based on the existing gender-based stereotypes. Unsurprisingly, such committees are often considered less important and less prestigious. For example, Shapira et al.'s study which examined the assignment of female MKs to the permanent Knesset committees in the 18th Knesset showed that the highest ratio of female MKs (33 percent) was found in the group of committees categorized as social affairs committees—the Immigration Committee, the Education Committee and the Labor and Social Welfare Committee—and in the Status of Women Committee (also 33 percent).

Contrarily, the ratio of female participants was much lower in the group of committees categorized as economic and foreign affairs committees (17.5 percent). The Foreign Affairs and Defense Committee—considered one of the most important and prestigious committees—was only 12.5 percent female in its composition. This is an improvement, considering the fact that until the 13th Knesset in 1992, no women had ever set foot in this committee, yet it is by no means satisfactory. In committees that are considered important and that confer power and prestige on their members—such as the House Committee and the Constitution

Committee—the percentage of female members remains a mere 10 percent (Shapira et al. 2016). These findings are consistent with those of Yishai (1997), who found that women are pushed onto less important parliamentary committees, which are considered to be the "province" of women. Thus, in spite of the growing presence of women in the Knesset in the last two decades, gender segregation remains unchanged, even when women leave the home and make inroads into fields that were once considered exclusively masculine (Herzog 1999).

The substantive representation of women in Israeli politics

While the previous section addressed what is known as the descriptive representation of women—their number or proportion only—this section will address a different type of representation—substantive representation. When examining the substantive representation of women, by women, researchers examine what women do when they enter parliament, or in other words, gauge their "impact." Do women represent and promote the interests of women in society? Do they promote a feminist agenda? Do they present a different set of policy priorities compared to men? While this is a popular and growing field of research, studies of the substantive representation of women have yielded ambiguous results, leading scholars to claim that the relationship between descriptive and substantive representation is often context dependent (Koch and Fulton 2011). In other words, that there are no guarantees: shifting identities, differences amongst women, partisan loyalties and institutional factors are all seen to play a part in shaping and constraining an inclination and capacity to "act for women" (Mackay 2008, p.127). Despite these drawbacks, many of the studies in this field do find differences between male representatives and female representatives, sustaining the notion of the substantive representation of women, by women (Childs and Krook 2009).

While only a few studies have examined this issue in Israel, it appears that Israeli female legislators do behave differently to male legislators, focusing more on issues related to the private sphere, as well as issues pertaining to women and their status in society. A recent study examining the parliamentary behavior of male and female Knesset members in the 17th and 18th Knesset terms found that female MKs contribute more than their male counterparts to the volume of legislation on issues related to women and their status in society, as well as to issues related to children and family. Male MKs, on the other hand, contribute more to the volume of legislation on issues related to national security (Itzkovitch-Malka and Friedberg 2016).

Contrarily, a different study, which focused on gender-related legislation promoted during the 18th Knesset, found that less than a third of female MKs played a role in passing gender-related legislation. Unsurprisingly, these MKs were feminist women who belonged to left or center parties (Golan and Melman). These findings go hand in hand with those of Herzog (2004, p. 216) who claimed that: "women who were elected were women in politics, but women who did not necessarily implement women's politics." Yes, female MKs support and promote legislation and policy affecting women and their status in society, but not as a result of a comprehensive feminist worldview or ideology which rejects the existing gender structure.

Cultural, social and contextual factors affecting women's participation and representation in public life

The representation of women in formal politics is affected by many factors. Some are institutional, such as the electoral system, the party system or the existence of gender quotas, while others are of a more socio-cultural nature, such as religion, social structure or political culture. The most important institutional factors expected to affect women's representation in politics are the electoral system and the nomination procedures for party candidates. The Israeli electoral system is based on a proportional representation (PR) electoral formula, a single nation-wide electoral district—encompassing the entire Israeli legislature and numbering 120 MKs—and a relatively low electoral threshold. While the PR electoral formula supposedly favors the representation of women in parliament compared to majoritarian electoral systems, because women find it easier to get elected in multi— rather than single—member districts (Kittilson 2011), the extremely large electoral district, combined with the low legal electoral threshold, apparently harms their representation. This is because such institutional conditions allow for the representation of many medium and small-sized parties in parliament. Given that women are usually placed in relatively low positions on party lists, the percentage of women who will serve in parliament on behalf of these parties is likely to be particularly low (Matland 1998).

The nomination procedures used by Israeli parties are extremely diverse, as there is no regulation regarding the type of candidate selection methods parties should adopt. Today, Israeli parties are characterized by a dichotomy, using one of two extreme candidate selection methods: either highly exclusive methods, usually selection by the party leader, or highly inclusive methods, usually party primaries; intermediate methods are used by a small minority of the parties (Rahat 2010). The exclusive methods are often considered more beneficial to female candidates, as they tend to produce more representative party lists. Inclusive methods, on the other hand, have the potential to impair the representation of female candidates (Rahat and Hazan 2010). As a result, as part of the democratization of the candidate selection process, many Israeli parties have adopted voluntary gender quotas. Nevertheless, such quotas are usually modest in their scope (ranging from 20 percent to 33 percent in most cases) and do not set a high enough bar for the representation of women.

Notwithstanding the importance of the above-mentioned institutional factors, this essay adopts the socio-cultural approach and addresses those non-institutional factors that clearly affect women's representation in formal politics, as well as their status in other realms of Israeli society. Adopting this approach allows to examine and address several of the most basic characteristics of Israeli society, their relevance to the gender structure, and their effect on women's participation in formal politics.

The predominance of the security discourse

The political and social repercussions of the prolonged Israeli–Palestinian conflict is a well-studied research area. Specifically of interest here are the effects of the conflict—and the predominance of the security discourse in Israeli society created by it—on the gender structure of Israeli politics and society. In short, there are two main paths by which the predominance of security affects the gender division of Israeli society and engagement with gender equality.

First, the ongoing conflict and the need to address what are almost unanimously perceived as life-threatening security concerns, overshadows most—and at times all—other everyday policy issues in Israel. Thus, the acute security threats Israel has to address on a daily basis, coupled with the dominance of the security discourse created as a result of this reality, perpetuates a constant distraction from other political concerns, such as the economy, social welfare, education and gender equality. This social climate, when everything is subordinated to security and its needs, ensures the struggle for women's rights and equality is significantly more challenging.

Additionally, the centrality of the security debate in Israeli society segments and divides women based on their stance regarding questions of security and foreign affairs. While the intersectionality problem of women as a social collective is present everywhere, the Israeli–Palestinian conflict aggravates this trend, forcing women to take a political stand on a dichotomous matter. This hampers the ability of women to act in unity as a collective, to promote their joint goals, further dividing Israeli women into different, competing political camps. The problem is even more acute when addressing women from both sides of the conflict: Jewish Israeli and Palestinian. In this case, the seeds of the conflict are so deeply rooted that it is almost impossible to spur the much-needed solidarity for collective action (Herzog 2004). This is especially concerning, as there is extensive common ground between the experiences shared by both Jewish Israeli and Palestinian women, which could potentially lead to a joint collective action for gender equality and women's rights on both sides of the conflict.

Second, the centrality of the security discourse helps to validate existing gender-based stereotypes and further marginalize women. This is not a new phenomenon, nor is it restricted to Israel alone, however the Israeli geopolitical context deepens and exacerbates this trend. Comparative scholarship on gender-based stereotypes argues that women are consistently perceived as more compassionate, kind, trustworthy, gentle and willing to compromise, whereas men are viewed as more aggressive, authoritative, powerful and self-confident (Wilson 2004). Women are also seen as more competent at handling such issues as education, welfare and healthcare, but less competent at what are perceived as "masculine" duties, such as the military, crime and foreign policy (Holman et al. 2011; Koch and Fulton 2011).

Because female legislators are stereotyped as holding different ideologies, character traits and issue competencies than men, they may confront credibility problems when dealing with issues perceived as masculine (Koch and Fulton 2011). This is especially true for national security, a policy issue that is highly dominated by men in most polities. This is the product of the framing of human conflict as largely a male pursuit (Tickner 2001), based on the common belief

> that military and foreign policy are arenas of policy-making least appropriate for women. Strength, power, autonomy, independence, and rationality, all typically associated with men and masculinity, are characteristics we most value in those to whom we entrust the conduct of our foreign policy and the defense of our national interest.
>
> *(Tickner 1992, p. 3)*

Unsurprisingly then, the military in Israel—a highly male institution which represents a powerful gender regime—is one of the prime institutions contributing to the construction of gender inequality, due to its central role and status within Israeli culture and society (Izraeli 1999).

The effects of the security discourse disadvantages women in many social and professional arenas, as well as in the political arena. Men in Israel have substantial leverage for a political career over women, due to their salience in the all-powerful military, especially in high-ranking or high-profile positions. A substantial number of Israeli MKs are from a military or security-focused background (Goldberg 2006), a fact which—in Israeli political culture—portrays them as more competent or qualified for politics than others. Moreover, it is not uncommon for politicians, both male and female, to face accusations of unsuitability for various high-profile political positions, based on the claim that they do not possess sufficient military/ security experience. Clearly, women face this accusation far too often, as they do not have access to most high-ranking military positions (Rahat and Itzkovitch-Malka 2012). While military service is mandatory for the vast majority of 18-year-old Israeli Jews, regardless of gender, this does not serve as a recruitment path or springboard to politics for women, as it does not provide the kind of military experience upon which they can build credibility to address national security policy areas. Women usually serve for only two years, generally in non-combative, administrative positions. It is only those who develop a military career—a minority within a male-dominated, privileged group of society—that usually enjoy a fast track to national politics and can claim credit and credibility to engage in national security policy issues.

Furthermore, the effect of the security discourse expands beyond matters of security per se. The securitization of politics—which brings to the forefront security considerations or military thinking, even in matters which do not strictly have to do with security—exacerbates the gender order and empowers stereotypical sexist perceptions. As a result, in a spillover effect, women are often perceived as less competent to engage in politics *as a whole*, and not just in security matters.

Social-political traditions

A common assumption in feminist literature is that women, wherever they are, are marginalized and discriminated against on the basis of their gender (Abdo 2011). This is mainly due to patriarchal social structures, which are still present in modern societies and contribute to the exclusion of women. For instance, the patriarchal family is considered a prime institution for male domination and control. The patriarchal nature of Israeli society—both Jewish and Arab—thus contributes to the further marginalization of women. Both societies are often described as traditional, attributing significant importance to familial values, while preserving and reproducing the public–private sphere dichotomy. According to those traditional worldviews—which are still considered highly popular in the Israeli social and political contexts—the distinction between the public and the private overlaps the gendered differentiation between men and women.

Traditionalist perceptions of gender, especially within the family, are opposed to the idea of women entering the public sphere, and support their exclusion from the political life. Not only does the Jewish tradition grant women fewer rights in matrimony compared to men, it also draws strict borders between the public and private spheres. While men are allowed to operate in both spheres, and are even expected to do so, women are limited to the private sphere only and are thus blocked from entering public life (Golan 2004). The upsurge in religious extremism, as witnessed within several sub-sections of the religious Zionist Jewish population, serves to strengthen these dichotomous divisions. For example, it is now considered acceptable to publicly question whether women should be allowed to sing, or young girls to dance, in official public ceremonies, despite the fact that this was an accepted norm for years in Israeli society.

In the political world, which is one of the most prominent arenas of the public sphere, this private–public dichotomy is particularly vivid. The clearest examples are those of the Jewish ultra-Orthodox parties and some of the Arab parties, mentioned in the previous section, which completely deny women the opportunity to seek political office and serve as elected representatives. According to their worldviews, politics (along with the entire public sphere in general) is not an appropriate arena for women to engage in.

The lack of separation between religion and state within Israel supports and replicates existing patriarchal patterns. In other words, it is not just a matter of culture: the gendered discrimination against women in Israel is also embedded in the political and legal arrangements of the country. The decision not to separate religion and state represents the focal point of Israel's identity as a Jewish state. According to the status quo agreements, which reiterate this decision, personal status law is entrusted in the hands of religious legal bodies—whether Jewish, Muslim or Christian. The religious courts thus hold judiciary authority on matters related to marriage, divorce, support, etc. As could be expected, the religious laws—determined and implemented by male-dominated institutions—are generally patriarchal and traditional in nature, and readily adopt the traditional perceptions regarding the nature and role of women, thus replicating and sustaining the public–private sphere dichotomy.

Female participation in public life is also hampered by a spillover effect from personal status laws to other arenas of legislation, often the result of the political influence of religious parties. For example, women are often deprived representation in various religious institutions, such as religious councils. In 2013, an amendment to the Rabbinical Judges (Dayanim) law was passed, overcoming substantial institutional resistance. The amendment sought to increase the participation of women on the Rabbinical Judges Appointment Committee, a body which elects judges for all rabbinical courts in Israel. At the time of writing, four out of the eleven committee members are now women. The political power of the ultra-Orthodox Jewish parties extends to affect Arab women's participation in public life as well. In 2015, a bill for female judicial participation in Sharia courts was opposed by the government, due to a concern among ultra-Orthodox members of the coalition that supporting the bill would create a precedent that could later be applied to Jewish rabbinical courts.

Women in the service of demography

Israel is a family-oriented society (Halperin-Kaddari 2004). Family—and family values—play a central normative role in the lives of individuals and the collective (Fogiel-Bijaoui 1999). Despite significant upward trends in levels of female education and workforce participation, the marriage rate and birthrate in Israel remain high and the divorce rate remains relatively low, compared to other post-industrial democracies. Furthermore, the centrality of family and family values is not limited to the more traditional sub-groups among Israeli society, such as the Orthodox Jew or Muslims—though it may be more salient among these groups—and is the common normative framework for most Israelis (Fogiel-Bijaoui 1999).

Israel's composition as a pronatalist society is reflected in the available data. While the fertility rates in all population sub-groups in Israel have decreased in recent decades, they remain significantly higher compared to other post-industrial Western societies. In 2014, the total fertility rate in Israel averaged at 3.08 children per woman. Taking religion into account, Jewish women averaged 3.11 children, compared to 3.35 children for Muslim women. Taken together, Israel's total fertility rate is the highest among OECD countries and is substantially higher than the OECD average, which stands at 1.7 children on average, per woman. It is no surprise then, that motherhood represents the heart of the female normative experience in Israel and many women feel that motherhood, or a lack thereof, socially defines them. Few women in Israel do not have any children, and those that do are often categorized as strange or miserable (Anat-Shafir 2011).

On an institutional level, having children is considered a contribution to the strengthening of the nation, the state and the collective. This is because having children in Israel is constructed as part of the Jewish–Arab conflict and is expressed in terms of the demographic balance (Halperin-Kaddari 2004). Substantial resources have been invested in encouraging fertility through a variety of economic, medical, educational and legal arrangements. The encouragement of fertility by the Israeli establishment is evident in different aspects of the relations between the state, fertility and women. The state is involved with the economic and constitutional aspects of fertility: it does not sponsor birth-control products, but invests millions in extremely expensive fertility treatments. The Israeli government encourages fertility by economic subsidies and grants, and it boasts one of the worlds' most liberal legislation regimes for surrogacy, despite the difficulties this issue raises in questions of religion and state (Wilamovski and Tamir 2012).

As a result, the role of women in the Israeli collective is determined mainly by their social roles as wives and mothers. It is motherhood that grants women their "entry ticket" (Herzog 2004) to citizenship and the basis for their equal rights and citizenship status. In other words, women are not considered equal citizens due to egalitarian principles which see them in gender-blind glasses as equal standing human beings, nor are they seen as a social collective with political interests other than those relevant to their roles as wives and mothers. This affects, among other things, the behavioral patterns of women in politics. Since the prevailing societal paradigms in Israel acknowledge women as a social category only based on their roles as wives and mothers, they deny women the opportunity to make political claims for women on the basis of normative principles, such as equality and justice.

Conclusion: prospects and challenges

To summarize, the status of women in Israel has indeed improved over the years, but the political, social and cultural reality demands more action in order to achieve true gender equality. Much work is still needed to reduce wage gaps between women and men; to promote the status of mothers in the labor market; to impart true social security for women and to improve the presence and representation of women in the public sphere. Judging by the experience of the last few decades, it is safe to assume that the status of women in Israeli society will continue to improve incrementally, in large part due to the continuous efforts of feminist organizations.

Nevertheless, the distinctive features of Israeli society and culture reviewed in this essay posit substantial challenges and obstacles on the road ahead. To a large extent, Israel is a venue for two parallel sub-cultures with regards to gender and gender equality. This is often expressed in what can be considered "a shift of a pendulum": from the adoption of some of the most advanced gender-related legislation in the Western world in many fields on the one hand, to various backlash phenomena, such as excluding women from performing in official ceremonies, or forbidding them from singing in front of IDF soldiers, on the other. The religious–secular cleavage—which is often referred to as the "culture war" in Israeli society—is well reflected in the struggle for gender equality and will probably continue to play a major role in it in the foreseeable future.

In other words, the feminist struggle is not over yet, and there is still a long way to go. This struggle should be fought in multiple arenas simultaneously. However, many advocates for women's rights would agree that the Knesset should be one of the main arenas for targeted feminist activity, since the legislation it produces forms a normative basis for conduct. The main challenge, in this respect, is twofold: first, to further increase the representation of women in the Knesset and second, to encourage those elected—both male and female—to adopt a feminist agenda or promote a gender-oriented policy. As for the first challenge, while we could simply hope that the incremental improvement in the representation of women in the Knesset will continue on its own and will result in more women being elected to the Knesset, there is only one way to guarantee it: the adoption of legal gender quotas. That is, to have the Knesset legislate a law obligating parties to ensure equal representation to both genders in their candidate lists before elections. Such a mechanism is highly accepted and popular in many Western democracies as a means to increase the representation of women in parliament. In Israel, however, while there had been many attempts to table such legislation, starting from the 13th Knesset onwards, it was never seriously promoted or considered, in part due to the massive objection such legislation raises among ultra-Orthodox parties.[4]

The second challenge is to implement gender mainstreaming practices in the Knesset and in government, as a means to achieve greater gender equality. Like gender quotas, gender mainstreaming has also become a widely accepted global strategy for the promotion of gender equality, and in this respect as well, Israel lags behind, though signs of improvement are visible. In 2007, the Knesset adopted a Gender Impact Assessment (GIA) law, granting the Authority for the Advancement of the Status of Women the mandate to assess the gendered impact of any suggested legislation, by incorporating gender mainstreaming in the process of regulatory impact assessment. Additionally, beginning in 2013, the Knesset made its first steps in gender budgeting, performing a gendered examination of the national budget. Advocates for women's equality hope that the adoption of such strategies, along with a continued increased in the percentage of female MKs and the public activity of feminist organizations, will bring greater gender equality in Israel, both in the Knesset and outside of it.

Notes

1 Excluding some clear outliers such as those of Asian or African developing countries in which women's political representation was institutionally engineered to achieve gender equality; however their status in other realms of society remains rather low. See, for example, the case of Rwanda, in which women constitute 64 percent of the legislature, a fact which is not mirrored in their low status in society.
2 Three more women legislators joined the Knesset as a result of personnel changes since the March 2015 elections. This is why the number of women in 2016 is larger than the number presented in Figure 10.1, which only includes the number of female MKs on the day the Knesset was installed.
3 Aside from a short period in which Shulamit Aloni, the leader of Ratz party, was appointed as a Minister without Portfolio during the first Rabin government, a position from which she resigned a few months later.
4 some of the parties in Israel have introduced voluntary party quotas, but those are easily changeable and do not produce a high enough ratio of female representation.

References and further reading

Abdo, Nahla. 2011. *Women in Israel: Race, Gender and Citizenship.* London/New York: Zed Books.

Anat-Shafir, Liora. 2011. "Motherhood?" in Tal Tamir (ed.), *Women's Body: Health, Body, Sexuality, Relations.* Ben-Shemen: Modan, pp. 397–587. [Hebrew]

Brichta, Abraham. 1975. "Women in the Knesset: 1949–1969." *Parliamentary Affairs.* 28, pp. 31–50.

Chazan, Naomi. 2011. "Gender, Power and Politics in Israel: Translating Political Representation into Meaningful Empowerment for Women." *Palestine-Israel Journal of Politics, Economics and Culture.* 17(3–4), pp. 42–45.

Childs, Sarah and Mona Lena Krook. 2009. "Analysing Women's Substantive Representation: From Critical Mass to Critical Actors." *Government and Opposition.* 44(2), pp. 125–145.

Druckman, James N. and Paul V. Warwick. 2005. "The Missing Piece: Measuring Portfolio Salience in Western European Parliamentary Democracies." *European Journal of Political Research.* 44(1), pp. 17–42.

Falk, Erika and Kate Kenski. 2006. "Issue Saliency and Gender Stereotypes: Support for Women as President in Times of War and Terrorism." *Social Science Quarterly.* 87(1), pp. 1–18.

Fogiel-Bijaoui, Sylvie. 1992. "On the Way to Equality? The Struggle for Women's Suffrage in the Jewish Yishuv, 1917–1926," in Deborah S. Bernstein (ed.), *Pioneers and Homemakers— Jewish Women in Pre-State Israel.* Albany, NY: State University of New York Press, pp. 261–282.

Fogiel-Bijaoui, Sylvie. 1999. "Families in Israel: Between Familism and Post-Modernism," in Dafna N. Israeli, Ariella Friedman, Henriette Dahan-Kalev, Sylvie Fogiel-Bijaoui, Hanna Herzog, Manar Hasan and Hannah Naveh (eds.), *Sex, Gender, Politics.* Tel Aviv: Hakibbuz Hameuhad, pp. 107–167. [Hebrew]

Golan, Galia. 2004. "Gender Quotas for Women in Politics," in Anat Maor (ed.), *Affirmative Action and Equal Representation in Israel.* Tel Aviv: Ramot—Tel Aviv University, pp. 315–330.

Golan, Galia and Lavi Melman (forthcoming). "What do they do when they get there? Women of the 18th Knesset, or Descriptive vs Substantive Representation," in Michal Shamir, Hanna Herzog and Naomi Chazan (eds.), *The Gender Gap in Israel.* Jerusalem: The Van Leer Institute.

Goldberg, Giora. 2006. "The Growing Militarization of the Israeli Political System." *Israel Affairs.* 12(3), pp. 377–394.

Halperin-Kaddari, Ruth. 2004. *Women in Israel: A State of their Own.* Philadelphia, PA: University of Pennsylvania Press.

Herzog, Hanna. 1999. *Gendering Politics.* Ann Arbor, MI: University of Michigan Press.

Herzog, Hanna. 2004. "Women in Israeli Society," in Uzi Rebhun and Chaim I. Waxman (eds.), *Jews in Israel: Contemporary Social and Cultural Patterns.* Hanover: Brandeis University Press, pp. 195–220.

Holman, Mirya R., Jennifer L. Merolla and Elizabeth J. Zechmeister. 2011. "Sex, Stereotypes, and Security: A Study of the Effects of Terrorist Threat on Assessments of Female Leadership." *Journal of Women, Politics & Policy.* 32(3), pp. 173–192.

Inter-Parliamentary Union (IPU). "Women in National Parliaments." Available at: www.ipu. org/wmn-e/world.htm (accessed June 3, 2016).

Israel Central Bureau of Statistics. 2016. "Data for the International Women's Day 2016." Available at: www.cbs.gov.il/reader/newhodaot/hodaa_template.html?hodaa=201611055 (accessed June 5, 2016).

Itzkovitch-Malka, Reut and Chen Friedberg. 2016. "Gendering Security: The Substantive Representation of Women in the Israeli Parliament." European Journal of Women's Studies, DOI: 1350506816684898

Izraeli, Dafna N. 1999. "Gendering the Labor World," in Dafna N. Izraeli, Ariella Friedman, Henriette Dahan-Kalev, Sylvie Fogiel-Bijaoui, Hanna Herzog, Manar Hasan and Hannah Naveh (eds.), Sex, Gender, Politics. Tel Aviv: Hakibbuz Hameuhad, pp. 167–215. [Hebrew]

Izraeli, Dafna N. 2003. "Gender Politics in Israel: The Case of Affirmative Action for Women Directors." Women's Studies International Forum. 26(2), pp. 109–128.

Kittilson, Miki Caul. 2011. "Women, Parties and Platforms in Post-Industrial Democracies." Party Politics. 17(1), pp. 66–92.

Koch, Michael T. and Sarah A. Fulton. 2011. "In the Defense of Women: Gender, Office Holding, and National Security Policy in Established Democracies." Journal of Politics. 73(1), pp. 1–16.

Krook, Mona Lena and Diana Z. O'Brien. 2012. "All the President's Men? The Appointment of Female Cabinet Ministers Worldwide." Journal of Politics. 74(3), pp. 840–855.

Lawless, Jennifer. L. 2004. "Women, War, and Winning Elections: Gender Stereotyping in the Post-September 11th Era." Political Research Quarterly. 53(3), pp. 479–490.

Mackay, Fiona. 2008. "'Thick' Conceptions of Substantive Representation: Women, Gender and Political Institutions." Representation. 44(2), pp. 125–139.

Matland, Richard E. 1998. "Enhancing Women's Political Participation: Legislative Recruitment and Electoral Systems," in A. Karam (ed.), Women in Parliament: Beyond Numbers. Stockholm: International Institute for Democracy and Electoral Assistance, pp. 65–88.

Rahat, Gideon. 2010. "The Political Consequences of Candidate Selection to the 18th Knesset," in Asher Arian and Michal Shamir (eds.), The Elections in Israel 2009. New Brunswick, NJ: Transaction Publishers, pp. 195–224.

Rahat, Gideon and Reuven Y. Hazan. 2005. "Israel: The Politics of an Extreme Electoral System," in M. Gallagher and P. Mitchell (eds.), The Politics of Electoral Systems. Oxford: Oxford University Press, pp. 333–351.

Rahat, Gideon and Reut Itzkovitch-Malka. 2012. "Political Representation in Israel: Minority Sectors vs. Women." Representation. 48(3), pp. 307–319.

Reynolds, Andrew. 1999. "Women in the Legislatures and Executives of the World: Knocking at the Highest Glass Ceiling." World Politics. 51(4), pp. 547–572.

Shapira, Assaf, Ofer Kenig, Chen Friedberg and Reut Itzkovitch-Malka. 2016. The Representation of Women in Israeli Politics—A Comparative Perspective Jerusalem: The Israel Democracy Institute.

Tickner, Anne J. 1992. Gender in International Relations: Feminist Perspectives on Achieving Global Peace. New York: Columbia University Press.

Tickner, Anne J. 2001. Gendering World Politics. New York: Columbia University Press.

Wilamovski, Inbal and Tal Tamir (eds.) 2012. Women in Israel: Between Theory and Reality. Tel Aviv: The Israel Women's Network. [Hebrew]

Wilson, Marie. C. 2004. Closing the Leadership Gap: Why Women Can and Must Run the World. New York: Penguin.

Yishai, Yael. 1997. Between the Flag and the Banner: Women in Israeli Politics. Albany, NY: State University of New York Press.

PART III

Security, geopolitical and foreign policy challenges

11

SECURITY CHALLENGES AND OPPORTUNITIES IN THE TWENTY-FIRST CENTURY

Charles D. (Chuck) Freilich

Israel's changing strategic environment

Israel is a tiny state, of around 20,000 square kilometers in size, about the size of New Jersey, or Slovenia. It is surrounded by an Arab, and broader Muslim, world which is either fundamentally hostile to its existence—including states such as Egypt and Jordan, which have concluded formal peace treaties with it—or explicitly committed to its destruction and actively engaged in warfare against it. Israel's eastern borders, the West Bank and Golan Heights, are hilly areas, whose control would provide its adversaries with a commanding military presence over most of its territory and virtually the entire population and industrial base of the country. Israel's precarious geography is further exacerbated by its elongated shape, which makes it no more than fifteen kilometers wide at its center and much less in other areas.

Regional and global developments in recent decades have, however, transformed Israel's strategic environment. Peace with Egypt removed the most powerful Arab state from the ongoing military conflict and once Egypt no longer considered the use of force against Israel, the other Arab states no longer had a conventional military option against it. Indeed, after fighting four wars against Israel during the first twenty-five years of the state's existence, all with Egypt's participation, the Arab states have not fought a single one ever since. Moreover, in a dramatic transformation of Israel's strategic fortunes, it no longer faces existential threats and is unlikely to face one again in the future, unless Iran, or another regional actor, acquires nuclear weapons.

Egypt's domestic turmoil in recent years initially endangered the peace treaty and weakened its control over the Sinai Peninsula, leading to a number of terrorist attacks against it by Islamic State (IS) factions active there. Even if Egypt stabilizes politically, and avoids becoming a failed state in the near term, its dire poverty and burgeoning population mean that the long-term danger to its stability, and consequently to the peace with Israel, remains significant.

Jordan has weathered the regional upheaval of recent years comparatively well. Nevertheless, unrest continues and Jordan's fundamental challenges, especially its poverty and the ongoing tensions between the traditional Hashemite population and Palestinian majority, continue to pose threats to its long-term stability. This has been further exacerbated by the violence in Syria and Iraq, which has led to a huge influx of refugees to Jordan, the emergence of radical Islamist entities on Jordan's borders, and its penetration by radical Islamists. For Israel, Jordan's location as a bulwark against the more radical, Iranian-dominated states it borders, and the extensive bilateral security cooperation that has developed in response, have turned it into a de facto ally and its ongoing viability into a foremost Israeli interest.

Egypt and Jordan have now been at peace with Israel for decades. The bilateral relationship with both is cold and devoid of virtually any normalization, other than the long-term deal Jordan concluded with Israel for the purchase of natural gas. Nevertheless, both countries' commitment to peace has successfully withstood a number of significant challenges and a cold peace is infinitely better for all actors concerned than a hot war.

Military cooperation, surprisingly perhaps, has increased significantly with both Egypt and Jordan in recent years and is the one area in which the picture for bilateral cooperation is bright. Israel, Egypt, and Jordan share important strategic interests today regarding the rise of Iran and its allies in the region; radical Sunni forces, such as IS; jihadi elements operating in Sinai; and Hamas. Israel has thus repeatedly acceded to Egyptian requests to deploy forces in Sinai in excess of those permitted by the peace treaty, in order to help Egypt restore its control over the area. According to media reports Israel has conducted drone strikes, with Egypt's blessing, against the Islamic State in the Sinai and has supplied attack helicopters to Jordan, in conjunction with the United States, as well as drones. Israeli drones have reportedly also used Jordanian airspace to monitor events in Syria and the two countries have participated in multilateral military exercises.

The Soviet Union, which provided the Arab states with massive military, diplomatic and economic assistance, disappeared, further undermining the Arab capability to wage war against Israel. Moreover, the regional turmoil that began with the "Arab Spring" has weakened many of the remaining threats Israel faced, while also producing new ones. Indeed, the primary threat Israel faces today is no longer the strength of the Arab states, but their weakness and the consequent danger that domestic instability, combined with weak and failing governments, will lead to hostilities. Each individual actor may be weaker than the more centralized Arab states of the past, but overall the region may be characterized by a growing number of radical actors, including non-state groups, increasingly willing to use force and empowered by modern military technology to do so.

The Syrian Civil War has devastated Syria and its military, heretofore the primary military threat Israel faced. With the fighting now dying down, Syria's long-term future is unclear, but at least for the medium term it appears to have become a strange hybrid of a Russian and Iranian-dominated country. Russia is likely to have heightened ongoing influence in Syria and a larger military presence, restricting

Israel's military freedom of maneuver and furthering complicating matters diplomatically. Iran and its proxy, Hizbollah, Israel's two foremost enemies today, will increasingly use Syria to widen their base of operations against Israel and create one long front from Lebanon, as part of a "Shiite crescent" extending from Iran, all the way to the Mediterranean. After over forty years of quiet, since the 1973 Yom Kippur War, the Golan Heights may once again become an active and particularly combustible front. The Syrian regime's heinous character notwithstanding, its repeated defeats at Israel's hands had the benefit of making it risk-averse and cautious in recent decades.

Lebanon has been a failed state for decades and its ongoing inability to control the terrorist organizations that have operated against Israel from its territory—the Palestine Liberation Organization (PLO) until the early 1980s and Hizbollah ever since—has led to repeated military confrontations. Hizbollah, a radical jihadist organization avowed to Israel's destruction, was founded by Iran and is largely armed, trained and financed by it to this day. Over the years, Hizbollah has become the most powerful actor in Lebanon, politically and militarily, far more than the government itself. Hizbollah has been deeply involved in the fighting in Syria in recent years, in the attempt to save the regime of Bashar Al-Assad from collapse, but its mammoth rocket arsenal and other capabilities remain directed at Israel, and renewed hostilities are likely.

Iraq no longer poses a direct threat to Israel. Its internal dislocations do, however, constitute a growing danger to the stability of Jordan and Saudi Arabia, two of Israel's neighbors whose behavior towards it has long been moderate, and thus an indirect threat to its security. Moreover, Iraq has come under growing Iranian influence and the emergence of an Iranian-dominated arc stretching through Iraq, into Syria and Lebanon, would pose severe challenges to Israel. Iran is the most dangerous adversary Israel has ever faced, with a sophisticated long-term approach towards its ultimate destruction. Moreover, Iran has not abandoned its nuclear aspirations, despite the 2015 nuclear deal, and remains the only regional actor that may acquire nuclear weapons in the near term, certainly after the agreement expires. An Iranian-dominated Syria and Iraq would thus be a highly negative outcome for Israel.

The Gaza Strip and the West Bank are ruled by rival Palestinian governments, neither of which has a monopoly over force in its territory. The long-term future of the Palestinian Authority (PA) in the West Bank is unclear, whether because of internal divisions, its fecklessness as a governing entity, or the failure of the peace process. After the terrorist ravages of the Second Intifada in the early 2000s, Palestinian terrorism against Israel dropped precipitously for a decade, only to increase somewhat once again in 2015.

Israel conducted a complete, unilateral, withdrawal from Gaza in 2005, at least partially in the anticipation of an improvement in the security situation. In practice, Gaza, under Hamas, has become a radical, theocratic and impoverished mini-state, which has continued periodic rocket fire at Israeli population centers, leading to ongoing low-level hostilities and also to three major confrontations—in 2008, 2012 and 2014—in which Israel sought to diminish the rocket threat and restore a period of calm. Although Hamas's rocket arsenal is far smaller than Hizbollah's, it is still potent and can cause a severe disruption to everyday life and the economy in Israel.

The Palestinians have rejected a number of dramatic proposals for peace, including the Camp David Summit and Clinton Parameters in 2000, as well as then-Prime Minister Ehud Olmert's proposal of 2008, beyond which there is little Israel could add. This raises a fundamental quandary for Israel, whether the conflict with the PA is, indeed, over a number of specific issues, whose resolution would lead to peace, or still over Israel's very existence. As for Hamas, there is no question it not only does not seek peace, but explicitly calls for Israel's destruction. In any event, as long as the West Bank and Gaza remain divided, and the PA, the recognized Palestinian government, cannot speak for all Palestinians, a final peace agreement is not possible. After a decade of deep and growing separation, the prospects for reunification remain bleak.

Saudi Arabia faces a period of change and possible instability, due to rapid domestic change, fluctuating energy prices and external challenges, primarily the rise of Iran. One of the world's most radical states domestically, Saudi Arabia has not posed a significant threat to Israel to date, a situation that could change rapidly in the event of regime instability or change. A combination of the Saudis' petro-influence, large arsenal of the most sophisticated American weapons, and possible future decision to develop nuclear ones, makes them a potential major threat to Israel.

Libya, Sudan and Yemen are already failed states. Advanced weapons from Libya's former military forces have already made their way to Gaza and not all of the Libyan chemical arsenal has been secured. Tunisia and Morocco, in the past the Arab states most amenable to a relationship with Israel, both face significant problems of domestic stability, as does Bahrain.

Failed states further present a threat to Israel's security, because of the heightened opportunities they afford for external intervention. For example, Iran, Saudi Arabia, Hizbollah, IS and Qatar, as well as Russia and the US, have all been deeply involved in the Syrian Civil War. Failed states also provide fertile ground for terrorist organizations, as a refuge and source of activists. Syria and Iraq have become focal points for al-Qaeda, ISIS, Hamas took over Gaza. Most dangerously, failed states may be unable to ensure effective control over their WMD capabilities.

The primal clash between the Sunnis and Shia has been a driving force in the region in recent decades and is likely to remain so, with Iran's pursuit of regional hegemony facing the countervailing spread of radical Sunni ideologies and forces. Israel is the one issue the warring sides all agree on. To date, they have been too preoccupied with their immediate conflict to join forces against it, but this may change and Israel could find itself caught between tectonic forces, which profoundly affect its national security, but over which it has little, if any, influence.

American influence in the Middle East is at a decades-long nadir and long-term regional trends will pose ongoing challenges to it. Changes in American policy, as well as regional and international developments, could restore the US's stature, but it will take time and resolute action in the face of the many challenges the region poses today. For Israel, whose national security is intimately linked to American global and regional influence, the ramifications are significant. The US is an ultimate guarantor of Israel's security, only it can lead international efforts to confront such major threats as the Iranian nuclear program, or the situation in Syria, and only the US has successfully brokered peace agreements between Israel and its adversaries.

As US influence in the region has waned, Russia's has grown, especially as it has turned the Middle East into a primary arena of renewed US–Russian competition. Russia has become the single most powerful player in Syria, having saved the regime from near-collapse with its military intervention in 2015. Russia has also long been a close ally of Iran, selling it arms, cooperating diplomatically and defending Iran from attempts to isolate and punish it for its nuclear program, although Russia did in the end join the nuclear deal the major powers reached with Iran in 2015. Russia has also been working assiduously to strengthen its ties with other countries in the region, including major American allies such as Egypt, with whom it has signed a deal to provide a nuclear reactor and possibly resumed military sales, as well as Saudi Arabia and Jordan. On a variety of important issues, including the Iranian nuclear program, the Syrian civil war, the peace process, and arms sales to regional actors, Russia's policies have been, and are likely to continue being, deeply inimical to Israeli interests. Nevertheless, the Russian constraint on Israeli policy remains much more limited than that of the Soviet Union in the past. Russia has become a friendly state and has shown at least some willingness to take Israeli strategic interests into account at times.

Europe has become an increasingly important actor for Israel. The EU is Israel's primary trading partner and Israel enjoys extensive political, socioeconomic and military ties with a variety of European states. Europe played an important role in the Iranian nuclear issue, initially constraining American and Israeli efforts to impose penalties on Iran, but ultimately adopting hard-line positions that contributed to the 2015 nuclear deal. Europe's long-standing opposition to Israel's policies on the Palestinian issue has been a source of growing bilateral friction, contributing to the deterioration of Israel's international standing. Without any positive developments in the peace process, relations are likely to become even more tense, with growing pressures for sanctions and other measures against Israel.

China has mostly stayed out of regional diplomatic and security issues and has therefore yet to become a major factor in Israel's strategic calculus, though economic ties are blossoming. Nevertheless, as a permanent member of the Security Council, where it generally opposes sanctions and other forms of direct intervention, China has taken positions on a number of regional issues that have been highly problematic for Israel, particularly the Iranian nuclear program, the Syrian civil war and the Israeli–Palestinian peace process.

One of the greatest challenges Israel faces today is from growing international isolation. Partly, this is simply a result of the controversial policies it has pursued in regard to the settlements and West Bank generally. It is, however, also very much a result of a concerted campaign of diplomatic warfare and delegitimization that the Arab states have conducted against Israel ever since it was established, increasingly joined in recent years by the PA, pro-Palestinian activists and NGOs around the world, and the growing use of international law as a diplomatic weapon (so-called "lawfare").

Israel is singled out for international opprobrium as no other nation and is the subject of intensive efforts to delegitimize everything about it, including its very existence as a state. Votes on Israel at the UN and other international forums are fundamentally and outrageously biased, with an automatic majority of Arab, Muslim and Third World states willing to condemn Israel for every transgression, real or imagined, while willfully ignoring those of the rest of the world. To illustrate, twenty-two of the twenty-six resolutions the General Assembly adopted in 2012 in regard to human rights violations had to do with Israel, with a similar pattern repeated in 2013, where twenty-one out of twenty-five resolutions concerned Israel.

It is not just in the UN and other international forums that Israel faces diplomatic opprobrium and isolation. Israel's relations with virtually all countries would be better, were a peace agreement reached with the Palestinians, or even just significant progress made. Many countries, including Arab, Muslim and Third World ones, would clearly like to establish relations today, or upgrade existing ones, subject to progress in advancing peace between Israel and the Palestinians. Relations with Egypt, Jordan, Turkey and Europe, in particular, have been adversely affected by the Palestinian issue. Various European countries have at times imposed partial or complete arms embargoes on Israel, including Britain, France and Germany, even without formal EU decisions to this effect. European anger has been brewing for decades and has begun manifesting itself in recent years in concrete, if still limited, measures.

No issue has undermined Israel's international standing more than the West Bank settlements. There is, however, more to international opprobrium towards Israel than just this issue. For decades, the Arab countries maintained a formal boycott on relations with Israel—diplomatic, economic, or social—and refused to have any contact with it whatsoever. Long before the Six-Day War and the beginning of the "occupation," in reality ever since Israel's establishment, they have waged an ongoing campaign designed to portray it as an illegitimate, brutal and racist state. Positive Israeli attributes and actions, including the vibrancy of its democracy and society, have long been denied or discounted, failures and weaknesses greatly magnified. It was not the West Bank and settlements, or Israel's specific borders that was the problem, but the fact that some Arab countries, as well as Iran, Hizbollah, Hamas, NGOs in the Arab and Muslim worlds, and beyond, have yet to reconcile to Israel's existence and still seek its destruction.

The diplomatic and delegitimization campaign has two primary objectives. In the short term, the campaign seeks to create international pressure on Israel to change its policies, and foster legal, political, and normative obstacles designed to circumscribe Israel's diplomatic and military freedom of maneuver. In the long term, delegitimizers seek to weaken and ultimately defeat Israel by eroding its international standing, isolating it and undermining the credibility of its positions.

To this end, the diplomatic and delegitimization campaign promotes a campaign of boycotts, divestments and sanctions, as part of a broader effort to convince Western publics that Israel pursues policies that violate Western values.

The media have also become an essential component of the delegitimization campaign, further exacerbated by the problematic character of the irregular confrontations with Hizbollah, Hamas and the PA. The causes of the hostilities are often blurred by the conflicting claims and seemingly endless cycles of hostilities. The inevitable loss of innocent lives caused by Hizbollah's and Hamas's use of their civilian populations as human shields, leads to a blurring of moral judgment and an inversion of power. Israel, which is forced to respond to attacks on its civilian population, but which has an organized military, looks powerful and oppressive, while its adversaries appear to be heroic underdogs. Moreover, Israel's enemies intentionally manipulate the damage and casualties caused to undermine the legitimacy of Israel's military operations and create pressure on it to end them prematurely. As a result, Israel is increasingly constrained in its ability to wield military power effectively. The long-term change in the international perception of Israel has had a devastating impact on its standing. Remarkably, a 2013 poll of citizens in twenty-five nations found Israel to be the fourth most unpopular country in the world. Only Iran, Pakistan, and North Korea had more unfavorable ratings.

The reality, however, is more complex. If one looks both at the number of states Israel has relations with today, as well as much of the quality of these relations, Israel is far from isolated. Israel had formal diplomatic relations with 158 countries in 2016—more than ever before—and a vast increase from ninety-eight in 1967. Moreover, Israel has particularly strong ties with Canada, Australia, Germany, Poland, Italy, Russia, India, and Singapore, to name just a few, a booming economic relationship with China and above all, a "special relationship" with the US. Military cooperation with Egypt and Jordan is at an all-time high and a shared fear of Iran has led to signs of an initial thaw in Saudi attitudes towards Israel. The Arab League has repeatedly reaffirmed the 2002 "Arab Peace Initiative" and even though some of its elements are non-starters for Israel, such as a demand that it withdraw completely from all territories occupied in 1967, including the Golan Heights, the fact that it suggests the entire Arab League may be willing to accept the existence of Israel is a welcome change, especially compared with some of the League's past declarations.

Despite the tensions in relations with Europe, Israel enjoys an advanced Association Agreement with the EU, which was further upgraded in 2008 and 2012. Germany has probably become Israel's second closest ally after the US, selling to it and partially financing submarines that can reportedly carry nuclear missiles. Britain is now Israel's second largest trading partner. Ties with France, long tense over the Palestinian issue, have improved in recent years. All three hold strategic dialogues with Israel, with whom they share a growing array of strategic interests.

Relations with India have developed rapidly, especially on the economic and military levels, making it a country of strategic importance for Israel. By 2015, India had become Israel's largest or at least second largest market for weapons exports: bilateral trade grew more than fortyfold in the first twenty years of bilateral relations. Ties with other countries in the Far East and Africa are also expanding rapidly, for example Japan, South Korea, and Kenya.

Israel's relationship with the US is so broad that it, alone, largely counter-balances the processes of diplomatic isolation and delegitimization. The importance of the US for Israel's national security cannot be overstated. Total US assistance to Israel, from 1949 to 2016, amounted to a whopping $124 billion, making it the largest beneficiary of American military aid in the post–World War II era. In 2016, a further ten-year $38 billion military aid package was concluded.

Moreover, the US and Israel engage in extensive strategic dialogue and cooperation, for example, on the Iranian nuclear program, missile defense, counter-terrorism, homeland security, bilateral and multilateral military exercises, and joint development and production of weapons. The US also uses its diplomatic leverage to protect Israel from an endless array of injurious resolutions in international forums, such as the United Nations Security Council. The two countries have worked extensively over the years to promote the peace process, in very close sync part of the time. Nevertheless, relations have been strained when the policies of Israeli governments were not aligned with those of the US. Above all, there is a long-standing assumption, not formally codified, that the US would come to Israel's assistance if its existence were to be threatened. Thus, Israel appears to enjoy a de facto US security guarantee that arguably serves as a regional deterrent.

One would hardly expect a complete confluence of interests between a global superpower and a small regional player, and the history of the bilateral relationship is replete with cases of disagreement and even ongoing discord in certain areas. It is a mark of the relationship's fundamental strength that it has always bounced back from these disagreements and progressed to ever-deeper ties.

The changing nature of military threats

The overall positive change in the military balance with the Arab countries has been at least partially offset by the growing irregular and asymmetric threats posed by Iran, Hizbollah, and Hamas. With the important exception of Iran, the threat today is from non-state actors, motivated by radical Islamist ideologies, rather than states, with whom the likelihood of large-scale conflicts is now low.

Iran, Hizbollah, and Hamas have concluded that decisive victory, and Israel's destruction, are beyond their near and mid-term capabilities and have instead adopted a long-term strategy of attrition. In the meantime, they make use of a variety of weapons and tactics designed to largely neutralize and withstand Israel's military superiority in each round, deny it victory, and enable them to survive and rebuild for the next conflict. To this end, Hizbollah and Hamas pursue a dual approach. They intentionally place their rocket arsenals among their civilian populations, thereby making it very difficult for Israel to locate and destroy them. In so doing, they also force Israel to cause civilian casualties when it responds to attacks and create international pressure on Israel to end the fighting, before having achieved its military objectives. Concomitantly, Hizbollah and Hamas focus their own offensive efforts primarily against Israel's civilian population, through massive and protracted rocket attacks, and are designed to promote demoralization and psychological exhaustion, which erode Israel's societal resilience. Finally, these actors seek to use the threat of large-scale casualties to deter Israel from conducting a full-scale war against them, in which they are clearly the weaker side.

Hizbollah is estimated to have a staggering 130,000 rockets today. In a future war, it may fire as many as 1,500 rockets a day at Israel, for some thirty days. This would amount to an unprecedented 30,000 to 45,000 rockets, potentially causing exceptional damage to Israel's population centers. Hamas's arsenal is far more limited in size, but still potent. The range of its rockets is also more limited, but like Hizbollah, Hamas can now hit all of Israel's population centers, as well as the nuclear reactor in Dimona. Both organizations are constantly at work to extend the ranges, payloads and, especially, the precision of their rockets.

The new precision rockets Iran has provided Hizbollah, still a small but growing percentage of its overall arsenal, present a possible game changer. For the first time, one of Israel's enemies has the ability to target specific sites and thereby disrupt the mobilization of the reserves, the primary component of Israel's military forces, its offensive operations and the national-political and military decision-making processes. To this end, Hizbollah may attack, inter alia, mobilization centers, weapons stores, air-bases, and command and control facilities, such as the Ministry of Defense and the Prime Minister's office. It may also attack sensitive national infrastructure sites, such as power plants, or communications and transportation nodes, thereby shutting down much of Israel's economy and society. Israel's rocket defenses, such as the Iron Dome, will mitigate the damage, but cannot neutralize a mammoth arsenal the size of Hizbollah's. The fear of potentially massive destruction has already had a significant impact on Israeli decision-making, creating a form of mutual deterrence and forcing Israel to invest far more heavily in defensive measures than in the past.

Iran's ongoing nuclear program remains the greatest potential threat to Israel's security, whether through the actual use of nuclear weapons, or just the threat thereof. The very hint of nuclear weapons would raise the level of a confrontation to the potentially existential, with dire ramifications for Israel's strategic calculus and freedom of maneuver. The dangers of Iran proliferating nuclear weapons to other radical states and even terrorist organizations, or of losing control over its nuclear capabilities in a scenario of regime change or internal disarray, also cannot be discounted. Moreover, a nuclear Iran may be a catalyst for a regional nuclear arms race.

Setting aside the nuclear program, the primary threat Iran poses to Israel is indirect, through Hizbollah. Iran is relatively far away and its conventional military capabilities, including its air force, which would be crucial to any attack against Israel at these distances, are limited. Iran has embarked on a military build-up, including advanced Russian anti-aircraft systems, and its involvement in Syria provides it with new possibilities for positioning forces near Israel's border. It will, however, be a long time before Iran can present a major, direct, conventional threat to Israel. Should it wish to attack Israel, nevertheless, Iran's ballistic missile arsenal is the primary means available to it at this time. As long as the missiles are armed with conventional warheads, the threat they pose is painful, but limited, and pales in comparison with Hizbollah's rocket arsenal, which remains the primary means by which Iran seeks to deter Israel, and especially to deter it from attacking its nuclear program.

At the time the nuclear deal was sealed in 2015, most credible experts believed that Iran was a matter of weeks or months away from having sufficient fissile material for a first nuclear bomb and a further period, a few years at most, from being able to miniaturize a nuclear warhead to be placed on ballistic missiles. Had the deal been observed by all sides, a period of ten to fifteen years might have been gained before Iran could have crossed the nuclear threshold, a not insignificant, but also not truly lengthy period of time. In 2018, however, with Israel's strong support, the Unites States withdrew from the deal, leaving the entire future of the issue in doubt. The US and Israel charged that the deal left Iran's nuclear infrastructure largely intact and that once its restrictions expired, , Iran would remain a nuclear threshold state, capable of crossing the threshold in a very short period of time. they additionally charged that the deal failed to address Iran's ballistic missile program and expansionist behavior in the region. Both countries argue what they see is a new and better deal, which will address the failures of the previous one.

The Sunni states also harbor deep fears of Iran's nuclear program and hegemonic ambitions in the region. While there are no signs of an immediate decision by any of the Sunni states to acquire nuclear weapons in response, a number have initiated civil nuclear programs, which could be the basis for military programs in the future. Given the nature and instability of the regimes in the region, their tense relations with each other, fundamental enmity towards Israel and lack of any channels of communication with it, the possibility of a multi-nuclear Middle East is a nightmare scenario, which makes the complexity of the US-Soviet nuclear rivalry pale in comparison, if not in destructive capacity.

In the past, Syria, Libya and Iraq all had nuclear and chemical weapons programs. Syria's nuclear reactor was destroyed by an Israeli airstrike in 2007. Its chemical weapons arsenal, the third largest in the world, was largely dismantled in 2014 under international pressure, but Syria retains a residual chemical capability. Libya and Iraq's WMD programs were dismantled following the 2003 Gulf War. Together with the, at least temporary, suspension of Iran's nuclear ambitions, the overall WMD threat to Israel has therefore decreased significantly in recent years.

Nevertheless, a significant conventional arms build-up is also underway in the region, especially led by Saudi Arabia, whose military expenditures between 2000 and 2014 totaled an unprecedented $1.1 trillion. In addition, Iran, the other Gulf states, Egypt and Jordan have also increased defense spending (IISS data, as adapted from Cordesman 2015). The Egyptian army remains a potentially formidable foe, the largest Arab military, most of which is equipped with advanced American weaponry. The Saudi army, though smaller, is still sizable and is equipped with large quantities of cutting-edge American weaponry. Given the uncertain future stability of these countries, the build-up is a source of deep concern in Israel.

The percentage of Israel's population killed by terrorism is higher than in any other democracy and few other countries, certainly no democracy, has ever confronted a greater terrorist threat than the Second Intifada (Byman 2011). Terrorism was a primary factor—in a number of cases the decisive factor—in most of the electoral outcomes during the last two decades, it caused a significant hardening of both public and leadership attitudes towards the Palestinians, and had a major impact on Israel's negotiating positions, repeatedly forcing it to reconsider and even back away from possible concessions. It has also caused frequent disruption of civilian life, but has not, with a few short-term exceptions, had a significant impact on Israel's economy. As such, terrorism has never posed an existential threat for Israel, but it has become a strategic one. Contrary to a common misperception, terrorism did not start in response to Israel's occupation of the West Bank in 1967, but has been the preferred Arab and Palestinian modus operandi from the earliest days of the conflict, long before Israel gained independence.

As an advanced state, which relies heavily on cyber-technology, Israel is particularly vulnerable to cyber-attacks and has been a primary target thereof, facing a nearly constant barrage of attacks from Iran, Hizbollah, Hamas, Palestinians, Turkey, and more. The danger from non-state actors and "cyber-activism" by individuals and groups is also growing. In a comparatively short period of time, Israel has put in place an impressive array of cyber-defenses, making it one of the world leaders in this realm. To date, Israel has succeeded in preventing highly disruptive cyber-attacks, but has identified the cyber-realm as one of the primary threats it faces today.

Demography has become a direct threat to Israel's future character as a Jewish and democratic state and thus to its national security. The issue stems primarily from the possible demise of the two-state solution, either due to Palestinian rejection of any and all peace proposals to date, or Israel's own settlement policies, which are creating a situation of de facto annexation of the West Bank and a "one-state" reality. Jews already constitute just 79 percent of Israel's total population today and if the West Bank Palestinian population is added to Israeli Arabs, the Jewish population is reduced to just 60 percent of the total. There is no agreed definition in Israel regarding the percentage of the population that should be Jewish in order for Israel to retain its Jewish character. An Israel, however, in which just over half the population is Jewish, hardly constitutes a Jewish state by any definition.

Demography has also had an effect on Israel's military strategy. Israel no longer seeks to conquer territory in battle, largely in order to avoid having to assume control of additional hostile populations and further undermine its demographic balance. Territorial conquest has long been, and remains, the primary means of achieving military victory and in its absence the IDF has encountered severe difficulties in achieving its objectives in all of the past rounds of fighting with hostile actors.

Challenges and prospects for Israeli national security

At 70, Israel continues to face a daunting array of military threats (unlike virtually any other state in the world), fundamental Arab enmity to its very existence, and deep international opprobrium. Israel has, however, won the battle for its existence and is stronger militarily and more secure today than at any other time in history. Furthermore, Israel has ties with more states than ever before, including a unique relationship with the US, and a vibrant economy that has grown rapidly in recent decades, turning Israel into an international leader in "hi-tech."

Peace with the Palestinians remains the foremost challenge Israel faces and is also the key to the achievement of its other primary national objectives. Peace with the Palestinians will greatly mitigate the conflict with much of the Arab world, reduce, but unfortunately not end, much of the terrorism and other forms of violence against it, and enable Israel's at least partial acceptance and integration into the region. It will further enable a restoration of Israel's international standing, ensue the future vitality of its relationships with its allies, including the US, and lead to dramatic socioeconomic growth, as already happened after the partial agreements with the Palestinians in the 1990s. Most importantly, it is the key to ensuring Israel's fundamental character as a primarily Jewish and democratic state.

The success of the peace process is not just up to Israel. The Palestinians have repeatedly rejected dramatic proposals for peace, to the point that it is not clear, diplomatic grandstanding aside, whether they truly aspire to a two-state solution, if this requires living alongside a Jewish Israel, or if the Palestinians are still committed to Israel's demise. In any event, and unrelated to Israeli policies, a final agreement is not possible as long as the West Bank and Gaza remain divided, restricting Israel's options.

Peace with the Palestinians, however, is a vital Israeli self-interest and it must pursue every option to achieve it. At a bare minimum, this requires a freeze on settlement activity outside of the three so-called "settlement blocs" and Jerusalem. In so doing, Israel would be able to achieve two vital objectives. First, maintaining the status quo in the West Bank for as long as necessary, until the Palestinians are willing to reach a two-state solution, without endangering Israel's Jewish and democratic character. Second, such a policy would convince the international community, at least the US, that it is the Palestinians who are the obstacle to peace, not Israel, thereby reducing its international isolation.

Israel cannot allow Iran, or any enemy state, to acquire nuclear weapons. Following the US withdrawal from the Iran nuclear deal in 2018 the prospects of a diplomatic resolution of the issue are unclear and the likelihood of the need for military action, even by the US or Israel, appears to have grown. Either way, close strategic dialogue and cooperation with the US are key to addressing the issue and the "special relationship" with the US remains essential for Israeli national security.

After seven decades, a combination of Israel's military superiority and strategic necessity, primarily a shared fear of Iran's hegemonic ambitions and ongoing nuclear program, have resulted in a growing willingness on the part of some Arab states to accept Israel's existence and even cooperate to a limited degree. It is a reluctant and equivocal acceptance, but an important change, nevertheless. Israel should pursue the options for ties and cooperation with the Sunni states to the extent possible, limited though this is likely to turn out, both as a supporting mechanism to help achieve peace with the Palestinians and as means of containing Iran.

The price of a truly remarkable relationship with the US has been a significant loss of Israel's independence. In effect, the US and Israel long ago reached an unwritten understanding; the US provides Israel with a de facto security guarantee, massive military assistance and broad, but not complete, diplomatic support. In exchange, Israel is expected to consult with the US prior to taking action and accord American positions, overriding importance, demonstrate military restraint and diplomatic moderation and even make concessions. Israel does act independently at times, possibly more often than might be expected in an asymmetric relationship of this sort. Nevertheless, with just a few exceptions, limited either to matters of existential consequence, or the highly politically charged issues, domestically, of the future of the West Bank, US policy has been the primary determinant of virtually all major national security decisions Israel has made in recent decades. It is a price worth paying.

Israel should be deeply concerned by the growing signs of dissatisfaction in the US with its policies and the nature of the relationship. There is no danger of Israel "losing" the US, at least for the foreseeable future, but even a modulation of American support would have grave consequences for Israel. Preserving the relationship is a fundamental Israeli national objective.

Israel's long-standing assumption, that the conquest of territory would bring the Arabs to negotiate peace, has proven fully substantiated only in regard to Egypt. Israel's willingness to withdraw from the Golan Heights in the negotiations during the 1990s and the Geneva Summit of 2000, did not prove sufficient to entice the Syrians into making a deal. Similarly, Israel's willingness, on at least three occasions, to withdraw from all of Gaza and virtually all of the West Bank (Camp David Summit 2000, Clinton Parameters 2000 and Olmert proposal of 2008), was also insufficient to close a deal with the Palestinians.

In these circumstances, there is certainly no point in trying to acquire additional territory for negotiating purposes. Moreover, there are large and deeply hostile populations on all of the potential military fronts today (Gaza, Lebanon, Syria) and to avoid further an exacerbation of the demographic challenges it faces, Israel has thus refrained from conquering them in any of the recent conflicts. The desire to avoid the acquisition of additional territory, however, poses a fundamental dilemma for Israel's defense doctrine; it is exceedingly difficult to win military conflicts without territorial conquest and Israel has been unable to do so in any of the rounds of fighting with Hizbollah and Hamas. Finding an effective military response to the threats these groups pose to Israel, especially its civilian population, is one of the foremost challenges it will face in the coming years. Defense alone is insufficient.

The root causes that gave rise to the "Arab Spring"—a demographic explosion, large numbers of young people with limited prospects, absence of political freedoms and effective governance, and deep income disparities—will continue to generate political and military upheaval in the region for years, if not decades. This will have severe ramifications for Israel, but also pose some opportunities. An Arab world preoccupied with domestic crises, for example, will be less able to mount credible threats to Israel. There is, however, little, if anything Israel can do to affect the dramatic processes underway in the Arab world, other than do its utmost to stay out of them.

References and further reading

Byman, Daniel. 2011. *A High Price: The Triumphs and Failures of Israeli Counterterrorism*. Oxford: Oxford University Press, 372 pp.

Cohen, Avner. 2010. *The Worst Kept Secret: Israel's Bargain with the Bomb*. New York: Columbia University Press.

Curtis, Michael. 2012. "The International Assault Against Israel." *Israel Affairs*. 18(3), pp. 344–362, 351.

Freilich, Charles D. 2012. Zion's Dilemmas: How Israel Makes National Security Policy. Ithaca, NY: Cornell University Press.

Freilich, Charles D. 2017. *Israeli National Security: A New Strategy for an Era of Change*. Oxford: Oxford University Press.

Gilboa, Eytan. 2006. "Public Diplomacy: The Missing Component in Israel's Foreign Policy." *Israel Affairs*. 12(4), pp. 715–747, 724–725.

Haaretz. 2016. "Report: Israel Launched Numerous Drone Strikes in Sinai." Available at: www.haaretz.com/israel-news/1.730167.

IISS. 2015. *Military Spending and Arms Sales in the Gulf*. Data adapted from A. Cordesman, April 28. Washington, DC: Center for Strategic and International Studies, 10 pp.

Inbar, Efraim. 2008. *Israel's National Security: Issues and Challenges Since the Yom Kippur War*. London: Routledge.

Inbar, Efraim. 2013. "Israel is Not Isolated." *Mideast Security and Policy Studies*. No. 99. UNWatch. November 23. Available at: http://blog.unwatch.org/index.php/2013/11/25/this-years-22-unga-resolutions-against-israel-4-on-rest-of-world/.

Klieman, Aaron S. 1990. *Israel and the World After Forty Years*. Washington, DC: Pergamon-Brassey.

Kober, Avi. 2009. *Israel's Wars of Attrition: Attrition Challenges to Democratic States*. London: Routledge.

Maoz, Zeev. 2006. *Defending the Holy Land: A Critical Analysis of Israel's Security and Foreign Policy*. Ann Arbor, MI: University of Michigan Press.

Ross, Dennis. 2015. *Doomed to Succeed: The US–Israel Relationship from Truman to Obama*. New York: Farrar, Straus and Giroux.

Shelah, Ofer. 2015. *Dare to Win: A Security Policy for Israel*. Tel Aviv: Miskal. [Hebrew]

12

THE CHALLENGE OF PEACE

Galia Golan

Introduction

One may contend that there were few—if any—possibilities for Israel to make peace with its neighbors prior to the "Six-Day War" of June 1967. For the Arab world, Israel was the "Zionist entity" to be boycotted and possibly destroyed militarily; for the Palestinians, the objective was not a state in line with the 1947 UN Partition Plan in Palestine, but rather sovereignty over all of the former British Mandate of Palestine. This helped shape Israel's view of the Arab world as a community inexorably hostile to the very existence of Israel.

The Six-Day War ended with Israel's control over millions of Palestinians in the West Bank (including East Jerusalem) and the Gaza Strip. But by ending with Israel in possession of lands belonging to Jordan, Syria, and Egypt, the war created the possibility of a land-for-peace deal with these states, without having to sacrifice any land held by Israel within its de facto borders, set by the 1949 armistice lines.

The initial challenges

In deliberations immediately after the war, the Israeli national unity government decided upon returning the Golan Heights to Syria and the Sinai to Egypt. Israeli policymakers hoped to annex the Gaza Strip after the relocation of its large Palestinian refugee population. Menachem Begin, the right-wing member of the government, agreed to these positions presumably because he did not consider the Golan and Sinai part of the historical "Land of Israel" (*Eretz Yisrael*). The explicit belief held by virtually the entire cabinet was that the Arab states would never make peace with Israel, and therefore Israel's conditions for peace with Egypt and Syria were essentially hypothetical.[1] Indeed, they were reversed within a year.[2] This conviction of unwavering Arab hostility and rejection of the legitimacy of the Jewish state guided Israel's decisions for decades to come, according priority to perceived security considerations over peace.

Jordan

In its post-1967 war decisions, the government also decided to annex East Jerusalem. This policy was implemented for historic and religious reasons, but also to symbolize Jewish legitimacy in this region, given the Biblical link between the Jewish people and Jerusalem. The only other decision made regarding the West Bank was the determination of the Jordan River as Israel's eastern border, that is, the border with Jordan, and Israeli sovereignty over the adjacent Jordan Rift Valley. The reason for this decision was to have a security precaution against the possible collapse of a future peace agreement or an invasion of the West Bank by a third army (Israel State Archives). For the remainder of the West Bank, the idea of Palestinian autonomy or limited statehood was suggested and even discussed with local Palestinians. Inasmuch as this proposal envisaged a state consisting of enclaves within the West Bank, surrounded territorially by Israel, the local Palestinians rejected it. Returning some of the territory within the West Bank to Jordan was also discussed by the government and even proposed in the Allon Plan presented to Jordan in 1968.

However, the demand for Israeli control over the Jordan Valley, along with the annexation of East Jerusalem, constituted deal-breakers for any peace agreement with Jordan. Talks with Israel had been initiated by King Hussein (with Egyptian approval) as early as the July 2, 1967, and they continued intermittently for decades, but Israeli demands remained unchanged. Both Jordan and Egypt accepted United Nations Security Council Resolution 242 of November 1967, which asserted the right of "every state in the area ... to live in peace within secure and recognized boundaries free from threats or acts of force" but also called on Israel to withdraw "from territories" taken in the June war. Israel's resistance to this, specifically the decision to hold onto major parts of the West Bank, initiated King Hussein to claim that he could not understand Israel's fixation with security (holding onto the Jordan Valley) when it could have peace.

While the Israeli conviction remained that the Arabs would never make "true peace" with Israel, as Prime Minister Yitzhak Rabin was to say to American President Gerald Ford in 1974, Israel did not entirely eschew visions of peace. Indeed, Rabin explained that this could change, subject to testing Arab intentions. And the declared policy of the Labor government was in fact "land for peace," although Labor refused to consider withdrawing from all the land taken in 1967; any Israeli withdrawal would thus not constitute a return to the pre-war June 4, 1967 lines sought by Arab leaders and the international community.

Aside from an interest in maintaining a Jewish majority in whatever area Israel was ultimately to control, the willingness to concede some land may have reflected an expectation that Jordan might one day accept Israel's terms or, alternatively, that Israel might be forced by the international community to evacuate conquered areas, as happened after the 1956 Sinai war. Therefore, the Labor government created

Jewish settlements in those parts of the occupied territories that it decided should remain under Israeli control: the Jordan Valley, East Jerusalem and its environs, as well as the Golan Heights. While the movement of Israeli settlers to these areas violated the Fourth Geneva Convention (which dealt with the responsibilities of an occupying power), the position of the government was that the West Bank was not occupied, but rather disputed territory, inasmuch as there had been no recognized sovereign there prior to 1967. Thus, Israel claimed the territory was not occupied, as it had no previous recognized owner, from which Israel could have taken the territory. This claim was based on the fact that only two countries, Britain and Pakistan, had recognized Jordan's 1950 annexation of the West Bank after the British Mandate and the war of 1948.[3]

The West Bank ceased to be an issue between Jordan and Israel when Jordan relinquished its claim to the area (excluding East Jerusalem) in favor of the Palestine Liberation Organization (PLO) in 1988. This was due to Jordanian-Palestinian relations, and the first Intifada linked to the moderate change in Palestinian policy (to be discussed below) as well as the PLO declaration of a Palestinian state for the West Bank and Gaza. Subsequently, the beginning of Israeli talks with the PLO in 1993 provided sufficient legitimacy for Jordan to sign a peace agreement with Israel in 1994, ending the state of war between both sides.

Egypt

The other post-1967 challenge for Israel was pursuing peace with Egypt. After Egyptian President Gamal Abdel Nasser's death in September 1970, his successor, Anwar Sadat, communicated several proposals to Israel via the Americans, including one internationally guaranteed peace proposal. All were rejected by Israeli Prime Minister Golda Meir. Similarly to the case with Jordan, Israel refused to withdraw from the entire Sinai, clinging to security-based territorial demands rather than opting for a peace agreement. The result of these Israeli red lines was the Egyptian (and Syrian) attack on Yom Kippur in 1973, which sought to break the diplomatic deadlock by military action. After the war, there was a limited Israeli withdrawal from the Suez Canal as a result of troop disengagement talks followed by further, but also limited, territorial withdrawals in 1975, in response to US pressure. However, then-Prime Minister Rabin repeated Israel's opposition to returning to the 4 June 1967 lines, in favor of what he deemed "defensible borders."

The 1977 Israeli elections brought the right-wing leader—Menachem Begin—to power. Begin believed that the 1967 war had "liberated" lands that had been part of the historical *eretz Yisra'el*, and he initiated a massive settlement campaign throughout the territories. Nonetheless, deeply affected by Israeli losses in the 1973 war, Begin sought a peace agreement with at least one of Israel's neighbors. Israel had always preferred dealing with one Arab state at a time in negotiations, not only to avoid pressure but mainly to avoid linkage between agreements, especially linkage to the Palestinian issue, which would necessitate the discussion of withdrawal from the West Bank. Thus, Begin sought a separate peace with Egypt to avoid pressure for broader steps, as President Carter began organizing an international conference that would seek a *comprehensive peace*. Working through intermediaries such as Romania and Morocco, secret meetings between Israel and Egypt laid the groundwork for Israeli–Egyptian negotiations. When plans for Carter's conference faltered, Sadat moved on the bilateral track and made his historic visit to Israel in November 1977, much to the surprise of the US administration.

The overwhelming public response in Israel to Sadat's gesture substantiated Sadat's analysis that Israeli intransigence stemmed mainly from psychological factors. In his speech to the Israeli Knesset, Sadat directly addressed the existential fears of Israelis about Arab acceptance of the country's basic legitimacy in the region. He repeated several times that Egypt considered Israel part of the region, a respected neighbor and friend. While he continued to press for withdrawal from all the territories conquered in 1967, including East Jerusalem, and the creation of a Palestinian state, he won over the Israeli public with his calls for "no more war" (Arian 1995, p. 102). According to public opinion polls, opposition among Israelis to returning the Sinai fell from 39 percent at the end of 1976 to just 16 percent at the end of 1977, one month after Sadat's visit (Arian 1995).

However, the drama of the visit did not entirely allay the government's concerns, nor totally dispel the mistrust regarding Arab intentions. Subsequent bilateral talks floundered, prompting President Carter to organize a summit at Camp David in September 1978 in order to broker a peace deal. Begin and Sadat met face to face only at the outset of the meeting, their mutual antagonism forcing the Americans to mediate and draft proposals. Principles for a peace treaty were drawn up, calling for complete Israeli withdrawal (including settlers) from the Sinai, along with a five-year autonomy plan for the West Bank, during which time Jordan, Israel, and local Palestinians were to negotiate the future status of the territory. A peace treaty between Egypt and Israel on this basis was ultimately signed in March 1979. While technically there was linkage between the treaty and the autonomy plan, implementation of West Bank autonomy was not made a precondition and was eventually ignored.

The Palestinians

For Begin, the evacuation of Sinai constituted Israel's fulfillment of UN Security Council Resolution 242 (which had called for Israeli withdrawal "from territories" not "the" or "all the" territories occupied in 1967). However, far more difficult challenges for peace lay ahead: peace with Syria, the one remaining state that could constitute a military threat to Israel, and, also, resolution of the conflict with the Palestinians, the core issue of the Arab–Israeli dispute. Many factors contributed to Israel's decision to take on these challenges when Labor returned to power in 1992, under the leadership of Yitzhak Rabin. Among these were a deterioration in relations with Washington due to a stalemate in US peace efforts. More importantly, the First Intifada that broke out in the West Bank and Gaza Strip in December 1987 resulted in a discernible shift in Israeli public opinion toward compromise, as a result of the growing threat to personal security (Shamir and Shamir 2000). Furthermore, Israel was shifting from a welfare state and a collective ethos to free market competition and individualism. Within this atmosphere, many Israelis were according less importance to the territories and losing interest in the continuing conflict, preferring more concrete individual interests.

An additional factor for Rabin was his concern about the decline in resilience in the Israeli population[4] and, still more importantly, he saw international and regional changes that made peace both possible and imperative. The collapse of the USSR and the emergence of the US as the sole superpower meant not only the loss of Soviet backing for Israel's adversaries, but also a broader Arab interest in cultivating ties with the world's sole superpower: America. The PLO had also been weakened by its loss of Saudi financial backing, due to Arafat's support for Saddam Hussein in the 1991 Gulf War. Furthermore, the rise of Islamism and the Iranian effort to develop a nuclear weapon made it important to remove Israel from the focus of Middle Eastern extremism. All of these international, regional and domestic factors led Rabin to seek a peace agreement in response to what he saw as both dangerous trends and a window of opportunity that might not remain open indefinitely.

Syria

When elected in 1992, Rabin promised to deal with both the Syrian and Palestinian issues but began with Syria, primarily in order to facilitate the withdrawal of Israeli troops deployed in Lebanon since the 1982 war.[5] These talks, conducted under US mediation, were plagued by Rabin's mistrust of the intentions of Syrian President, Hafez al-Assad, mirrored to a large degree by Assad's own suspicions and his view that the security measures demanded by Israel were excessive in the context of what would be peaceful relations with Israel.

The decisive issue preventing progress in Israeli–Syrian talks was the location of the border. Resolution 242 referred to territories occupied in 1967, which the Arab states interpreted to mean that Israel should must withdraw from all of the Golan Heights, to the lines of the 4th of June 1967, prior to the outbreak of the Six-Day War. Those lines would place Syria directly on the northeastern corner of Israel's Sea of Galilee, with access to the sea itself. It remains unclear if Rabin in fact agreed to a future Israeli withdrawal to the 4 June lines, but faced with growing opposition from the Israeli public and even within his own party, largely based on the view that the Golan was a critical strategic asset, Rabin announced that he would put any decision on a withdrawal to a referendum. Syrian President Hafez al-Assad saw this as a deliberate move to prevent an accord, and the negotiations between the two countries broke down. Thus, by the time that Rabin was assassinated in November 1995, the Israeli–Syrian peace effort was in full crisis.

While Rabin had chosen a slow, deliberate path—testing Assad while demanding security measures as a "safety net" for a peace agreement—his successor, Shimon Peres, hoped to move swiftly. Peres sought a dramatic achievement that he could present to the Israeli electorate in the elections scheduled for late 1996. Therefore, he sought some public gesture from Assad, particularly a summit that would demonstrate progress and Syrian seriousness of intent. Assad continued to resist such a meeting, but he did authorize trilateral talks that began in 1996. Despite some progress, however, in mid-February Peres called early elections for May 1996, primarily because of domestic, party considerations. Assad saw this as an indication of Israel's lack of genuine interest in an agreement, and the talks effectively came to an end.

Peres and the center-left Labor Party lost the May 1996 elections by a miniscule margin. Beginning anew, the new prime minister, Binyamin Netanyahu—of the right-wing Likud Party—authorized secret talks, conducted by American businessman Ron Lauder. These produced two draft peace treaties that reportedly included full withdrawal from the Golan Heights. Netanyahu denied this claim and in fact rejected the plan Lauder negotiated. The ideological opposition of his own party to any land-for-peace deal, along with Israeli public opinion against withdrawal from the Golan, apparently held Netanyahu back.

In 1999, the Labor Party returned to power; Labor leader Ehud Barak promised to end Israel's unpopular 17-year occupation of southern Lebanon within a year. To do this, he sought security assurances through a peace treaty with Damascus, given Syria's patronage of Hizbollah, the Shia Islamist movement that had been fighting Israeli forces in southern Lebanon. Consequently, Barak undertook a series of US-led meetings with the Syrian Foreign Minister, Farouk al-Shara. The Americans believe that these meetings, held in Washington at the end of 1999 and in Shepherdstown in early 2000, could have succeeded. American participants also claim that Barak agreed to withdraw to the 4 June line, but backtracked unexpectedly due to concern over negative public opinion in Israel. The Syrians perceived Barak's retreat as a sign of duplicity. Moreover, since 1967, the waters of the Sea of Galilee had receded, and it was not clear where the pre-Six-Day War line lay. Barak therefore began to speak of the two countries' simply agreeing arbitrarily to a line of separation. Assad, already seriously ill, apparently saw this vague formulation as further deceit. With no agreement in sight, Barak unilaterally withdrew Israeli forces from Lebanon on May 24, 2000. Assad died two weeks later.

Doubts remain regarding Assad's intentions, but there is some agreement among Israeli experts that once Assad fell ill, he was anxious to close a deal. Barak, too, wanted an agreement, but he was arrogant in his manner and over-confident about his ability to gain Assad's acquiescence to Israeli conditions. More importantly, Barak feared that he could not win over the Israeli public,[6] with several successive polls indicating a majority opposed to a withdrawal. Official negotiations between Israel and Syria were not to resume until 2007, although the Syrians (under Assad's son Bashar) initiated informal contacts as early as 2004.

Further negotiations with the Palestinians

In 1991, the US had pressed Israel, then led by Likud Prime Minister Yitzhak Shamir, to attend an international conference in Madrid, aimed at securing a comprehensive peace agreement that would resolve the Israeli–Palestinian conflict. Local Palestinians were invited as part of the Jordanian delegation. Following the ceremonial opening, the conference broke into bilateral and multilateral meetings, the latter focusing on issues such as arms control, water, and refugees. Concrete results, however, depended upon the bilateral talks, which soon faltered. In January 1993, with Labor back in power, then Foreign Minister Shimon Peres authorized secret talks with high-level PLO representatives in Oslo, outside the framework of the Madrid process. In the spring, Prime Minister Rabin agreed to elevate the talks, sending Uri Savir—the Director General of the Ministry of Foreign Affairs—to lead the team. The Oslo Declaration of Principles, signed on the White House lawn on 13 September 1993, was the result.

The same window of opportunity that Rabin had perceived with regard to Syria, born of changes in the international and regional arena as well as within Israel, had led to a reversal of his previous rejection of contacts with the PLO. An additional factor was the PLO's 1988 declaration that it sought to create a state *next to* Israel, limited to the West Bank and Gaza, with East Jerusalem as its capital. The PLO termed "historic compromise" thus supplanted the Palestinians' previous hard-line positions that rejected the existence of Israel.

Perhaps the most important achievement of the Oslo Accords was the exchange of letters of recognition between Rabin and PLO Chairman Arafat, in which Arafat stated that the "PLO recognizes the right of the State of Israel to live in peace and security," and promised to abrogate the clauses of the PLO Charter that violated this principle, whilst renouncing the use of terrorism (Golan 2007, pp. 165–166). For his part, Rabin recognized the PLO as the legitimate representative of the Palestinian people. Rabin did not go further in his letter since he viewed—and designed—the Oslo Agreement in keeping with his mistrust of his opponent. He had spoken in the past of the need for a testing period, and so Oslo was actually a five-year interim agreement, during which the final status of the occupied territories was to be negotiated.

The Oslo Accords deferred divisive issues to the final status talks that were to begin within three years, concerning security arrangements, borders, Jerusalem, refugees, settlements, and water. In the meantime, Israel was to withdraw its forces gradually but maintain security for Israeli citizens in the West Bank and Gaza, as well as to maintain control over the roads used by both the settlers and the IDF. According to the Oso Accords, the Palestinians were to create a governing authority, with an elected council and a limited police force, to administer autonomy in the West Bank and Gaza. Jerusalem was explicitly excluded, although an arrangement was found to enable East Jerusalem Palestinians to vote for the council. While Israel refused to halt settlement building in this period, the Oslo Accords determined that nothing would be done in the interim period "to prejudice or preempt the outcome of the final status talks."

In 1995, the "Oslo II" agreement was negotiated, with the help of the Americans, to guide implementation of the original Accords (Declaration of Principles). It included a timetable for Israeli withdrawals and laid out the responsibilities of each side. In the Palestinian towns from which Israel withdrew, termed Area A, the new Palestinian Authority (PA) would have control over security as well as civil matters; in Area B, mainly West Bank villages but also the Gaza Strip, from which most of the IDF had withdrawn earlier, the PA would have only civil control; and in Area C, which included most of the Israeli settlements but also some 50,000 to 60,000 Palestinians, Israel was to have full control. These were temporary delineations; Israeli withdrawals were to continue, so that parts of Area C would become B and B would become A, with the permanent borders to be determined in final status talks. Rabin was assassinated a little over a month after Oslo II was signed, and subsequent political paralysis left this delineation of areas in the West Bank frozen in time. Israel continues to maintain full control over Area C, comprising 60 percent of the West Bank, territorially encircling the edges of the West Bank, including the Jordan Valley.

The Oslo Accords were racked with problems, disagreements and delays, such as inadequate monitoring of implementation, which led to further delays and violations by both sides. More critically, there were other serious flaws in the agreements themselves. The first serious problem was the interim Accords. Intended as a test period, during which trust would be built between the two sides, the extended interim period allowed opponents of the Accords on both sides to mobilize. While approximately 65 percent of both Israeli and Palestinian publics initially supported the Process, hard-line political opposition on both sides launched devastating campaigns to spoil the Accords. The Islamic Jihad and Hamas carried out massive terror attacks inside Israel. The violence of the Palestinian Islamists, which Arafat condemned but could not or would not prevent, played into the hands of Israeli spoilers, who argued that the peace process undermined security and that a peace accord would give terrorism a free rein.

At the same time, the Palestinians wondered if the continued settlement building, increased checkpoints, and the imposition of a permit system for the Palestinian entry to east Jerusalem constituted what Israel meant by "peace." Israeli settlers, bolstered by their political supporters, demonstrated and railed against the government, on one occasion massacring Muslim worshippers in the West Bank. The Palestinian terror attacks took a larger toll, but the vociferous right-wing campaign against the government sought to delegitimize the entire process. Opponents of the Oslo Process frequently accused Rabin of treason, ultimately creating an atmosphere in which a religious Jewish student shot and killed Rabin in Tel Aviv, on November 4, 1995.

Another significant flaw in the Oslo Accords was the absence of a clear "endgame." Neither Israelis nor Palestinians knew if the process would in fact conclude with an end to the occupation, an independent Palestinian state, and the end of the conflict. Indeed, both sides continued to harbor suspicions as to the intentions of the other, whilst also possessing very different conceptions of what an end-game scenario would look like. Perhaps if these key issues had been addressed, rather than deferred until final status talks, there might have been greater willingness—on both sides—to tolerate the setbacks and violence.

Actually, Rabin himself may not have had a clear vision of the end-game. One month before his assassination, Rabin told the Knesset that he envisaged a "Palestinian entity which is less than a state," a united Jerusalem that would remain under Israeli sovereignty, and Israel's security border to be located in the Jordan Valley "in the broadest meaning of the term" (Israel Ministry of Foreign Affairs 1995). It is possible that Rabin's views would have changed had he lived, as suggested by his occasional references to possibly limiting Israeli control of the Jordan Valley to a period of thirty years. Nonetheless, his positions at the time of his death were little different from those of the Israeli cabinet in June 1967, clinging to security measures such as territorial control of all the borders surrounding the Palestinians and holding onto enclaves of land inside the West Bank, such as the large settlement area of Gush Etzion, south of Jerusalem.

Post-Oslo challenges

Rabin's successor—Shimon Peres—implemented some of the previously delayed steps of Oslo, but he gave priority to the Syrian track; these talks failed to yield an agreement, as described above. In addition, lacking Rabin's security credentials, Peres' support was unable to withstand the particularly harsh Hamas and Jihad terrorist attacks that occurred, and he lost the elections to Netanyahu in May 1996. Under US pressure, the new right-wing Prime Minister Netanyahu signed agreements, such as the Wye Memorandum of 1998, for further withdrawals, but he did not fully implement them. Like Likud leaders before him, Netanyahu sought to retain as much as possible, if not all, of the West Bank.

It was only when Labor returned to power in May 1999—under Ehud Barak—that the peace process with the Palestinians was resumed. Barak, however, skipped the final withdrawals promised by Oslo, preferring to go directly to final status negotiations, unwilling, as he said, to give up assets before an agreement was reached. Preparatory talks were held with the Palestinians, but the sides were still far from full agreement when Barak decided to try for a final accord at a summit in July 2000, hosted by the US administration, led by President Clinton. Arafat did not believe the talks had sufficiently advanced to warrant a summit, but with Clinton leaving office at the end of the year, both Barak and the Americans were anxious to conclude the process.

As with the 1978 Camp David conference between Sadat and Begin, the two leaders barely met, leaving it to the Americans to mediate. Israel retreated from some of the understandings reached in earlier, lower level talks regarding territorial issues, leading the Palestinians to retreat on the controversial issue of compromise on the "right of return" of Palestinian refugees. Nonetheless, Barak was prepared to go further than any previous Israeli leader in specifying how much land Israel would annex from the West Bank in the effort to keep as many settlers in place as possible (and maintain certain security interests). Unexpectedly, he was also willing to concede authority over some outlying neighborhoods of East Jerusalem as well as the Muslim and Christian Quarters of the Old City.

Barak later retreated from some of these positions, but Arafat had rejected them, anyway, as insufficient. For his part, Arafat grossly underestimated the symbolic import-ance of Jerusalem as a source of legitimacy for Israel. But in Arafat's view, Israel was proposing *mutual* compromises when the Palestinians had already made their "historic compromise" in 1988 by abandoning their claim to all of Mandatory Palestine, in favor of a state limited to the West Bank and Gaza. Moreover, Barak demanded a continued Israeli presence in the Jordan Valley for 10-12 years and early warning stations with access roads that would effectively divide the West Bank into three separate areas or enclaves, plus Israeli control of the airspace over the West Bank. In Palestinian eyes, a continued Israeli military presence along the Jordan River meant not only that large pieces of land would remain under Israeli rule, even for a limited period, but also that Palestinian sovereignty would be compromised as all land entrances and exits would be controlled by Israel; thus the occupation would appear to continue. Thus, once again, security measures threatened the chance for peace. In essence, little if anything was agreed at Camp David. The final dispute revolved around the holy places in East Jerusalem, with neither side willing to concede sovereignty.

The failure at Camp David need not have ended the peace process; bilateral talks did resume in the fall. The decisive blow, however, was the assertion, by Barak and Clinton at the end of Camp David that there was no partner on the Palestinian side. Neither public knew much of what had actually been said at Camp David, but the "no partner" conclusion was to have a lasting effect. Polled after the meeting, 65 percent of Israelis held the Palestinians mainly or wholly responsible for the failure (Peace Index 2000, July poll). Israelis genuinely believed that Barak had made "a gen-erous" offer and that Arafat's rejection meant that the Palestinians continued to seek Israel's destruction, primarily by insisting on the "right of return" of the refugees. Israelis understood this to mean inundating the country with Palestinian refugees, eventually outnumbering the Jewish population of Israel, thereby rendering the Jews a minority. In fact, the refugees had not been a major topic at Camp David, although the Palestinians had retreated from earlier, more flexible positions on the issue when Israel had appeared to retreat on previously agreed border issues. This fact was both unknown and irrelevant to Israeli public opinion, after the failure of the July Camp David summit.

The Second Intifada broke out at the end of September, fortifying Barak's "no partner" claim. The uprising was triggered by a provocative visit by Ariel Sharon, then leader of Israel's parliamentary opposition, to the Temple Mount/Haram al-Sharif (the location of the Al-Aksa Mosque). The situation had become significantly tense since the collapse of the Camp David talks, and Arafat had personally urged Barak to prevent the visit, but Barak did not comply. What followed was a violent Palestinian uprising, in which some 3,000 Palestinians and 1,000 Israelis lost their lives. There was controversy over Arafat's support (in fact his absence of support) for the outbreak of the Second Intifada, but both the Israeli military and Arafat did little to moderate or contain it once it broke out.

At the end of December 2000, before leaving office, Clinton presented what came to be known as the Clinton Parameters for a peace agreement. The US suggested that the parameters had to be accepted, within a short deadline, as the basis for the future accord. They consisted of the following: Israeli withdrawal from 94 to 97 percent of the West Bank and 1:1 land swaps to compensate the Palestinians for the areas annexed by Israel; a demilitarized Palestinian state, with an international force on the Jordan River for a limited period; the resettlement of refugees either (a) where they were, (b) in the future Palestinian state, (c) in third countries, or (d) in Israel—in all cases subject to numbers decided by the host countries. Regarding Jerusalem, the Jewish neighborhoods in East Jerusalem would be under Israeli sovereignty, Arab neighborhoods and the Haram al-Sharif (Temple Mount) under Palestinian sovereignty, with Israeli sovereignty over the Western Wall below.

Barak met the short deadline, accepting the Parameters, albeit with the addition of numerous reservations. Arafat, too, posed many questions but basically left the proposal unanswered. Both the deadline and Clinton's presidency came to an end without further progress and with the Intifada still raging. Perhaps believing that something could still be saved prior to Israeli elections (in which Barak was expected to lose), Israel and the Palestinians met in Taba, Egypt at the end of January 2001, for a week of intensive negotiations. While reportedly some progress was made on the refugee issue, little was in fact agreed, most likely because the Palestinians were aware that Barak was about to lose the upcoming Israeli election. Indeed, in February 2001, Ariel Sharon, then head of the right-wing Likud, became Prime Minister of Israel.

The Clinton Parameters became something of a model for a future agreement, but other initiatives followed as efforts were made to end the violence. The most significant was the Arab Peace Initiative (API) initiated by Saudi Arabia and adopted unanimously by the Arab League in February 2002, later endorsed by fifty-seven Islamic states at a conference in Tehran. Reiterating the usual demands for Israeli withdrawal from all the lands taken since June 4, 1967 (later the possibility of land swaps was added) and the creation of a Palestinian state with East Jerusalem as its capital, the text employed a new formulation for the refugee issue, calling for a "just solution ... *to be agreed* in accordance with United Nations General Assembly Resolution 194" (Muasher 2008, pp. 121–122, *127–128*). The new phrasing was designed to reassure Israel that it would not be forced into a refugee solution with which it did not agree. Nor was there an explicit demand for "the right of return." In exchange for the above conditions, the Arab states offered Israel: a peace agreement, end of the conflict, and normal relations, along with security for all states in the region. However, coming as it did just after a deadly terrorist attack during a Passover service (precipitating a limited Israeli invasion of previously evacuated areas of the West Bank), the API received little attention in Israel. In fact, ever mistrustful, Israel continued virtually to ignore the Arab Peace Initiative, failing to this day even to bring it to a cabinet discussion.

The API was evoked in subsequent proposals by other actors, including a Performance Based Road Map for Peace proposed in 2003 by the US and the newly formed Quartet, a group composed of representatives from the US, UN,

EU and Russia. Designed to end the violence of the second Intifada and to revive negotiations, the Road Map laid out a series of mutual steps, in three phases. The first phase necessitated the return of Israeli forces to the pre-Intifada positions, a freeze on settlement-building and a cessation of violence, alongside reform and democratization of the PA and consolidation and control of its security forces. The second phase of the Road Map spoke of an option to create a Palestinian state in temporary borders prior to the commencement of final status negotiations (the third and last phase) in the framework of an international conference. The Road Map was officially accepted by the government of Israel, albeit with fourteen reservations. The Palestinians accepted the Road Map without formal reservations, although they rejected the option of an intermediate state in temporary borders.

These steps toward Palestinian statehood followed dramatic changes that had taken place earlier. In September 2001, then Prime Minister Sharon declared that Israel wanted to give the Palestinians something that no one had offered them in the past—the possibility to establish a state. President George W. Bush followed this with a "vision" of the two-state solution, endorsed by UNSC resolution 1397 (Reuters 2001). Following his unexpected acceptance of a Palestinian state, Sharon implemented a "unilateral disengagement" from the Gaza Strip in 2005, including the evacuation of all the settlements there, alongside four small settlements in the West Bank. Some months later, however, Sharon fell into a coma and never regained consciousness.

It was never clear just how far Sharon had meant to go, but there is evidence that he intended further, possibly even massive, evacuations from areas in the West Bank. He was apparently motivated by the violence of the second Intifada, as well as internal pressures from former military and security figures, who had spoken out against Israel's policies in the occupied territories. As a pragmatist, not an ideologue, Sharon's primary concern most likely was the demographic issue: Jews being eventually outnumbered by Arabs between the Mediterranean Sea and the Jordan River and the possibility of sliding into a bi-national state if the occupation continued. In the spring of 2005, he even used the term *occupation* from the podium of the Knesset, a first for a right-wing leader, arguing that continued occupation was bad for Israelis as well as Palestinians.

In the face of strong opposition to his disengagement plan from within the Likud, Sharon had created a new party—Kadima—in 2005, taking with him Ehud Olmert, who succeeded him as prime minister in January 2006. Initially, Olmert sought to continue unilateral disengagement, envisioning withdrawal from settlements within the West Bank up to the line of a planned security barrier, while leaving the IDF in place. He abandoned this idea after four soldiers were kidnapped by Hizbollah in the north, precipitating the "Second Lebanon War." Hizbollah had continued to be a threat since Barak's unilateral withdrawal from Lebanon in 2000, and with the outbreak of the war, unilateralism was discredited and abandoned. Instead, Olmert launched a new peace process with the Palestinians. At the urging of the Americans, it was initiated at an international conference in Annapolis in November 2007, but Olmert preferred to conduct the subsequent negotiations bilaterally, with US Secretary of State Condoleezza Rice participating intermittently.

Israeli Foreign Minister Tzipi Livni and PLO negotiator Abu Ala conducted the official talks, but Olmert conducted a private channel with PA President Mahmud Abbas (Abu Mazen), striving to create an atmosphere of personal trust. Olmert and Abbas actually came closer to agreement than any previous leaders. In a plan presented to Abbas in their negotiations, Olmert proposed Israeli annexation of 6.5 percent of the West Bank, with 5.8 percent of the annexed land to be compensated through land "swaps." Seeking contiguity for the Palestinian state, Abbas countered with 1.9 percent to Israel, based on the Palestinian calculation of the actual areas of the Israeli settlements. Both leaders later said they believed they could have easily reduced their differences on this issue.

Regarding Jerusalem, both leaders claimed to have reached near-agreement on international trusteeship over the Holy Basin, with the Arab neighborhoods of East Jerusalem to be under Palestinian sovereignty and the Jewish neighborhoods under Israeli sovereignty, although the settlement of Har Homa, built after the signing of Oslo, remained disputed. It is not clear what was agreed or even suggested regarding the refugee issue, but Abbas repeated often that the Palestinians did not intend to change the nature of Israel—namely, flood Israel with refugees. Olmert spoke of allowing 15,000 refugees to return over a ten-year period; Palestinians spoke unofficially of 150,000, over ten years. The only firm agreement reached was on the critical issue of security. Olmert agreed to a NATO force under US command to guard the Jordan River border, compromising on the traditional demand for an Israeli presence. His willingness to forgo the Jordan Valley was based on his conviction that missile warfare made a land presence less important, although there would be demilitarization of the Palestinian state and reciprocal early warning stations in both states.

In September 2008, Olmert presented Abbas with his proposed map, but refused to let him take a copy. Abbas said he would return with a map expert the next day, but instead he traveled to Jordan and Egypt, presumably to discuss the offer. He never gave Olmert a final answer, but he later maintained that despite the Israeli attack on Gaza that began in December 2009, there were plans to meet—or for their representatives to meet—to discuss their differences. Olmert claimed to have no knowledge of such plans.

There are many views on why the negotiations ended in September 2008. By then, Olmert had announced his resignation in the face of pending corruption charges; President Bush was also near the end of his term. Abbas may have been hesitant to proceed under such circumstances. Rice and others later claimed that Israelis had told the Palestinians to wait for the new Israeli prime minister, expected to be Tzipi Livni. At one point after the talks, Abbas said the two sides had been too far apart, but subsequently both he and Olmert claimed they could have finalized an agreement "within two months" (Birnbaum 2013; Reuters 2001).

Olmert, beginning his political journey from within the Likud, had come to the realization that Israel could not both maintain a Jewish majority and remain a democracy, if it continued to hold onto the occupied territories. Like Sharon, Olmert saw that granting citizenship to the millions of Palestinians under occupation would have meant the creation of a bi-national state, with Jews quickly becoming a minority, possibly even a persecuted minority. Denying citizenship while continuing to keep the territories would constitute apartheid (as Rabin had actually admitted in the past). Olmert's willingness to compromise did not stem from diminished security concerns, or greater trust in the Palestinians than his predecessors. Rather, like Rabin, and possibly even Sharon, he perceived continued occupation, with its demographic consequences, to be a greater threat to Israel's future than the risks involved in a peace agreement. Unlike Barak, Olmert did not seem concerned about public opinion. His concept of leadership was that if one leads, the public will follow. It helped that 70 percent of the Israeli public supported negotiations with the Palestinians and the two-state solution, although Olmert did not have the security credentials (and therefore public confidence) that Barak could have commanded (Peace Index 2007BIB-007, February poll).

The situation was slightly different with regard to Syria during Olmert's tenure. Those negotiations, begun in February 2008 via Turkish mediation, were kept secret for many months, but by December 2008 negotiations showed signs of progress. At that time and in Olmert's presence, the Turkish Prime Minister held a telephone conversation with Bashar al-Assad, in which it was agreed that their two foreign ministers would hold direct negotiations on security and delineation of the elusive 4 June 1967 line. While never publicly confirmed, the general principles of the deal were that Israel was to return the Golan, and Syria was to limit its relations with Iran and Hizbollah. A joint statement was also to refer to peace and normalization of relations with Israel. However, just days after the phone call, Olmert launched the attack on Gaza which, according to the Israeli press, surprised and angered Turkey, halting the plans. Although contacts continued, the Syrians may have subsequently concluded (perhaps similarly to Abbas) that Olmert would not be in office long enough to make, or implement, a deal.

Following the Israeli election, it was Netanyahu, not Livni, who succeeded Olmert in 2009, leaving little expectation that Israel would pursue a genuine peace process with any of its adversaries. Both Netanyahu and Assad proposed some form of talks, but once civil war broke out in Syria, Israel considered the Golan off the agenda. In May 2016, Netanyahu held a cabinet meeting on the Golan itself and ceremoniously declared the area, already officially annexed by Israel in 1981, an integral part of Israel.

The Palestinian issue was another matter. One of Barack Obama's first steps as US President was to appoint George Mitchell as Special Envoy to the Middle East. Obama called for a settlement freeze, and Mitchell declared the Arab Peace Initiative to constitute official US policy. Presumably it was these signs from Washington that prompted Netanyahu to make a startling announcement of support for the two-state solution in June 2009, seemingly reversing his previous record of intransigence. He spoke of negotiations without preconditions, signaling, however, that he would not resume talks where Olmert had left off. In addition to the usual demands for demilitarization of the Palestinian state and Israeli control of the airspace, Netanyahu revived the position that Jerusalem is the indivisible and eternal capital of Israel, referred to the need for "defensible" borders, including an Israeli military presence in the Jordan Valley, and rejected the return of any refugees to Israel. Netanyahu added a new demand, saying some six times in his two-state speech that the Palestinians must recognize Israel as the homeland of the Jewish people, on later occasions calling it the "nation state of the Jewish people."[7] Since the PLO had already recognized Israel's right to exist in peace and security, this new demand was interpreted by many as a tactic to further impede negotiations.

In November 2009, Obama obtained Israeli agreement to a 10-month halt in settlement-building, so that negotiations could take place. The freeze, however, did not include construction that had already begun, building for "natural growth" and construction of public buildings such as schools. Thus, some 3,000 housing sites as well as public buildings were completed during this time, causing friction with both the Palestinians and the US administration (Israeli settlement-building in East Jerusalem particularly strained US–Israel relations). As a result, negotiations did not begin until roughly a month before the end of the freeze, despite many efforts by Mitchell to open the talks. The Palestinians balked at negotiating while settlements were being built, especially in East Jerusalem, and Israel refused to broaden or extend the freeze. Only a Palestinian decision to seek full UN membership for Palestine as a state (a move that failed) finally prompted direct Israeli–Palestinian talks, but they were plagued by haggling over agenda and topics, and no progress was made over the following two years.

Although the Americans supported Israeli opposition to Palestinian efforts to internationalize the conflict via UN organs and thwarted Palestinian efforts to gain international recognition of Palestine as a state, US interests were not identical to those of the Netanyahu government. Washington was not completely comfortable with Israel's positions, and the relationship between Obama and the Israeli leader steadily deteriorated. Obama adopted Netanyahu's "Jewish homeland" phrasing, but supported talks based on the 1967 lines and full, phased Israeli withdrawal.

In 2013, Washington undertook a new peace initiative, led by Secretary of State John Kerry, aimed at achieving a peace agreement by mid-2014. Indirect talks took place, with Kerry meeting with each side separately, usually in the region. As the deadline neared and the gaps remained wide, Kerry lowered his sights and sought a framework agreement, rather than a peace treaty.[8] The details of the talks have not been officially revealed, but by all accounts Palestinian demands reflected deep mistrust of Netanyahu. Moreover, Abbas later claimed that Kerry had sought foremost to find solutions satisfactory to Netanyahu, ignoring the needs and demands of the Palestinians.

The last weeks before the deadline saw little progress, but the end came when Netanyahu delayed the final installment of Palestinian prisoner releases. Israel had agreed to prisoner releases, in exchange for a Palestinian commitment to suspend moves to join international agencies, such as the International Criminal Court.

Israeli insistence upon phasing the releases presumably was meant to ensure progress in the talks, but controversy over which prisoners, specifically Palestinian citizens of Israel held in Israeli prisons, was a constant issue. With the fourth and last release in sight—and the fact that the disputed prisoners could no longer be passed on to the next release—vociferous right-wing opposition led Netanyahu to balk. At this impasse, just before the deadline, Israel also announced another construction tender, for 700 units in East Jerusalem. Following these moves, Abbas submitted applications for admission to fifteen international bodies and opened new reconciliation talks with Hamas. Israel called an end to the Kerry led negotiations and the initiative came to a close.

Little is known as to what actually was or was not agreed in the talks. In a speech two years later, Kerry laid out points believed to have comprised the ideas presented to the two leaders. Most accounts agree that by the time of a White House meeting between Abbas and Obama, the Palestinian leader had begun to despair of reaching an agreement primarily over the issue of the release of prisoners, but also out of deep distrust of Netanyahu, and what the Palestinians saw as US collaboration with the Israelis. Regardless, Abbas gave a negative response to the Kerry proposals, and the talks ended with the crisis over prisoner releases and the announcement of renewed settlement-building in East Jerusalem.

Few in either Israel or Palestine were surprised. Opinion polls had continued to show a mutual lack of faith, and a majority belief that there was no partner on the other side. Abbas pointed to continued settlement-building as proof of Israel's duplicity, while Netanyahu fed Israeli skepticism, by arguing that the Palestinians were not out to end the occupation but to eliminate Israel. Netanyahu pointed to Hamas's shelling from Gaza as a sample of what happens when Israel withdraws, ignoring the fact that the Gaza withdrawal was unilateral, and had not been carried out within the framework of a peace agreement. Following the Arab Spring and the ensuing instability in the Arab world, Netanyahu spoke increasingly of the danger of radical Islam, presenting Islamic terrorism as the reason Israel would have to control all of the West Bank "for the foreseeable future."[9]

At the time of writing, a resumption of peace negotiations continues to face two critical challenges—primarily from within Israel. The first and perhaps foremost is the basic, persistent mistrust of the Palestinians, or perhaps Arabs in general, shared by the Israeli leadership and public alike. Failed efforts of previous negotiations, particularly Oslo and Camp David 2000, followed by the violence of the Second Intifada and rocket attacks from Gaza, have fortified this mistrust. The Israeli public has shifted sharply to the right, preferring a staunch Israeli government out of the persistent conviction that Palestinian hostility is immutable.

Netanyahu has been feeding this fear, as demonstrated by his statement that Israelis must "live by the sword, forever." The second major challenge is the belief held by Netanyahu and much of the public that all of the ancient Land of Israel belongs to the Jewish people—exclusively. This concept of entitlement differs from the more general belief that the homeland of the Jewish people lays in the holy land of Biblical times. The more pragmatic streams of Zionism were and remain willing to forego exclusivity and to divide the land, though their views on where the lines should be drawn vary. Many see possibly insurmountable practical challenges such as the evacuation of thousands of settlers. Yet the major challenges of the past—the zero-sum game approach of the Palestinians and the Arab world—were long ago eliminated by the peace treaties with Egypt and Jordan, by the PLO's recognition of Israel's right to exist, and by the Arab Peace Initiative. The primary challenges for peace may now lie within Israel itself.

Notes

1 No evidence can be found that these proposals were ever conveyed to the Arab states.
2 In fact, Israel began settling the Golan Heights in July 1967.
3 Jordanian annexation of East Jerusalem was not recognized. Nor was Israeli annexation of the areas beyond the 1947 Partition Plan lines, namely the post-1948 Armistice lines. Israel still has no recognized eastern border.
4 Civilian reaction to the SCUD attacks during the 1991 Iraq war and to the Intifada led to this concern.
5 A Labor led unity government under Shimon Peres had moved these troops from Beirut to southern Lebanon in 1984, but pressure remained within Israel for total withdrawal due to continued IDF casualties.
6 Uri Sagie, *Ha-yad she-kaf'ah* (*The Hand that Failed*), Tel Aviv, Yedioth Sfarim, 2011, 121; Danny Yatom, *Shotaf l'Sod* (*Party to the Secret*), Tel Aviv, Yedioth Sfarim, 2009, 221 or in English, Shlomo, Ben Ami, *Scars of War, Wounds of Peace*, New York, Oxford University Press, 2006, 243. See also, Bill Clinton, *My Life*, New York, Vintage Books, 2005, 886; Martin Indyk, *Innocent Abroad*, New York, Simon and Shuster, 2009, 251.
7 This demand had appeared in Israel's fourteen reservations to the Road Map.
8 The following account is based on interviews and Y-Net (*Yedioth Aharonot*), 2 May 2014; *Al Monitor*, December 2, 2013; *Haaretz*, December 6, 2013, March 16, 2014, April 11, 2014; *Times of Israel*, February 13, 2015; *New York Times*, December 23, 2014.
9 Speaking to the Knesset Foreign and Security Affairs Committee, *Haaretz*, October 26, 2015.

References and further reading

Arian, Asher. 1995. *Security Threatened: Surveying Israeli Opinion on Peace and War*. Cambridge: Cambridge University Press, p. 102.
Birnbaum, Ben. 2013. "The End of the Two-State Solution." *The New Republic*. March 11.
Golan, Galia. 2007. *Israel and Palestine: Peace Plans and Proposals from Oslo to Disengagement*. Princeton, NJ: Marcus Weiner Publishers, pp. 165–166.
Israel Ministry of Foreign Affairs. 1995. *Prime Minister, Yitzak Rabin: Ratification of the Israel Palestinian Interim Agreement*. The Knesset, October 5.
Israel State Archives. "Stenographic Minutes of the Meetings of the Government, 18 and 19 June 1967." Documents 1–6 a-8164/7, a-81647/8, a-8164/9 Government Publications, *Periodic History*. [Hebrew]
Muasher, Marwan. 2008. *The Arab Center*. New Haven, CT: Yale University Press, pp. 121–122, 127–128.
Reuters. 2001. Sharon, November. Available at: www.pmo.gov.il/PMO/Archive/Speeches/2001/09/Speeches8394.htm.

Shamir, Jacob and Michal Shamir. 2000. *The Anatomy of Public Opinion*. Ann Arbor, MI: University of Michigan Press, 171 pp.

The Peace Index. 2000. *Israel Democracy Institute*. July poll. Available at: https://en.idi.org.il/centers/1159/1520.

The Peace Index. 2007. *Israel Democracy Institute*. February poll. Available at: https://en.idi.org.il/centers/1159/1520.

13

BORDERS AND THE DEMARCATION OF NATIONAL TERRITORY

David Newman

Introduction

Despite the huge amount of media attention which Israel attracts, the total land area of Israel and the Occupied Territories (the West Bank, the Gaza Strip and the Golan Heights) is no more than 25,000 square kilometers. Being enclosed by the Mediterranean Sea to the west, and Arab countries to the north, south and east, makes Israel vulnerable in terms of its strategic location. Such vulnerability is multiplied by the fact that Israel's international borders have not, entirely, been demarcated and formally ratified by all of its neighbors. Thus seventy years after the establishment of the State of Israel, the territorial question, which is largely a passé issue in contemporary global geopolitics, remains central to any understanding of the Israel–Arab conflict.

This chapter, and the next, will examine two related aspects of Israel's territorial politics: borders and settlement landscapes. This essay on borders discusses the ways in which Israel's outer configuration is determined vis-à-vis its neighbors, while the essay on settlement landscapes discusses the way in which the territory within the borders is controlled in terms of Jewish–Arab demographic and territorial object-ives. Each essay is a unit in its own right, but the impact of settlements on borders indicates the essential interrelationship between the two.

The basic territorial question facing Israel/Palestine has not changed in over eighty years, dating back to the first British attempts to partition the Mandate into distinct national territorial entities, as witnessed through the attempts of both the Peel and Woodward Commissions in the late 1930s and through to the UNSCOP partition proposal (ratified in November 1947). It is often forgotten that the Partition Resolution legitimized the creation of separate Jewish and Arab states, along with the internationalization of Jerusalem into a "corpus separatum." However, in reality, the Arab refusal to accept the partition, and the subsequent War of Independence (also known as the Naqba which took place through 1948–1949), resulted in only one of these three decisions being actually implemented: the establishment of the Jewish State, to be known as Israel. This state would exist within borders which were significantly larger than those outlined in the original UNSCOP proposal. It is this border that has become accepted as the ultimate determinant of Israel's sovereign territory within the international community.

While the outer territorial configuration of the area to be partitioned, stretching from the Mediterranean Sea in the west to the Jordan River in the east, and from the border with Lebanon in the north to the border in Egypt in the south, has remained the same throughout this period, two other dimensions—demography and power relations—have undergone significant change. Such change has made it all the more difficult for the territorial question to be resolved.

With respect to power at the time of the Mandate, Britain ruled the area. Beneath the British rule, both communities, the Jews and the Arabs, had little or no power other than administrative procedures with respect to their own communities. Eighty years down the road and power hegemonies within the territory are vastly different, with the sovereign State of Israel recognized by the international community but very little formal recognition of an Arab-Palestinian State.

With respect to demography, the population of this small territory (including the Occupied Territories) has increased from less than a million, almost tenfold to just under ten million. Demographic ratios between the two populations have undergone significant change during this period. Within the boundaries of the State of Israel, there is an approximate ratio of 80–20 between Jews/Israelis and Arabs/Palestinians, while this ratio is closer to 60–42 when taking the West Bank and Gaza Strip into account. Given differential demographic growth rates, it is the demography–territory balance which has highlighted the "demographic" problem facing Israel in the long term if it insists on retaining control of all those territories captured in 1967. This "demographic" problem has given rise to the two-state discourse on the part of Israel's leaders—from both the right wing to the left wing of the political spectrum.

Israel's borders

Israel has five potential international borders—with each of the neighboring states—Lebanon, Syria, Jordan and Egypt, and a potential boundary with a future Palestinian state. Of these five, only two—with Egypt and Jordan—have the status of internationally agreed lines, by virtue of the peace treaties with each of these countries, with Egypt in 1979 (the Camp David Accords) and with Jordan in 1995 (Cohen 1987; Collins-Kreiner et al. 2006; Newman 2013). The borders with Lebanon, Syria, and the West Bank remain the armistice lines which were drawn up in Rhodes immediately after Israel's War of Independence. However, Israel's conquest of the Golan Heights and the West Bank in 1967, the subsequent expansion of settlements in both these regions, and the unilateral construction of the Separation Barrier during the post 2000 period, mean that in reality the borders as such are managed from alternative locations.

Historically, Israel's borders date back to the partition of the region between the respective French and British mandates at San Remo in 1920, following World War I and the final dissolution of the Ottoman Empire (Biger 2004, 2008; Brawer 1988). The lines drawn up at San Remo were based on the principles of the Sykes-Picot Agreement from 1917, in which the allied powers agreed to divide up the Levant and the Middle East according to the realpolitik interests of the Western European powers. The divisions which took place at that time remained the territorial basis for the system of states which have constituted the Middle East during the past hundred years. The French divided their own territory into two separate states, Lebanon and Syria, based on their desire to have a country with a Christian majority which, they argued, was the case in Lebanon based on the 1932 population census. For their part, the British divided the Mandate territory of Palestine along the River Jordan, thus creating the new state of Transjordan to the east, awarding control to the Hashemite tribes who had, in turn, been driven out of Arabia by the Saudis and lost control of the holy sites of Islam. The Hashemite support of the British during the war resulted in their being rewarded by the British who carved out an entirely new state territory, largely desert and largely unpopulated at that time, which became the State of Jordan. The State of Jordan has been ruled by the descendants of the Hashemite monarchy until the present period.

As with the creation of new nation-states in Europe in the aftermath of World War I, and according to Woodrow Wilson's doctrine of a state for every nation, the new boundaries did not always entirely reflect the distribution of the local ethnic populations and tribes. Nonetheless, the borders became sacrosanct within a relatively short period of time, and they have continued to form the basic territorial building blocks around which the state system in both these regions (as well as in Africa) has continued until the present period. Following the partial fragmentation of some of these boundaries in the wake of the Arab Spring, the rise and fall of the Islamic State (crossing the boundaries of Iraq and Syria and encroaching on the boundaries of Turkey and Iran), and the establishment of Kurdish autonomy and self-rule, the question of the potential of boundary modifications that takes into account these new regional and geopolitical interests still remains to be resolved.

Israel–Egypt

The current Israel–Egypt boundary was formalized as part of the Camp David Peace Agreement signed between Israel and Egypt in 1979 (Kliot 1995). Israel withdrew from the Sinai Peninsula which it had conquered in 1967, dismantling settlements, especially in Northern Sinai (renamed the Yamit region) and returning to the course of the boundary which had been drawn up by the British in the early part of the century. The unresolved issue of Taba was taken to international arbitration, which ruled in the favor of Egypt, establishing Israel's southernmost point at the port city of Eilat where, in effect, four boundaries come together: Israel, Egypt, Jordan and Saudi Arabia. The result of this ruling generated limited territorial waters for each of these countries in the Red Sea, but enabled maritime access to all of the countries by mutual agreement.

For almost twenty-five years after the implementation of the Israel–Egypt peace agreement, no fence or physical barrier was constructed along the boundary. Along the Egyptian–Israel border, security or terrorist incidents were and remain rare. This status quo is primarily the result of administrative and military coordination between both countries, who work together to pre-empt threats. The line of the border was visible from early satellite maps due to the differential policies concerning ease of access to the border by the local Bedouin populations. Access was restricted on the Israeli side, while access was enabled on the Egyptian side. This resulted in grazing on the Egyptian side of the border, thus denuding the desert vegetation, while on the Israeli side the desert scrub remained untouched. The depleted vegetation due to grazing shows up clearly as light and dark colors on satellite images, defining the precise line of the border, even in a period without fences or walls.

In the 2000s, and following the beginning of the construction of the Israel–West Bank separation barrier, the Israeli government decided to construct a fence along the course of the Israel–Egypt boundary as a means of preventing the further movement of migrants from Africa fleeing Somalia, Sudan and Ethiopia. The formation of ethnic migrant communities in the south of Tel Aviv was opposed by many Israelis and by the right-wing Israeli government who sought both to expel those who had already arrived and to prevent the continued arrival of new migrants fleeing war-torn countries and seeking safety and/or economic improvement. One of the solutions was the construction of a physical barrier along the course of the boundary. The idea of a physical barrier tied in with the rise of ISIS and the movement of Islamic fundamentalist groups into the Sinai peninsula, both of which destabilized Egypt on the one hand and threatened the border with Israel on the other. A terrorist incident which took place along the border in 2012 pushed the Israeli government into completing the border fence, secured and patrolled by highly sophisticated surveillance techniques which can detect movement across the border at almost every point.

A territorial addendum to the Israel–Egypt border concerns the border separating and hermetically sealing Gaza from Israel to the east and north, and from Egypt to the south with the Mediterranean Sea, with the maritime waters closely patrolled by both countries, to the west. The Oslo II Accords in 1995, called for safe passage routes which would allow residents of Gaza access and travel to the West Bank through Israeli territory. But, following the unilateral withdrawal of Israel from Gaza and the forced evacuation of all Israeli settlements (numbering some 7000 inhabitants), the border has been effectively closed, with all transport of goods and food being subject to stringent cross-border inspections at the Erez crossing point. The former Philadelphi line between Gaza and Egypt also remains closed and patrolled by Egypt, effectively transforming Gaza into a closed territory. Gaza's isolation has resulted in attempts to build tunnels, in the case of Israel constituting a terrorist threat and in the case of Egypt enabling the transportation of goods and military equipment into Gaza. The sea embargo imposed by Israel has also made it almost impossible to transport goods from Europe, culminating in the violent events surrounding the 2010 flotilla in which ships from Turkey were forcefully stopped, boarded and diverted to Israel's sea port in nearby Ashdod. Gaza has continually requested permission to construct their own independent sea port which would enable the free movement of goods and people and could, potentially, serve a Palestinian state in the West Bank if acceptable safe passage routes linking the two territories were to be demarcated and managed without mutual security concerns.

Israel–Jordan

The Israel–Jordan border has its historical roots in the decision by the British government to partition the Mandate area of Palestine and to create the State of Transjordan in 1921. The line of division was along the course of the River Jordan, from the Syrian Mandate area in the north (at the confluence of the River Yarmoukh) as far south as the port of Aqaba at the head of the Red Sea. Following the Rhodes Agreements in 1949, Jordan undertook the administration of those territories occupied by their own troops to the west of the River Jordan, thus giving rise to the name "the West Bank." Jordan's attempt to annex the West Bank and extend its own sovereignty to the region was recognized by only two States: Britain and Pakistan. The West Bank remained under Jordanian administration until the Six-Day War in 1967 when it was captured by Israel. The Jordanian army retreated to the line of the River Jordan, creating Israel's de facto eastern border for the next fifty years.

It was this line which constituted the concept of defensible borders to the East as elaborated by Yigal Allon, Israel's deputy prime minister and former commander of the elite Palmach troops, in his famous Allon Plan, drawn up shortly after the Six-Day War.

Allon argued that the populated mountainous interior of the West Bank should become an autonomous area, to be administered by Jordan, and to be linked to Jordan by means of a territorial corridor running from Ramallah to Jericho and across the Allenby Bridge. The strip of land along the border itself should remain under Israeli control and, reflecting the defensive posture of that period, be fortified by the establishment of Israeli agricultural communities/colonies along the course of this inhospitable region. The Allon doctrine remained central to Israeli strategic and territorial thinking for the next decade until the rise of the country's first right-wing government under the leadership of Menachem Begin (Allon 1976), although notions of what exactly constitutes defensible borders have changed over time and according to the respective Israeli or Palestinian perspectives (Saadi 2010; Gold 2012).

The Israel–Jordan Peace Treaty of 1995 formalized the course of the boundary in two sections, one from the northernmost point of the West Bank to the border with Syria, and the other from the southernmost point to the twin post cities of Aqaba and Eilat. Although the course of the entire border is clear along the River Jordan (through which hardly any water flows) Jordan refused to sign the map which demarcated the border between the West Bank and Jordan, arguing that this could only be undertaken between Jordan and a future Palestinian State. As with the Israel–Egypt boundary, much of the southern section of the Israel–Jordan boundary remained unfortified for the next two decades, although there have now been calls (from Prime Minister Binyamin Netanyahu, for example) to complete the security fencing of Israel by constructing a fortified fence and barrier along the entire course of the eastern boundary. For a short period following the Israel–Jordan peace treaty, attempts were made to implement cross-boundary cooperative projects in fields relating to water, ecology and agriculture, as a sign of better relations. However, these attempted cooperative initiatives did not prove successful and most have now been abandoned (Arieli and Cohen 2013).

Israel–Lebanon

The course of the Israel–Lebanon boundary also dates back to the territorial partitioning of the region between the two Mandate powers in the post-World War I era. This boundary line, with only some slight deviations, remained constant throughout the ensuing period. Following the Rhodes Agreements, the course of the border became an armistice line. Initially the armistice line was controlled by the Lebanese army with few incidents between the two countries. But this changed after the influx of Palestinian refugees to the south of the country. Following the major political changes which took place in this region as a result of Israel's invasion of the area in the Second Lebanon War in 1982, fundamentalist Shi'a groups such as the militant Hizbollah organization have largely retained control of the region through to today.

The British desired to move the northern border of their Mandate territory further to the north in order to have control of the waters of the River Litani, but this move was rejected by the League of Nations. The same idea emerged during the 1980s, following Israel's invasion of South Lebanon: detractors argued that Israel would never relinquish control of the region because of its need for additional water sources for its growing population, arguing that secret tunnels were being constructed which linked the Litani to the north of Israel. Although these rumors proved to be completely false, they reflect the critical geopolitical importance of the region's limited water resources and location vis-à-vis the course of the country's boundaries.

The significance of water in regards to boundaries was also reflected in Israel's bombing of the dams which were being built by Syria in 1965 on the River Yarmoukh and which would have prevented the free flow of water into the headwaters of the River Jordan, the transfer of water from Israel to Jordan as part of the Israel–Jordan peace agreements, and the sensitivity around the underground water aquifer which underlies Israel and the West Bank in the center of the country. But, as Israel has moved more strongly into the desalination of seawater in recent years, the geopolitical importance of the scarce water resources has declined.

When Israel withdrew from South Lebanon in 2000, it returned to the course of the original Israel–Lebanon line (Hof 2001). A minor territorial issue exists in the fate of the area known as the Sheba'a farms, not least because it is unclear whether they will eventually be part of Lebanon or transferred to Syrian control. Nonetheless, this issue proves relatively insignificant in comparison to other issues, and it remains an issue to be resolved under any future bilateral territorial and border negotiations between the two countries.

Israel–Syria

The Israel–Syria border is contested more strongly than any of the previous three borders as a result of Israel's capture of the Golan Heights during the Six-Day War of June 1967. The initial armistice line created a border almost on the Sea of Galilee/ Lake Kinneret, with the Golan Heights as part of Syria. The region overlooked much of northern Israel and was the source of many incidents during the 1949– 1967 period. Israeli communities in the north of Israel were often subjected to artillery fire into their homes and this constituted a major strategic threat for Israel and, during the Six-Day War, Israel conquered the entire region. In the 1973 October (Yom Kippur) War, the region was nearly retaken by the Syrian army. A disengagement agreement followed immediately after the 1973 War and was negotiated by American Secretary of State Henry Kissinger, resulting in the return of the city of Kuneitra to Syria while letting the rest of the Golan Heights remain under Israeli control. In order to strengthen their hold of the region, Israel proceeded to establish more settlements (some had already been established between 1967 and 1973). As a direct government response to what was perceived as an act of weakness in returning the whole of the Sinai Peninsula to Egypt without any concessions, the Israeli parliament (Knesset) passed a law extending civilian control to the Golan Heights—in effect, a law of territorial annexation. This law, recognized only by Israel, provides the internal justification for the direct administration and development of the region through the normal civilian and government channels without the need for the additional involvement of the military authorities, unlike the case in the West Bank (with the exception of East Jerusalem).

Though the West Bank (Judea and Samaria) is tied up with a combination of both security and religious/historical discourses, which right-wing groups use to justify their attempts to annex the territory as part of a Greater Israel, the Golan Heights is, in contrast, purely a security issue. Its strategic location overlooking the entire eastern area of Northern Israel and the pre-1967 experiences of artillery firing into the settlements in the valley below mean that there is greater consensus within Israel against any form of territorial withdrawal from this region and against a return to the course of the original armistice line. It was surprising therefore that Israeli Prime Minister Ehud Barak, a former Chief of Staff and one of Israel's most decorated war heroes, was prepared to negotiate an Israeli withdrawal from the Golan as part of a future Israel–Syria peace agreement. Any withdrawal from this region would necessitate, as was the case of the unilateral withdrawal from Gaza, the evacuation of approximately 25,000 settlers/Jewish residents from the region, although this figure is only a quarter of the 100,000 indigenous residents of the region who left their homes in 1967 and became refugees in Syria.

Israel–West Bank/Palestinian state

The most contentious of Israel's border issues concerns a border which does not yet exist: the future border between Israel and a Palestinian state when—and if— a two-state solution to this ongoing conflict is negotiated and ratified (Brawer 2002; Newman 2011). The formal armistice line separating Israel from the West Bank, known as the Green Line, was also demarcated as part of the Rhodes Agreements, negotiated between representatives of Israel and Jordan. Although this line has become the "default" line for an Israel–Palestine border, it is an artificial boundary, reflecting only the distribution of Jordanian and Israeli armies after the first Arab–Israeli war of 1948–1949. Apart from being influenced by these military realties, this artificial "border" made little sense in 1949 and makes even less sense today.

The border was known as the Green Line because of the green pen that was used to demarcate the line on the maps. All official Israeli maps between 1949 and 1967 depicted the line in green, although myths have also grown up around the fact that the green signified the fact that Israel planted forests on their side of the line, especially in unsettled border regions so as to make a statement concerning territorial control. In some areas, such as the Lahav and Yattir afforestation regions in the south, this cultivation of vegetation on the Israeli side has become a reality and is quite clear on satellite imagery or when driving along the border roads. However, this is not the reason for the name. Furthermore, in other regions, such as in the "no mans land" area around Latrun and the Canada Park, trees have been planted on both sides of the line, thus obliterating the original course of the line, as the "no mans" areas have been annexed de facto to Israel.

Although the Green Line was opened in the immediate post-1967 period, it was never formally deleted, not least because Israel never attempted to annex the territory or to unilaterally extend its sovereignty over the West Bank (Newman 1995, 2009). Successive Israeli governments after 1967 realized the demographic implications of any form of annexation and the addition of hundreds of thousands (now millions) of Palestinians as full citizens. Moreover, in the immediate aftermath of the 1967 War, the Labor government of the time believed that it would be able to negotiate a peace settlement with Jordan, which would comprise the return of most of the conquered area as a Palestinian autonomous zone linked to Jordan, as laid out in the Allon Plan drawn up by Yigal Allon, the former Palmach Commander. Under the plan Israel would retain control of the Jordan Valley (an area seen as the country's new "defensible border" in the east), while relinquishing itself of the concern for the densely populated Palestinian mountainous interior of the region where most of the local population resided.

The administrative nature of the Green Line remained the same as before, even in the period prior to the reconstruction of fences and walls. Israel civilian law and citizenship applied to all residents—Jewish and Arab—residing inside Israel, while the Arab residents of both the West Bank and Gaza Strip remained stateless Palestinians even as Israeli settlers in the West Bank retained their full Israeli citizenship. The impact of the imposed Green Line boundary offers a good example of how artificial borders, even in the modern era, create new realities. Prior to 1948, all of the Arab-Palestinian population residing in this region were part of a single ethnic national space within which there were commercial, transportation and family links. In such a space there was no difference between Qalqiliya and Tayibe or between Jenin and Um el Fahm. But following the demarcation of the Green Line, those Arabs residing on the Israeli side became full Israeli citizens, while those residing on the West Bank side became stateless Palestinians under Jordanian rule. Each was subject to different educational, economic and welfare policies, such that by the time the Green Line was "opened" in 1967, the two populations displayed completely different socioeconomic and educational profiles, even though they shared the same language, religion and family affiliations.

Fifty years after the Six-Day War, the laws applying to the Arab-Palestinian populations on each side of the line still remain different, one applied through the normal civilian authorities of the State of Israel, the other through the agency of Israel's Military Administration, even when it relates to civilian matters. The division of the West Bank into different types of area "A," "B" and "C" as a result of the Oslo Accords has not changed this situation, although Palestinians living in Areas "A" enjoy full autonomy and security control (Areas "A" include approximately 85 percent of the Palestinian population of the region and all the major towns with the exception of East Jerusalem; partial autonomy in areas "B"; while areas "C" remain under full Israeli control). The fragmentation of the West Bank into areas "A," "B" and "C" has resulted in a map consisting of disconnected exclaves and enclaves, connected by safe passages and security routes which the local citizens have to negotiate on a daily basis. In this way, Israel successfully retains control over large swathes of the territory: direct control over Areas "C" and indirect control over Areas "A" and "B." As such, "A" and "B" areas allow Israel to relinquish direct control of the population and the need to adequately provide public and welfare services for this large and growing population.

While Israeli citizens can travel in Areas "C," they are not allowed to enter Areas "A." For their part, Palestinians can travel throughout the West Bank but are no longer allowed to cross the border into Israel unless they have employment permits which enables them to enter (and requires them to return) on a daily basis, and even then, only on foot. They are collected by their Israeli employers on the "other" side of the boundary early in the morning (who return them to the checkpoints at the end of the day) and are required to go through the inspection process on a daily basis. Since the construction of the separation barrier the number of Palestinian workers allowed to work inside Israel has been greatly reduced and replaced within the Israeli employment market by cheap labor imported from elsewhere (the poorer countries of Europe, the Philippines and illegal migrants from Africa), all of whom are perceived as constituting a lesser security threat.

Following the increase in terrorist incidents in the post-Oslo period, the Israeli government decided to construct a physical barrier to separate the West Bank from Israel. The Barrier is, for much of its course, a set of electrified fences with infrared surveillance which detects movement from one side to the other. For smaller portions of the fence, the barrier constitutes a concrete wall, particularly in those areas where the Palestinian towns and villages are in close proximity to the border as well as in large swathes of Jerusalem. There are five major crossing points along the course of the fence/wall which, over time, have in effect become international crossing points. At these crossing points, all vehicles (especially those of Palestinians), are checked, Israelis and Palestinians cross at separate checkpoints, and trucks and lorries carrying goods have to be unloaded on one side and the goods transferred to trucks from the other side, leading to much delay and cost.

The separation barrier deviates from the course of the Green Line along some 25 percent of its course, notably in those areas where Israeli settlements (see Chapter 14) are in close proximity to the border. Thus the de facto border which has been superimposed upon the region has, effectively, reduced the area of the West Bank. Some Palestinians have become spatial hostages in that they are located in communities on the eastern side of the Green Line, and they do not possess the necessary documents to cross the barrier into Israel. And for those located on the western side of the barrier, they are unable to directly cross into the Palestinian areas and are required to undertake significant time-consuming detours to arrive at their destination. This constitutes a basic human rights problem relating to the imposition of spatial and territorial change.

Jerusalem and its borders

The borders of Jerusalem are tied up with the broader issue of West Bank borders, but given the intense political sensitivity surrounding almost every square meter of this highly contested city, Jerusalem can be said to constitute a separate border issue (Dumper 2014; Yacobi and Pullan 2014). The city which, in the original UNSCOP partition proposal, was intended to be internationalized under neither Jewish nor Arab control was nonetheless divided into a western and eastern section as a result of the 1948 War of Independence. The Old City, with its Jewish, Moslem and Christian holy sites became part of the Jordanian controlled eastern part of the city, resulting in the expulsion of the Jewish population from the Jewish Quarter of the city. Israel did retain control of a territorial exclave on Mount Scopus, the site of the original Hebrew University and the Hadassah hospital, and they were allowed, under United Nations protection, to maintain a small garrison of soldiers to guard the site.

Immediately following the Six-Day War, Israel declared the "reunification" of the City into a single municipal entity with the slogan, consistent until today, that Jerusalem is the "eternal capital of the Jewish people, never again to be re-divided." The Israeli Knesset passed a law annexing the eastern portions of the city, and the municipal borders were withdrawn to include the Old City and areas to the east, north and south of the city which had previously been under Jordanian control. The boundary also included Atarot airport to the north, which the government hoped would be transformed into an international airport, but the airport never materialized due to its sensitive and problematic location. During the pre-1967 period, urban planning had concentrated on expansion to the west, the only direction open to Israel. The construction of a new hospital, a new university campus, and the government complex including the Knesset building, exemplify this westward growth. In the post-1967 era, successive Israeli governments focused on expanding new neighborhoods, notably Ramat Eshkol and Ramot to the north, Gilo and East Talpiot to the south, effectively eradicating any previous physical separation of the city.

Areas beyond the city have also been expanded, notably the Gush Etzion settlement bloc to the south of Bethlehem, and Maa'leh Adumim, a city of over 40,000 inhabitants, some fifteen kilometers to the east on the road to the Dead Sea and Jericho. This is part of territorial policy aimed eventually at expanding the municipal area in all directions so as to ensure future retention of the entire city. Especially contentious is the area to the east of the city known as E1 which links Jerusalem to Maaleh Adumim and which Israel desires to include within its future borders. Also contentious is the more recent settlement neighborhood of Har Homa, to the south of the city, effectively creating a continuous built-up zone between South Jerusalem and the neighboring Palestinian city of Bethlehem.

Nowhere has the construction of the separation barrier been as contentious as in Jerusalem. A concrete wall has been built in the heart of East Jerusalem, separating Palestinian neighborhoods. The course of the wall indicates the municipal boundaries which Israel desires to demarcate in the future, arguing that many of the "newer" (sic) Palestinian neighborhoods on the other side of the wall are not really part of Jerusalem, unlike the many Jewish neighborhoods which have been constructed during the same period. Municipal boundary commissions which deal with boundary changes in the areas surrounding the city (especially to the west inside Israel proper), have to take account of the political objectives and imperatives of the government in addition to the normal planning, infrastructure and transportation problems. This complex dynamic makes the long-term planning of the "united" city—a city which effectively remains divided between Israeli and Palestinian ethnic and functional neighborhoods—exceedingly difficult. The transportation network and systems of commerce remain separate, and it was thirty years before the electricity grid was united. Most Israelis do not travel to the east of the city out of fears for their safety, while Palestinians from the east of the city come to the western areas to find employment but maintain their social and family lives within their own separate neighborhoods. The construction of the light railway partly along the major transportation artery separating West Jewish Jerusalem from East Palestinian Jerusalem, links the center of the city to the newer neighborhoods of Pisgat and Givat Zeev in the north of the city, beyond the Green Line. Though it has improved the transportation options open to city residents, the light railway remains politically contentious, becoming the target for stone-throwing attacks by some Palestinian residents, as it passes near their own neighborhoods.

Transportation infrastructure plays a major role in the strengthening of internal borders in and around the city of Jerusalem. The light railway's course runs from Bayit Vegan in the west of the city through eastern parts of the city on its way up to Mount Scopus and from there to the Jewish neighborhoods which have been built beyond the Green Line. As just mentioned, the railway has been the target of a number of stone throwing attacks on or around the interface between the east and west of the city. The new fast railway from Tel Aviv into Jerusalem will, for the time being, stop at the entrance of the city in the west. But plans have been proposed to extend it as far as, and even into and underneath, the Old City, a plan which would cause major international opposition once it crosses the border from the pre-1967 west of the city into the eastern sections, especially considering the stone throwing incidents already occurring.

While the city is divided into interspersed Jewish and Arab neighborhoods, there remain hardly any mixed neighborhoods, with Abu Tor in the west of the city being an exception. The previously divided village of Bet Tzafafa reunited into a single functional entity after 1967. However, Bet Tzafafa has once again experienced physical separation in recent years with the Begin highway extension south towards Gush Etzion, dissecting the heart of the village against the wishes of the residents and through compulsory expropriation and purchase of land. Such a project was ostensibly for the "public good" but affected only one population sector. It is now possible to travel from the heart of the city to the Gush Etzion settlements south of the city, inside the West Bank, on the new highway within twenty minutes, thus erasing any former impact of borders between "better" roads in the west and "worse" roads in the east. Similarly, the new highway—which links the north of Jerusalem, through area E1, to the growing settlement city of Maaleh Adumim to the east—also erases any form of previous border as successive Israeli governments seek to make de facto changes in the territorial and border allocations.

The Old City remains unique. Its territorial extent is determined by the impressive ancient walls of the city but is divided internally into Christian, Moslem, Jewish and Armenian quarters. The holy religious sites—The Al Aqsa Mosque, the Dome of the Rock, the Church of the Holy Sepulchre and the Western (Wailing) Wall—remain open for religious worship, attended by hundreds of thousands throughout the year. No side is prepared to even consider forfeiting ultimate control over the holy sites: Israel refuses to relinquish control over the entire Old City; the Jewish Quarter has been rebuilt and repopulated in the fifty-year period since the Six-Day War; more radical groups have also attempted to purchase houses and expand into neighboring quarters. Ideas have been circulated concerning a city without any form of national flags, open to all religions and ethnicities, and managed jointly by religious authorities, but given the nature of the conflict in which religious groups have promoted extremist and violent nationalist positions, as contrasted to messages of peace and forgiveness, this seems highly unlikely at the time of writing. Any attempt to extend the new rail systems into the Old City as far as the Western Wall—or other holy sites—may from a transport and infrastructure perspective. But such an attempt runs in the face of any geopolitical logic which is aimed at reaching conflict resolution and an ultimate peace agreement for as long as such projects are unilaterally imposed by one side on the territory and space which remains under contention.

Conclusion

Despite its small, even miniscule, territorial size, this chapter has shown the multi-faceted nature of borders, both in terms of their diverse locations with neighboring states, as well as the hierarchy of scales ranging from the interstate borders down to the level of intra-regional (West Bank) and intra-city (Greater Jerusalem) lines of separation. Not all of these borders have visible walls or fences but the lines—be they political, administrative or municipal—nonetheless function as places of separation and division. They demarcate spaces as well as determine the nature of the activities, functions and citizenships which take place on either side. That the functional dynamics of the borders are as, or perhaps even more, important than the actual location, is indicative of the way in which borders have undergone change throughout the world in recent decades. At the same time, while the demarcation of borders and related territorial disputes has largely disappeared from much of the world today, basic territorial issues remain central to the way in which the Israel–Arab–Palestinian conflict is managed and is eventually to be resolved.

References and further reading

Allon, Yigal. 1976. "Israel: The Case for Defensible Borders." *Foreign Affairs.* 55(1), pp. 38–53.

Arieli, Tamar and Nissin Cohen. 2013. "Policy Entrepreneurs and Post-conflict Cross-border Cooperation: A Conceptual Framework and the Israeli–Jordanian Case." *Policy Sciences.* 46(30), pp. 237–256.

Biger, Gideon. 2004. *The Boundaries of Modern Palestine. 1840–1947.* London: Routledge.

Biger, Gideon. 2008. "The Boundaries of Israel—Palestine Past, Present, and Future: A Critical Geographical View." *Israel Studies.* 13(1), pp. 68–93.

Brawer, Moshe. 1988. *The Borders of Israel.* Yavneh Press. [Hebrew]

Brawer, Moshe. 2002. "The Making of an Israeli–Palestinian Boundary," in Clive Schofield, David Newman, Alasdair Drysdale, and Janet Allison-Brown (eds.), *The Razor's Edge.* London: Kluwer Law International.

Cohen, Saul B. 1987. *The Geopolitics of Israel's Border Question.* Boulder, CO: Westview Press.

Collins-Kreiner, Noga, Yoel Mansfeld and Nurit Kliot. 2006. "The Reflection of a Political Conflict in Mapping: The Case of Israel's Borders and Frontiers." *Middle Eastern Studies.* 42(3), pp. 381–408.

Dumper, Michael. 2014. *Jerusalem Unbound: Geography, History, and the Future of the Holy City.* New York: Columbia University Press.

Gold, Dore. 2012. "U.S. Policy toward Israel in the Peace Process: Negating the 1967 Lines and Supporting Defensible Borders." *Jewish Political Studies Review.* 24(1/2), pp. 7–22.

Hof, Frederic. 2001. "A Practical Line: The Line of Withdrawal from Lebanon and Its Potential Applicability to the Golan Heights." *Middle East Journal.* 55(1), pp. 25–42.

Kliot, Nurit. 1995. *The Evolution of the Egypt-Israel Boundary: From Colonial Foundations to Peaceful Borders.* Monograph Series, *Boundary and Territory Briefings*, No. 8, International Boundaries Research Unit: University of Durham, England.

Newman, David. 1995. "Boundaries in Flux: The Green Line Boundary Between Israel and the West Bank—Past, Present and Future." Monograph Series, *Boundary and Territory Briefings*, No. 7, International Boundaries Research Unit: University of Durham, England.

Newman, David. 2009. "The Renaissance of a Border which Never Died: The Green Line between Israel and the West Bank," in A. Diener and J. Hagen (eds.), *Border Lines: History and Politics of Odd International Borders.* Plymouth: Rowman & Littlefield.

Newman, David. 2011. "From Bilateralism to Unilateralism: The Changing Territorial Discourses of Israeli–Palestinian Conflict Resolution," in Elizabeth Mathews, David Newman and Mohammed Dajani (eds.), *The Israel–Palestinian Conflict: Parallel Discourses.* London: Routledge, pp. 51–66.

Newman, David. 2013 "Territory and Borders," in Joel Peters and David Newman (eds.), *A Companion to the Israel–Palestine Conflict.* London: Routledge, pp. 135–144.

Saadi, A. 2010. "U.S. Policy toward Israel in the Peace Process: Negating the 1967 Lines and Supporting Defensible Borders." *Asian Journal of Social Science.* 38(1), pp. 46–59.

Yacobi, Haim and Wendy Pullan. 2014. "The Geopolitics of Neighbourhood: Jerusalem's Colonial Space Revisited." *Geopolitics.* 19(3), pp. 514–539.

14

SETTLEMENTS AND THE CREATION OF POLITICAL LANDSCAPES

David Newman

Introduction

The discussion of borders presented in Chapter 13 showed that territorial changes over time have resulted in the need to modify the course of Israel's borders, as facts on the ground have led to de facto border changes. The changes in settlement landscapes over time can be thought of in stages: from the earliest period of Zionist agricultural settlements in the late nineteenth and early twentieth centuries; the post-State national development of planned settlement, both urban and rural, in border locations and other peripheral regions, along with the creation of development towns to absorb the hundreds of thousands of new immigrants; and the post-1967 settlement of the West Bank, now numbering over 400,000 settlers (Kimmerling 1983; Kellerman 1993). In addition, there has been a general transformation of the human landscape from a rural idealism to an urban and exurban country which closely resembles a city state, with Tel Aviv and Gush Dan in the metropolitan center, linked to the rest of the country through sophisticated road and rail systems. Ideological politics dictating settlement priorities in the immediate pre- and post-state periods has been replaced by planning dynamics which are characteristic of all post-industrial Western technological societies, the growth of cities and the suburbanization of the surrounding areas. This essay examines the changing settlement patterns of Israel during the past 100 years, against the backdrop of the geopolitical imperatives—borders and demography—which necessitate strong government intervention in determining investment and construction priorities in the formation of the human and political landscapes of the country.

Between the establishment of the State of Israel in 1948 and the Six-Day War in 1967, a period of nineteen years passed during which the country underwent stages of physical development. During this period of development, Israel focused on the "bolstering" of the border regions through settlements and the dispersal of the population through the establishment of development towns in both the Negev in the south and the Galilee in the north of the country. The areas within which development could take place were limited by the location of the borders. The natural metropolitan hinterland of the Tel Aviv area was limited in the west by the sea and in the east by the Green Line and the West Bank. The development of the area took place in a north–south strip along the coastal plain, laying the foundations for the country's metropolitan core known as Gush Dan as well as setting the stage for the eventual transformation of the country into a city state with improved transportation links (both road and more recently rail) linking the country's peripheral regions to the metropolitan core.

But the construction of towns, villages and other settlement types has always been perceived as constituting part of a political policy through which land is managed and controlled by a state engaged in ethnic conflict. Land is strongly contested between Arabs and Jews, not only in the West Bank, but throughout Israel, especially in densely populated Arab regions such as the Galilee in the north and the Bedouin communities and encampments of the Northern Negev in the south of the country.[1] The expropriation of land, the granting of zoning and building permits and the establishment of municipal authorities whose task it is to provide municipal services is therefore as much a political issue as it is a banal question relating to planning efficacy and population size thresholds. In particular, there is intense contestation of land in the Bedouin regions where the indigenous local population are only partially settled in permanent townships, and where they do not have formal documentation of their historical land rights and proofs of ownership. This essay focuses on the ways in which settlements are constructed and expanded for political purposes and the relationship between settlements, borders and related issues.

Settlements as defense

The earliest forms of Zionist settlement in the late nineteenth and first half of the twentieth centuries focused on the establishment of rural and agricultural communities throughout the periphery, especially in the north, known as Kibbutzim and Moshavim. There were also some private enterprise agricultural communities known as Moshavot. The basis for the urban infrastructure of the country took place in the new city of Tel Aviv and in some smaller urban townships. Not only was this part of the socialist utopia of the early Zionist migrants, but it was also seen as a policy through which land could be brought under control for political purposes. Agricultural communities required relatively few people who could control large swathes of land as contrasted with urban communities where large numbers of people controlled relatively small areas of land in densely populated communities. As Erik Cohen noted in a seminal paper which was published in 1970, the earliest forms of settlements were spurred on by an anti-urban ideology reflected in the political priorities of the ruling elites and planners (Cohen 1970; Troen 1994).

Historians maintain that the eventual delineation of the borders and the decisions by the fledgling government in 1948 concerning which areas were prioritized in the military tactics focused on those areas in which there was Jewish settlement. This meant focusing on the coastal plain, the northern Jezreel and Huleh valleys and the Northern Negev. The interior mountainous region, which became transformed into the West Bank after the War of Independence, was largely devoid of Jewish settlement and was not therefore considered to be a priority region at the time. When Ben-Gurion and his temporary government needed to decide which areas to bring under their control between the first and second stages of the War, they opted for the sparsely populated Negev region of the south. They believed the sparsely populated region would be the area for future development, rather than the densely populated Palestinian region of the interior mountains—the West Bank. Thus Israel extended its control southwards to the port city of Eilat rather than eastwards to the Jordan River.

Not only did existing settlements and communities determine military policy during the War of Independence, but they also played a major role in bolstering the control of these regions in the post-War period and during the first three decades of statehood, until the 1970s and the immediate post-1967 era (Kimmerling 1983; Newman 1989). Settlements were seen as constituting an integral part of defensive policy and, as such, were established or expanded throughout the peripheral regions of the country and along the state's new borders. An important army program (in a country of obligatory conscription), known as the Nahal, promoted the idea of army service alongside the establishment of new peripheral communities. Following the completion of their three to four year army service, these groups often opted to remain within the new communities they had helped establish, transforming them into civilian agricultural settlements with a significant military and defensive component. The defensive knowledge of the former soldiers was then put to use at times of crisis or in keeping a watch along the borders. At the same time, these former Nahal soldiers farmed land which was in contested regions or in which it was necessary to demonstrate a physical presence to the "other" side.

The defensive dimension of new settlements was an integral part of the Allon Plan which was later proposed for the West Bank in the aftermath of the Six-Day War. But the defensive importance of the settlements was increasingly put to the test with the advent of modern sophisticated weaponry and the change in the conception of warfare. At the time of the War of Independence, outlier settlements such as Yad Mordekhai in the south, Ramat Rahel on the outskirts of Jerusalem, or Deganya and Kineret in the north had held up the advance of the Egyptian, Jordanian and Syrian armies, respectively, until larger military forces could arrive at the scene. With changing military tactics, it was no longer considered necessary to conquer every single small community, but rather advance rapidly to the main population centers and outskirt these communities altogether. More sophisticated rocket and tank technology could wipe out an entire settlement with a single hit, while—as was experienced in the Golan Heights during the 1973 Yom Kippur War—the army had to use its scarce manpower resources to evacuate the resident population to safety when threatened by the advancing Syrian army. Thus, this particular aspect of defensive policy became outdated by the 1970s, although settlements retained other land colonization and territorial presence functions, which equally served the political objectives of the State.

The political objectives of settlement and the formation of national landscapes

The establishment of settlements in contested territories serves an important geo-political objective, namely, the long-term civilian control of land. Although the functions of such control have changed over time as a result of both technological and social change, nonetheless the basic geopolitical principle remains the same. Within the Israel/Palestine context, the establishment of settlements has tradition-ally served the purpose of bringing land under control as a means of laying claim to the territory. As such, the earliest kibbutzim and moshavim (which were established throughout the Mandate territory based on agricultural pursuits) were much more effective in laying claims to large swathes of territory than were the towns and the urban developments, despite the fact that they only ever included a relatively small percentage of the Jewish population. Kibbutzim in particular, which were based on the collective farming of land and the fencing in of large areas of territory, proved to be the most effective form of political land control. A relatively small group of settlers were able to control a relatively large area of land. This was repeated in a different form in the Golan Heights following the Six-Day War, when large areas of land were fenced in for the purposes of "pasture," thus essentially excluding local Arab or Druze populations from reclaiming their land. The fencing of land is in itself a practice of bordering which enables control, inclusion and exclusion as a means of obtaining geopolitical objectives.

Settlements also constitute a presence in the landscape, even in situations where agricultural pursuits are limited due to difficult soil or climatic conditions. The establishment of settlements in peripheral regions, or areas contested by competing national claims, rather than leaving difficult terrain empty and unsettled, was an important means through which the pre-state Zionist movement extended its con-trol over territory to be included in the future state. Following the establishment of the state, the establishment of settlements in all areas which were suddenly part of the *de jure* sovereign State of Israel became a major element in the state's policy of regional development as a means of ensuring that the legal right of control was transformed into an effective de facto presence, not least along the border areas. This same policy of effective de facto presence generating legal right of control was at the forefront of the immediate post-1967 Allon Plan, promoted by the Labor Government between 1967–1977, and aimed at strengthening "Israel's defensible borders" along its new eastern front along the entire length of the Jordan valley. This policy then underwent change from the 1980s onwards as the social desirability of collective and agricultural settlement receded within the Israeli psyche, and as the security function of settlements in border regions were no longer deemed as effective in an era of changing military technology.

A third political objective of settlement was to change the demographic balance of regions throughout the country in favor of the Jewish population. In direct contrast to the extension of territorial control, the influx of large numbers of people could be achieved through the establishment of urban centers covering a relatively small area. Although the rural ideology of the early state period, promoting collective and cooperative agricultural-based communities as the ultimate form of Zionist expression was favored by the political elites of the Labor and Mapai governments, they never contained—even at their peak—more than 7 percent of the country's population, with that figure falling below 5 percent by the 1960s. In contrast, the enforced dispersal of immigrants in the 1950s, following the mass migrations from North Africa and Iraq, contributed to the establishment of development towns in both the south (the Negev) and the north (the Galilee) as a means of ensuring demographic hegemony. Ensuing social and economic problems emerged within these politically deprived communities and contrasted with the political objectives of their establishment. This same policy was adopted in the 1990s, following the immigration of almost one million immigrants from the former Soviet Union, with large numbers of the new arrivals, especially those lacking the necessary financial resources, opting for houses in the metropolitan center of the country. Given the changed technological conditions and the significant improvement of transportation and accessibility, this enabled the bolstering and strengthening of many of the development towns which had, during the previous four decades, become the symbol of social and economic deprivation, leading to the constant outflow of residents from the periphery to the center of the country.

Population dispersal and the settlement of the periphery

Since the establishment of the State, Israeli planners and policymakers have attempted to implement population dispersal away from an over-concentration of the population in the metropolitan center of Gush Dan, as a means of promoting and strengthening the peripheral regions of the Galilee in the north and the Negev in the south. In the case of the Galilee, the policy of population dispersal has been perceived as a means of creating a demographic balance between Arabs and Jews, especially in the densely populated mountainous regions where the major Arab towns, such as Nazareth and Shefar'am, are located. The Negev, which occupies 50 percent of the country's territory but holds no more than 11 percent of the country's population, has always been perceived as the region within which the future development of the country would take place. For this reason Israeli historians have argued that Prime Minister Ben-Gurion insisted the sparsely populated desert region of the Negev be taken by the Israeli army during the War of Independence in preference over the densely populated West Bank.

Furthermore, the establishment of development towns in both regions to house the migrant population was a major factor in the population dispersal policy (Tzfadia 2006). This was seen as an effective means of populating the periphery especially as most of the newly arrived migrants were poor and destitute, having arrived as refugees from North Africa and Iraq, and were therefore dependent on government assistance in providing them with housing. Even though in the first stages the migrant population was temporary in transit camps, they were later to be transformed into development towns in the same locations. However, the lack of long-term employment opportunities did not enable their long-term development. Consequently, with high levels of unemployment and under-employment and an ongoing outflow of population, the metropolitan center, wherein employment and social opportunities were greater and more varied, was clearly favored by the second and third generations.

Development towns were built in Israel during the 1950s in order to provide permanent housing to a large influx of Jewish immigrants from Arab countries and Holocaust survivors from Europe and other new immigrants (Olim), who arrived to the newly established state. The towns were designated to expand the population of the country's peripheral areas and to ease development pressure on the country's crowded center. The towns are the results of the Sharon plan—the first master plan for the regional development of Israel. The majority of such towns were built in the Galilee in the north of Israel, and in the northern Negev desert in the south.

The first development town was Beit Shemesh, founded in 1950, around twenty km from Jerusalem. The newly established towns were mostly populated by Jewish refugees from Arab and Muslim countries—Morocco, Iraq, Iran, Egypt, Libya, Yemen, Syria and Tunisia—many of them replacing the temporary "maabarot" camps which had been set up in order to accommodate the hundreds of thousands of migrants. These immigrants had arrived in Israel in a relatively short period of time before the state could adequately deal with the physical housing requirements. Development towns were also populated by Holocaust survivors from Europe and Jewish immigrants, who came to the newly established State of Israel. Despite businesses and industries being eligible for favorable tax treatment and other subsidies, with the exception of Arad, most of the towns (particularly those in the south) have fared poorly in the economic sense, and feature amongst the poorest Jewish Areas in Israel.

The influx of one million new migrants from the former Soviet Union in the 1990s was also used as a means to bolster the population of the development towns, enabling demographic growth in places which had remained stagnant, or in some cases experienced population decline as many of the second-generation immigrants opted to relocate to the metropolitan center of the country. The government attempted to learn from many of the mistakes it had made in the earlier periods of development in the 1950s and began investing greater resources in better housing conditions and more long-term employment opportunities, and vastly improved transportation links between the towns and the metropolitan center, thereby enabling higher levels of commuting on a daily basis. The improved transportation infrastructure now links the rail system with most of the development towns, no longer known by that name, in the south and the north of the country, while the release of land for private detached housing development has encouraged many residents of these towns to remain and build their own houses. In some cases, it has even encouraged residents of the center of the country to opt to build large detached houses on cheap land plots as an alternative to a crowded apartment block in the heart of the city. Thus the cheaper land and housing prices, better transportation links, along with the higher educational levels of the Russian migrants, have provided a boost for many of the development towns and has partially alleviated the growing demographic imbalances between center and periphery. At the same time, the influx of one million immigrants from the Soviet Union has also given rise to ethnic tensions between North African and Russian communities who now compete for hegemony and political power within local government.

In both periods of mass immigration, the government has played a central role in developing the country's peripheral regions since the immigrants have largely arrived without financial resources of their own and have been dependent on government for providing them with initial housing solutions. As such, the central government has been able to determine the location of the new housing infrastructure in accordance with its geopolitical priorities. But unlike the period of the 1950s, wherein the immigrants from Iraq, the Yemen and north Africa came without any resources of their own, this was not the case with respect to the mass Russian immigration. The Russians were more directly involved in their own absorption process, since they were relatively westernized and often better educated than previous immigrant groups. Many were given the option of renting flats in the center of the country, while many others went to bolster the demography of the development towns. The private market played a greater role in providing housing solutions for the 1990s' migrants than it did in the 1950s, as would be expected from a country which had undergone forty years of rapid economic and technological growth in the interim period. The shrinking of functional distances due to new roads, new trains and high car ownership in what was now a middle-class society, has also contributed to changed perceptions of core and periphery, even though that area of the country comprising the Negev with over 60 percent of the land surface still only contains some 12 percent of the country's population.

The recent improvements in the country's transportation infrastructure—especially the Cross Israel Route 6, the expansion of the rail network to take in many of the development towns in the south, and the upgrading of the road and rail links between Tel Aviv and Jerusalem—have meant that an increasing number of people can now remain within the peripheral communities (not just the development towns) and work within the metropolitan center of the country. A job in Tel Aviv no longer necessitates a residential move. People opting to live in development towns and commute often do so because housing opportunities are both cheaper and more varied than in the densely populated and expensive small apartments of Tel Aviv and the surrounding metropolitan area. Thus, although this reflects a lack of adequate employment opportunities within the towns themselves, given the resulting lower levels of local taxation and provision of municipal services, such a situation does allow for residential and housing opportunities for people who opt to reside and remain in these locations.

Another population factor in the periphery has been the growth of some ultra-orthodox communities, especially in towns such as Arad, Ashdod and Ofakim. The ultra-orthodox population is the most rapidly growing sector within the country. Housing prices in their traditional core areas of Jerusalem and Bnei Brak (adjacent to Tel Aviv) are beyond their means and they have sought to establish communities in more distant locations where housing prices are significantly lower. This is not a random dispersal—the community leaders earmark specific towns within which new communities are rapidly established and they too compete for power within local government, often creating new tensions between secular and religious inhabitants of these towns with their contrasting needs for municipal services, schools and public services. Given the exponential growth of the ultra-Orthodox population, this trend can be expected to continue as a major factor in the country's population dispersal in the next two to three decades.

Settling the West Bank and the creation of an exurban Israel

The major focus of "settlement activity" in the post-1967 period has been the West Bank. As of 2017, the number of Jewish residents in the West Bank numbered some 400,000, not including the suburbs of East Jerusalem, which are also located beyond the Green Line.

Since the onset of the West Bank settlement project, and especially through the first two decades, the settlement leaders and ideologues have attempted to portray their actions as constituting the "true" (sic) continuation of the Zionist settlement activities of the early part of the twentieth century, a period during which many remote rural communities were established throughout the area of mandate Palestine, as a means of gaining control ("achizah") of the land.

The early kibbutzim and moshavim served a double purpose. On the one hand they were part of the socialist and cooperative Zionist experiment of creating communal communities which experienced a "return to the land" based on agricultural self-productive labor. But on the other hand their dispersed locations were aimed at expanding the territorial control on behalf of the Zionist project, later to be transformed into an independent state. The two objectives were intricately interlinked with each other. A pre-technological and geographically isolated society, which lacked easy communication and transportation links within and between each other, these communities were able to hold together as a consolidated unit against external threat through their internal solidarity and communalism. Thus, the social structure of the communities constituted an important factor in the meeting of wider territorial and political objectives. The ideological hegemony of the rural cooperative settlements extended through to the post-state period for the first two to three decades of statehood. Despite the fact that these rural agricultural cooperatives never contained more than 5 to 6 percent of the total population at its peak, this hegemonic structure was sharply in contrast with the political power enjoyed by this community within the leadership of the Zionist community and its governmental frameworks (Troen 1994).

The post-1973 settler movement portrayed itself as the continuation of the pre-State pioneering activities around which there was, at the time, consensus. It was important for them to be seen as constituting part of the Zionist enterprise, an enterprise which the *Gush Emunim* movement argued was now bereft of idealism and the torch of which would now be taken up by the ideologically motivated generation of national-religious settlers in the West Bank. Thus, despite the fact that the West Bank, especially those areas settled by *Gush Emunim* (in contrast to the unsuccessful attempt to settle the Jordan valley with traditional rural agricultural cooperatives within the framework of the Allon Plan), was located in the geographical center of Israel/Palestine and, further, despite the fact that roads and technology enabled ease of access and communication, the settlers always portrayed the region as remote, isolated and "unsettled" (by Jews). They then portrayed themselves as the modern day pioneers who were taking up the challenge of the pre-state settler pioneers.

The long-term success of establishing new settlement networks is dependent not only on the supply of affordable housing, but also on the creation of long-term employment opportunities which will enable new residents to work close to home rather than to seek alternative housing in areas where such employment opportunities exist. The alternative is to adopt the commuting model which, for political and ideological reasons, had not been favored by Israeli governments prior to the 1980s. It was this commuting model, the adoption of classic Western suburbanization processes, with cheaper land plots away from the city center, which proved to be the reason behind the move of many non-ideologically motivated residents to the West Bank, especially to those areas in closest proximity to the Green Line and their places of employment in the Gush Dan metropolitan region. Slogans such as "five minutes from Kfar Sava" expressed the geographical reality whereby the settlements were located just "five minutes" (in reality there was no settlement closer than twenty to thirty minutes' commute) from the former densely populated towns of the metropolitan center. But, this short distance provided cheaper land, larger land plots, detached housing and more generous government mortgages (Newman 1996, 2017). As such, the Green Line constituted an important border of discontinuity between the cost of housing in Tel Aviv to that in the West Bank (Reichman 1986). However as time has passed, the western areas of the West Bank have also become highly attractive for families seeking to relocate from the center of the country and who no longer perceive the western margins of the West Bank as being problematic from a geopolitical perspective, convinced that any future political arrangement will involve a redrawing of the boundaries in such a way that their new communities will remain inside of Israel.

The *Gush Emunim* settler ideologues of the 1970s and early 1980s strongly promoted the establishment of exurban communities based on commuting. They were fully aware on the one hand that the mountainous and densely populated West Bank did not lend itself to the sort of agricultural communities which were typified by the kibbutzim (and a lesser extent by the moshavim), but on the other hand they were equally aware of the fact that third generation Israelis were no longer interested in the "pioneering" challenge of cooperative and communal communities and were seeking alternative, less rigid, less centralized, forms of living in an Israel of social and generational change (Newman 2005, 2013). The physical and locational realities of the West Bank lent themselves to the adoption of a new style of *rurban* communities, enabling the young families, who were not ideologically opposed to moving beyond the Green Line and who equally had no interest in exchanging their urban middle-class lifestyles for that of a rural agricultural cooperative community, to coincide.

Within the short space of one decade, the demand for change in residential modes was an experiment which began with the new *rurban Kehillati* communities in the West Bank and very quickly slipped back beyond the border into Israel itself. The *mitzpim* project in the Galilee in the late 1970s and early 1980s latched onto some of these new settlement ideas, as did the eventual transformation of most of the country's kibbutzim and moshavim into *rurban* communities, especially those along the coastal plain. Agricultural land plots were converted into sites for detached housing, the role and importance of agriculture in the national economy became far less important than in the past. Furthermore, those engaged in agricultural activities were commercial firms and large landowners rather than individuals. Consequently, by 2017 the "rural" landscape was unrecognizable from that which existed in the late 1970s, having undergone an exurban transformation of a type which could not have been imagined at the time but which, in retrospect, is no more than could have been expected from a society undergoing rapid internal social and economic change along the classic Western patterns of evolving human landscapes and settlement patterns. One can no longer travel through the center of the country and see vast expanses of citrus orchards—indeed, it is difficult to find expansive citrus orchards in any part of the country, as much of the citrus-growing areas having been replaced with housing (low and high density) and out-of-town commercial and shopping malls.

The policies put into practice to promote West Bank settlement have dispelled the earlier settlement objectives aimed at population dispersal to the peripheral regions of the country, such as the Negev in the south and the Galilee in the north. Successive governments have promoted the settlement of the West Bank through the provision of cheap land, low interest mortgages and a range of other benefits to entice new settlers, directly competing with similar benefits which were offered to residents of the country's true peripheries in the Negev and the Galilee. The result has been unfair competition between the "real" (sic) periphery within the national consensus, to the "new" periphery which was outside the political consensus and which is geographically located in the exurban regions of the metropolitan core.

Government policy favoring the exurban West Bank resulted in a situation termed "double centrality" in which a geographical center was strengthened even further by the package of economic benefits and conditions. Why would someone opt to relocate to a "real" periphery such as the Galilee or the Negev, when they could receive the same benefits by relocating just beyond the metropolitan core region within the suburban commuting belt? The promotion of suburban middle-class communities in the West Bank, a geographically central region, explains why this region is so attractive to the population; they do not oppose relocating in the West Bank for political reasons and no amount of benefits and cheap land will induce them to move.

Since the early 1980s, and the earliest *Gush Emunim* settlement plans, the West Bank has enjoyed these locational advantages. The economic advantages explain the ability of the settler leaders to attract tens of thousands of settlers who are not necessarily attracted by the ideological or political challenges of the West Bank, but have opted for the economic and residential advantages of improving their housing conditions while remaining within the suburban belt of commuting opportunities. The transportation and road infrastructure in the West Bank has also experienced significant improvement during the past two decades, so that those areas previously considered as too remote and too interior, have now been drawn into the expanding exurban reach of the metropolitan center. Thus the opportunities of the suburban belt have become self-perpetuating as the friction of distance decreases, along the classic models of suburbanization and commuting zones.

On numerous occasions during the past twenty years, successive governments have announced a "settlement freeze" as the price necessitated for entering into political negotiations with the Palestinians, usually after a period of pressure on the part of a third party (often the USA). This is, as expected, opposed by the settlement leadership and has been portrayed as a dangerous step on the way to future territorial concessions and enforced settlement evacuation. Regardless of occasional settlement freezes, the settlement population has continued to grow almost unchecked, both as a result of the internal demographic growth of many young religious families with large numbers of children, as well as along with new arrivals of settlers from within Israel as new generational cohorts of young religious settlers set up their first homes in existing, or new, hilltop communities.

But settlement freezes have almost entirely applied to the establishment of new settlements, rarely to the expansion and consolidation of existing settlements, within which the major growth has taken place. The first years of rapid settlement growth in the late 1970s and 1980s were characterized by a rush to create as many small communities, dispersed throughout the region, as possible. This gave rise to functional and administrative problems of small communities. Few of these small communities reached the minimum economic thresholds necessary for stand-alone economic sustainability, even with the relatively high levels of public subsidization. It was therefore important for the settlement planners to ensure the long-term sustainability of the settlements over and beyond the immediate short-term political objectives. The so-called settlement freeze, while opposed politically, enabled the planners to focus on the expansion and consolidation of the existing communities, arguing that they had no other choice because of government policy. This resulted in the transformation of many of the smaller communities into larger settlements with a threshold size that enabled them to function as independent communities and that enabled the transformation of some settlements into fully fledged townships and independent municipalities.

Even in the West Bank, the growth of the townships, as in previous Zionist settlement policy within Israel, attracted the largest numbers of residents. This enabled demographic growth on a relatively small area of territory, as contrasted with the widespread dispersal of smaller communities throughout the region. Towns such as Kiryat Arba, Ma'aleh Adumim, Emanuel, Betar Illit, Efrata and Ariel contain the bulk of the settler population. Some of these towns, notably Emanuel and Betar Illit, have been populated by an ultra-orthodox spillover from Jerusalem and Bnei Braq, as their populations grow exponentially and they are unable to afford the cost of housing in the major cities. Others have offered cheaper housing solutions for people faced with high, and growing, prices, such as are found in Tel Aviv and the Gush Dan metropolitan core. Some, such as Efrat, offer middle-class housing communities, with high house prices, located at the center of a secondary residential area in Gush Etzion, fifteen minutes south of Jerusalem, and comprise almost twenty middle-class suburban communities.

It is these areas, such as Gush Etzion or the Elkana–Alphei Menashe region in the center of the country, which have attracted the larger groups of settlers and where the residents are convinced that any future boundary changes arising from a peace settlement with the Palestinians will leave them inside Israel. They are convinced that they will not be forced, under any circumstance, to evacuate their homes as was the case in Northern Sinai in the early 1980s, or in the Gaza strip in 2005. In conclusion, the dynamic and changing nature of settlement patterns in Israel can only be properly understood through an analysis of the combined impacts of socioeconomic processes of Westernization and suburbanization on the one hand, combined with geopolitical imperatives and the prioritization of certain regions over others on the other. It is the fusing of the two which makes the emergence of the country's political landscapes so different from many other countries undergoing their own settlement and town planning expansion.

Settlements, borders and the two-state solution

The rapid growth of the West Bank settlements has had a major impact on the mechanics of border demarcation. At the time of the signing of the Oslo Accords, there were less than 200,000 Jewish residents of the West Bank (excluding east Jerusalem) but this number has more than doubled in the interim period. While the settlement leaders bemoaned the Oslo Accords as the ultimate failure of their geopolitical aspirations, namely the extension of Israeli sovereignty throughout the entirety of the West Bank, the location, dispersion and growth of the settlements has nevertheless made it increasingly difficult, some would say impossible, to envisage any clean line of separation—a border—between two distinct territorial entities or States (Falah 2005).

The idea that a territorial configuration of the two-state solution that would simply require a return to the Green Line and the evacuation of all settlements which have been constructed in the region since 1967 is unrealistic, even for those on the Israeli left who believe that the settlement network is illegal, immoral and should never have taken place from the outset. No Israeli government, even one of the left, would be able to undertake such an enormous evacuation; the cost of major political unrest inside the country is perceived by many as being a greater danger than the unclear benefits of a total territorial withdrawal. This perception has been enforced in the wake of the unilateral withdrawal from Gaza in 2005 and the forced evacuation of the 7,000 Israeli settlers. The ensuring rocket attacks, two wars and many fatalities has meant that many Israelis who supported territorial concessions in principle, believing that this would bring them greater security, have now shifted their political positions. Indeed, many Israelis have shifted their political positions on withdrawal from the left to the center and from the center to the right, and there is no longer support for a similar withdrawal from even part of the West Bank, let alone the forced evacuation of tens, perhaps hundreds, of thousands of settlers many of whom will refuse to accept economic compensation and will actively oppose any attempt to force them out of their homes. There can be no comparison between the relatively successful and smooth evacuation of the Gaza Strip and the potential unrest, violence and even fatalities that could result from a similar policy in the West Bank. The region carries with it far greater religious and historical emotions than Gaza. The radicalized youth of the hilltop settlements have made it clear that they will not listen to their own leaders (the national-religious Rabbis) as they did in Gaza, while the sheer numbers involved (over 400,000 as compared to 7,000) are incomparable.

Much of the discussions of the past twenty years, aimed at demarcating a border in which both sides would be equally dissatisfied, has focused on the notion of boundary re-demarcation along the lines of current geopolitical realities. Such geopolitical realities are, namely, the settlement infrastructure and the idea that an appropriate exchange of territories between the two sides is to ensure that the total area encompassed by a Palestinian state would be no less than it is at present, even if the ultimate territorial shape would be different to that of the present West Bank.

Different cartographic exercises have proposed the redrawing of the border in such a way that anything between 60 and 70 percent of the existing settlement network, most of which are in relatively close proximity to the Green Line (due to the exurbanization processes outlined above) could be included on the Israeli side of the border in as little as 8 to 12 percent of the territory. Proposals for territorial exchange have focused on three distinct micro areas:

1. The south of the region, in the Guvrin-Metar area, where there is relatively little Jewish/Israeli presence and which would not necessitate evacuation of Jewish communities. However, in recent years there has been a concerted attempt on the part of the government to bolster and expand Jewish communities in this region, not only because of the border issue but also because of the competing and contested claims for land control between the local Jewish and Bedouin populations, the latter of whom form a majority in the border region. The settlement of Carmit has been added to the existing community of Metar to ensure an Israeli/Jewish presence hugs the border in such a way as

to create territorial "wedges" between the Arab communities on each side of the border.

2.   The north of the region in the area of the "Triangle" where, it is argued by right-wing politicians, including the present Defense Minister Avigdor Lieberman, that the border could be redrawn in such a way as to effectively "transfer" a significant part of the Arab-Palestinian residents of Israel proper on to the Palestinian side of the border. Such a transfer would thus increase the demographic ratio between Jewish and Arab populations inside Israel in favor of the Jewish population. Instead of an 80–20 ratio, it could effectively change to approximately 87–13 in favor of Israeli Jews, simply by redrawing the border and without having to physically or forcefully evacuate anyone from their houses. However, such a policy is adamantly opposed by the local Arab population who have stated categorically that they have no interest in becoming part of a Palestinian state, whose structure, nature of governance and potential fundamentalism is unclear.

3.   The expansion of the Gaza land base into Western Israel or even over the border into Egypt, with potential availability of unsettled land and where territorial compensation could even be larger than the amount of land which would have been given up in the West Bank. This would also allow for the expansion of the territorial land base of one of the most densely populated micro regions in the world. However, the relative location of this area in the periphery, away from the main urban and commercial centers in the West Bank itself, along with a clear statement by Egypt that it does not see such a solution as having any bearing on Egyptian sovereign territory and that it would have to take place (if at all) only on the Israeli side of the border, both raise a new series of unsolvable questions.

There is also a major geopolitical irony in all attempts at the redrawing of borders and the proposals for territorial exchanges. Regardless of how the border would be redrawn and whatever percentage of the settlements could remain on the Israeli side of the border, there would always be some 30 to 45 percent of settlers on the "wrong" side of the border who would have to undergo evacuation (assuming they are not interested in remaining under Palestinian control). It is precisely these interior areas of the West Bank, which encompass the more ideological and committed of the settler population and the leadership of the entire settlement movement, and they would refuse to be evacuated under any circumstances, causing major civil strife inside Israel and possible violent confrontation with the Israeli military forces sent to remove them. By contrast, many of the settlements which are located in close proximity to the border and which would remain in situ by virtue of the new border, are precisely those which could have been evacuated given adequate monetary compensation, as many of them moved to these locations for economic or quality of life considerations rather than ideological or religious ones. One should be careful not to interpret this as being 100 percent binding for either of these two populations, but it certainly affects the majority and offers a dose of tragic irony.

Given the significant increase in settlements during the past decade, it is by no means clear whether it is possible to draw any form of border which would adequately separate two territorial political entities, even allowing for complex territorial exchanges. A new discourse has begun to focus on the idea of an a-territorial political solution, returning to notions of federalism or confederalism, wherein each of the two national populations would have allegiance to separate political authorities while remaining in their existing communities. Different from a single bi-national secular state, such a configuration would consist of two separate states, composed of many internal exclaves, enclaves and territorial outliers. This is only the beginning of a new discourse which at present seems fictional rather than tangible, but has resulted from the almost impossible task of creating new borders in the light of the rapid geographical changes and settlement evolution which have taken place in the region since 1967.

Note

1   This essay only discusses the Jewish landscapes. Arab—Palestinian settlement landscapes are not included although they too require a full analysis. In reality the settlement landscape of the country is characterized by ethnic and national duality, with two diverse settlement patterns operating within a single national space, often in close proximity, but with little functional connections between them.

References and further reading

Allegro, Marco, Ariel Handel and Erez Maggor (eds.) 2017. *Normalizing Occupation: The Politics of Everyday Life in the West Bank Settlements*. Bloomington, IN: Indiana University Press.

Cohen, Erik. 1970. *The City in the Zionist Ideology*. Centre for Regional and Urban Studies. Jerusalem: Hebrew University of Jerusalem.

Efrat, Elisha. 1986. *Urbanization in Israel*. London: Croom Helm.

Efrat, Elisha. 2006. *The West Bank and Gaza Strip: A Geography of Occupation and Disengagement*. London: Routledge.

Falah, Ghazi-Walid. 2005. "The Geopolitics of 'Enclavisation' and the Demise of a Two-State Solution to the Israeli–Palestinian Conflict." *Third World Quarterly*. 26(8), pp. 1341–1372.

Gonen, Amiram. 1995. *Between City and Suburb: Urban Residential Patterns and Processes in Israel*. Avebury: Aldershot.

Hirschhorn, Sara Yael. 2017. *City on a Hilltop: American Jews and the Israeli Settler Movement*. Cambridge, MA: Harvard University Press.

Kellerman, Aharon. 1993. *Society and Settlement: Jewish Land of Israel in the Twentieth Century*. New York: SUNY Press.

Kimmerling, Baruch. 1983. *Zionism and Territory: The Socio-territorial Dimensions of Zionist Politics*. Institute of International Studies. Oakland, CA: University of California Press.

Newman, David. 1989. "Civilian and Military Presence as Strategies of Territorial Control: The Arab-Israel Conflict." *Political Geography Quarterly*. 8(3), pp. 215–227.

Newman, David. 1996. "The Territorial Politics of Exurbanisation: Reflections on Thirty Years of Jewish Settlement in the West Bank." *Israel Affairs*. 3(1), pp. 61–85.

Newman, David. 2005. "From 'Hitnachalut' to 'Hitnatkut': The Impact of Gush Emunim and the Settlement Movement on Israeli Society." *Israel Studies*. 10(3), pp. 192–224.

Newman, David. 2013. "Gush Emunim and the Settler Movement," in Joel Peters and David Newman (eds.), *A Companion to the Israel–Palestine Conflict*. London: Routledge, pp. 255–266.

Newman, David. 2017. "Settlement as Suburbanization: The Banality of Colonization," in *Normalizing Occupation*. Indiana, IN: Indiana University Press, pp. 34–47.

Reichman, Shalom. 1986. "Policy Reduces the World to Essentials: Reflections on the Jewish Settlement Process in the West Bank Since 1967," in David Morley and Arie Shachar (eds.), *Planning in Turbulence*. Jerusalem: Magness Press.

Troen, Ilan. 1994. "The Transformation of Zionist Planning Policy: From Rural Settlement to an Urban Network." *Planning Perspective*. 3, pp. 3–23.

Tzfadia, Erez. 2006. "Public Housing as Control: Spatial Policy of Settling Immigrants in Israeli Development Towns." *Housing Studies*. 21(4), pp. 523–537.

15

ISRAEL IN THE WORLD

The quest for legitimacy

Joel Peters

As with all states, the primary purpose of Israeli foreign policy and diplomacy is the promotion of the national interest of the state on the global stage. From the early days of statehood, Israel's foreign policy objectives have coalesced around five broad themes: (i) enhancing security and ensuring the survival of the state; (ii) seeking international legitimacy and political support; (iii) the promotion of peace with Israel's neighbors; (iv) the development of trade and commercial relations; and (v) the protection of world Jewry. Far greater emphasis, however, has been given to the quest of security than the pursuit of the four other goals, which have been relegated, at best, to a secondary supportive role.

Over the years, foreign policy and diplomacy have become the handmaiden of Israel's security interests, with the defense ministry and intelligence agencies playing a central role and frequently sidelining the foreign ministry. In accordance with the importance Israel places on security interests, the defense ministry and intelligence agencies lead Israel's foreign policy and diplomacy efforts in determining the nature and scope of Israel's foreign relations. As a consequence, this essay argues, arms sales, military training, and intelligence sharing have become the leitmotif of Israeli relations with countries around the world.

A common, almost unchallenged narrative exists in Israel concerning the nature of its foreign policy and the international system writ large. Born out of conflict, Israel and its leaders perceive their surrounding neighborhood, as well as the international environment, as one of danger and threat. The narrative of an Israel under constant besiegement and threat has led to a foreign policy driven by realpolitik, pragmatism and expediency.

Realist framings of the anarchic nature of international politics, coupled with the scars and memories of Jewish history, impact significantly on the nature and direction of Israeli foreign policy. Although Israel seeks the support of external powers, most notably the United States, a narrative of military power and self-reliance dominates contemporary Israeli security culture and its thinking on foreign affairs. For Israel, foreign policy is determined by the pursuit of interests and not principles. Pragmatism driven by short-term opportunism guides foreign policy. Israel's leaders see Israel as possessing few foreign policy choices, and thus consider Israel compelled to seek out friends and allies wherever they present themselves, regardless of the nature of the regime or the content of the ties that are developed. Foreign policy is largely reactive, with the pursuit of short-term opportunities outweighing any long-term strategic planning or any real public debate over the country's foreign policy orientation and of Israel's role in the world. Israel has been more willing than the majority of Western nations to overlook human rights abuses and foster relations with military dictatorships and autocratic regimes. Israeli decision makers have frequently legitimized these questionable relations and arms sales by invoking pragmatism and security, fed by a cynical, realist-tinged view of international politics. Israel has not hesitated in placing its national interests first, regardless of any immediate negative political fallout, and has, at times, even placed those interests ahead of the concerns of Jewish communities in the Diaspora.

Israeli foreign policy 1948–1991

During the early years of statehood, Israel sought to navigate the emerging rivalry between the United States and the Soviet Union through the adoption of a policy of *Non-Identification*. The *Non-Identification* balancing act did not survive for long as Israel quickly shifted to a de facto alignment with the Western powers (Bialer 1990). Initially, Israel looked to Great Britain and France (who until 1967 was Israel's prime supplier of arms), leading to its participation in the ill-fated 1956 Suez campaign. Although the United States had been one of the first countries to recognize Israel, the USA initially rebuffed Israel's offers of friendship. Whilst Israel enjoyed widespread support among the American people, its foreign policy elite saw overt support for Israel as undercutting broad US strategic interests in the region, especially securing access to the oil reserves of the Persian Gulf. In the face of massive political, military and economic support of the Soviet Union, the United States began to respond to Israeli overtures and demonstrate an increased sensitivity to Israel's defense requirements. This led to the delivery by Presidents Kennedy and Johnson of major weapons systems to Israel—most notably the sale of the Hawk anti-aircraft missile system in 1962 and Phantom jets in 1968. These arms deals established the United States as Israel's principal arms supplier. The arms deals also marked the beginning of the US policy of giving Israel a *qualitative* military edge over its neighbors.

In the early years of statehood, Israel saw itself as sharing a common destiny with the newly emerging, post-colonial nations in Africa and Asia. Israeli policymakers hoped that diplomatic recognition by the "Third World" would grant Israel international legitimacy and thereby bypass the political isolation that the Arab countries were trying to impose. In particular, Israel sought to develop close ties with India and China. However, early efforts to forge diplomatic links were quickly rebuffed.

By contrast, Israel was far more successful in cultivating relations in Africa, quickly establishing relations with the newly independent states. By the early 1970s, Israel maintained diplomatic ties with thirty-two African states, one of the largest diplomatic networks on the continent. Israel's presence in Africa positively transformed its image in the international community (Curtis and Gitelson 1976; Peters 1992).

However, Israel's global standing began to falter, following its victory in the Six-Day War of June 1967. Immediately following the war, the Soviet Union and the communist countries of Eastern Europe (with the exception of Romania) severed diplomatic relations. The Yom Kippur War of October 1973 inaugurated the worst period of diplomatic isolation in Israel's history. Under pressure from the oil-producing Arab world, nearly all the African states broke off ties during the war. Two years later, Israel's global standing reached its nadir with the passing of the UN General Assembly resolution equating Zionism with racism. Relations with Western European states also began to nose-dive, reaching a low point in 1980 with the passing of the Venice Declaration, which called inter alia for Palestinian self-determination and the inclusion of the PLO in any peace talks.

While other states turned their back on Israel during the Yom Kippur War, the United States took the unprecedented step of airlifting crucial arms and ammunition during the fighting. In subsequent years, US–Israel strategic cooperation began to take root and collaboration between the two countries' defense establishments evolved into an important, if not central component, of the overall web of bilateral political, economic and cultural ties. The Carter administration took the first steps to allow for cooperation in defense production, the transfer of US technology to Israel, and for Israeli military exports to the United States. Israel was increasingly seen as an important strategic asset and the only reliable ally of the United States in the Middle East. The Reagan administration formalized and institutionalized the burgeoning Israel–US strategic relationship with the signing of a series of memorandums of understanding in 1981 and 1983, leading to greater cooperation in defense research, joint planning, and combined military exercises.

Aside from its relationship with the United States, Israel remained isolated in the aftermath of the Yom Kippur War, leading a drive to cultivate ties with military dictatorships in Latin and Central America. Israel's reputation as a military power resulted in a massive growth in Israeli arms exports in the 1970s, with the volume of Israel's arms sales surging from an estimated $100 million in 1970, to $1.25 billion by the end of the decade. But arms sales were a double-edged sword: Israel's relationship with the military dictatorships throughout the 1970s and early 1980s further undermined its political standing in the world, adding only to Israel's political isolation. During those years, Israel even sold arms to the military Junta in Argentina, despite Argentina's record of anti-Semitism and its persecution of the Jewish community, and a US-led embargo on arms sales to Argentina. Israel rationalized those ties as driven by political necessity, arguing that the well-being of its military industries, which was dependent on those arms exports, was crucial to Israel's security and survival (Klieman 1985). The same rationale was offered for the development of an overt set of warm ties with the apartheid regime in South Africa during the 1970s, a relationship highlighted by the visit of South African Prime Minister John Vorster to Jerusalem in April 1976.

But towards the end of the 1980s Israel was beginning to emerge out of its international isolation. African states were beginning to resume diplomatic ties with Israel, and tentative openings were being developed with India and China. The end of the Cold War accelerated this process. However, it was with the signing of the Oslo Accords in September 1993 that Israel's global standing was radically transformed. The prospect of peace with the Palestinians, and the Arab world, opened up a range of new opportunities for Israel.

Israel and Russia

The end of the Cold War led to the restoration of relations with Eastern European states which had been severed in the immediate aftermath of the Six-Day War in 1967. Released from the shackles of communist rule, relations have flourished. The eastern European states have often displayed greater understanding and support for Israel in respect to the peace process than their western European counterparts. Diplomatic relations were also renewed with Russia in October 1991, just prior to the collapse of the Soviet Union. The demise of communism led to the mass immigration of Jews from the former Soviet Union. Israel boasts nearly 1 million Russian-speaking citizens—one out of nearly every seven Israelis—many of whom were permitted to leave the former Soviet Union in the early 1990s. Their arrival not only impacted significantly on all spheres of political, social and economic life in Israel, but led to the development of an intensive web of relations with Russia as well as with the new states emerging from the former Soviet Union. Moscow has become an important destination of the foreign travel itineraries of Israeli ministers and almost every sitting Israeli head of government and state visited Russia. Under Putin, Israeli–Russian relations have intensified, with Putin visiting Israel twice: in 2005 and 2012. Bilateral trade has more than doubled between 2009 and 2013, reaching $3.5 billion (though this is a relatively low figure, compared to Israel's trade with the United States, the European Union, China and India). Most critically, Russia is Israel's second largest oil supplier.

However, relations have been fraught with tension over Russia's policies in the Middle East. Russia's extensive engagement in Middle Eastern affairs has consequently compelled Israel into a delicate balancing act, causing it, at times, to defer to Russia's geostrategic interests. In the 2008 Russo-Georgian War, Israel suspended military cooperation and halted arms sales to Georgia. Similarly, Israel absented itself from the UN General Assembly vote on the 2014 crisis in Ukraine and, to the chagrin of the United States, failed to condemn Russia for its annexation of Crimea. Specifically, Russia's selling of arms to Syria, its support for Bashar Assad, and above all, Russia's role in the development of Iran's nuclear capabilities, have strained relations between the two countries. Israel and Russia have been walking a tense tightrope over developments in Syria (Etzion 2016). Although both countries have displayed a shared interest in preventing the overthrow of the Assad regime, Israel has expressed its concerns over Russia's support for and arming of Hizbollah forces in Syria and Iran's attempt to increase its influence in Syria. In order to ward off potential collisions between its forces in Syria, a series of high-level meetings have been held and the two countries' militaries have established close communications to avoid such an occurrence. At the same time, Israel has openly warned Moscow that it would not refrain from taking military action in Syria should it feel that its security interests were threatened. Russia's alliance with Iran—recently improved by signed agreements to collaborate on "strategic" energy deals worth up to $30 billion involving energy groups such as Rosneft and Gazprom—also puts Israel ill at ease.

Israel and the Caucasus region

With the break-up of the Soviet Union, Israel was also quick to establish relations with the newly independent states in the Central Asia and Caucasus regions. Most notably, Israel's relations with Azerbaijan and Kazakhstan, two predominantly Muslim states, have garnered considerable attention in recent years (Guzansky 2014). The two countries are critical suppliers of oil to Israel (accounting for over 50 percent of Israel's oil imports), and the trade balance with Azerbaijan totaled over $4 billion in 2012. Primarily, shared concerns about containing Iranian influence have drawn the countries together, with Israel reportedly securing consent to use Azerbaijan's airfields for any strike against Iranian nuclear facilities. In February 2012, Israel and Azerbaijan confirmed the signing of an arms-supply agreement valued at $1.6 billion, to include Israeli drones and anti-aircraft/missile defense systems, whilst Israel and Kazakhstan penned a comprehensive defense agreement at the start of 2014. In November 2015, Israel entered into a free-trade zone with the Eurasian Economic Union (EEU). With their openly neutral stance in the Israel–Palestine conflict and opposition to radical Islamic movements, both Azerbaijan and Kazakhstan are likely to be chief beneficiaries of Israel's closer ties with the EEU. By 2016, Azerbaijan had already purchased close to $5 billion worth of defense equipment alone from the Jewish state. In December of 2016, Binyamin Netanyahu became the first Israeli prime minister to visit Azerbaijan and Kazakhstan to cement ties with both countries.

Israel and Turkey

Israeli–Turkish relations have always been complicated, oscillating with the dynamics of the Arab–Israeli conflict. Historically, Turkey enjoyed open relations with Israel and in 1949 was the first predominantly Muslim country to recognize the Jewish State. The development of relations with Turkey formed part of Israel's "Periphery Doctrine," a strategic vision developed by Israel's Prime Minister David Ben-Gurion in the 1950s. This called for close strategic ties with non-Arab Muslim states in the Middle East to counteract the opposition of Arab states to the existence of Israel. This doctrine led to the establishment of close ties with Iran, which lasted until the overthrow of the Shah in 1979 (Alpher 2015).

Following the Oslo Accords in 1993, Israeli–Turkish relations flourished with the exchange of ambassadors and the visits of Prime Minister Ciller and President Demirel to Israel, in 1994 and 1996 respectively. The core of the relationship was always covert and military-strategic in nature. In February 1996, Israel and Turkey signed a military training and cooperation agreement, which allowed for military technology transfers, joint military research, intelligence-sharing, regular strategic-policy dialogue and joint military exercises. Turkey rapidly became a lucrative market for the Israeli defense industry, as bilateral trade boomed, rising from $100 million in 1991, to $2 billion by the end of the decade.

The collapse of the peace process and the outbreak of the Second Intifada created a visible deterioration of Turkish–Israeli relations. Some degree of cooperation continued, especially in the military and intelligence-sharing sphere, but Turkish leaders became increasingly critical and hostile in tone, openly excoriating Israeli policies vis-à-vis the Palestinians. Relations reached a low point in May 2010 with the Gaza Flotilla Incident, wherein nine Turkish activists in a fleet of ships seeking to enter Gaza were killed by Israeli soldiers. The fallout saw Turkey withdraw their ambassador, cancel joint military exercises and freeze arms deals, including a $5 billion contract. Israel formally apologized for the "Flotilla Incident" in May 2013, but bilateral ties remained frozen until June of 2016 when Israel and Turkey signed a deal to resume normal diplomatic relations after the six-year freeze (Arbell 2014).

Shared strategic concerns—most notably the turmoil arising from the civil war in Syria, instability in Iraq and the growing influence of Iran in the region—were without question the prime drivers behind the resumption of bilateral relations. But the Turkish–Israeli reconciliation was also driven as much by the prospect of lucrative Mediterranean gas deals as by mutual fears over growing security risks. It is notable in this respect that the first Israeli minister to visit Ankara after the formal renewal of diplomatic ties was Israel's minister of energy Yuval Steinitz. Even while diplomatic relations were frozen, Israel–Turkey bilateral trade rose to $4.1 billion in 2015, almost double the 2009 figure. The exponential increase of trade between the two nations during the freeze testifies to the robust commercial relations between Turkey and Israel and the capacity of economic ties to weather their political differences. By 2016, Turkish exports to Israel amounted to almost $3 billion, making Israel one of Turkey's largest export markets. Yet at the same time, political relations remain volatile. At the end of December 2017, Turkish President Erdogan hosted a meeting in Istanbul, under the auspices of the Organization of Islamic Cooperation (OIC) in response to President Trump's decision to recognize Jerusalem as Israel's capital, deeming the move a "red line" for Muslims and threatening to cut off (once again) diplomatic ties with Israel.

Israel, Greece and Cyprus: the new geopolitics of energy

Turkey's freezing of ties with Israel in 2010 was followed by a blossoming in relations with Greece and Cyprus, two countries that had traditionally cold-shouldered Israel. Relations between Greece, Cyprus and Israel remain strong today, with talk of collaborating on new natural gas resource projects. Binyamin Netanyahu became the first Israeli Prime Minister to visit Greece in 2010 and Cyprus in 2012, visits that were reciprocated by the Greek Prime Minister George Papandreou and Cypriot President Nicos Anastasiades in 2014. Israel–Greece defense cooperation forms a prominent part of the new relationship, with Greece replacing Turkey's place in joint maneuvers with the US Navy. Cyprus president Nicos Anastasiades visited Israel in June of 2015. In July of 2015, Greece Defense Minister Panos Kammenos visited Israel and signed a status of forces agreement (SOFA) between the two nations, an agreement which Israel maintains with only one other state— the US. Shortly after the SOFA agreement with Greece, Netanyahu flew to Cyprus, underlining the emerging triadic relationship between Greece, Cyprus and Israel (Guzansky 2014).

Essentially, it is the discovery of natural gas fields in the Eastern Mediterranean in 2009 that has provided a natural incentive for increased ties between Israel, Greece and Cyprus and potentially Turkey. Israel, Greece and Cypress signed the Tripartite Energy Memorandum in 2013, pledging cooperation in the exploitation of gas resources in the region and joint protection of these resources. The memorandum included a declaration of intent to lay an electric cable to link Israel and Cyprus's electricity grids, whilst commentators have discussed the potential to export gas to Europe, via a pipeline running from Israeli territory through Cyprus. Israel has also been working with Turkey and Cyprus about potential tri-lateral cooperation to export gas to Europe. The EU has also been closely monitoring the gas politics and opportunities surrounding the natural gas fields in the Mediterranean. The cooperation regarding gas resources between Turkey, Greece, Cypress and Israel has caught the EU's attention as both a peacekeeper and a potential buyer: the EU hopes that the gas fields will provide a way in which the European Union can encourage ever more peaceful diplomatic relations in the region whilst gaining for Europe the economic benefits of energy diversification. In April 2017, energy ministers from Italy, Israel, Greece and Cyprus, together with the EU's Commissioner for Climate Action and Energy, pledged to move forward with plans for the world's longest undersea gas pipeline, extending from the eastern Mediterranean to southern Europe. The proposed pipeline would take gas from Israel and Cyprus's recently discovered offshore gas reserves to Europe, thereby potentially reducing European dependence on Russian energy (Baconi 2017; Tanchum 2015).

Israel's share of the gas is concentrated in two hydrocarbon fields: Tamar and Leviathan. The Tamar field alone provides 40 percent of Israel's electricity needs, with Leviathan said to be able to take Israel from net gas importer to a net exporter. In February of 2017, Israeli developers reached a Final Investment Decision (FID) to develop the first phase of the Leviathan field, setting themselves up to extract 12 billion cubic meters (bcm) per year beginning in 2019. The discovery of the gas reserves in Israeli waters opens the possibility for greater regional cooperation. Israel has already agreed energy deals with traditional rivals, including $15 billion with Jordan, at least $500 million with Egypt and even $1.2 billion to the Palestinian

Authority. Thus, the gas reserves serve a plethora of foreign policy objectives, ranging from self-sufficiency, the diversification of resources, regional peacemaking, and realigning the geopolitics of the Eastern Mediterranean.

Israel's Asian pivot

The most pronounced shift in Israel's foreign policy orientation has been the ever-increasing importance of India and China, leading commentators to talk of an "Israeli Asian pivot." At the end of 1991, Israel established diplomatic relations with both India and China, formalizing a process that had been underway for several years. Commercial ties between India and Israel have flourished throughout the past two and a half decades. The level of Indian–Israeli bilateral trade crossed the $1 billion mark in 2000 and rose to $4.4 billion in 2013, with Israel emerging as India's principal trading partner in the region. Israel has also become one of the largest foreign investors in India.

Military cooperation is the bedrock of this newfound India–Israel friendship. The scope of activities in this field range from Israeli arms sales to India, cooperation in intelligence gathering and counterterrorism activities, joint military exercises, through to joint research and the development of new weapons systems. Israel has become India's second largest defense supplier, and India is now Israel's largest buyer of military hardware. In 2001, Israel and India signed a series of defense contracts worth over $2 billion, for the supply of Israeli weapons systems and ammunition to India, whilst in 2004, India and Israel signed a contract worth $1.1 billion for three Phalcon radar systems. In 2007, India and Israel unveiled a joint project worth $2.5 billion for the development of a new air defense system based on the Barak missiles, for use by the Indian air force and army. Relations are intensifying: in April 2017, Israel Aerospace Industries announced that it signed the largest defense contract in Israeli history: a mega-contract with the Indian Army worth 1.6 billion for advanced air and missile defense systems, medium range surface-to-air missiles, long range surface-to-air missiles, and air and missile defense systems for Indian aircraft carriers. Israel and India also partner on many joint development projects, such as the Barak-8 air defense system, in which Israel collaborates with local Indian companies (Inbar and Ningthoujam 2014).

The Israeli–Indian relationship has been cemented by a series of high-profile state visits. At the end of 2016, Israeli President Reuven Rivlin flew to New Delhi to mark the twenty-fifth anniversary of the opening of diplomatic relations. This was followed by Indian Prime Minister Narendra Modi's momentous visit to Jerusalem in July 2017, the first ever visit by an Indian Prime Minister to Israel (he balanced his trip by including visits to Gulf nations and by hosting the Palestinian President Abbas in New Delhi) and a reciprocal visit by Israeli Prime Minister Binyamin Netanyahu in January of 2018. Netanyahu returned the visit within 7 months in January of 2018. Netanyahu's visit was received warmly, and with great fanfare in both Israel and India. This despite India having voted only weeks earlier for the United Nations resolution condemning President Trump's decision to recognize

Jerusalem as Israel's capital, and India's significant ties with Iran, most notably oil imports and economic and defense cooperation (Kumaraswamy 2017).

In a similar vein, relations have expanded with China. The rapidly deepening relationship between Israel and China is based on an accelerating economic partnership; the countries diverge greatly in many diplomatic matters, and China has often condemned Israel for their settlement activity and often votes against Israel in the United Nations. Due to strategic (and oft-times controversial) arms sales diplomacy and trade incentives, multiple high-level political visits by both sides have been matched by a dramatic growth in economic cooperation and trade. In 2001, the level of trade exceeded $1 billion and by 2013 this figure had risen to over $10 billion per year, with China becoming Israel's third largest trading partner. In 2010, Israeli non-military exports to China increased 95 percent to $2 billion annually. Since 2011, China's investment in Israeli technology has reached a staggering $15 billion. It is perhaps telling that in November 2017 China opened their first Cultural Center in Tel Aviv. As recently as December 2017, the Technion, (Israel's Institute of Technology), opened a campus in Shantou, becoming the first Israeli university with a campus in China (Evron 2014).

Arms sales have been a prominent, though highly controversial, aspect of this new relationship. In particular, Israel's willingness to sell arms to China and upgrade its weapons systems has been a source of friction between Israel and the United States. American concerns over Chinese military developments led to intense pressure from Washington, strongly encouraging Israel to shy away from exploring potential arms deals with China. Most notably, this pressure forced Israel to rescind the sale of the Phalcon early warning system to China in July 2000. Despite this, restricted military ties have continued quietly. In June 2011, Israel's defense minister visited Beijing to hold talks with his Chinese counterparts. This was soon followed by the first ever visit by the head of the Chinese armed forces to Tel Aviv in August 2011. Relations received a further boost when Prime Minister Netanyahu visited Beijing in May, 2013, leading to the signing of a new series of cooperation agreements between the two countries (Chen 2012).

The China–Israel cooperation reached the next level in 2016 when Israel and China courted the idea of a free-trade agreement (Israel currently has free-trade agreements only with the US and the EU). The free-trade talks between the nations officially began in 2016 and were continued by Netanyahu's recent visit in March 2017 where both sides announced the setting up of the China–Israel "innovative strategic partnership." During his visit, Netanyahu also proposed that a fast track be established for Israeli and Chinese investors. Indeed, the rising trajectory in trade between the two nations would seem to substantiate the speculation of a free-trade agreement being reached in the near future (Rajiv 2017).

Israel's relations with Africa and Latin America

With the opening of new opportunities for Israel in Asia, relations with African and Latin American countries took a back seat until recent times. Although several

African states renewed diplomatic ties in the 1980s, Israel's (re)discovery of Africa really began in September 2009, when Avigdor Lieberman became Israel's first foreign minister for over two decades to travel to Africa, visiting Ethiopia, Ghana, Kenya, Nigeria and Uganda. In the past two years Prime Minister Binyamin Netanyahu has traveled three times to Africa; first in July of 2016 to Uganda, Kenya, Rwanda and Ethiopia and then again in June of 2017 in order to attend a meeting of the Economic Community of West African States (ECOWAS) in Liberia. Netanyahu's July 2016 visit marked the first time in twenty-nine years in which a sitting Israeli leader visited Africa. During his 2016 July visit, the Prime Minister also brought along eighty business leaders from more than fifty companies—a testament to Israel's desire to increase trade and business partnerships on the African continent. Netanyahu kept up Israel's strong diplomatic push to the continent when he attended the inauguration of Kenya's president Uhuru Kenyatta, in November 2017, where he also met with eleven other African leaders while in Nairobi.

Israel's renewed interest in Africa has mirrored the pattern of earlier years: the garnering of political support in the hope of favorable votes in the United Nations and bolstering Israel's image within the international community. And, as in the 1960s and 1970s, Africa has become a political battleground. King Mohamed VI of Morocco pulled out of the ECOWAS summit in response to Netanyahu's attendance and the first ever Israel–Africa Summit, planned for October 2017 in Togo, was canceled, ostensibly due to logistical reasons, but in reality as a result of threats of a boycott by a number of countries following pressure from the Palestinians and Arab states. Equally, the providing of military and intelligence training to security forces in numerous countries throughout the continent, regardless of the suppressive nature of some of those regimes, is a prominent feature of these burgeoning relationships. Equally, much of the economic links being forged in Africa comprise the sale of military hardware. Arms sales to Africa in 2016 totaled over $275 million, an increase of 60 percent compared to the previous year.

In the 1990s, Israel's relations with Latin America received little attention. Geographical distance and the Latin American economies' difficult stabilization efforts meant that the region was low on Israel's radar. The past ten years, however, have witnessed a deepening in the bilateral ties between Israel and Latin American countries, and in particular with Brazil. It has been a decade marked by a series of high-profile ministerial visits, the signing of a number of cooperation agreements, a growth in trade and above all a high degree of military cooperation and arms sales.

In May 2009, deputy foreign minister Danny Ayalon attended the annual summit of the Organization of American States in Honduras, the first time in over a decade that Israel had sent such a high-level representative to the meeting. This was followed by a 10-day, four-nations tour—Brazil, Argentina, Peru and Colombia—by foreign Minister Avigdor Lieberman in July, and a visit by Israel's President Shimon Peres to Argentina and Brazil at the end of the year. The following year, in March 2010, Brazilian President Lula da Silva became the first Brazilian President to visit Jerusalem. And more recently, Binyamin Netanyahu visited Argentina, Columbia and Mexico in 2017.

Israel's interest in developing ties on the continent can be explained, in part, as a concerted effort to counter the support of Latin American states for Palestinian statehood and the growing influence of Iran on the continent. But as in the 1980s, the sale of advanced weapons systems and security cooperation has been a central feature of the burgeoning ties on the continent, and in particular, a centerpiece of the Israeli–Brazilian relationship. Gaining a foothold in expanding the Brazilian defense sector became an important goal for Israeli defense companies, especially once Israel's alliance with Turkey, a major and profitable arms market, collapsed in 2009. Those efforts received a significant boost in December 2010 with the signing of a security cooperation agreement between Israel and Brazil. Brazil has emerged as a lucrative market for Israel and recently became the fifth largest importer of Israeli arms, with defense contracts estimated at being worth over $1 billion (Datz and Peters 2013).

But relations with Latin American countries have continued to encounter difficulties at the political level, with many of those countries remaining in steadfast opposition to Israeli policies and actions against the Palestinians. In July 2014, Ecuador, Brazil, Peru, Chile and El Salvador have withdrawn their ambassadors to Israel in protest at Israel's military campaign in Gaza (Operation Protective Edge), Bolivia rescinded its visa-free policy for Israeli travelers, and Chile suspended free-trade negotiations with Israel. And in 2016, Brazil rejected Israel's choice of Dani Dayan, a former head of the West Bank settler Yesha council, as its ambassador there. Israel eventually backed down, reassigning Dayan to a position in New York instead. Nonetheless, trade has remained robust between Latin American countries and Israel, and Lieberman's and then Netanyahu's landmark visits are indicative of Israel's eagerness to increase cooperation militarily, diplomatically and commercially with Latin America.

Israel and Europe: uneasy neighbors

Israel's relations with Europe have consisted of a number of conflicting trends that have resulted in a highly problematic and volatile relationship: one characterized by a strong and ever-increasing network of economic, scientific and cultural ties, yet marked at the political level by disappointment, bitterness and anger. Israel was one of the first countries to engage with the European Economic Community, signing a free-trade agreement in 1975. Shortly after the Oslo Accords, Israel and the European Union signed a new Association Agreement, which gave a significant boost to the economic and research links between the EU and Israel, and resulted in European leaders talking of affording Israel a "special status" in its relationship with the EU. In 2008, negotiations began over formally upgrading relations between Israel and the European Union, though those negotiations quickly stalled over the impasse in the Israeli–Palestinian peace process.

In spite of their differences over the peace process, relations between Israel and Europe are robust and are thriving. In 2016, the value of EU–Israel trade was €34.6 billion (consisting of €13.2 billion in Israeli imports to the EU and €21.6 billion

European exports to Israel. The EU is Israel's main trading partner, accounting for one-third of its total trade. Beyond trade, Israel and the EU have developed close cooperation in agriculture, aviation and a wide variety of research and development fields, including nanotechnology, health, the environment and communications. Israel's high-tech industry and its expertise in counter-intelligence and cyber security is highly valued in European circles. In 1996, Israel became the only non-European country to be included as a full partner in the EU Research and Development Framework Programme; and in June 2014, Israel also joined the EU's follow-up research and innovation program, Horizon 2020. Further, the recent discovery of natural gas fields off the Israeli coast now makes Israel a potentially important energy resource for Europe.

But sharp differences over the Israeli–Palestinian peace process have soured Israeli–European relations; bilateral relations have over the years become hostage to the vicissitudes of developments in the peace process. Relations with Europe deteriorated in the 1970s and 1980s over disagreements concerning the Middle East peace process, in particular over the status of Jerusalem and the inclusion of the PLO in the negotiating process. The signing of the Oslo Accords seemingly resolved those differences, but European leaders and civil society have been frustrated by the lack of progress in the peace process over the past twenty-five years, for which they place the blame primarily on Israeli intransigence. They have also been resentful of the way in which Israel has marginalized the EU's role and have argued strongly that it should be afforded a role commensurate with its global standing.

It is the issue of Israeli settlements in the West Bank undoubtedly that casts the longest shadow. European states regard Israeli settlement-building as illegal, and undermining possibilities for the emergence of a viable Palestinian state. Though falling short of full-scale economic sanctions, Israeli products from settlements are excluded from the free-trade agreement with the European Union. More recently, and to the ire of the Israeli government, the European Union has begun to take measures to differentiate its dealings between Israel and the West Bank by bringing its practices towards Israeli settlements in line with its principles and with European legislation. This can be seen in the drawing up of clearer and more categorical rules over the labeling of Israeli products and goods produced in Israeli settlements, and in the guidelines over the funding of projects within the Horizon 2020 research and development program. Those guidelines, to the chagrin of Israel, excluded the funding of any research projects which included Israeli settlements.

Israelis are contradictory in their views about their relationship with Europe. Israeli leaders acknowledge the importance of Europe to the Israeli economy and have displayed a genuine desire to strengthen ties with Europe and to be fully included as part of the European project. Some even talk of Israel applying for EU membership at some point, an idea that has received a large degree of support amongst the Israeli public. On the other hand, they are deeply suspicious of European policies, and are untrusting of Europe's intentions towards the Arab–Israeli conflict and to the region as a whole. Israel frequently accuses European leaders of being indifferent to Israel's security concerns, of not fully recognizing Israel's hostile strategic environment, in particular the threat posed by Iran, and of ignoring the policy dilemmas it faces in trying to protect its citizens from Palestinian terrorism. The differences between Israel and Europe are not simply over immediate policy choices but reflect a deeper clash over strategic culture. Indeed, for many in Israel, Europe has become a "lost continent." Europe's projection of normative power, its stress on human security and on cooperative practices, is dismissed in Israel as hollow and an expression of its weakness and of its lack of will and capacity to act on the global stage. Many on the right wing of the Israeli spectrum dismiss the long-term strategic importance of Europe and point to Asia as an alternative and more lucrative market for Israel.

The issue of anti-Semitism features prominently in the discourse of Israeli–European relations. It is impossible to speak of Israeli–Europeans relations in terms of just another set of "normal" bilateral ties. The nature of the relationship will, for the foreseeable future, be framed by the Jewish experience in Europe, the Holocaust and by that shared history. The media coverage in Israel of European affairs focuses almost exclusively on anti-Semitism or how Europe views the Israeli–Palestinian conflict. In response to European criticisms of its policies, Israeli leaders have not shied away from invoking memories of the Holocaust and the tragedy of the Jewish experience in Europe. They are quick to rebuke European leaders over the growth of anti-Semitism in Europe, and have castigated them over a lack of genuine efforts by Europeans to undertake effective measures to counter this phenomenon, presenting this as a further sign of underlying European antipathy to Jewish concerns and interests, and by association, Israel's long-term security.

At the same time, Israelis are attracted to the European lifestyle and culture. Europe and its cities are a favored destination for Israeli holidaymakers. Contemporary European studies, once marginal, are now flourishing at Israeli universities. Numerous public opinion surveys show that large segments of the Israeli public, especially the academic, scientific and business communities, are favorably disposed towards Europe, and attach great importance to the strengthening of relations with the EU. In short, there is a marked dissonance between the daily interactions of much of the Israeli public with Europe and the public rhetoric, and the indifference—bordering at times on disdain—of much of Israel's political elite, especially within right-wing and religious circles.

Europe displays an equally ambivalent attitude concerning the nature of its ties with Israel. The EU has spoken of its desire to develop a "special relationship" with Israel and to afford Israel a separate standing from other countries in the Middle East. Yet it has failed to articulate what such a status might actually entail. Europeans want Israel to embrace the European project, to adopt its values and act according to those goals. In its policies the EU treats Israel as an outsider. Europeans do not regard Israel as belonging fully to Europe and believe that Israel's future lies within the Mediterranean and the Middle East. At the civil society level, Israel's (over)reliance on military action to secure its defense (especially the extent of its military operations in Gaza) is seen in European circles as disproportionate, often in breach of international law and a contributory factor to rising tensions in the region. This understanding has led to increasing calls from European civil society that the EU needs to be more assertive in its approach and use its economic leverage on Israel to bring about a resolution to the conflict, calls which so far have been resisted by Europe's political leaders. In the same way that coverage of European events in Israel is refracted through the lens of anti-Semitism, so European views of Israel are shaped through the prism of its policies towards the Palestinians. This discourse has resulted in a volatile and uneasy relationship between Israel and Europe. It has created a very distorted reality, and one that frequently overlooks the substantive and positive ties that have been developed within European and Israeli business, scientific and security circles.

Israel and the United States

Although the European Union is Israel's largest trading partner and India, China and Brazil offer new opportunities and markets for Israel, relations with the United States remain the centerpiece of Israeli foreign policy. Contemporary Israel–US relations are sustained by overwhelming support of the US public for Israel, ideological affinity underlined by a set of shared and common values, the unique role and influence of the American Jewish community, and the deep affinity of Israelis for America.

Through the cultivation of political and personal relationships, especially among the evangelical Christian right, and the adroit lobbying by AIPAC, Israel enjoys rock-solid bipartisan support for its economic welfare and security. For Israel, American military aid is critical for maintaining Israel's qualitative military superiority and in the development of new weapons systems. The United States has been consistently supportive of Israel's security concerns. Whenever Israel has faced international pressure at the UN, the US has stood firm in defending Israel's use of military force to counter Palestinian terrorism and rocket attacks on its citizens by Hamas in Gaza and Hizbollah in Lebanon. The US has frequently resorted to vetoing UN Security Council resolutions critical of Israel's actions and policies (Freedman 2012).

The United States has played an instrumental role as a mediator in the Israel–Arab peace process. Resultantly, American mediation is also seen as key to achieving a peace agreement with the Palestinians, and serving as the guarantor of any agreement. At the same time, Israel and the United States have often differed and clashed over policy issues, most notably over the building of Israeli settlements in the West Bank. For example, in 1991, the George H. Bush administration refused to provide Israel with the $10 billion in housing loan guarantees that was needed to assist in the absorption of Jews arriving from the former Soviet Union, until all settlement expansion was halted.

Tensions were particularly fraught during the Obama presidency, again over settlement-building and over negotiations to secure a nuclear deal with Iran. One of the guardrails of Israeli foreign policy is that disputes with the US should be kept behind closed doors and Israeli leaders should work to maintain the strong bipartisanship support for Israel. During the Obama years that understanding became increasingly frayed. There was unconcealed antipathy and distrust between President Obama and Israeli Prime Minister Binyamin Netanyahu, bordering at times on outright contempt. Controversies between the Israeli and American leaders were almost continual. This led to talk of Israeli–US relations reaching an all-time low, a wavering in American Jewish support for Israeli policies and a questioning as to the nature of the US–Israel "special relationship": were relations a "strategic partnership" of shared values and interests, as supporters would argue, or an unequal burden and product of a disproportionately powerful "Israel lobby," as detractors claim?

Israel actively worked to thwart negotiations by the Obama administration with Iran over its nuclear weapons program. Relations reached a low point in March 2015, when Binyamin Netanyahu, in an unprecedented move, addressed a joint meeting of Congress to rally support against the signing of any agreement with Iran. At the tail end of the Obama administration, Secretary of State John Kerry apportioned blame for the impasse in the Israeli–Palestinian peace process to Israel, and in December 2016—marking a stunning departure from previous policy—the United States abstained from voting on a United Nations Security Council resolution which called for an immediate halt to all Israeli settlement construction in the West Bank and East Jerusalem, thereby enabling the resolution to pass.

Yet, in spite of talk of a growing crisis in US–Israeli relations during the Obama administration, US–Israel security ties remain strong, marked by US financial support for the development of the Iron Dome missile defense system, the signing of the United States–Israel Enhanced Security Cooperation Act in the summer of 2012, and the unanimous passing by Congress at the end of 2014 of the United States–Israel Strategic Partnership Act.

Donald Trump's election as US President in November 2016 was greeted with relief in Israel, despite Hilary Clinton's long-standing support for Israel. Right-wing circles celebrated Trump's victory as an opportunity to press ahead with their agenda of expanding settlements. Some even talked openly that Trump's victory would allow Israel to annex parts of the West Bank. He has not disappointed. His visit to Israel in May was met with great fanfare. Budget proposals presented by the new administration in March called for vast reductions of US foreign aid programs, with the sole exception of Israel. And to the delight of most Israelis, President Trump announced at the end of his first year in office, his intention to relocate the US embassy from Tel Aviv to Jerusalem and formally recognize Jerusalem as the capital of Israel, a move upending nearly seven decades of American foreign policy.

But Israel needs be careful not to be seen as a cheerleader for Trump. American politics has become deeply divided, and close identification with President Trump for short-term political gain runs the danger of undercutting bipartisanship support for Israel in the long run, and of alienating American Jewry, who voted for Hilary Clinton in large numbers and who oppose Trump's domestic policies, especially those on immigration.

Conclusion

In his address to the United Nations in September 2016, Binyamin Netanyahu spoke of Israel's diplomatic standing in the world as undergoing a major revolution. For Netanyahu, Israel's global isolation was now a thing of the past: more and more nations were beginning to change their attitude towards Israel and were beginning to look upon it as a potent partner, and as a force for change in global affairs.

In particular, Netanyahu has pointed to changes in the views of Arab states, and the growing number of meetings between Israeli officials and representatives from the Gulf states and Saudi Arabia as emblematic of Israel's growing international stature. Much has been made of those contacts leading to the emergence of a new discourse in certain quarters of an emerging Israeli–(moderate) Sunni alliance in the Middle East to counter the threat of ISIS and Iran. In reality, those contacts have been limited, and the promotion of such an "alliance" is designed more for domestic consumption rather than reflecting a sea change in the geopolitics of the region (Jones and Guzansky 2017).

It can be argued that the balance sheet of Israel's foreign relations is positive. Israel maintains diplomatic relations with over 160 nations, almost a threefold increase from the low point of its diplomatic isolation in the 1970s. Equally, foreign statesmen have become frequent visitors to Jerusalem and Israel's leaders are welcomed in capitals across the globe. But there is an underlying fragility to those relations. In contrast to Netanyahu's assertion about Israel's newfound global standing, the Israeli public holds a much more pessimistic outlook. In a 2017 survey on foreign policy attitudes, nearly 50 percent of those polled deemed Israel's global standing as either "poor" or "rather poor" and only 17 percent saw it as "good." Overall, the Israeli public regards the government's handling of foreign policy as, at best, mediocre (The Mitvim Institute 2017). There is an overriding sense that the development of Israel's foreign policy is guided by pragmatism, a foreign policy driven by short-term opportunism rather than any long-term strategic design or principles.

The conduct of Israel's diplomacy has a transactional quality. The array of relations highlighted in this essay has not been translated into the political support, legitimacy and normalization that Israel craves. European leaders seek out Israeli expertise in cybersecurity and counterterrorism. At the same time, they are sharply critical of Israeli policies towards the Palestinians, settlement-building in the West Bank, its actions in Jerusalem, and of Israeli domestic legislation that might potentially limit the freedom of dissent, and the rights of Israel's Palestinian citizens. India looks to Israel for defense cooperation but continues to maintain close ties with Iran and remains a strong advocate for Palestinian statehood. Africa welcomes Israeli overtures but Senegal was a co-sponsor of a UN Security Council resolution in December 2016, which condemned the construction of Israeli settlements in the West Bank and east Jerusalem. Nothing is more illustrative of the weakness of Israel's global standing than the vote in the UN General Assembly in December 2017 condemning the US decision to recognize Jerusalem as Israel's capital. Some

128 countries voted in favor of a resolution condemning the US and calling on countries to avoid moving their embassies to Jerusalem. Only nine states voted against the resolution.

The Israeli foreign policy system is weak and dysfunctional. Diplomacy in recent years has become hostage to domestic and coalition politics. For the past three years, Israel has operated without a full-time foreign minister, with Prime Minister Binyamin Netanyahu retaining the portfolio. Moreover, the foreign ministry has been stripped of much of its functional authority, with many of its primary functions parceled out to other ministries to placate ministers of the ruling Likud party and coalition partners. This has led to a lack of coordination, competing agendas and continuous bureaucratic turf wars. As a consequence, it is the defense establishment that has taken the lead in determining the nature and scope of Israel's foreign relations.

But it would be wrong to attribute the failings of Israeli diplomacy solely to the weakness of the foreign ministry. Foreign policy is not simply an instrument designed to achieve the realization of a state's national interests, however narrowly or broadly they are defined. A state's foreign policy reflects the balance between acquiring security, economic and other material needs with the promotion of core values on the global stage. It is the outcome of ongoing domestic narrative over values, identity and location and on how a society sees itself, and its place in the world and its immediate surroundings. Such a debate has been sorely lacking in Israel's public discourse. It can be argued that such an exchange is the luxury of states at peace. However, until Israeli society embarks on a discussion over its foreign policy orientation and its place in the world, then Israel's foreign policy will remain reactive, one driven by expediency and impacted by the vicissitudes and the needs of other states.

References and further reading

Alpher, Yossi. 2015. *Periphery: Israel's Search for Middle East Allies.* Boulder, CO: Rowman & Littlefield.

Arbell, Dan. 2014. "The US–Israel–Turkey Triangle." *Center for Middle Policy.* Washington, DC: Brookings Institution.

Baconi, Tareq. 2017. "Pipelines and Pipedreams: How the EU can support a regional gas hub in the Eastern Mediterranean." (Policy Brief). The European Council on Foreign Relations. Available at: www.ecfr.eu/page/-/ECFR211_-_PIPELINES_AND_PIPEDREAMS.pdf.

Bialer, Uri. 1990. *Between East and West: Israel's Foreign Policy Orientation, 1948–1956.* Cambridge: Cambridge University Press.

Chen, Yiyi. 2012. "China's Relationship with Israel, Opportunities and Challenges." *Israel Studies.* 17(3), pp. 1–21.

Curtis, Michael and Susan Aurelia Gitelson (eds.). 1976. *Israel in the Third World.* New Brunswick, NJ: Transaction Books.

Datz, Giselle and Joel Peters. 2013. "Brazil and the Israeli—Palestinian Conflict in the New Century: Between Ambition, Idealism, and Pragmatism." *Israel Journal of Foreign Affairs.* 7(2), pp. 43–57.

Etzion, Eran. 2016. "Israel–Russian Relations: Respect and Suspect." *Middle East Institute.* August 3.

Evron, Yoram. 2014. "Chinese Investments in Israel: Opportunity or National Threat?" *INSS Insight* (No. 538, April 8, 2014).

Feiller, Gil and Kevin Lim. 2014. "Israel and Kazakhstan: Assessing the State of Bilateral Relations." *Middle East Security and Policy Studies.* Begin-Sadat Center for Security Studies. (Report No. 107).

Freedman, Robert O. (eds.). 2012. *Israel and the United States: The First Six Decades.* London: Routledge.

Guzansky, Yoel. 2014. "Israel's Periphery Doctrine 2.0: The Mediterranean Plus." *Mediterranean Politics.* 19(1), pp. 99–116.

Inbar, Efraim and Ningthoujam Alvite. 2014. "Indo-Israeli Defense Cooperation in the Twenty-First Century." *Mideast Security and Policy Studies.* Begin-Sadat Center for Security Studies. (Report No. 93).

Jones, Clive and Guzansky, Yoel. 2017. "Israel's Relations with the Gulf States: Toward the Emergence of a Tacit Security Regime?" *Contemporary Security Policy.* 38(3), pp. 398–419.

Klieman, Aaron. S. 1985. *Israel's Global Reach: Arms Sales as Diplomacy.* Washington, DC: Pergamon-Brassey's International Defense Publishers.

Kumaraswamy, P.R. 2017. "Redefining 'Strategic' Cooperation." *Strategic Analysis.* 41(4), pp. 355–368.

Pardo, Sharon and Joel Peters. 2009. *Uneasy Neighbors: Israel and the European Union.* Lanham, MD: Lexington Books.

Peters, Joel. 1992. *Israel and Africa: The Problematic Friendship.* London: British Academic Press.

Rajiv, Samuel. 2017. "Israel–China Ties at 25: The Limited Partnership." *Strategic Analysis.* 41(4), pp. 355–368.

Tanchum, Michael. 2015. "A New Equilibrium: The Republic of Cyprus, Israel and Turkey in the Eastern Mediterranean Strategic Architecture." *PRIO Cyprus Centre* and *Friedrich-Ebert-Stiftung.* Occasional Paper Series, 1.

The Mitvim Institute. 2017. The 2017 Israeli Foreign Policy Index. Available at: www.mitvim.org.il/images/English_Report_-_The_2017_Israeli_Foreign_Policy_Index_of_the_Mitvim_Institute.pdf.

16

ISRAEL AND THE JEWISH PEOPLE

Dov Waxman

Introduction

There is one crucial respect in which the State of Israel is unlike any other state in the world—it is a Jewish state. The state's Jewish identity was clearly expressed from the moment of its establishment on May 14, 1948, when David Ben-Gurion, Israel's first prime minister, read from the Declaration of Independence, beginning with the first sentence: "The Land of Israel was the birthplace of the Jewish people." Since then, the Jewishness of the State of Israel has been reflected in the official symbols of the state (such as the seven-tiered candelabra [the Jewish *menorah*] and the "Star of David"), in its national anthem (the *Hatikvah*), in state ceremonies, and in numerous laws (most notably the 1950 Law of Return, which grants automatic citizenship to any Jew emigrating to Israel).

As the world's only Jewish state, Israel has a unique and special relationship with the Jewish people. Whereas most states regard themselves as serving only the interests of their citizens, Israel's Jewish identity means that it regards itself as the only state representing all Jews around the world. In Ben-Gurion's words: "Israel is the state of and for a world people" (Brecher 1972, p. 231). Israel, then, is the nation-state of the Jewish people, wherever they live. Its self-appointed mission, therefore, is to represent the Jewish people on the world stage, protect them, and promote their welfare and well-being. According to the dominant Zionist ideology in Israel, only a state can do this effectively in the world today. Although the Jewish people lacked a state for most of their long history, Zionism insists—and most Jews now agree—that Jews need a state of their own. Without one, many fear, Jews will be as vulnerable as they were during the Holocaust, when a third of the Jewish people (two-thirds of the Jewish population living in Europe at the time) were annihilated. More than anything else, the Holocaust has proven the need for a Jewish state to Jews around the world (and also to many non-Jews).

While most Jews want Israel to be a Jewish state, there is much less agreement about the kind of relationship it should have with Jews who live outside of Israel (commonly referred to as the "Jewish Diaspora," although not all "Diaspora Jews" regard Israel as their "homeland") (Aviv and Shneer 2005). Should Israel also cater to their interests and needs, and if so, how important should these be in the state's policymaking? Should Diaspora Jews have a say in Israeli policymaking, and are they entitled to criticize Israel's policies? What loyalty, if any, should Diaspora Jews have to the Jewish state, and how can they reconcile this with loyalty to their countries of citizenship? These questions have been a source of recurrent tension between Israel and Diaspora Jewry, and among Diaspora Jews themselves.

This essay focuses on the relationship between Israel and Jews living outside Israel, which is where the majority of the world's Jewish population still lives (there are nearly 16 million Jews in the world today, with about 6.5 million in Israel, and the rest located mainly in North America and Europe, mostly in the United States). This relationship is much more complex than many believe. It is often assumed, for instance, that all Jews around the world passionately support Israel. In fact, as I will argue in this chapter, Diaspora Jewish support for Israel, though strong and enduring, is more complicated, and increasingly more ambivalent, than the popular view suggests. It is also widely believed that Israel is very concerned with the security and welfare of Diaspora Jews, that it often acts on their behalf, and that this is a major determinant of its foreign policy and its relations with other states. In this essay, I will also challenge this popular belief, as I will argue that the interests of Diaspora Jews have almost always been a secondary concern to Israeli policymakers, and that Israel's foreign policy is primarily guided by raison d'état.

Israel and Diaspora Jewry

Ironically, for a state that would not have been created were it not for the Jewish Diaspora—the Zionist movement was born in the European Jewish Diaspora and Diaspora Jews played a crucial role in its success[1]—Israel has historically harbored a disdainful, even scornful, attitude towards Diaspora Jews. Despite the fact that Israel's population was for decades mostly composed of foreign-born Jews immigrating to Israel from the Diaspora, Israel's leadership (often non-natives themselves) traditionally regarded Diaspora Jews as somehow inferior to Jews in Israel, and they perceived Jewish life in the Diaspora in largely negative terms. This attitude was rooted in the traditional Jewish view of Diaspora Jewish existence as a condition of exile (*galut* in Hebrew), which involved a perpetual longing for a return to the Jewish homeland. It was also a product of the extremely disparaging portrayal of Diaspora Jewry in early Zionist ideology. Classical Zionism insisted that there was ultimately no future for Diaspora Jewry. Due to the twin pressures of anti-Semitism and assimilation, Jewish life and culture in the Diaspora was destined to disappear. Although some prominent Zionist thinkers like Ahad Ha'am believed that the creation of a Jewish homeland could also ensure a future for the Jewish Diaspora, most Zionists shared the view of Theodore Herzl, the visionary founder of the Zionist movement, that there was no future for the Jewish Diaspora after the establishment of a Jewish state (Herzl believed that Jews would either move en masse to the Jewish state or else assimilate into oblivion outside of it). Jacob Klatzkin, the editor of *Die Welt*, the official journal of the World Zionist Organization, expressed the typical attitude of classical Zionists towards the Jewish Diaspora:

> Without this raison d'etre, without the goal of a homeland, the Galut is nothing more than a life of deterioration and degeneration, a disgrace to the nation and a disgrace to the individual, a life of pointless struggle and futile suffering, of ambivalence, confusion and eternal impotence. It is not worth keeping alive.
>
> *(Klatzin 1971, p. 325)*

The antipathy of classical Zionism to the Jewish Diaspora was summed up in the concept of the "negation of Diaspora" (*Shlilat Ha-galut* in Hebrew).[2] This entailed not only a concerted effort to end Diasporic Jewish existence by encouraging all Jews to "return" to the Jewish homeland and establish their own state, but also a strong desire among early Zionists to rid themselves, and other Jews, of the alleged negative qualities and characteristics of Diaspora Jewishness. As A.D. Gordon, one of the early Zionist thinkers, declared: "what we seek to establish in Palestine is a new, recreated Jewish people, not a mere colony of Diaspora Jewry, not a continuation of Diaspora Jewish life in a new form" (Liebman 1977, p. 220). Israel's early leaders, especially Ben-Gurion, shared this view. What this meant, in practice, was that during the first few decades of the state's existence, Israel's leadership insisted that the Jewish Diaspora should no longer exist, and that all Diaspora Jews should make *aliyah* (meaning "to ascend") and "return" to Zion. In the words of ex-Prime Minister, Golda Meir: "One must not acquiesce in the idea that the diaspora will be permanent" (Shimoni 1995, p. 15).

Although more than three million Jews from over ninety countries have moved to Israel since its establishment (many of them, perhaps most, more out of necessity than choice),[3] millions of other Jews, the vast majority of them living in Western democracies, have chosen not to move to Israel. This fact has compelled Israel's leaders to pragmatically alter their attitude towards Diaspora Jewry. Instead of insisting that all Diaspora Jews relocate to Israel, they have gradually come to accept the existence of a Jewish Diaspora, if only reluctantly. Over the years, classical Zionism's negation of the Diaspora has been largely discarded, and replaced by an acceptance of the Jewish Diaspora and even a growing recognition among Israeli leaders and government officials of Diaspora Jewry's importance, especially American Jewry. The Israeli public's attitude towards the Diaspora has also softened over time, as Israeli Jews have come to identify more with Jews in the Diaspora, although most Israeli Jews still have little interest in or knowledge about Diaspora Jewish life (Sheffer 2004). Nevertheless, traditional derogatory Zionist attitudes toward the Jewish Diaspora still persist among some Israeli Jews (perhaps the most famous exponent of such views is the Israeli author A.B. Yehoshua).

Today, while Israel accepts the existence of the Jewish Diaspora, it still considers it to be less important to Jewish life and to the future of the Jewish people than the Jewish state. Israel claims to be the center of the Jewish world, the sun around which Diaspora Jewish communities should revolve. Whether or not this is really the case, the belief in Israel's centrality in Jewish life is widely held by Israeli Jews and Israeli policymakers. This belief, which can be termed "Israel-centrism," shapes Israel's relationship with the Jewish Diaspora and with different Jewish communities within it. According to this belief, Diaspora Jewry ultimately depends upon Israel for its survival, and hence Israel's interests and needs take precedence over those of Diaspora Jewry's. In other words, since Israel's well-being is the paramount interest of the Jewish people, all other considerations are to be subordinated to it.

This attitude posits that fundamentally, the Jewish Diaspora should be subservient to Israel, not vice versa. This belief underlies the typical instrumentalist view held by Israeli policymakers towards Diaspora Jews, whereby the latter are primarily seen as a valuable source of economic and political support for Israel. If they are unwilling to move to Israel (which is still seen as desirable, but not imperative), Diaspora Jews, especially American Jews, are expected to at least donate money to Israel, publicly advocate for it, and lobby on its behalf. Throughout Israel's history, this generally implicit expectation has guided Israeli governments, whatever their political makeup, in their various dealings with Diaspora Jewish communities, at least those located in safe, prosperous, Western liberal democracies. By contrast, more vulnerable and poorer Jewish communities in the Diaspora are simply expected to relocate to Israel.

Thus, in stark contradiction to classical Zionism's denigration of the Jewish Diaspora, Israeli leaders, and many Israeli Jews, have come to view the Jewish Diaspora as one of Israel's most important strategic assets, because of the financial and political support Israel receives from Diaspora Jewry. As Naftali Bennett, Chair of the Jewish Home Party and Israel's current Minister for Education and Diaspora Affairs (there is an official position in the Israeli government that deals specifically with the Jewish Diaspora) has written: "The Israeli government sees the connection between Israel and the Diaspora as a strategic asset, both for the Jewish people and the State of Israel" (Bennett 2016). Instead of "negating the Diaspora"—expecting and hoping for its eventual demise—Israeli policymakers now want to sustain the Jewish Diaspora and maintain its connection with Israel.

Hence, Israeli policymakers now stress the importance of strengthening Jewish identity and attachment to Israel among Diaspora Jews, and they promote and fund a variety of projects and initiatives that are designed to do this, most notably the Taglit-Birthright Israel program, which sends young Diaspora Jews (aged 18–26) on a free, ten-day tour of Israel. Rather than calling upon all Diaspora Jews to move to Israel, therefore, Israeli policy now merely tries to encourage and enable them to remain Jewish outside of Israel, while maintaining and developing meaningful ties with Israel. Thus, the Zionist movement's historic mission to save the Jewish people by bringing Diaspora Jews to live in Israel (the "ingathering of the exiles" in Zionist terminology) has been slowly transformed into Israel's current mission to save the

Jewish people by bringing young Diaspora Jews to visit Israel, and preserving the Jewish Diaspora.[4]

Israel's attitude towards the Jewish Diaspora, therefore, has changed in some important respects over the years. What has not really changed is the way in which Israeli policymakers have considered the interests and needs of Diaspora Jews when formulating their policies. As a Jewish state, Israel has a self-appointed mission to protect and defend Jews everywhere. Consequently, Israeli foreign policy is not just concerned with securing the interests of its own citizens (as most states are), but also Jewish citizens of other countries.[5] As Ben-Gurion told a meeting of Israeli ambassadors on July 17, 1950:

> So long as there exists a Jewish Diaspora […] Israel cannot behave as other states do and take into account only its own geographic and geopolitical situation or limit its concerns to its own citizens and nationals only. Despite the fact that the Jews living abroad are in no legal way part and parcel of Israel, the whole Jewish people, wherever it resides, is the business of the State of Israel, its first and determining business. To this Israel cannot be neutral: such a neutrality would mean renouncing our links with the Jewish people.
>
> *(Avineri 1986, p. 11)*

The clearest historical instance in which considerations of the welfare of Diaspora Jewry affected Israeli foreign policy was in Israel's relations with the Soviet Union (USSR). Although it is difficult to gauge the extent of its impact upon Israeli policy towards the USSR, the large number of Jews residing there was a major consideration for Israeli policymakers, especially because the welfare of Soviet Jewry was highly precarious (they were subject to numerous restrictions by the Soviet regime, most notably, the ability to freely leave the country). Shimon Peres, for instance, stated in 1966: "When it comes to Soviet Jewry the consideration of local Jewry is dominant, because of the real danger to their survival" (Brecher 1972, p. 236). But Israel's sustained effort to secure the freedom of Soviet Jewry was motivated by Israel's own needs (especially its need to increase Israel's Jewish population to counterbalance a high Palestinian birthrate) as much as, if not more than, the needs of Soviet Jews. This is demonstrated by Israel's opposition in the 1980s to allowing Soviet Jews to emigrate to the United States, rather than to Israel.

Israeli leaders have frequently expressed the belief that Israel is responsible for world Jewry. For instance, when visiting a Nazi concentration camp in 1999, then-Prime Minister Ehud Barak declared: "We will always defend ourselves and every Jew, wherever they may be."[6] Declarations of concern by Israeli policymakers for the security and welfare of Jews abroad, however, do not mean that Israeli foreign policy has actually been predominantly guided by this concern. Like policymakers elsewhere, Israeli policymakers have sought to advance the interests of their state, above all else. If there is a conflict between the interests of a particular Jewish community and those of the State of Israel, the interests of the latter have almost always prevailed in determining policy. For example, in the late 1970s and early

1980s, Israel had close relations with the military Junta in Argentina and with the Pinochet regime in Chile, despite the severe measures these authoritarian regimes took against some members of their country's Jewish communities. Israel also maintained a close relationship with the Apartheid government in South Africa, against the wishes of many South African Jews (Sheffer 1996).

The preference accorded to Israel's interests by Israeli policymakers finds its justification in their belief that the interests of Israel are ultimately identical with those of Diaspora Jewry, since the survival of the former ensures the survival of the latter. As Ben-Gurion stated:

> It was *always* my view that we have to consider the *interests* of Diaspora Jewry—any Jewish community that was concerned. But there is one crucial distinction—not what *they* think are their interests, but what *we* regarded as their interests. If it was a case vital for Israel, and the interests of the Jews concerned were different, the vital interests of Israel came first—because Israel is vital for world Jewry.
>
> *(Brecher 1972, p. 232)*

There is no reason to suspect that this is simply a rationalization for the narrow pursuit of Israel's interests. Numerous statements by Israeli policymakers attest to the sincerity of their conviction that the welfare of Jews around the world is inextricably tied to the welfare of the Jewish state. Ya'acov Herzog, the Director General of the Prime Minister's Office under Levi Eshkol, Golda Meir and Menachem Begin sums up this view:

> The Israeli elite looks upon Israel as the bastion of the collective Jewish group and, as such, it takes into account the interests of its part. But it places primary value on the whole and, to that end, the survival and enhancement of the bastion.
>
> *(Brecher 1972, p. 232)*

In addition to consistently prioritizing Israel's interests over those of Diaspora Jews in Israel's foreign policy, Israeli policymakers have also consistently ignored the views of Diaspora Jews about Israel's policies, except those that directly affect Diaspora Jews themselves, most notably its policies that touch upon the question of "who is a Jew" and affect the status of non-Orthodox Jews in Israel. The prevailing attitude among Israeli policymakers has always been to insist that Jews in the Diaspora are not entitled to any formal role in Israeli politics since this is restricted to Israeli citizens. Israeli policymakers are also generally unwilling to grant Diaspora Jews even an informal role or say in Israeli policymaking, on the grounds that they are not entitled to involvement, because they choose not to live in Israel. Thus, although Jews in the Diaspora, especially a few very wealthy individuals,[7] have become much more involved in domestic Israeli politics in recent years, the input of Diaspora Jews in Israeli policymaking remains minimal. In recent years, this fact has become a source of growing frustration among many Diaspora Jews, particularly those in the United States, as their criticisms of Israeli policies have intensified.

Diaspora Jews and Israel

Just as the continued existence of a Jewish Diaspora after Israel's establishment has posed ideological and policy challenges to Israel, so too has the existence of a Jewish state posed a host of challenges to Jews who live outside of it. Israel's existence raises some unprecedented questions for Diaspora Jews: How important should Israel be to them? What obligations, if any, do they have to Israel? Must they support Israel and, if so, how? Must they always support Israel, regardless of what it does? Most Diaspora Jews care about Israel; some intensely, others less so. For many, Israel has become a part of their Jewish identity; in fact, for some, it is the central component of their Jewishness. Only a small minority of Diaspora Jews opposes the Jewish state's existence, or rejects having any kind of relationship with Israel.

Indeed, it is almost impossible for Diaspora Jews to ignore Israel, even if they wanted to. Very few Diaspora Jews can remain apathetic about what is happening there. They are almost obligated to have an opinion about Israel and about the Israeli–Palestinian conflict, especially since it has become a major, almost obsessive, issue for Western public opinion. For better or worse, many Diaspora Jews often feel somehow implicated in what Israel does. As a self-declared Jewish state, Israel claims to act not only on behalf of its own citizens, but also on behalf of Jews world-wide. What Israel does, what happens to Israel, and what happens in Israel, there-fore, affects Diaspora Jews around the world. That is why the subject of Israel has dominated the agenda of Diaspora Jewry since 1948, and to this day Israel continues to be at the center of Diaspora Jewish political discussion and debate.

The Jewish Diaspora has existed for over 2,600 years, since its beginnings during the Greek and Roman empires. During this long history, Jewish communities of varying sizes have been established all over the world. Today, there are Jewish com-munities in around a hundred different countries, some numbering just a few dozen Jews, others hundreds of thousands. The largest Jewish communities are in North America and Western Europe. By far the biggest Jewish community in the Diaspora is the American Jewish community, comprising roughly 6–7 million Jews,[8] almost 70 percent of Diaspora Jewry. Given the diversity of the Jewish Diaspora, it is impossible to generalize about its relationship with Israel. Different Jewish com-munities have different relationships with Israel, some are very close—marked by a strong emotional attachment to Israel, a high volume and frequency of visits to Israel, and a lot of political and financial support for the country—others are more distant. The kind of relationship that exists depends upon many factors, such as the size, location, and demographics of the community, its history, and its relationship with the society and state in which it is based. In states that are hostile to Israel, for example, it is difficult and sometimes dangerous for members of the local Jewish community to maintain active relations with Israel: the Soviet Union, for instance, once contained the third largest Jewish community in the world, but until the late

1980s, Jews there were forbidden from maintaining any kind of relationship with Israel.

This essay will focus on the American Jewish relationship with Israel, since American Jewry is the largest, richest, and most powerful Diaspora Jewish community in the world, and the one to which Israel pays by far the most attention. Since Israel's establishment in 1948, and even before then, American Jews have made an incalculable contribution to the country's development, if not its very survival. Over the years, they have donated vast sums of money to Israeli governments, and to a multitude of Israeli charities, hospitals, universities, schools, and other Israeli institutions. Although American Jews give to a host of causes, to this day more money from American Jewish donors goes to Israel than to any other cause (Nathan-Kazis 2014). Indeed, it is estimated that American Jews give more than a billion dollars every year to organizations and charities in Israel.[9] For many years, American Jews have also channeled large sums of money to their own elected officials, in order to encourage them to support Israel, and they have energetically lobbied American policymakers on Israel's behalf. In the public arena, American Jews have vigorously defended and justified Israel's policies and actions to the American public at large. They have also done this in the international community, as major American Jewish organizations frequently act as unofficial emissaries and interlocutors for Israel to foreign governments and groups.

The American Jewish relationship with Israel has changed considerably over time. Contrary to the common belief that American Jews have always been strong supporters of Israel, in fact, the extent and intensity of American Jewish support for Israel has significantly fluctuated. American Jewry, for the most part, did not initially embrace Zionism, and relatively few American Jews joined the Zionist movement. However, by the end of World War II, the vast majority of American Jews had come to wholeheartedly support the establishment of a Jewish state in Palestine, largely in reaction to the mass murder of European Jewry in the Holocaust. As a result, American Jews became a vital source of economic and political support for the *Yishuv* (the pre-state Jewish community in Palestine) as it sought to achieve sovereignty and prepared for war with the Palestinians and surrounding Arab states. American Jewish lobbying also helped convince President Truman to support the United Nations' partition plan of 1947 and then to officially recognize the State of Israel, against the advice of his own State Department, when it declared independence in May 1948. In addition to energetically lobbying the Truman Administration, American Jews also provided the *Yishuv* with large amounts of money and arms that were crucial to ensuring Israel's victory in the 1948 war (Rosenthal 2001).

But while American Jews played an important part in Israel's creation, they quickly lost interest afterwards. After the initial euphoria that American Jews, like Jews everywhere, felt when the Jewish state was born, American Jewish excitement and enthusiasm for Israel soon died down and was followed by a long period of indifference. Israel was of little interest and concern to most American Jews during the early years of Israeli statehood, from 1948 to 1967. This was a time of upward mobility, suburbanization, and assimilation for American Jews, and the needs of a foreign country thousands of miles away were a lot less pressing to them than their own needs for prosperity, security, and belonging—especially as American Jews still frequently faced domestic discrimination and anti-Semitism.

Thus, most American Jews were simply preoccupied with their own immediate concerns and did not think about Israel very much. Nor was supporting Israel the most important item on the political agenda of the American Jewish community during this period. Although raising money for the fledgling state (through the sale of "Israel Bonds" and annual fundraising campaigns) was a communal priority, and pro-Israel advocacy in Washington DC (led by the American Israel Public Affairs Committee [AIPAC] and the Conference of Presidents of Major American Jewish Organizations) became an ongoing activity, the organized American Jewish community as a whole was generally more concerned with advancing Jewish rights and security in the United States than supporting Israel. It was only after 1967 that supporting Israel came to dominate the Jewish communal agenda.

The "Six-Day War" of June 1967 transformed the American Jewish relationship with Israel. The widespread fear of a second Holocaust prior to the war, followed by the relief and jubilation felt after Israel's swift and stunning victory, led to a spontaneous outpouring of support for Israel from American Jews. Ironically, although Israel dramatically displayed its military might in the 1967 war and emerged as arguably the dominant regional power in the Middle East, American Jews became much more concerned with Israel's survival after the war than they were before. This heightened concern with Israel's survival, coupled with the newfound pride of American Jews in the Jewish state's military prowess, propelled Israel to the top of the American Jewish communal agenda. Not only was there a huge surge in fundraising and political advocacy for Israel (and a brief surge in emigration to Israel), but also Israel became a central element in the "civil religion" of American Jewry, and a potent symbol of Jewish recovery after the Holocaust and of Jewish power. Israel also became a central component in American Jewish identity, especially for secular Jews, for whom supporting Israel effectively became a kind of substitute religion and a new way of being Jewish. In the absence of shared religious ties, support for Israel became the one thing that almost all American Jews had in common.

If American Jews fell in love with Israel during the 1960s and early 1970s, by the end of the 1970s and throughout the 1980s, the romance was wearing off. "The American Jewish love affair with Israel" was short-lived, lasting only about ten years (Rosenthal 2001, p. 21). What followed it was not so much disaffection, but disillusionment and dissent over Israeli government policies (especially those of right-wing, Likud-led governments). This period of disillusionment has lasted to the present day, much longer than the brief period of intense and uncritical devotion to Israel.

Why have growing numbers of American Jews become disenchanted with Israel and increasingly critical of it since the late 1970s, particularly since the first Lebanon war in 1982? Undoubtedly, part of the reason for this shift in American Jewish attitudes is that Israel has changed in ways that have disappointed, disturbed, and even angered many secular, liberal American Jews. Instead of being the secular, social-democratic, egalitarian, idealistic, and peace-seeking country that American Jews once perceived from afar (whether accurately or not), a different, altogether less attractive, Israel appeared from the late 1970s onwards. Israel became more right wing, more religious, more unequal, and more expansionist than the Jewish state that American Jews had fallen in love with. But Israel was always more flawed in reality than the vast majority of American Jews realized—it was certainly not the paragon of democracy and egalitarianism in its early decades that American Jews imagined it to be (for one thing, it maintained military rule over its own Arab citizens until 1966). Why, then, was it not until the 1980s and 1990s that American Jews became disillusioned with Israel?

The main reason for this shift in perceptions is that more American Jews have been visiting Israel, learning about Israel, and paying closer attention to what is happening there than in the past, when American Jews knew very little about Israeli history, politics, society, and culture. As a result, there is now greater familiarity with Israel and more knowledge about it among American Jews than ever before. To be sure, many American Jews remain quite ignorant about Israel, but more and more of them are gaining some knowledge of Israeli politics and society due to extensive foreign news reporting about Israel and the easy accessibility of English-language versions of major Israeli newspapers on the internet. Hence, as American Jews have become more able to regularly read about social issues, economic problems, and political debates in Israel, they have gradually become better informed. American Jews are also learning more about Israel by actually visiting the country. There has been a significant increase in travel to Israel, with the number of American Jews who have visited the country rising from just 14 percent in 1970, to 27 percent in 1990, to 35 percent in 2000.[10]

As American Jews read about Israel more often and travel there in increasing numbers, their views of the country inevitably change—becoming less idealistic, and more realistic (Sasson 2009). Increasing engagement with Israel by American Jews has, therefore, led to a less rose-tinted view of the country and a more critical attitude toward it. As American Jews have got to know Israel better, they have become more critical of those aspects of Israel that conflict with their own values and beliefs (such as its settlement-building in the West Bank, its treatment of its Arab citizens, and its ultra-Orthodox-dominated religious establishment).

Many American Jews are becoming particularly uncomfortable with Israel's actions in its conflict with the Palestinians and increasingly worried about Israel's ability to be a Jewish and democratic state. This is especially true for younger American Jews (those between the ages of eighteen and thirty-five), who make up about a quarter of the total American Jewish population. Born long after the Holocaust and Israel's founding, they have no nostalgic memory of Israel's early years and no experience of the emotional highs and lows of the Six-Day War. Instead, they have grown up during the years of the Second Intifada, and Israel's wars with Hizbollah and Hamas, and consequently they look at Israel through a very different lens than those of older American Jews. Young American Jews are more inclined to see Israel as powerful, not weak and endangered, and their atti-tude toward Israel tends to be more critical (especially of Israel's behavior toward the Palestinians).

Growing disillusionment with Israel among American Jews, however, has not yet led to growing alienation from Israel. Despite their disagreements with Israeli government policies, American Jews have not turned away from Israel. In regular surveys from the 1980s until the present day, between three-fifths and three-quarters of American Jews have consistently reported feeling "close to Israel" (Sasson et al. 2010). In a large survey of American Jews conducted in 2013, just over two-thirds said they were either very (30 percent) or somewhat (39 percent) attached to Israel, while an overwhelming 87 percent said that caring about Israel was either an essen-tial (43 percent) or important (44 percent) part of what being Jewish meant to them personally (Pew Research Center 2013). Although levels of American Jewish attachment to Israel have fluctuated slightly from year to year, overall, attachment to Israel has been remarkably stable and there has been no decline.

Rather than growing more disconnected from Israel, American Jews have actu-ally become more actively involved with Israel over the past two decades. They are more engaged with Israel than were previous generations whose connection with Israel was largely limited to donating money every year. The major change that is currently taking place in the American Jewish relationship with Israel is that American Jews are now critically engaging with it. For decades, most American Jews had a deferential attitude toward Israeli governments, uncritically accepting and endorsing whatever they did. Instead of questioning or challenging Israeli gov-ernment policies and actions, American Jews saw their roles as providing financial and political support for whatever goals or policies the Jewish state chose to pursue.

This is no longer the case today. Nowadays, there is much more public questioning and heated debate about Israel within the American Jewish community than in the past. Feeling deeply troubled by developments in Israel, more and more American Jews are starting to believe that supporting Israel no longer necessarily means supporting its government's policies. In fact, it may even involve actively and vocally opposing those policies. Increasing numbers of American Jews who are critical of Israel's policies in its conflict with the Palestinians are now speaking up and mobilizing politically, as demonstrated by the rapid rise of the liberal advocacy group called J Street, which bills itself as "pro-Israel, pro-peace." As this is occurring, the pro-Israel consensus that once united American Jewry is eroding, and a bitter and divisive conflict over Israel is developing within the American Jewish commu-nity (Waxman 2016).

It is not only American Jews who have been publicly questioning and chal-lenging Israeli policies and actions in recent years. So too, have Jews elsewhere, particularly in other liberal democracies in Western Europe, Canada, and Australia. While Jews in these places tend to be even more attached to Israel (unlike most American Jews, the vast majority of British, French, Canadian, and Australian Jews, for instance, have visited Israel at least once), there has also been growing Jewish criticism of Israeli policies and a growing debate about Israel, and particularly about the Israeli–Palestinian conflict. Within the Jewish communities in all of these countries, Israel is becoming a major source of intra-communal tension and controversy, linked in some cases to rising concerns over a resurgent anti-Semitism. To be sure, this is not the case everywhere in the Jewish Diaspora. In some parts of the Diaspora, such as in South America, the traditional pro-Israel consensus still largely prevails and there is little public debate about Israel among Jews. But, in general, Israel is no longer the great unifier of Diaspora Jews that it once was. Instead, Israel is increasingly becoming a source of division, rather than unity, for Diaspora Jewry.

Conclusion: challenges and prospects

For both ideological and pragmatic reasons, Israel has always maintained a close relationship with the Jewish Diaspora (a relationship that many other states have sought to emulate with their own diasporas). This relationship has been mutually beneficial. For Israel, the financial, political, and moral support it receives from the Jewish Diaspora has been an immensely valuable resource—something that Israeli policymakers have come to recognize and publicly acknowledge. For Diaspora Jewry, support for Israel has been the single most important and common expression of Jewish identity around the world. Visiting Israel, donating to Israel, and lobbying for Israel have all become ways in which many Diaspora Jews not only express their solidarity with the country, but also their own Jewish identity. And in an age when the religious and cultural ties that once united them have steadily diminished, Israel has been the focus of a lot of political, cultural, educational, and religious activity for Jews worldwide. In addition to helping sustain Jewish identity in the Diaspora and serving as a common rallying point for Diaspora Jews, Israel has also provided refuge to vulnerable and persecuted Jews and provided reassurance to those fearing persecution.

Will the relationship between Israel and the Jewish Diaspora remain as close in the future? Arguably, both sides still need each other: the Diaspora, especially American Jewry, provides Israel with reliable political support (something it sorely needs in the world today), and Israel helps to provide Diaspora Jews, especially the more secular, with a strong sense of Jewish identity (although sending young Diaspora Jews on trips to Israel is unlikely to be enough to secure the future of Diaspora Jewish identity, even if it strengthens their identification with Israel). But while both Diaspora Jewry and Israel have good reasons to maintain a close relationship, it will probably become harder to do so in the years ahead. Jews in the Diaspora, especially younger Jews, have become less deferential toward Israeli governments, and more inclined to form their own opinions about what Israel should or should not do, and also more willing to voice these opinions, believing that they have the right and even the obligation to do so.

Indeed, fewer Diaspora Jews are content to quiescently accept whatever Israeli governments do, and to simply send their money to Israel and lobby on its behalf. Instead, more now want to have a bigger say in Israel's future, if only from afar. The old relationship between Diaspora Jews and Israel, marked by Diaspora Jewish acquiescence with Israeli policies, is becoming anachronistic. The era of uncritical support, of "Israel right or wrong," is over. Israeli policies are now highly divisive in the Diaspora, just as they are in Israel. Indeed, nowadays Diaspora Jewish identity is often expressed by arguing about Israel, rather than simply by supporting it. In the years ahead, therefore, Israel–Diaspora relations will surely be challenged as Diaspora Jews develop a new, more critical and contentious relationship with Israel.

Notes

1 Although the vast majority of Diaspora Jews were not Zionists before Israel's establishment and only a tiny minority actually moved to Palestine, Diaspora Jewry played a crucial role in Israel's creation. Their charitable donations provided the Zionist movement with funds to buy land, build agricultural settlements and towns, and purchase arms, and their political lobbying and advocacy activities helped the Zionist movement gain international support and diplomatic backing.

2 On the concept of Shlilat Ha-galut in Zionist thought see, Yosef Gorny, "Shlilat Ha-Galut: Past and Present," in Allon Gal and Alfred Gottschalk (eds.), *Beyond Survival and Philanthropy: American Jewry and Israel* (Cincinnati, OH: Hebrew Union College Press, 2000), pp. 41–58.

3 The largest waves of Jewish immigration to Israel have come from Jewish communities facing persecution and poverty. First, survivors of the Holocaust languishing in Displaced Person camps, then Jews from Arab countries in the 1950s, then Jews from the former Soviet Union in the 1970s through to the 1990s, and Jews from Ethiopia in the 1980s and 1990s. There has been much less immigration to Israel from Jews in Western Europe and North America (less than 10 percent of the total).

4 This shift is evident in the activities of the Jewish Agency for Israel, a quasi-governmental organization, which is now less focused on encouraging Jewish immigration to Israel and more oriented to promoting Jewish identity in the Diaspora and strengthening Jewish attachment to Israel.

5 On Israel's policy towards the Jewish Diaspora see, Dov Waxman, "The Jewish Dimension in Israeli Foreign Policy," *Israel Studies Forum* 19, 1 (2003); Alan Dowty, "Israeli Foreign Policy and the Jewish Question," *Middle East Review of International Affairs* 3, 1 (1999); Gabriel Sheffer "The Elusive Question: Jews and Jewry in Israeli Foreign Policy," *Jerusalem Quarterly* 46 (Spring, 1988); Efraim Inbar, "Jews, Jewishness and Israel's Foreign Policy," *Jewish Political Studies Review* 2, nos. 3–4 (Fall, 1990).

6 Barak was speaking at the Sachsenhausen concentration camp in Germany. Reuters, 22 September 1999.

7 For example, individuals like Sheldon Adelson, Ronald Lauder, and S. Daniel Abraham.

8 The size of the American Jewish population ranges widely depending on who you count as being Jewish. The most recent figure estimated the total Jewish population to be 6.7 million, including 4.2 million adults who are "Jewish by religion," 1.2 million adults of no religion, and 1.3 million children being raised as Jews or partly as Jews.

9 In 2010, the figure was estimated to be $1.45 billion. In 2007, before the great recession, American Jews donated more than $2 billion to Israel.

10 Uzi Rebhun, "Recent Developments in Jewish Identification in the United States: A Cohort Follow-Up and Facet Analysis," *Papers in Jewish Demography 1997*, Sergio DellaPergola and Judith Even (eds.), The Avraham Harman Institute of Contemporary Jewry, The Hebrew University of Jerusalem, Jerusalem, 2001, p. 268; Jonathon Ament, "Israel Connections and American Jews: United Jewish Communities Report Series on the National Jewish Population Survey 2000–01," p. 41.

References and further reading

Ament, Jonathon. "Israel Connections and American Jews." *United Jewish Communities Report Series on the National Jewish Population Survey 2000–2001*, p. 41.

Avineri, Shlomo. 1986. "Ideology and Israel's Foreign Policy." *The Jerusalem Quarterly*. 37, p. 11.

Aviv, Caryn and David Shneer. 2005. *New Jews: The End of the Jewish Diaspora*. New York: New York University Press.

Beilin, Yossi. 2000. *His Brother's Keeper: Israel and Diaspora Jewry in the Twenty-First Century*. New York: Schocken Books.

Ben Moshe, Danny and Zohar Segev (eds.). 2007. *Israel, the Diaspora and Jewish Identity*. Brighton: Sussex Academic Press.

Bennett, Naftali. 2016. "Minister Naftali Bennett on Why Diaspora Jews Matter to Israel." *Ha'aretz*. July 12.

Brecher, Michael. 1972. *The Foreign Policy System of Israel: Setting, Images, Process*. New Haven, CT: Yale University Press, pp. 231.

Dowty, Alan. 1999. "Israeli Foreign Policy and the Jewish Question," *Middle East Review of International Affairs*. 3, 1.

Gal, Allon and Alfred Gottschalk (eds.). 2000. *Beyond Survival and Philanthropy: American Jewry and Israel*. Cincinnati, OH: Hebrew Union College Press.

Gorny, Josef. 2000. "Shlilat Ha-Galut: Past and Present," in Allon Gal and Alfred Gottschalk (eds.), *Beyond Survival and Philanthropy: American Jewry and Israel*. Cincinnati, OH: Hebrew Union College Press, pp. 41–58.

Halkin, Hillel. 1998. "The Jewish State and the Jewish People(s)." *Commentary*. May, pp. 50–55.

Inbar, Efraim. 1990. "Jews, Jewishness and Israel's Foreign Policy," *Jewish Political Studies Review*. 2(3–4) (Fall).

Klatzin, Jacob. 1971. "Boundaries," in Arthur Hertzberg (ed.), *The Zionist Idea*. New York: Atheneum, pp. 325.

Liebman, Charles S. 1977. *Pressure Without Sanctions: The Influence of World Jewry on Israeli Policy*. Cranbury, NJ: Associated University Presses, 220 pp.

Nathan-Kazis, Josh. 2014. "26 Billion Bucks: The Jewish Charity Industry Uncovered." *The Forward*. March 28.

Pew Research Center. 2013. "A Portrait of Jewish Americans: Findings from a Pew Research Center Survey of U.S. Jews." October 2013. Available at: www.pewforum.org/2013/10/01/jewish-american-beliefs-attitudes-culture-survey/.

Rebhun, Uzi. 2001. "Recent Developments in Jewish Identification in the United States: A Cohort Follow-Up and Facet Analysis," in Sergio DellaPergola and Judith Even (eds.), *Papers in Jewish Demography 1997*. The Avraham Harman Institute of Contemporary Jewry, The Hebrew University of Jerusalem, Jerusalem, 268 pp.

Rosenthal, Steven T. 2001. *Irreconcilable Differences? The Waning of the American Jewish Love Affair with Israel*. Hanover, NH: Brandeis University Press, p. 21.

Safran, William. 2005. "The Jewish Diaspora in a Comparative and Theoretical Perspective." *Israel Studies*. 10(1), pp. 36–60.

Sasson, Theodore. 2009. "The New Realism: American Jewish Views About Israel." New York: American Jewish Committee.

Sasson, Theodore. 2014. *The New American Zionism*. New York: New York University Press.

Sasson, Theodore, Charles Kadushin and Leonard Saxe. 2010. "Trends in American Jewish Attachment to Israel." *Contemporary Jewry*. 30.

Sheffer, Gabriel. 1988. "The Elusive Question: Jews and Jewry in Israeli Foreign Policy," *Jerusalem Quarterly*. 46 (Spring).

Sheffer, Gabriel. 1996. "Israel Diaspora Relations," in Michael Barnett (ed.), *Israel in Comparative Perspective: Challenging the Conventional Wisdom*. New York: SUNY Press, p. 74.

Sheffer, Gabriel. 2004. "The Israelis and the Jewish Diaspora," in Uzi Rebhun and Chaim I. Waxman (eds.), *Jews in Israel: Contemporary Social and Cultural Patterns*. Hanover, NH: Brandeis University Press, pp. 426–427.

Sheffer, Gabriel. 2012. "Loyalty and Criticism in the Relations Between World Jewry and Israel." *Israel Studies*. 17(2), pp. 77–85.

Shimoni, Gideon. 1995. "Reformulations of Zionist Ideology Since the Establishment of the State of Israel," in Peter Medding (ed.), *Values, Interests and Identity: Jews and Politics in a Changing World*. New York: Oxford University Press, 15 pp.

Waxman, Dov. 2003. "The Jewish Dimension in Israeli Foreign Policy," *Israel Studies Forum*. 19(1).

Waxman, Dov. 2016. *Trouble in the Tribe: The American Jewish Conflict over Israel*. Princeton, NJ: Princeton University Press.

Yakobson, Alexander. 2008. "Jewish Peoplehood and the Jewish State, How Unique?—A Comparative Survey." *Israel Studies*. 13(2), pp. 1–27.

INDEX

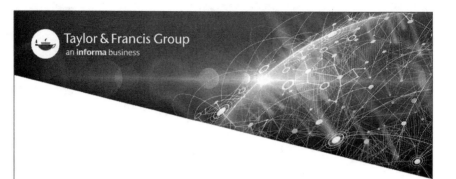